After the cult

AFTER THE CULT

Perceptions of other and self in West New Britain (Papua New Guinea)

Holger Jebens

Berghahn Books
New York • Oxford

First published in 2010 by

Berghahn Books

www.berghahnbooks.com

© 2010, 2013 Holger Jebens
First paperback edition published in 2013

Library of Congress Cataloging-in-Publication Data
Jebens, Holger.
After the cult : perceptions of other and self in West New Britain (Papua New
  Guinea) / Holger Jebens.
    p. cm.
Includes bibliographical references and index.
ISBN 978-1-84545-674-0 (hbk.)–ISBN 978-0-85745-798-1 (pbk.)
1. Cargo cults–Papua New Guinea–New Britain Island. 2. Papuans–Papua New
  Guinea–New Britain Island–Psychology. 3. Papuans–Papua New Guinea–
  New Britain Island–Attitudes. 4. Self-perception–Papua New Guinea–New
  Britain Island. 5. Whites–Papua New Guinea–New Britain Island–Public
  opinion. 6. Public opinion–Papua New Guinea–New Britain Island. 7. New
  Britain Island (Papua New Guinea)–Social life and customs. I. Title.
GN671.N5J42 2010
306.6'999212–dc22

                                                                    2010006693

British Library Cataloguing in Publication Data
A catalogue record for this book is available from the British Library

Printed in the United States on acid-free paper.

ISBN: 978-0-85745-798-1 (paperback)
eISBN: 978-0-85745-831-5 (retail ebook)

Contents

List of maps and figures

Maps

Figures

Acknowledgements

The present work is based on the research project 'Constructions of "cargo": on coping with cultural otherness in selected parts of Papua New Guinea', generously sponsored by the Volkswagen Foundation.

I would like to thank the relevant authorities in Papua New Guinea for providing me with a research permit. Members of the following institutions have kindly supported my work: the Archives of the Missionaries of the Sacred Heart (Münster and Hiltrup), the Michael Somare Library (Port Moresby), the National Archives of Papua New Guinea (Port Moresby), the National Museum and Arts Gallery (Port Moresby), the Pacific Manuscripts Bureau (Canberra) and the University of Pennsylvania Museum Archives (Philadelphia). In addition, Fr. Reiner Jaspers made available materials from the Archives of the Archdiocese of Rabaul (Vunapope).

Karl-Heinz Kohl has accompanied my efforts over a long period of time and in various capacities, as initiator and supervisor of the research project mentioned above, as a fellow traveller and visitor in Papua New Guinea, and as a demanding but also helpful superior at the Frobenius Institute (Frankfurt am Main) and the New School University (New York). My thanks go to him as well as to others who have also supported me with both friendly interest and critical advice: Bärbel Högner, Dan Jorgensen, Joel Robbins, Hartmut Zinser, and above all Susanne Lanwerd, from whose perceptivity and understanding I have profited greatly.

The photographs were printed by Peter Steigerwald and the maps prepared by Gabriele Hampel. Astrid Hünlich, Dirk Lang and Robert Tonkinson did a preliminary proofreading of the text. I also thank Robert Parkin for his help in translating the German manuscript. This translation was made possible in part through a grant from the Hahn-Hissink'sche Frobenius Foundation.

Lastly and most of all, however, I would like to thank the inhabitants of Koimumu and the surrounding area, and in particular, Francis Ave, Peter Mape, Titus Mou, Otto Puli, Augustin Sande, Joe Sogi and Alphonse Mape, who became a good friend of mine. Many of my interlocutors have insisted that I do not make village and personal names anonymous. It is out of respect and gratitude that I agree to this request, especially as I feel that there is no danger of anyone being harmed by my doing so. Without the hospitality and helpfulness on the part of the inhabitants of Koimumu and the surrounding area, the present work would never have come to fruition: *taritigi sesele*.

1
Introduction

Topic of research

Kago *and* kastom

The period of colonisation and missionisation in Melanesia has long since become part of the past. Papua New Guinea achieved independence as a state more than a quarter of a century ago, and in many places white people exist only in the memory or the imagination. Dealing with cultural difference, however, has in no way lost its significance. What Joel Robbins (2004a: 171) states with respect to the Urapmin of Sandaun Province certainly applies to most other societies in the region as well: 'the opposition of black and white skin is now as important in organizing thought as are those other classically Melanesian dichotomies, male/female, kin/affine, and friend/enemy'.[1]

In the context of the present work, I examine cultural perceptions of Other and Self, particularly with reference to indigenous constructions of *kago* and *kastom*. Both terms come from the neo-Melanesian Tok Pisin, a lingua franca that emerged towards the end of the nineteenth century in the context of the plantations and the stations of the colonial administration and the missions, and is now widespread in many parts of present-day Melanesia.[2]

Like the similar-sounding word 'cargo', 'kago' signifies consignments of industrially manufactured Western goods brought by ship or aeroplane, which, from the Melanesian point of view, are likely to have represented a materialisation of the superior and initially secret power of the whites.[3] These goods therefore appear as emblematic of the differences between the cultures that encountered or conflicted with one another in the wake of colonisation and missionisation. In addition, 'kago' refers to almost innumerable religiously based social movements, which, especially in the coastal and island parts of New Guinea, were feared or combated as 'cargo cults' or 'cargo movements' by early planters, traders, colonial officials and missionaries. For a no less innumerable number of anthropologists, these phenomena have become the object of a changing but recently revived and increasing fascination.[4]

Like 'kago', 'kastom' refers to both verbally expressed ideas and observable actions. In this sense, theoretical and practical constructions of *kago* and *kastom* respectively can be distinguished. However, while in the case of *kago* cultural perceptions of the Other are foregrounded, in the context of *kastom* this is mostly a matter of the objectification of one's own traditional culture, that is, of cultural representations of the Self. One of the reasons why 'kastom' has established itself in the corresponding literature might be that, unlike 'vaka vanua', 'fa'aSamoa', 'Maoritanga' or other locally used terms, it sounds much like the English word 'custom'.[5]

Following an analysis of indigenous constructions of *kago* and *kastom*, I compare indigenous and Western perceptions of Other and Self, the latter being articulated in previous research on these constructions. With respect to the view of the cultural Other, Roy Wagner (1981: 31) already suggested such a comparison in the 1970s when he wrote:

> If we call such phenomena 'cargo cults', then anthropology should perhaps be called a 'culture cult', for the Melanesian 'kago' is very much the interpretive counterpart of our word 'culture'. The words are to some extent 'mirror images' of each other, in the sense that we look at the natives' cargo, their techniques and artefacts, and call it 'culture', whereas they look at our culture and call it 'cargo'.[6]

Chris Gosden and Chantal Knowles (2001: 209) even describe the inhabitants of New Guinea as 'true anthropologists', since, in relation to the whites, they have allegedly been more ready and willing to learn something about their opposites.[7]

At first sight, however, one cannot help acquiring the impression that similarities predominate. My thesis is that both ethnographers and the people with whom they work move in a field of tension characterised by mutual influence between their respective cultures. Both grasp the Other according to their own respective models and patterns, which are thereby changed. Furthermore, both parties refer to each other by speaking, among other things, of material goods, secrecy and the importance of individuals in shaping history.

However, when comparing indigenous and anthropological perceptions of Other and Self, the question arises as to whether the similarities may not be more apparent than real, obscuring one's view on the differences between, for example, 'kago' and 'cargo' or 'kastom' and 'custom'. It is perhaps precisely in these differences, that is, in the relational definition and ambivalent evaluation of indigenous notions and concepts, that the 'cultural Self' articulates itself. This 'cultural Self' should be taken seriously, explicated and made fruitful for a critique of Western culture itself. Although the occasional demand to recognise intercultural similarities may be justified, I assume that it is, rather, the differences which hold the promise of contributing to intercultural understanding.

Koimumu and the surrounding area

My analysis of indigenous constructions of *kago* and *kastom* – that is, my comparison of indigenous and anthropological perceptions of Other and Self – focuses on the village of Koimumu and its environment. Here, in 1996 and 1997, I carried out a total of eleven months of fieldwork divided into two periods.[8] Koimumu lies at the eastern end of the Hoskins Peninsula, part of the north-east coast of West New Britain Province, which itself belongs to the island of New Britain and thus to Papua New Guinea.[9]

At the time of my first field trip, some 550 individuals were living in Koimumu. Most of the ninety or so houses are on stilts and are generally built out of palm leaves.[10] Wooden houses, roofed with corrugated iron (*kapa*) and thus corresponding to a Western model, are the exception.[11] They belong to the villagers who represent modern forms of authority, such as the president of the Pulabe Local Government Council, Alphonse Mape (Figure 13); the representative of Koimumu in the local government, George Tautigi; and the headmaster of the local school, Lawrence Olpitarea.[12] Koimumu is divided into four wards, Guria, Lakuba, Malebulu (Figure 4) and Taivel, the latter consisting of two smaller subdivisions, Tailabolo and Vela. In recent years further settlements have emerged, but although they have their own names (Kalibaga, Gere, Kovia), so far they comprise only one or two houses each and do not yet have the status of separate wards. The villagers belong to a total of nineteen different matrilineal clans.[13] According to Paul Gar (Figure 12), who was introduced to me as the leading Big Man and thus as an expert in traditional culture, some of these clans came originally 'out of the bush', others 'from the coast'.[14] However, even before the arrival of the first whites, their members were said to have intermarried, then migrated through a number of places that are no longer inhabited, and finally settled down where Koimumu is now situated.[15]

As in the pre-colonial period, the villagers live on taro, sago and fish they catch themselves, and they hold large-scale feasts on the beach or in the men's house (*haus boi*). Referring to these occasions, they speak of 'wokim kastom', that is, of 'making' traditional culture.[16] What people do not mention, however, is the fact that in Koimumu almost all relationships appear to be mediated through kinship; everyone thus seems to be able to place everyone else genealogically through an appropriate reference or address term.[17] In addition to subsistence, today there is also the money economy: next to 'food from the village' (*kaikai bilong ples*), 'food from the store' (*kaikai bilong stua*), i.e. rice and tinned fish or meat, is becoming increasingly important. Sources of income include the cultivation of cash crops such as cocoa, copra production (Figure 10), the planting of oil palms and the running of a shop or a passenger transport vehicle. Such 'public motor vehicles' (PMV) ply the recently asphalted road between Koimumu, other villages on the Hoskins Peninsula and Kimbe, the provincial capital. In addition, in the 1960s land was sold for commercial logging and the establishment of large oil palm plantations.[18] My interlocutors stressed that the Big Men of the time had been comparatively reluctant to pursue these activities, so that today there is much less shortage of arable land in Koimumu than around Kimbe or Hoskins.[19]

The inhabitants of Koimumu and neighbouring villages call themselves 'Nakanai', a term used for both the ethnic group of around 10,000 individuals and their Austronesian language.[20] To date, the major contributors to Nakanai ethnography have been Ann Chowning, Ward Goodenough, Raymond Johnston and Charles Valentine. Chowning, Goodenough and Valentine stayed in Galilo and Rapuri respectively in 1954 and were working in the immediate neighbourhood of Koimumu, while, from 1971 on, Johnston lived in Karapi, where he was employed by the Summer Institute of Linguistics to translate the Bible.[21]

Chowning, Goodenough and Valentine describe the people of the Koimumu area, together with their dialect of Nakanai, first as 'West Nakanai' and then as 'Lakalai', since in this dialect 'Nakanai' would become 'Lakalai'.[22] Johnston initially adopted this label in a manuscript dated 1973, but then rejected it in his dissertation, which was submitted in 1978 and reworked for publication in 1980: 'The Nakanai have now had fifty years of literacy, however, and are familiar with the sound [n]. Whilst it still may not be differentiated phonemically, [n] is nevertheless recognised as a distinct orthographic symbol, and to avoid using it in spelling the name "Nakanai" is regarded by many as being at once humorous and patronising.'[23]

Johnston (1973: 38) differentiates between an area stretching from Koimumu to Makasili and another from Gavatu to Kwalekessi. The first, which Johnston called the 'Kulabe area', corresponds roughly to the present-day Pulabe Local Government Council and the second to the present-day Garua-Bileki Local Government Council.[24] For the latter, as well as for the dialect spoken by 6,477 people in the entire region, Johnston suggests the term 'Bileki'.[25]

When I asked my hosts and informants in and around Koimumu about the numerous labels used in the literature, they assured me that they had never heard the word 'Lakalai' and that it meant nothing to them. In contrast to Johnston's account, they referred to the inhabitants of the Garua-Bileki Local Government Council only as 'Bileki', but identified themselves with the so-called 'Muku tribe', whose members are said to live between Koimumu and Kwalekessi, that is, throughout the area of Johnston's 'Bileki dialect'.[26] At the same time, and out of a mixture of self-irony and pride, people in Koimumu called their own village 'the last village' (*las ples*). This name is written on a PMV based in Koimumu, and it alludes not only to the geographical position of the village but also to the fact that, as Alphonse Mape (12 April 1997) told me, the few children from Koimumu who used to attend the community school in Vavua had usually been abused by their teachers as 'bottom bilong basket', that is, as 'those who remained behind' or 'the very last latecomers'.

The Hoskins Peninsula, like the whole of New Britain, belonged to the colony of German New Guinea from 1884 to 1914. From 1914 to 1921 it was subject to Australian military administration, and from 1921 to 1941 to Australian civil administration as part of the Mandated Territory of New Guinea.[27] With respect to missionisation, the members of the Australian Wesleyan Missionary Society were always slightly ahead of their Catholic rivals, the Missionaries of the Sacred Heart. In 1903 they 'acquired' land near Malalia, in 1918 they sent two Samoan pastors to Galilo, and in 1923 they opened a station in Malalia, where Edgar and Elsie Anderson became the first white people to live permanently in the region.[28] The Catholics 'purchased' their first land in 1918 near Vavua and Valoka. In 1919, two catechists from the Gazelle Peninsula travelled to Tarobi and Vavua respectively, and in 1924 Fr. Josef Stamm founded a station in Valoka, which, from the Catholic point of view, later came to be regarded as the 'centre of the Muku-Nakanai'.[29] In the course of the Second World War, Japanese soldiers occupied large parts of New Britain. After their defeat by the American and Australian allies in 1944, the entire region was returned to Australian administration, as part of, first, the United Nations Trust Territory of New Guinea, and, after 1949, the Trust Territory of Papua and New Guinea, before the independent state of Papua New Guinea came into existence in 1975.[30]

During the post-war period, the coast of the Hoskins Peninsula was known to Westerners first and foremost as the home of a man called Batari, who, according to a history of the Methodist mission, 'started a cargo cult in 1940 and led many people to destroy their gardens, fruit trees and animals, in the hope that the spirits of their ancestors would send an unlimited supply of "cargo" (the general name for European-introduced goods)'.[31] In the autobiographical recollections of the Catholic Bishop Leo Scharmach and the colonial officer Keith McCarthy, the so-called 'Batari movement' is presented as a typical 'cargo cult', and it has also entered the anthropological literature as such.[32] In particular, Lucy Mair's claim that Batari had 'scored a strong point on one occasion when a crate marked "battery" was unloaded from a ship – but not delivered to him' (1948: 66), was widely cited. Peter Worsley (1957: 206) mentions this in his influential monograph, *The trumpet shall sound*, as does Andrew Lattas (1998: 48–49), who describes the spread of the 'Batari cult' among the Kaliai in north-east New Britain.[33]

By the beginning of the 1950s, Batari's prophecies and activities belonged to the past. However, the Australian colonial administration still feared that they might be revitalised in the form of a movement called

'Kivung'.[34] Thus on 25 February 1953, in a 'Report on unrest, West Nakanai Sub-Division', Patrol Officer E.S. Sharp notes that the adherents of the Kivung had built small round houses at prominent places in several villages where they would assemble under the leadership of Lima of Rapuri, in order to discuss the arrival and later distribution of the cargo. According to Sharp, Lima's followers were in the majority, but what was perhaps the most important faction of their opponents was led by a man called Boas, known throughout the sub-district for having taken the side of the Allies during the war and for currently supporting the administration. Sharp writes that he himself had turned against the Kivung, and was feeling uncomfortable concerning its further development:

> The writer gave talks to the natives re the outbreak and pointed out to them the silliness of the whole idea. The talks had the desired effect for the present at least, but it is my opinion that unless something is done to REMOVE the cause of the unrest this sub-division will always be a thorn in the Administrations side. Perhaps at some future date we will not be as lucky as the past and the outbreak will get out of hand. From what I have observed and from reports by other Officers it appears evident that at one stage they will eventually get out of hand. (PRT 1952/53–7: 2; capitals in original)

Just one year afterwards, Ward Goodenough led an expedition whose members were to be based for several months in Galilo or Rapuri, and it is against this background that he commissioned Charles Valentine, whom he remembers today as 'probably the brightest, most promising graduate student we had', to study the Kivung.[35]

Referring to Valentine

For me, Valentine's work offers a historical perspective with respect to both indigenous constructions of *kago* and *kastom* and anthropological perceptions of Other and Self. Although there was a period of more than forty years between our respective first arrivals in the field, a great deal of what my interlocutors in and around Koimumu told me about their recollections of the Kivung, their complaints about the decline of their traditional culture and their performances of masked dances, called *tumbuan* (Tok Pisin) or *valuku* (Nakanai), was also referred to in Valentine's texts and field notes.

Valentine had submitted a report on his research on the Kivung, entitled 'Cargo beliefs and cargo cults among the West Nakanai of New Britain', to the colonial administration. The text exists in three unpublished and mostly identical versions. The first one (1955a), dated 15 January 1955, was completed less than three months after Valentine's return from his first field trip. Apart from a systematically revised paragraph, to which I shall return later, in the second version (1955b) there is merely the removal of a few references to the colonial administration, and the names of several missionaries and a trader have been anonymised, incidentally in contrast to those of the villagers.[36] Finally, in the third version (1956a), written after a second field trip, Valentine leaves his account of the Kivung essentially unaltered but shifts it from the present into the past.[37] He also adds a chapter bringing things up to date ('The current situation, 1955–56'), in which he goes into developments since 1954.[38]

I examined the field notes of Valentine, Chowning and Goodenough in the University of Pennsylvania Museum Archives.[39] Some five hundred of a total of around a thousand typed pages, each provided with a date, contain entries by Valentine concerning the Kivung or the Batari movement. They range from brief accounts, observations or quotations to extensive reproductions of conversations or entire stories. In contrast to Goodenough and Chowning, Valentine increasingly used a form of Tok Pisin shorthand, which obviously enabled him to record faithfully the statements of his interlocutors without interruption or omission and with all details and repetitions.[40] In reading them I felt somewhat taken aback from time to time, because there seemed to be something manic about some passages that stretched over several pages, often without line breaks or paragraphing. On the other hand, I often thought of my own interlocutors and could vividly imagine hearing what I was reading. In this sense Valentine's shorthand is certainly an appropriate way of reproducing the characteristics of how people express themselves on the ground.[41]

Contexts

Transformation

Beyond concentrating on the concrete example of Koimumu and neighbouring villages, I hope that the present work will also contribute to the ethnography of the Nakanai in general. At the same time, I do not attempt to reconstruct a supposedly untouched 'tradition', but to examine the culture-specific, local manifestations of a process of transformation that extends from the historical experience of colonisation and missionisation to what is now often invoked as globalisation and modernisation.

In the Koimumu area, however, people speak of a Western influence, which, triggered by the representatives of colonisation and missionisation, leads to assimilation and is ultimately supposed to turn the villagers into whites. As a consequence, the indigenous understanding of cultural change presupposes more or less specific ideas of what it means to 'be white'. Since the 1990s, such ideas or constructions of 'being white' or of 'whiteness' have been examined by the so-called 'whiteness studies' that have emerged in various disciplines. Until then, works on the themes of 'race' and 'race relations' had instead tended to focus on disadvantaged minorities, leaving the privileged or dominant majority out of consideration.[42] At present, however, the very omission of the fact that 'white' is as much a 'racial category' as 'black' is seen as a factor that contributes fundamentally to the perpetuation of social inequality.[43] In the context of an overview of the literature, John Hartigan (1997) pleads for the heterogeneity and complexity of 'whiteness' to be taken into account in an anthropological perspective and, under the title of 'Whiteness in the field' (2000b), he presents a collection of articles as 'disparate reflections on the local uses of "whiteness" in making sense of conflict, power, desire, and anxiety in culturally distinct places'.[44]

In one of these articles, Ira Bashkow describes how the Orokaiva of Oro Province, Papua New Guinea, construct 'whiteness'.[45] He thus represents an exception within 'whiteness studies' in the sense that authors otherwise mainly restrict themselves to analyses of Western discourses.[46] According to Bashkow (2000: 286), the Orokaiva use the 'whitemen' in order to communicate about themselves or their own society in a thoroughly critical and differentiated fashion: 'Today, the Orokaiva construction of whiteness is charged with ambiguities that invert the virtues and vices that the Orokaiva see in themselves.'[47] Bashkow does not aim to compare the Orokaiva's ideas of the whites with the ideas that the whites in their turn develop with respect to the Orokaiva, for example, in the context of anthropological research. At the same time, however, he starts from the assumption that, while the Orokaiva construction of 'whiteness' in many ways corresponds to the 'Western conception of race', it cannot be traced back solely to such a source.[48] Bashkow notes that one might be inclined to take the similarities between indigenous and Western discourses as 'prima facie evidence of a Western hegemony'; at the same time, however, he warns against exaggerating the Western origins of indigenous discourses. Thus knowledge of the colonial origins of modern forms of racism in Papua New Guinea is not sufficient 'to specify the complexities of local racial dynamics or the peculiarities of how race is constructed'. Rather, it is the achievement of the Orokaiva to exploit the power of the whites according to local goals and relationships. Thus, Bashkow (2000: 322–24) continues, 'whitemen' are represented differently according to context, and the 'Orokaiva construction of whitemen, even where it subordinates Orokaiva to white men morally, paradoxically is itself a medium in which Orokaiva morality is perpetuated'.

Constructions of 'whiteness' are based, among other things, on specific encounters with Western traders, colonial officials, missionaries and anthropologists. However, while the period of representatives of colonisation and missionisation seems to be over, long-term fieldwork in single locations continues to be conducted. For some decades now, anthropologists have increasingly been encountering situations in which they are told about more or less famous colleagues who have previously worked in the same region or with the same ethnic group, such references emanating not only from within the scientific community but also from the people visited.[49] In and around Koimumu, for example, I was regarded as Valentine's successor, as I had realised by 28 April 1996 when I attempted to introduce myself and explain my intentions to an assembly of villagers. 'Yeah, Vali did that too,' they replied unanimously. 'You don't have to say any more. We already know what sort of work you're talking about.'[50] Further references to Valentine followed in time. Many of my interlocutors praised him for having been 'in every village' and for having eaten 'everywhere', while others represented him critically as a recluse who just sat in his house and took down stories.[51] Titus Mou, on the other hand, spoke of Valentine as having been regarded favourably in general, though he also confirmed the, as it were, local limitations of Valentine's activities:

> He ran around Rapuri and Vavua and was able to stay in the men's house from dusk to dawn. He sent messages to people in other villages like Kassia or Karapi that they should come at a certain time, and come they did. At that time, people regarded him as an important person, since, after all, he was a white … He was made a Suara, which was a mark of respect (*mak bilong rispekt*) … People saw him as an important person. He took part in many feasts, danced himself … he even took part in the *tumbuan* … So there were no bad feelings or anything like that.[52]

When anthropologists refer to the work of their predecessors, they arrive at different assessments. As an example of an uncompromising rejection, one might mention Susanne Kühling's dissertation (1998) on exchange in Dobu (Milne Bay Province, Papua New Guinea), in which she seeks to refute the picture of the islanders given in Reo Fortune's classic *Sorcerers of Dobu* (1932).[53] In contrast, Joan Larcom, whose fieldwork on Malekula (Vanuatu) began forty-five years after the death of Bernard Deacon, demonstrates a more nuanced judgement.[54] She writes that it was only thanks to her predecessor's notes that she was able to understand the local 'ideology of place'.[55] Attributing central significance to this ideology, Larcom (1983: 184) describes Deacon's 'emphasis on kinship as the paramount factor of social life' as 'misplaced', and yet she identifies a similarity between herself and Deacon: influenced by their respective field experiences, they had both moved away from the ideas and assumptions they had initially brought with them.[56]

   The impression of similarity or continuity also predominates with respect to Valentine and me: at a distance of a good forty years, two anthropologists, both shaped by the academic discourses of their respective times, contribute to the creation of the data they collect and they are simultaneously subject to the influence of their hosts and informants. Yet the academic discourse does not remain the same. Accordingly, as I shall show, I clearly differ from Valentine in the way I understand the relationship between the two cultures which met or collided with each other in the course of colonisation and missionisation.

As Karl-Heinz Kohl (1987) has elucidated, using the examples of 'fetish', 'totem' and 'taboo', the history of anthropology shows that notions which have been developed while analysing foreign ideas can, through a process of universalisation, move beyond their original context and be applied to Western modes of behaviour, attitudes and norms. Following Kohl, Heike Kämpf speaks of the 'repercussions of anthropological research ... that have shaped our society in its self-understanding and in its attitude towards itself' (2003: 87), as well as of a 'migrating back of the anthropological gaze which initially seemed to be directed to other people'.[57] Based on these approaches, but at the same time superseding them, here I am also concerned with the impact of anthropological notions on the society under study itself; that is, I examine the ways in which the inhabitants of Koimumu and neighbouring villages deal with such notions as an element of Western influence.

Recollection and memory

For the people of the Koimumu area, the Batari movement and the Kivung belong to the past, as do numerous elements of their traditional culture. In this respect, the analysis of indigenous constructions of *kago* and *kastom* is also a case study of recollection and memory, and thus of themes which have been intensively discussed for about a quarter of a century in the humanities and various natural sciences.[58] In this context, the concept of 'cultural memory' developed by the Egyptologist Jan Assmann and the literary scholar Aleida Assmann has emerged as particularly influential.[59] Both authors explain the 'boom' in so-called 'cultural memory research', for example, with reference to the fact that more and more witnesses of National Socialism and the Second World War are dying.[60] Thus it is possible for A. Assmann (1998: 18) 'to recognise in the thematisation of memory also a form in which those born later both inherit and work on the shocks of this century'.

Building on Maurice Halbwachs and Aby Warburg, who shaped the concepts of 'collective memory' and 'pictorial memory' or 'human memory' in the 1920s, and following Jurij Lotman and Boris Uspenskij, who define culture as the 'non-heritable collective memory', A. and J. Assmann regard 'cultural memory' as a fabric of ideas, actions and artefacts with which humans seek to construct and perpetuate a collective identity by going back to the past: 'Under the term "cultural memory", we are subsuming the inventory of repeatedly used texts, pictures and rituals, typical for every society and every epoch, through the "cultivation" of which this society stabilises and transmits its self-image, a collectively shared knowledge preferably (though not exclusively) about the past, on which a group bases its consciousness of unity and uniqueness.'[61]

A. Assmann (2004: 47) describes the notion of 'cultural memory' as 'multi-dimensional and dynamic', since it refers not only to memory but also to forgetting and thus to opposed but at the same time closely linked processes, among which there are, 'in addition, many grey tones and continuous displacements'.[62] In order to describe this dynamic better, A.

Assmann distinguishes between 'functional memory', which is determined by consciousness, reference to a group, value formation and an orientation towards the future, on the one hand, and 'storage memory' on the other. This 'storage memory' is understood as a more comprehensive resource of contents, which, stored for example in archives, is no longer or not yet again considered important.[63]

While J. Assmann (2000: 16) examines the 'interdependence of the three themes of "memory" (or reference to the past), "identity" (or political imagination) and "cultural continuation" (or the formation of tradition)' with respect to the early literate cultures of the Near East and the Mediterranean, A. Assmann (1998) deals with the further development of 'cultural memory' from antiquity to the present day. For A. Assmann (1998: 371) this development leads to a 'crisis', since culture 'does not remember its past and has also forgotten its lack of memory', and society is 'less and less able to define in a generally binding fashion the body of knowledge which is relevant for itself'.[64]

In the anthropology of Melanesia, if not the whole of Oceania, recollection and memory have so far mainly been approached with reference to the experience of colonisation and missionisation. Here, for example, Andrew Lattas (1996a: 257) pursues the goal of examining the 'politics of memory and forgetting' by editing a collection of articles.[65] Another collection, assembled by Jeanette Mageo (2001c), deals with the role of 'cultural memory' in both colonising and colonised societies. She suggests that 'intragroup' and 'intergroup' memories be distinguished.[66]

The term 'cultural memory' creates a different impression, but Mageo appears to be unaware of the Assmanns' work, and the same can be said with respect to Lattas and many other authors who have dealt with the history of colonisation and missionisation in Melanesia.[67] Thus, a hitherto unexplored link between 'cultural memory research' and Melanesian anthropology could be established, provided that the Assmanns' concept of 'cultural memory' can be used in analysing the constructions of *kago* and *kastom* recorded in and around Koimumu.

These constructions consist on the one hand of present-day memories of the Kivung and the Batari movement, and on the other of the objectification of one's own traditional culture, that is, of the complaint about its decline and of the performance of *tumbuan* and *valuku*. In both cases, the data collected by Valentine and by me more than forty years later can be compared, showing that present-day and earlier statements prove to be quite different. Following Johannes Fried (2004), one might therefore speak of a 'veil of memory'.[68] The data from Koimumu and neighbouring villages could be added to the 'examples of dealing with memory in oral or semi-literate cultures' presented by Fried (2004: 214). However, it is precisely the differences between present-day and earlier statements, that is, between Valentine's representations and the memories of my interlocutors, that help to shed light on the indigenous definition and use of the term 'cargo cult', initially imported by the whites.

Research on cargo and kastom

In addition to dealing with colonisation, missionisation, globalisation and modernisation on the one hand, and the themes of recollection and memory on the other, I take up some recently published works on indigenous constructions of *kago* and *kastom*. In agreement with these studies, I understand the corresponding notions as products to which ethnographers and the people with whom they work both contribute. This process can only be made conscious through self-reflexivity and discernible through ethnographic specificity.

In the context of 'cargo research', Charles Valentine is virtually unknown and could therefore be described as something of a discovery: from a contemporary perspective, he not only presents an extraordinarily rich and multilayered corpus of data but also anticipates the insights of, among others, Peter Worsley (1957), Kennelm Burridge (1960) and Peter Lawrence (1964). Even the title of Lawrence's influential monograph, *Road belong cargo* (1964), already appears as a formulation in Valentine's field notes ten years before that book was published.[69] Lawrence and Valentine met in Canberra when Lawrence had just returned from New Guinea and Valentine was preparing to go there.[70] However, Valentine was not able to use the opportunity to rework his report to the colonial administration and to turn it into a 'classic' of 'cargo research'. This is, as I shall show, mainly due to the fact that, during his first field trip, he had a quite serious conflict with the resident priest of Valoka, Fr. Heinrich Berger.

Moreover, using the example of Koimumu and neighbouring villages, I hope to comply with the demands raised by '*kastom* research' and demonstrate both the polyphony of cultural self-representations and the way verbally expressed ideas are translated into practice.

Structure

The past

In the first two sections of this first chapter, I have set out the topic of the present work and the contexts within which my data (based on field research and archival studies) can be viewed. In the second chapter, I begin by considering the prehistory of the expedition led by Ward Goodenough, in which Valentine participated and was assigned to study the Kivung. Although Goodenough described large parts of New Britain as an 'ethnographic *terra incognita*' (1962: vii; italics in the original), in some coastal villages of the Hoskins Peninsula people could already look back to around fifty years of more or less sporadic contacts with white missionaries, traders and colonial officials when Valentine first arrived in Rapuri.

While today the Kivung is history, for Valentine it was the present. Thus my predecessor was able to take part in numerous assemblies of Kivung adherents, and he worked on his field notes almost daily, recording individual observations, reporting various events in village life and documenting the statements of his interlocutors in the form of brief quotations or whole transcriptions. In the three versions of his report to the colonial authorities, Valentine then unfolded a picture of a coherent and continuous development, which, beginning with older beliefs, led via the Batari movement to the Kivung. Later, Valentine's interpretation was to change fundamentally: while in the 1950s he was still criticising the Kivung as an authoritarian system of compulsion, in 1979 he was praising it as a creditable form of social protest.[71]

The course of Valentine's first stay in Rapuri, or, more precisely, his conflict with Berger, not only proved disastrous for Valentine's future career, but also throws a characteristic light on the preconceptions that Valentine brought to Rapuri with regard to cargo cults in general and the Kivung in particular. At the same time, the way in which Valentine describes the beginning, the course and in particular the outcome of his conflict with Berger to the colonial administration differs substantially from the picture that emerges from his field notes.

The present

In Chapter 3 the view shifts, so to speak, from the present in the past to the past in the present, and thus to today's memories of the Kivung. I describe how my fieldwork in Koimumu began, how my relationships with my hosts and informants gradually changed and how I heard about the Kivung for the first time. Almost always, when people mentioned it in the following weeks and months, particular themes or basic elements recurred at different frequencies and levels of detail, including especially the pursuit of Christian and economic goals. Conversely, in only a few cases, and then only in a very allusive manner, did some of my interlocutors speak of a change to the Kivung, let alone its 'transformation into a cargo cult' or a 'return to the Batari movement'.

Chapter 4 concerns the indigenous interpretation of the Kivung. This interpretation can be deduced from a comparison of past external views with present internal ones, in other words, by confronting Valentine's representations with present-day memories. Regardless of all parallels and shifts in meaning, the inhabitants of Koimumu and neighbouring villages have been persecuted by the colonial administration as alleged adherents of cargo cults, a historical experience they react to by rejecting the term 'cargo cult' for themselves while simultaneously using it to describe others in the context of religion and politics.

As people reject the term 'cargo cult' for themselves, they also reject particular beliefs concerning, for example, a link between one's own ancestors and the whites or a possible way of gaining access to money or Western goods. This is not to say, however, that such beliefs are no longer expressed. On the contrary, they can be seen as underlying the activities of a man called Paga, which one of his former adherents assessed as having been almost successful, but which a sceptic described as the last chapter in the history of the Batari movement and the Kivung.

Perceptions of other and self

In Chapter 5 I relate statements about the Kivung and the Batari movement as constructions of *kago* to statements about one's own culture as constructions of *kastom*. At first sight these constructions do not have much in common, and yet in their context similar, highly ambivalent and closely interdependent images of 'whites' and 'blacks' are being articulated, as well as corresponding concepts of 'modernity' and 'tradition'.

In Chapter 6 I turn from indigenous to anthropological perceptions of Other and Self by examining Valentine's interpretation of the Kivung and subsequent research on indigenous constructions of *kago* and *kastom*. Here Valentine and I appear to some extent as both subjects and objects of a mutual influence between the cultures represented by ourselves on the one hand and by our hosts and informants on the other.

This mutual influence is equally experienced by ethnographers and the people with whom they work, as will become apparent when I compare indigenous and anthropological perceptions of Other and Self in the seventh and last chapter of this study. Similarities, however, may merely result from a process of transference, a certain propensity to grasp the Other according to the pattern or model of the Self. I therefore conclude with a plea to take into account the differences between, for example, indigenous and anthropological notions of *kago* and 'cargo', or *kastom* and 'custom'.

Notes

1. Similarly, Stephen Leavitt (1995: 177) writes, in an article with the revealing title, 'Political domination and the absent oppressor': 'I argue that Bumbita Arapesh ideas about identity have been significantly shaped by the relative absence, or social silence, of Europeans in the postcolonial era.'
2. On the history of Tok Pisin, see especially Mühlhäusler (1985a, 1985b). To the extent that Tok Pisin is today being learned as a first language, for example in urban contexts or by children from inter-ethnic marriages, it is increasingly developing from a 'pidgin' into a 'creole'. See Mühlhäusler (1985b: 148–63) and Verhaar (1995: 2).
3. Among these were clothing and steel tools, as well as torches and refrigerators. See Lindstrom (2004: 20).
4. The history of the relevant research begins with brief reports (Chinnery and Haddon 1917; Eckert 1937, 1940; Höltker 1941, 1946; Belshaw 1950; Guiart 1951a, 1951b; Lommel 1953), followed by the first comparative studies by Worsley (1957) and works by Burridge (1960), Schwartz (1962) and Lawrence (1964) based on fieldwork undertaken before anthropological interest seemed to wane in the 1970s and 1980s. This interest was then resumed around 1990, as is evidenced by the monographs of Lindstrom

(1993), Hermann (1995), Kaplan (1995) and Lattas (1998) as well as by the collections of articles edited by Trompf (1990), Lattas (1992c), Otto (1992c), Dalton (2000b) and myself (Jebens 2004d).

5. See the articles collected by Keesing and Tonkinson (1982), Linnekin and Poyer (1990b) and Jolly and Thomas (1992b), as well as Hanson (1989), Keesing (1989), Schindlbeck (1990), Otto (1991, 1992a), Thomas (1992), Keck (1993), and volume 109(2) of the *Journal de la Société des Océanistes* (1999). Linnekin (1990: 151) and Jolly and Thomas (1992a: 241) refer to the terms 'vaka vanua', 'fa'aSamoa' and 'Maoritanga'. Although 'kago' seems to sound as much like 'cargo' as 'kastom' seems to resemble 'custom', authors use the English term to refer to religiously based social movements and the Tok Pisin term for cultural self-representations. I therefore write 'cargo research' on the one hand and '*kastom* research' on the other.

6. This passage has often been cited: see Dalton (2004: 191), Jebens (2004a: 11n2) and Lindstrom (2004: 16).

7. Gosden and Knowles (2001: 8–9) also write: 'The difference between New Guinean views of whites and white views of locals was that whites were more inclined to pigeon-hole New Guineans into categories such as "natives", "savage" or "Stone Age", whereas New Guineans felt impelled to learn, so as to discover what sort of beings these were and how these incomers had such an access to objects, an access denied to them.'

8. The first trip lasted from May to October 1996, the second from April to September 1997. Further details of the circumstances of my fieldwork are given in Chapter 3.

9. See Map 1. Since this study is devoted especially to constructions of *kago* and *kastom* articulated in and around Koimumu, as well as to a comparison of indigenous and anthropological perceptions of Other and Self, I restrict the presentation of basic ethnographic data and the introduction of my most important informants to what is indispensable. I am reserving for a separate publication detailed descriptions of the social and political organisation of the villagers, their modes of livelihood and their religious convictions and practices.

10. See Map 2, in which I have only counted the houses actually occupied, not those under construction at the start of my fieldwork or those used only for cooking or storage. The names of the occupants of the numbered houses are listed in the appendices to the present work, along with information on gender and clan membership ('List of houses in Koimumu').

11. Unless otherwise stated, words given in italics within parentheses are Tok Pisin.

12. Alphonse Mape, who is around thirty-five years old, belongs to the Kevemuki clan and lives in the part of Koimumu known as Guria (house no. 5 in the 'List of houses in Koimumu'). In contrast to most other villagers, Alphonse completed several months of training at a police school in Pt. Moresby and in this context also spent some weeks in Australia. Often just called 'President' in Koimumu and the surrounding area, Alphonse enjoys a generally high status. Moreover, he represents the Pulabe Local Government Council, and has also been invested with the traditional title of 'Suara', which includes as its insignia an armband called 'meleki' (see Chowning 1965/66: 495–96; Chowning and Goodenough 1965/66: 458–62). Alphonse struck me as modest and serious but at the same time not a humourless man. In the course of my fieldwork, he became one of my closest friends (Chapter 3). Approximately as old as Alphonse, George Tautigi belongs to the Kurukuru clan. He lives in Taivel (Vela, house no. 41), as Koimumu's representative in the local government is often just called 'Member' and has some influence. Especially on my first field trip, I conversed with him frequently and came to know him as a mostly good-tempered and generally rather extrovert man. Lawrence Olpitarea, around forty years old, from East New Britain and attached to the Bualali clan, is married to Leoba, Alphonse's sister. Like George, he lives in Taivel (Tailabolo, house no. 46). The respect shown to him by most of the villagers is based on the fact that, in accordance with his position as headmaster, he has a certain education and appears to be relatively prosperous. In addition, at least Alphonse and his brothers and

cousins avoid using Lawrence's name, since they see him as an affine (*tambu*). After I moved into a house in the school grounds (Chapter 3), especially at the start of my first field trip, Lawrence obviously felt responsible for my well-being. Although personally I valued him as a simultaneously sympathetic and interesting informant, we had fewer contacts during my second field trip, though I cannot give reasons for this.

13. While the older literature speaks of 'sibs' (Chowning 1958: 215; Johnston 1973: 40), I follow my informants, who call these groups 'clan' in English, 'bisnis' or 'lain' in Tok Pisin and 'maratatila' in the local language. The names of the nineteen clans represented in Koimumu are: Ababe, Ailili, Baumonu, Baumu, Baumunu, Bobiso, Bualali, Gararua, Ilalao, Kabilimosi, Kabulubulu, Kakea, Kerakera, Kevemuki, Kurukuru, Mamapa, Mararea, Ugeuge and Vavaha. Although the Ailili see themselves as a clan in their own right, the Kevemuki refer to them as 'Kevemuki-Ailili' and thus as their subclan.

14. Like Alphonse, the approximately sixty-year-old Paul Gar belongs to the Kevemuki clan. He lives in Malebulu (house no. 70). Unlike other men of his age, Paul is said not to have worked on the plantations in East New Britain Province in his youth. Remaining in the village instead, as people told me, he was able to learn much from the old men who also remained there. In numerous conversations, but also in the context of public meetings, Paul emphasised his own significance and expertise with regard to different areas of traditional culture in a manner that was often as serious as it was energetic. When, shortly before my departure from Papua New Guinea in September 1997, I met him twice in Port Moresby, where he was visiting his son Cosmas Gar, then in the army, I came to appreciate a rather relaxed and humorous side of Paul, which up until then I had not known. It seemed that, away from Koimumu, he enjoyed not having to present himself as a Big Man and appeared to feel temporarily relieved from the demands that such prestige brings with it. 'Out of the bush', according to Paul, came the Kabilimosi, Kevemuki, Mararea and Vavaha, 'from the coast' the Bualali, Gararua, Ilalao, Kurukuru, Mamapa and Ugeuge. The members of all the other clans, however, had allegedly arrived only later or through marriage. Paul gave me this information in conversations that took place on 24 May 1996, 18 June 1996 and 27 August 1996, listed in the references ('Interviews and conversations'). I refer to this list when, in the following text, I supplement the statements of my informants with dates.

15. According to Paul Gar, one of the villages that is now deserted was also called Koimumu. When, at least as far as I know, the name is mentioned for the first time in a patrol report dated 6 September 1927 (PRY 1927-8: 2), the author, Ian McCallum Mack, is probably referring to this place. On I.M. Mack, see McPherson (2001).

16. Among the occasions for such feasts are, for example, the first harvest from the garden of a firstborn son or the tearing down of the house of someone recently deceased.

17. See Chowning (1958: 121). She describes the 'basic system' of the inhabitants of Koimumu and surrounding villages as 'Iroquois, with derivative bifurcate merging terminology in the parental generation' (1965/66: 484). The preferred residence is patrivirilocal (Chowning 1965/66: 493).

18. On the cultivation of oil palms in West New Britain Province, see Jonas (1972), Longayroux et al. (1972), Benjamin (1977, 1985), C. and B. Valentine (1979a), Hulme (1982) and Ealel (1984).

19. Among these interlocutors are Peter Mape (24 May 1996) and Robert Boko (28 June 1996). Peter Mape, around thirty-five years old, like Alphonse Mape and George Tautitigi, belongs to the Ilalao clan. He lives in Guria (house no. 19), has been employed for many years as a contract worker on Bougainville, where his wife comes from, and occasionally works for the church or the community administration as a carpenter. Personally, I liked Peter for being both humorous and intelligent, and, like Alphonse, he gradually became one of my closest friends.

20. Johnston (1980a: 1) refers to a census carried out by the provincial government on 4 March 1980 and gives a total figure of 10,403, of which 1,365 were allegedly not living in West New Britain Province.

21. Chowning and Valentine took part in an expedition led by Goodenough. I deal with this expedition and Valentine's fieldwork in the second chapter of the present work. Johnston (1980a: 130) wrote in 1980 that he had 'resided in Nakanai for nine years'. See also Johnston (1973, 1976, 1980b, 1980c).

22. Chowning and Goodenough (1965/66: 471n2). After a reconnaissance trip in the region from October to September 1951, as well as after his stay in the field in 1954, Goodenough only used the term 'West Nakanai' (1952: 16, 1955: 21). Moreover, one seeks in vain for the term 'Lakalai' in a report that Valentine submitted to the colonial administration after his return from the field (1955a, 1955b, 1956a), as well as in his and Chowning's field notes. This term does not start to appear consistently until Valentine's and Chowning's dissertations (both 1958) and in subsequent articles that both they and Goodenough (1965: 266) published. Daris Swindler, however, who took part in Goodenough's expedition as a physical anthropologist, refrained from replacing 'West Nakanai' with 'Lakalai' in his dissertation (1962). See Simmons et al. (1956).

23. Johnston (1980a: 19). In his previous adoption of the term, though, Johnston (1973: 3) had already added the following restriction: 'However, for the purposes of publications intended for consumption by the Lakalai people themselves, they should be referred to by the name "Nakanai", which spelling they have learnt to recognize and prefer.'

24. Koimumu, Rapuri, Vavua, Galilo, Makasili, Karapi and Gavuvu belong to the Pulabe Local Government Council, while the Garua-Bileki Local Government Council consists of Gule, Rikau, Malalia, Gavutu, Kololo, Valoka, Gavaiva, Vovosi, Porapora, Galeoale, Kassia, Vaisisi and Kwalekessi. Before the 1997 administrative reform, the Pulabe Government Council was called the 'Pulabe Constituency' and the Garua-Bileki Local Government Council the 'Garua-Bileki Constituency'.

25. Johnston (1980a: 14n1; see also 1973: 3, 1980b: 139). According to Johnston (1980a: 14), the Bileki dialect thus has more speakers than any other Nakanai dialect, and the area in which it is spoken is also more densely settled than those of the other dialects. Like the terms for the subdivisions of the Nakanai language, their boundaries are also controversial: Chowning refers to Melamela, spoken between Lolobau and Open Bay, as 'East Nakanai', while for Johnston (1980a: 20) this forms a 'separate and unitary linguistic entity' (Johnston is referring here to Chowning, 'The Austronesian languages of New Britain', *Pacific Linguistics* A-21: 17–45, 1969). However, at the same time, Johnston (1980b: 110) also speaks of 'Meramera', and thus one cannot help agreeing with his conclusion: 'Naming always seems to be a problem in New Britain languages' (1980a: 14).

26. Chowning and Goodenough do not mention this self-designation as 'Muku'. In their account, the 'Lakalai' are called 'Muku' only by their western neighbours and 'Bileki' by their eastern ones, while they themselves refer to the groups living to the west of them as 'Bileki' (1965/66: 471n2). This latter information is confirmed by Johnston, as well as by my own observations. At the beginning of the 1930s, Fr. Josef Hüskes of the Missionaries of the Sacred Heart (MSC) also used the term 'Muku' in subdividing the Nakanai into the 'Melamela Nakanai', 'Muku Nakanai' and 'Bola Nakanai'. He writes, 'We leave entirely aside here the garbled, meaningless "Lakalai" of the Muku, who do not recognise "n" in their language' (cited by Schumm 1932: 73n1; all translations from the German, H.J.). By way of contrast, Johnston writes that in 1924 Fr. Josef Stamm had indicated that the description 'Muku' was negatively valued and claimed that it constituted 'a derogatory word referring to the faces the Nakanai make when speaking and eating, caused by the heavy lip ornaments they wear'. Johnston (1980a: 18) is referring here to an unpublished manuscript by Stamm, entitled 'Grammatik der Lakalai-Sprache: West and Central Lakalai', of 1925. This title indicates that Stamm regarded the term 'Lakalai' less critically than Hüskes and Johnston were to do later.

27. On the German colonial period, see Moses and Kennedy (1977), Firth (1978, 1982, 1985), Hempenstall (1978, 1987), Sack and Clark (1979), Sack (1980, 1985), Knoll and Gunn (1987), Gründer (1995) and Hiery (1995a, 1995b, 2001a, 2001c), as well as the bibliographies of Carlson (1970) and Scheps and Liedtke (1992). Jose (1987), Mackenzie

(1987) and Hiery (2001b) deal with the end of the German colonial period and the First World War. Rowley (1958) describes Australian colonial policy after the First World War.

28. On the 'acquisition' of land, see C. and E. Valentine (1956: 3). They refer to the following sources: Reports of the Methodist Missionary Society: Annual Reports, Sydney; F.G. Lewis, Methodist Overseas Mission, New Guinea District, 1875–1934 (n.d.). Neville Threlfall mentions two Samoan pastors settling down in Galilo (n.d.: 1) and the opening of a station in Malalia (1975: 114, n.d.). On the history of the Methodist mission in general, see Williams (1972), Threlfall (1975) and Schütte (1986).

29. Schumm (1932: 77). Schumm mentions both the first 'land purchase' (1932: 74) and the founding of the station in Valoka (1932: 77). From letters written by Stamm (29 May 1922) and Fr. Zwinge (15 October 1923), it emerges that To Kopia, the catechist stationed in Tarobi, was adopted into the 'union of the Emeleki', as Stamm and Zwinge put it. This means that, just like Alphonse Mape today, he was made a Suara. On the history of the MSC, which in 1890 replaced the Société des Missionaires de Notre Dame du Sacré Coeur at the behest of the German colonial government in New Britain, see Missionare vom hlst. Herzen Jesu (1917, 1954, 1975, n.d.), Linckens (1921, 1922), Bley (1925), Hüskes (1932), Jaspers (1984), Waldersee (1995), Biermann and Pittruff (1977), Editions du Signe (1999), Steffen (2001) and Dunn (2004).

30. In the literature, the Second World War is described from the point of view of the Australians (Walker 1957; Long 1963; Dexter 1968; Wigmore 1968), the US-Americans (Miller 1959) and the villagers who were affected (David Counts 1989). On the Coast Watching Organisation, which was active during the Japanese occupation, see Feldt (1946) and Wright (1965). Reed (1943), Mair (1948) and Stanner (1953) refer to post-war Australian colonial policy. Historical overviews are provided by Valentine (1958), Hudson (1971), Griffin et al. (1979) and Lātūfeku (1989).

31. Threlfall (1975: 140). Williams's Methodist mission history also mentions Batari (1972: 152–53).

32. Scharmach (1960: 128–30, 235–39), McCarthy (1963: 180–83, 191, 210). In addition to his recollections, Scharmach also refers to Batari in a mission handbook, *Manuale missionariorum* (1953: 59–60, 62–63), in a chapter entitled 'Cargo madness' (1953: 58–65). See also the memoirs of Fr. Bernard Franke (1982: 65–66), who was stationed in Vavua and Valoka before the Second World War.

33. In the second edition of Mair's account of Australian colonial policy, published in 1970, the claim just quoted no longer appears. Lattas refers, among others, to Scharmach (1998: 33, 44–45) and McCarthy (1998: 46–48), claiming that the 'Batari cult' distinguished itself among the Kaliai through its military organisation and 'various forms of military discipline' (1998: 37). I discuss Lattas's research in Chapter 6.

34. In a patrol report of 1944/45, that is, before the Kivung began, it is said that 'Batari's influence has been removed' (PRT 1944/45-K2: 2). Yet Fr. Sebastian Schweiger, who was stationed in Valoka, complains in several letters written to his Bishop in Rabaul in 1947 and 1948 that his work was made more difficult by Batari, who, according to Schweiger (2 November 1947), is 'stirring up the people'. In addition, Schweiger (5 December 1948) writes that Batari had reported him to the colonial administration for hitting children.

35. Ward Goodenough made this assessment of Valentine when I interviewed him at the Museum of the University of Pennsylvania on 30 November 2001.

36. The second version is dated 'March 1955'. It has the same structure as the first version, and the individual chapters and sections have the same headings. The text merely has fewer line breaks and, having been typed differently, is shorter by twenty pages (fifty-seven instead of seventy-seven). Moreover, a general map is added ('New Guinea territory and adjacent regions'), and a map of the region, differently drawn, appears at the end rather than the beginning. The references to the colonial administration, which have been removed from the second version, can be found in the first version (1955a) on pp. 1–2, 8–9 and 62.

37. Thus the corresponding chapter is no longer entitled 'The present movement' but 'The post-war Kivung, 1946–54'. The third version is entitled 'Cargo beliefs and movements in

the Talasea Sub-District New Britain'. In it, Valentine continues the anonymisation of the second version. Only in one place is there an exception (1956a: 48), when, obviously inadvertently, he writes 'Fr. Wagner' instead of 'Fr. W'. In contrast to the second version, however, the third contains a key to the abbreviations used (1956a: 90). From it, however, presumably also inadvertently, 'Fr. G' (for 'Fr. Weigl') is missing, and Valentine admits that 'Fr. X' stands for 'Fr. Munzlinger', although previously he had replaced this name with 'Fr. Z'. The three main chapters of the first two versions of the text remain basically unchanged, apart from new headings and the addition of explanations for selected words. Only the first of these three chapters, entitled 'Early responses to a changing world, 1900–1938', replacing the previous 'Early cargo beliefs', has been supplemented more comprehensively and contains extra sections on the initial encounters between the Nakanai and Westerners, the beginnings of plantation work and missionisation, and general historical developments up to the period after the Second World War. In the second main chapter, Valentine writes about an encounter, not mentioned in the first two versions of the text, between Batari and McCarthy, which would later also feature in McCarthy's recollections (1963: 180–83).

38. Also added is a new introduction, a subsequent chapter with the heading 'The land and the people' and an appendix, whose respective parts Valentine numbers as chapters in their own right: 'Postscript on the role of Fr. B.', 'Acknowledgements' and 'Key to abbreviations in the text'.

39. Some of them copied several times, they were assembled in files, corresponding to a scheme of the Human Relation Area Files. In addition, Valentine's second wife Bettylou let me have a good one hundred pages of field notes from Valentine's second stay in Rapuri, which mainly deal with local history, from the first encounters with Westerners up to the Second World War.

40. See Figure 2. This shorthand had been devised by Theodore Schwartz (see Mead 1956: 483, 492), who studied with Valentine under Goodenough at Pennsylvania and who visited Valentine together with his wife Leonora in Rapuri in mid-1954. At this point, Schwartz was on his way back from fieldwork he had conducted on Manus to study the so-called 'Paliau movement' (Schwartz 1962). The date of Schwartz's stay in Rapuri is confirmed as 17 July 1954 (CV 17 July 1954. 4). Schwartz (20 February 1997) wrote to me that his stay had lasted some three to five days. On 23 July 1954, Valentine (CV 23 July 1954: 2) was already writing about Schwartz's visit in the past tense.

41. I return to these characteristics in Chapter 4 of the present work.

42. A comprehensive bibliography by Eske Wollrad (n.d.) is divided into various rubrics, among them 'history', 'science of literature', 'cultural sciences', 'philosophy', 'gender', 'education', 'sociology' and 'international studies' (however, one looks in vain for 'social' or 'cultural anthropology'). According to a research overview by Susan Arndt (2002: 3), the term 'critical whiteness studies' can be traced back to David Stowe. In fact, however, Stowe (1996: 68) writes in the article referred to by Arndt: 'It may not be premature to speak of a new humanities subfield: whiteness studies.'

43. Arndt (2002: 5) notes that 'being white is set as a norm'. This allegedly results in a tendency she calls 'colour blindness', according to which 'whites do not perceive their white cultural identity'. Stowe (1996: 70) cites the 'activist and writer Coco Fusco' (without giving the source) as follows: 'To ignore white ethnicity is to redouble its hegemony by naturalizing it.'

44. Hartigan (2000a: 269). According to Hartigan (2000a: 273), it is less a matter of what determines 'whiteness' than of examining, with the aid of fieldwork and ethnographic examples, the process through which 'whiteness' emerges and is applied: 'these articles trace how dimensions of race are deployed as modes of interpretation in certain situations'. This should lead to a 'comparative understanding of constructions of whiteness that would underscore the "cultural" ... rather than essential features of these constructions' (2000a: 276).

45. Here the focus is on the quality of 'brightness' that the Orokaiva attribute to the skin of the whites (Bashkow 2000: 291–318). Bashkow has taken the corresponding material,

partly literally, partly revised, from his dissertation (1999: 260–69), in which he also refers to the supposed 'lightness' of the 'whitemen' (1999: 79–113), their nourishment (1999: 114–221) and their 'softness' (1999: 224–60). Bashkow's dissertation was published by the University of Chicago Press in 2006 and it is based on a total of two years of fieldwork conducted between 1993 and 1995 (Bashkow 1999: 326n6).

46. Bashkow himself, who incidentally first writes 'whiteness studies' (2000: 282) and then 'critical whiteness studies' (2000: 318), correctly concludes: 'Few scholars have examined how whiteness is constructed by non-whites in places outside the West' (2000: 282). Indeed, the statement that the articles collected by Hartigan would deal with 'the status and uses of representations of "whites" by "natives", "Others" and subordinated populations' (Hartigan 2000a: 276) only applies to Bashkow.

47. Accordingly, Bashkow writes with reference to the Orokaiva: 'Depending on context, they may use white men as a foil for extolling their own virtues ... or they may use white men as a foil for criticizing their own moral failings and those of their society' (2000: 321).

48. The 'Orokaiva construction of whiteness' is, according to Bashkow, 'neither a variant of ... western hegemony, nor ... an instance of counter-hegemonic resistance' (2000: 283).

49. Thus Judith Macdonald (2000: 123n9), who carried out fieldwork on Tikopia some fifty years after Raymond Firth, writes: 'My thesis supervisor was well versed in the Tikopia corpus. Several times while reading drafts of my thesis she marked passages and said that I should acknowledge the quotation from Firth. With irritation, I replied that they had said it to me, too.'

50. I have already outlined this reaction elsewhere (2003a: 41, 2004b: 117). When, as in Koimumu and neighbouring villages, the people themselves refer to anthropological predecessors, this seems to be handed down orally rather than in writing within the scientific community. If references to anthropological predecessors are mentioned at all in the literature, they come rather from colleagues or, as in McDonald's case, from a supervisor.

51. Fred Golumu (26 May 1996), a Big Man from Vavua, expressed himself as follows about Valentine in one conversation: 'He was in all the villages, ate everywhere, went to all the mountains, took part in feasts, and already knew Tok Pisin when he arrived. Then he learned our own language (*tok ples*) and could say "good morning" and "good evening". He visited the Big Men, and the Big Men visited him. Then there couldn't be any noise, so the children had to be quiet or go away.' The idea that, in contrast, Valentine had stayed put in his own house eating and taking down stories was expressed by Leo Guvi (9 July 1997), a Big Man from Makasili.

52. 'So i no gat hard feelings, i no gat wanem' (interview with Titus Mou, 4 July 1996). Titus Mou, about forty-five years old, lives in Vavua. Employed at the start of the 1970s by the colonial administration and thereafter in various capacities in government service, he was introduced to me by Alphonse Mape. I came to appreciate him as a humorous and knowledgeable interlocutor. Displaying from time to time a tendency towards comparatively graphic expressions, he was able to perform valuable services for me, especially with respect to my research on the Kivung (Chapter 3).

53. Kühling's dissertation was published by the University of Hawaii Press in 2005. In her introduction, she refers to Fortune's allegedly insufficient and problematic fieldwork and accuses him of factual errors and inappropriate interpretations (1998: 14–19). Most of the subsequent passages in which she mentions her predecessor also appear to be designed as a contradiction. In her concluding chapter, she states: 'My thesis has attempted to deconstruct Fortune's image of the Dobuan' (1998: 323). Yet, if one consults Fortune's monograph itself (1932), which is nowhere represented in context by Kühling, one has the impression that Kühling is merely using her predecessor as a sort of negative foil and that, in misrepresenting Fortune, she tends to treat him in much the same way as she accuses him of treating the inhabitants of Dobu. I have sought to praise *Sorcerers of Dobu* elsewhere (Jebens 2001a).

54. Larcom (1983: 178) reports, in an article tellingly entitled 'Following Deacon', that on the very day of her arrival she was shown a ledger with the name of her predecessor on it.

Between 1926 and 1927 Deacon carried out fourteen months of fieldwork on Malekula, where he died before his departure (Larcom 1983: 178). Larcom landed on Malekula in 1972 and stayed there between 1973 and 1974 and again in 1981, as she states in an article on the changing evaluation of the local culture and the corresponding increase in Deacon's significance (1982: 331). On this article, see also Kohl (2000: 74–75). In his preface to Camilla Wedgwood's edition of Deacon's notes, Alfred C. Haddon (1934) gives biographical information on Deacon, while Deacon's friend Margaret Gardiner (1984) combines extracts from letters she received from him with her own recollections. On Gardiner's book, see also Clifford (1997). Langham (1981: 212–342) praises the results of Deacon's research. See also Terry Crowley (2001), who presented texts by Deacon to the people of Malekula in 1999 and who alludes to the possibility that they might have regarded him as a sort of 'ghost' of Deacon.

55. Following a rereading of Deacon's notes against the background of her own field experiences, Larcom (1983: 183) states: 'Deacon's records unlocked for me the depth of the ideology of place as a structure enfolding and extending kinship relations.'

56. Larcom (1983: 189) writes: 'Just as Deacon's field experience caused him to move away somewhat from his prior commitment to Rivers' theory, so fifty years later did my research in South West Bay also alter preconceptions carried to Mewun. If Deacon's search for a coherent social organizational system was disrupted by Malekulan concerns with place, so in a similar way my initial view of social change was shaken by the tenacity of native ideology about the same organizing construct – place.'

57. Kämpf (2003: 88). Kämpf (2003: 87) describes the 'generative or constructive power of notions and the processes of their formation' with regard to one's own identity as their 'theory effect'.

58. As Astrid Erll (2004: 1) writes in her introduction, 'Kollektives Gedächtnis und Erinnerungskulturen' (Collective recollection and memory cultures), 'around the turn of the century, the practice of memory and its reflection [became] an interdisciplinary and international phenomenon covering culture as a whole'. A specific research programme based at the Justus-Liebig University of Giessen, from which Erll's introduction stems (see Erll 2004: 34 37), is concerned with the 'contents and forms of cultural memory from antiquity into the twenty-first century' (2004: 34). The development of autobiographical memory from the perspective of both the neurological and social sciences is focused on by a research group being promoted by the Volkswagen Foundation (see Welzer and Markowitsch 2001; Oddo et al. 2003).

59. See, among others, J. Assmann (1988, 1991, 2000) and A. Assmann (1998, 2004). For Erll (2004: 13), the concept of 'cultural memory' has been 'the most effective in the German-speaking world and the most thoroughly worked out in international comparison'. According to A. Assmann, the term 'cultural memory' itself has 'become equally well-established' in French and Anglo-American discourses.

60. See A. Assmann (1998: 18) and J. Assmann (2000: 11). The former notes 'a constantly growing research literature that, in its bulk, is still not receding', as well as a 'continuing fascination with the theme of memory' (1998: 16) and a 'quality of the obsessive in memory research' (1998: 17). Erll (2004: v, *passim*) uses the term 'cultural studies memory research'.

61. J. Assmann (1988: 15). See J. Assmann on Halbwachs and Warburg in general (1988: 9–13), and on Halbwachs in particular (2000: 45–48). A. Assmann also deals with Halbwachs (1998: 131–32) and Warburg (1998: 225–26, 372–74). J. Assmann (1988: 13) criticises both authors as follows: 'As with Halbwachs the memory function of objectivised culture remains underexposed, the same is indeed true of Warburg and the sociological aspects of his pictorial memory.' Lotman and Uspenskij (1984: 3) write: 'In the widest sense of the word culture may be understood as non-hereditary collective memory.' A. Assmann (1998: 19) summarises this definition. Here 'non-hereditary' obviously means that the individual acquires memory or culture only after birth, in contrast, for example, to the 'collective unconscious' assumed by some authors. If one leaves aside the rather individual-focused approaches within psychoanalysis, interest in

the theme of recollection and memory receded after the publication of Halbwachs's and Warburg's works, before being revived in the 1980s, initially by Pierre Nora and his notion of 'sites of memory' (see Erll 2004: 23–26). In order to examine the reasons for the 'boom' in 'cultural memory research' more exhaustively, one would therefore have to go beyond referring to the fact that more and more witnesses of National Socialism and the Second World War are dying, and ask what the 1920s and 1980s might have in common.

62. Harald Weinrich (1997) presents a cultural history of forgetting. In addition, see the collection edited by Günther Butzer and Manuela Günter (2004) on 'media', 'rituals' and 'sites of forgetting', as well as a monograph with the title *Soziales Vergessen* (Social forgetting), in which Elena Esposito (2002) tries to apply the systems theory of Niklas Luhmann to the 'memory of society'.

63. A. Assmann (1998: 19, 133–42). For A. Assmann (1998: 136–37), the 'storage memory' can only emerge when people start to write, whereas it would not be possible for an 'oral culture of memory' to 'retain what is not needed for the identity of the group and what is therefore necessary for survival'.

64. A. Assmann (2004: 57). In comparison with J. Assmann, A. Assmann (1998: 15) refers perhaps rather more clearly to the conflict potential of 'cultural memory', that is, to the 'danger of the distortion, reduction or instrumentalisation of memory', which could 'only be countered by open criticism, reflection and discussion'. On the other hand, J. Assmann (2000:24) states, with reference to the 'space of memory', that it 'may enter into contradiction with the social and potential reality of a present', in order then to continue: 'we characterise this case with the notions of "kontrapräsentische Erinnerung" [counter-present memory] (G. Theißen) and "anachrone Strukturen" [anachronic structures] (M. Erdheim)'.

65. In this context, Lattas (1996a) ascribes both an 'oppressive nature' and a 'liberating potential' to the processes of remembering and forgetting.

66. Mageo (2001a: 4) defines 'intergroup memory' as a rather restrictive 'political tendency that comes into play in negotiations between groups', and 'intragroup memory' as a creative tendency that has a potential for resistance and 'that comes into play in the transformations of meaning within a group'. According to Mageo, these two 'genres of cultural memory' (2001b: 11) not only form 'apparent adversities', but also overlap and are each 'latent in the shadow of the other' (2001b: 26–27).

67. See, for example, Neumann (1992) and Hiery (2001c).

68. In his monograph of the same title, praised by J. Assmann (2004) as a 'path-breaking contribution to critical history', Fried attempts to sensitise historical science to the specific characteristics of processes of remembering. In doing so, he adopts the term 'cultural memory' (see, for example, 2004: 78, 85–86, 364, 390). Moreover, he refers to the changeability of content handed down orally (2004: 214–21).

69. In his Tok Pisin shorthand Valentine writes 'rt bl kako' (CV 23 August 1954a: 2). Incidentally Lawrence's monograph contains a foreword by McCarthy, in which the latter expresses himself as follows on cargo cult leaders: 'Some of them, like Batari of Talasea, New Britain, claimed that they were reincarnated spirits in human form (Batari claimed a like transformation in myself so that I was a spirit in a rather bulky human shape.)' (1964: vi)

70. Valentine (31 March 1954) mentions this meeting in a letter to Goodenough.

71. See C. Valentine and B. Valentine (1979a).

2

Valentine's Kivung

Prehistory

First contacts

The Western influence noted in and around Koimumu emanated from the nearby Gazelle Peninsula, where the ships of the first whites landed and from where they spread along the coast of the rest of New Britain.[1]

The trade in Western manufactured goods such as metal tools and calico became more intensive towards the end of the 1870s, before the so-called 'blackbirders' tried to recruit workers for plantations in Queensland and Fiji from among the inhabitants of the coast of New Britain.[2] At the end of the nineteenth century, trade and 'labour recruitment' became less important than the coconut plantations of the Gazelle Peninsula.

Although missionaries, traders, colonial officials, 'blackbirders' and travellers partly pursued different interests, in the eyes of the local population they must have seemed to belong to one and the same group, the more so since they often literally sat in the same boat. Thus, for example, in July 1897, Fr. Matthäus Rascher and the later imperial governor, Albert Hahl, travelled along the north-east coast of New Britain as far as the island of Lolobau, and Rascher was Hahl's interpreter during so-called 'punitive expeditions'.[3]

Rascher was the superior of the mission station of St Paul, founded as a sort of 'model village' in 1898 in the north of the Gazelle Peninsula. Here, the indigenous Baining were to be settled following the example of the Christian family: married to one another and 'expected', as Peter Hempenstall (1978: 147) writes, 'to function as cells of Christian peasant-farmers and artisans among their heathen compatriots'. The Baining themselves, however, brought Rascher's efforts to a sudden end when they attacked and killed him and nine other missionaries on 14 August 1904.

On the Western side, this event, described, for example, as the 'bloodbath of the Baining Hills' (Kleintitschen 1929) and the 'St. Paul Massacre' (Rohatynskyj 2000: 184), caused considerable unrest. Corresponding references and more or less detailed accounts can be found in contemporary publications of the colonial government and Catholic Church, as well as in later mission and colonial histories or ethnographic presentations.[4]

Colonial officials and missionaries accused one another of being partly responsible for the murder of Rascher and his colleagues through their mishandling of the Baining or their failure to act.[5] Moreover, in November 1904 Fr. Hubert Linckens noted a local 'conspiracy', allegedly 'aimed not directly at the mission but at the whites in general' (1904: 500) and led by a man called To Maria, whom Rascher had earlier taken to task over a case of adultery.[6] Some seventy-five years later, Reiner Jaspers (1979: 1) sought 'the reasons for this bloody deed' rather in the relations between the colonial government and the Catholic Church, as well as between the Baining and Tolai living on the coast.[7] The plan to have the victims of the 'bloodbath', 'massacre' or 'bloody deed' canonised has as yet been unsuccessful, but at least in present-day New Britain, they are revered as 'martyrs' by leading functionaries of the Catholic Church.[8]

All in all, during German colonial rule, Western influence was mainly restricted to the Gazelle Peninsula, while the Hoskins Peninsula could be approached only with great difficulty because of the north-west storms that rage for several months of the year and the presence of dangerous reefs offshore.[9] Thus F.E. Hellwig (1927: 136), the chronicler of the well-known Hamburg South Seas Expedition, writes in his log for 18 April 1909: 'The plan to run into Commodore Bay ... was dropped. Because of the enormous number of reefs and cliffs and the light at present, the captain does not want to risk entering after several failed attempts.'[10]

Yet, even before the first missionaries, traders, 'blackbirders' and travellers themselves encountered the Nakanai, of whom they had heard from the Tolai, who, in the pre-colonial period, had visited the Nakanai coasts to trade for the materials (*tambu*) needed for the manufacture of shell money.[11] For the Australian colonial officer P.M. Penhalluriack, the term 'Nakanai' itself can also be traced back to the Tolai:

In the old days, the Rabaul people came to the beach villages to trade for tambu. Their reception was not always as peaceful as it is nowadays. They were afraid to sleep ashore, and so kept moving, the only sleep they had being such as they could get on their canoes. They likened themselves to a seabird that sleeps on the water and is known in Rabaul language as 'akanai'. So that they soon came to know the place by that name. 'la' is the definite article in the Muku language, so that the place became known to them [as] 'lakanai' or Nakanai as it is now known.[12]

Referring to the Tolai's 'trading activities', which in his view 'frequently [have] the character of robberies', Parkinson (1907: 86) notes: 'That the mutual encounters are not always friendly is shown by the many spear wounds borne by those who return; it is equally certain that the "deaths" during the journeys are far from always having a natural cause.' Accordingly, the Tolai usually portrayed their exchange partners to the whites in a negative light. In their accounts, as Parkinson (1907: 202) further states, 'the Nakanai people are deeply subordinate to them, and they enjoy themselves in giving depictions in which they can represent themselves as better and more complete humans'.[13]

When the plan to enter Commodore Bay could not be realised, the ships of the Hamburg South Seas Expedition moved on to the Willaumez Peninsula on 18 April 1909, where the members of the expedition had already encountered apprehensive and reserved villagers a year before. The visit to a series of sand dunes on the northern shore of Hannam Bay was summarised with disappointment in the log: 'The scientific yield was small; the physical anthropologist in particular was only superficially successful. Even the production of his skin colour chart made people flee' (Hellwig 1927: 88). There were similar experiences on the other side of the Willaumez Peninsula, for, on 30 November 1908, Hellwig (1927: 90) reported as follows on entering a deserted village: 'Here too the natives had noticed our advance and had flown into the bush as quickly as possible. Only one remained behind, to call out to us "not got boy" and disappear the next minute. They had obviously taken us for a recruiting expedition.'

Accordingly, the image of the whites among the Nakanai hardly seems to have been any more positive than the image of the Nakanai among the Tolai. If, because of the depictions of the Tolai, the Nakanai had a bad reputation in the eyes of the whites, this was undoubtedly based on reciprocity.

Pupils and teachers

The first more permanent encounters between the Nakanai and the whites took place on the Gazelle Peninsula, more precisely at a mission station situated on the river Toriu run by Fr. Friedrich Hees. At the start of the 1910s, 'some boys of the Nakanai people' were to be 'taught and raised' here, as Hees (1913a: 104) writes, 'in order gradually to prepare even this poor tribe for conversion'.[14]

On the basis of his contacts with the total of six 'boys', five of whom came from the area of Mount Pago and one from around Lolobau Island, Hees published four brief reports in the Order's journal, the *Monatshefte*, in 1913 and 1914.[15] These texts, however, seem to be completely unknown in the English-language literature, since Valentine (1958: xxxiii), Chowning and Goodenough (1965/66: 472n8) and Johnston (1980a: 4) refer only to a collection of 'legends and tales' published by Hees in *Anthropos* in 1915/16.[16]

Nevertheless, Hees can be described as an 'ancestor of Nakanai research', that is, as a predecessor of Valentine. In addition, he did indeed contribute, at least indirectly, to the 'conversion of this poor tribe': before founding the first Catholic mission station on the Hoskins Peninsula (Chapter 1), Joseph Stamm visited Hees and his 'charges' on the Toriu in order to follow Hees in learning Nakanai from them (Johnston 1980a: 4).

To illustrate his comments on Nakanai culture, Hees frequently cites passages from their 'legends and tales'. Almost like an ethnographer, he describes individual incidents from his living together with the 'boys', and he quotes them first in obviously literal translations and then more and more in the original language, often also going into the context of the respective conversation or repeating whole passages of dialogue. Hees not only shows methodological care and a somewhat critical attitude vis-à-vis his sources, in the person of his six informants, but also allows the Nakanai to speak for themselves for the first time, after they had previously only been spoken or written about, whether by the Tolai or by Western travellers.[17]

Although Hees openly admits in his first report that he is primarily concerned with the 'conversion' of the Nakanai, he simultaneously contrasts his own perspective with that of his 'charges':

> The present relationship between them and me could be described briefly as one of pupils and teacher. However, I would like to refrain from the comfort of briefness, since it has not at all found the approval of the 'pupils' who believe they are degraded by such a view. They themselves explained to me by touching on the question of our relationship that although I would certainly teach them the *lotu* (service), they would teach me their language, so that we would be faithfully taking turns in being teacher and pupil. (1913a: 104)

Hees adopts this view himself when, at the end of his first report and following the reproduction of a myth, he states 'that not for nothing was it said at the outset that we are pupil and teacher to one another' (1913a: 108).

On the other hand, however, Hees (1913a: 107) hints with desirable clarity at different forms of violence used against the 'boys': 'Admittedly constant attention could not yet be found among them, but here and regardless of our friendship in other respects, I helped along occasionally and effectively with the pointer.' One morning, Hees (1913b: 344) writes, the 'pupils' packed bedrolls, dishes and bush knives and 'were already riding along in the heavy seas of the Toriu, when a worker surprised them and caused them to return immediately'.[18] In the same rather casual tone, Hees repeats the statement of one of the 'boys' that, as a member of the tribe of the 'E Holuhólu', he must not eat a particular species of shark, continuing as follows: 'coincidentally I came along and remarked to him that these fishes would be eaten here, and I had him fed with a good chunk' (1914b: 215).

Corporal punishment, deprivation of freedom and the requirement to break culturally specific food taboos can, of course, hardly be reconciled with the claim to be 'pupil and teacher to one another'. Accordingly, Hees himself viewed the Nakanai with not a little contradiction and ambivalence. He praises their 'fondness of and skill in storytelling' (1913a: 108, 1914b: 213), as well as their ability to observe, adapt and learn. He gives examples of their sense of honour and courage (1914b: 215) and stresses that one could 'only call satisfactory their behaviour, performance and submission to school discipline', while at the same time complaining that 'the native' would only recognise 'external force'. Without this, Hees (1914b: 216) goes on, 'his guides are traditional habits, mood and temperament, and his will, governed by unordered passions and malice, leaves no place for reason'.

Each of these different judgements corresponds to an aesthetic evaluation. Whereas Hees (1914b: 210) writes of the Nakanai that 'their large, powerful men and pretty, slim women are emphasised admiringly by all travellers', not even the tasteful colour composition of his body painting could do anything to alter the fact 'that the [individual] Nakanai in all his splendour still makes a repulsive impression on a European'.[19]

Despite all the contradiction and ambivalence, Hees apparently cannot deny a certain sympathy when he describes the desire of his 'charges' to return to where they were born: 'Who would wish to blame the boys when they frequently look down in the direction of their mountains … when in the melancholy mist of the mountains they only recognise a homeland wondrously courted by the hazy mood of fairy tales … and in their world of thoughts give prominence to the forthcoming joy of reunion?' (1914a: 161)

Here one cannot help receiving the impression that the homesickness of the 'boys' is in reality wanderlust on the part of Hees himself. He also looks 'down in the direction of their mountains' and is almost painfully aware of the fact that, as he asserts elsewhere, 'the entire way of life of the Nakanai and the environment the children came from [represents] an almost unknown new country' (1914b: 216). In one of his reports Hees writes that, 'from year to year, civilisation is knocking at the gates of the Nakanai with increasing impetuosity'(1914a: 162), and yet in 1915/16 he still states that the sea charts end 'directly beyond the island of *Lolobao* or Duportail' and that therefore 'the entire Nakanai region is a *terra incognita*' (1915/16: 36; italics in original).

Goodenough's expedition

From October to December 1951, some thirty-five years after the publication of Hees's collection of 'legends and tales', Ward Goodenough undertook a reconnaissance trip through different parts of New Guinea in order to select a site for future field research. In doing so, he spent a day in Galilo and visited several coastal villages, including Koimumu, in the company of a white trader.[20]

Goodenough's choice finally fell on New Britain. He believed that, in comparison with, for example, the Massim region, the island would be 'the less known, the more varied, and the more colorful' and that it would offer 'opportunities for every kind of ethnological interest' (Goodenough 1952: 37). Using the same term as Hees before him, Goodenough states that, although the Gazelle Peninsula was already known quite well, 'the rest of the island, with the exception of only one or two tribes has remained *terra incognita* to this day.[21] Accordingly, the main task of the research expedition led by Goodenough was to fill in 'white spots' on the ethnographic map.

On 13 March 1954, Goodenough arrived with two of his students, Ann Chowning and Daris Swindler, at the Methodist mission station in Malalia. Two days later, the group proceeded to Galilo and moved into a house built for the colonial administration (*haus kiap*).[22] Until the end of his stay on 21 June 1954, Goodenough focused on examining social organisation, in order, as he writes (1954: 41), to collect basic information as a background for the more specialised research of the other participants in the expedition. Chowning, who remained until 1 September 1954, concerned herself with the social and economic lives of the women, while Swindler, who had already departed a week before Goodenough, not only measured the inhabitants of the different villages as a physical anthropologist but also took numerous blood samples and teeth impressions.

Goodenough still recalls today that during his reconnaissance trip the Kivung had been a constant topic of conversation in Galilo, Koimumu and neighbouring villages. Thus, even before the start of his expedition, in 1952, Goodenough had already referred to cargo cults in order to explain why, out of New Britain as a whole, he had decided upon the coast of the Hoskins Peninsula for fieldwork:

> The West Nakanai are of special interest at the present time because of a strong nativistic movement. Movements of this kind have developed in many parts of the world as a reaction against Europeans and outside dominance. In New Guinea they began to appear before the war in a form which has given them the name of Cargo Cult. While Cargo Cults vary a great deal locally, they usually start with the emergence of a native prophet who claims that the ancestors, or some other divine agent, are going to send a great ship laden with all kinds of European cargo which will be distributed free to the natives. A new era will follow in which natives will have equal status with whites or in which whites will be driven from New Guinea. In the past decades Cargo Cults have sprung up among a number of tribes in the New Guinea territory. The West Nakanai are one of them. (Goodenough 1952: 16)

Goodenough knew that the colonial administration regarded the Kivung as a potential threat. A summary of the Patrol Report dated 7 April 1954 and classified as confidential, in which E.S. Sharp had articulated his corresponding disquiet (Chapter 1), can be found in the field notes of the expedition's participants, and Goodenough (1954: 40) writes in the same year that, although the Batari movement itself was no longer active at the time of his reconnaissance trip, the then Assistant District Officer, Ian Skinner, had received many indications that something similar was looming. A later statement of Goodenough's (1962: vii), in the foreword to Swindler's dissertation, may also refer to such fears: 'Finally, government officials considered the West Nakanai to be a problem group administratively. They expressed genuine interest in the possibility of broadening their knowledge and understanding of Nakanai ways and circumstances.'

In an interview, Goodenough (30 November 2001) told me how he had hardly arrived in Galilo when Lima, the supposed leader of the Kivung, visited him with his followers several times and reversed the planned roles of observer and observed by asking him about the Kivung: 'They sounded us out what we thought about this thing, very obliquely.' Already on the sixth day of his stay in Galilo, Goodenough found himself compelled to write an entry in his journal in which he first refers to Lima and his economic activities and then mentions Heinrich Berger, the resident priest of Valoka: 'Is his "company" more than just a copra set-up. Is there something of a cultish movement of which he is leader or a leader. If so, it would seem to have Father Berger's general blessing. ???. Something interesting seems to be present.[23]

The investigation of the Kivung – next to filling in the 'white spots' on the ethnographic map, the expedition's most important task – was to be assigned to Charles Valentine. He arrived with his first wife Edith in Galilo a good month after Goodenough, Chowning and Swindler, and a few days later, on 27 April 1954, they moved to Rapuri, Lima's home. While the inhabitants of Galilo, the only Methodist village and the largest village of the region, were known for never having joined either the Kivung or the Batari movement, Rapuri, much smaller and under Catholic influence, counted as less conservative or 'traditional' and as the centre of the Kivung. Until their departure in October 1954, both Valentines lived there in a house probably built on Lima's land and at his behest.

A second stay, again of about six months and again accompanied by Edith, followed in 1956. Between 1977 and 1979, Valentine finally returned one last time to Rapuri in the context of temporary employment at the University of Papua New Guinea, this time for a total of five months and together with his second wife Bettylou and their son Jonathan Ragi.[24]

However, even before his first arrival in Rapuri, Valentine must have heard not only of Goodenough's supposition that there was perhaps 'something of a cultish movement' with Berger's 'general blessing' but also of the fear of the colonial administration that the Batari movement might somehow be revitalised in the form of the Kivung (Chapter 1). Moreover, Valentine is most likely to have known the reference to cargo cults which Goodenough had used to explain his choice of the Hoskins Peninsula or the West Nakanai in 1952: when, in a letter of the same year, he informed his parents about his forthcoming fieldwork, Valentine followed Goodenough in mentioning the expectation of a ship full of Western goods.[25]

Report

The Batari movement

In his report to the colonial administration (Chapter 1), Valentine constructs a coherent and uninterrupted process of development which starts with older beliefs, proceeds via the Batari movement and for the time being ends with the Kivung. Even before the German colonial period was over, Valentines writes, most of the West Nakanai believed that their own ancestors had already been in possession of Western goods, that is, of cargo. Then the cargo had been lost, but it would eventually be returned to its legitimate or original owners. Moreover, the ancestors, who allegedly assume a white skin after death, were said to be living in Rome, where they would manufacture the cargo supernaturally. For Valentine (1955a: 6), the individual Nakanai increasingly came to see cargo no longer as a thing in itself but rather as a symbol of all he wanted but did not know how to get.

In Valentine's view, these ideas were picked up when, prior to the Second World War, the world market price for copra fell and caused a severe economic crisis. Two agents from Germany and Japan arrived in Rabaul on the Gazelle Peninsula, 'sent into New Guinea to prepare the native population for the inevitable invasion' (1955a: 10). One of them called himself 'Master Hitler' ('Masta Hitla' in Tok Pisin) and approached Batari, who was employed in Rabaul by the Catholic Church as a contract worker. He told him that the deceased Nakanai, white in skin colour, would stay in Rome to produce the cargo and wanted to send it to their descendants. The Europeans or the Australians, however, were appropriating the corresponding shiploads. Valentine (1955a: 14) further summarises Masta Hitla's message as follows:

> The dead ancestors want to return to the living, but they are prevented from doing so by the Europeans, and to hasten the return of the dead the living must defy their masters in every way. When the dead return they will bring with them all the material things of European culture, as well as European knowledge, social and political institutions, and freedom from European rule. The dead

will come in great armadas of ships and planes, and they will be known as Nippon or Japan.

Thus inspired, Batari completed his contract work and returned to his homeland, where in the meantime people had already begun to organise a cult on the basis of Masta Hitla's statements. But the Australian colonial administration stationed in Talasea regarded this as a 'disturbance' and imprisoned Batari, without, however, being able to deprive the 'Cargo Belief' of its force. Instead the cult organisation went underground and continued to develop until the control of the Australian colonial administration broke down at the beginning of 1942. Batari was released from prison and, according to Valentine, 'the Movement came out into the open'.[26]

Batari assumed supreme leadership and the title of 'King'. After him came two or three men designated 'Number Two', who led an 'army' of about five hundred men and spread the movement from village to village where other functionaries, including a 'Number One Kiap', a 'Number Two Kiap', a 'Police Master' and a 'Clerk', were appointed. Valentine sees this administrative organisation as 'a remarkable development of symbolic Europeanism' (1955a: 16).

One of the essential elements of the Batari movement was the 'rejection and destruction of certain aspects of the existing culture': people were encouraged to commit adultery or conclude new marriages, destroy food supplies and write down magical formulae (1955a: 14). Batari and his followers rejected existing relations with the whites, and resistance to the orders of the colonial administration, as well as rejection of plantation work and church attendance, was propagated. At the mission station in Valoka, Batari's 'soldiers' imprisoned and mistreated the Austrian Fr. Josef Weigl. In order to enter into contact with the deceased and bring about their return to the land of the living, the adherents of the Batari movement sought to avoid social conflicts. Villages were to be kept permanently clean, great feasts were put on at specially decorated cemeteries and dances described as traditional were held.

Then the Japanese did indeed march in. According to Valentine (1955a: 20), they were at first 'welcomed with some hopefulness if not great enthusiasm', but they soon made themselves unpopular because they ordered Weigl to be released and not only captured and beat up Batari but also deported him to prison in Rabaul. Robbed of its leader, the organisation of the Batari movement soon broke down, the Nakanai believing 'that Batari had perverted the true teaching of Master Hitler and so led them into ruin' (1955a: 21). When, from 1944 on, the Japanese in their turn had to retreat before the US forces, the aspirations initially directed towards the Japanese were quickly revived and transferred onto the Americans, who now came to be identified with the ancestors. When the war was over, however, the Australian administration returned. In its name, Batari and his office-holders were interrogated repeatedly, put before a court and sentenced to prison terms. The Nakanai took this merely as evidence of the fact 'that the white man was hiding the secret of the Cargo from them and penalizing those who sought to find it' (Valentine 1955a: 23). As a result, for Valentine the 'Cargo Belief' remained as strong as it had been before 'because none of the motives behind it had been removed and none of its fundamental tenets had been disproved'. Thus, Valentine (1955a: 23) continues, 'the Nakanai were very nearly back where they had started before the war, with a set of systematic beliefs but no organization by which to put them into effect'.

The Kivung

Even without being translated into practical actions, between 1944 and 1946 the beliefs underlying the Batari movement continually developed further into a 'complex mythology' (Valentine 1955a: 23) according to which blacks and whites had once lived together peacefully in a place on Nakanai territory called Rome, both made by God in the same way and both having unrestricted access to the cargo.[27] Then, however, a conflict broke out, and all the whites, together with some of the blacks, sailed away with the cargo in order to people the whole world and to found a city named after their home place. There they started a movement which, according to Valentine (1955a: 26), was obviously identical with the Catholic Church and which had the aim of preserving and spreading the advantages of one's old way of life. With this aim in mind, some whites had wanted to return to the Nakanai and to bring them the cargo and their superior way of life, but they were prevented from doing so by being killed while still en route. Nonetheless, the ancestors would continue to attempt to return, and the first success of these endeavours was the fortunate appearance of the liberating Americans towards the end of the Second World War. When the Australians forced the Americans to leave New Britain and the rest of New Guinea, however, the millennium was put off again. 'Following all this,' Valentine (1955a: 26) concludes his summary of the myth[28] in its 1946 version, 'the way to obtain cargo and the superior way of life associated with it is to heed the message of the Movement in Rome and draw the Americans back to the land of the Nakanai.'

In the same year, 1946, the same Berger mentioned by Goodenough was transferred by his superiors first to Vavua and then to Valoka. There he had the people tell him the myth summarised above, and he assured them that all this was correct, that under his, Berger's, leadership Batari would have been successful and that he, Berger, alone knew 'the true Secret of Cargo'. He offered to lead a new movement to attain the goals of the 'Cargo Belief', met with enthusiastic agreement and became what Valentine calls the 'organizing genius behind the present Nakanai Cargo Cult', first known as the 'Catholic Action Party' but later as the Kivung.[29]

For Valentine, Berger has the highest leadership position within the Kivung, he takes all the important decisions himself and he chooses and instructs the higher functionaries, including, first of all, Lima of Rapuri. Here, the idea that Berger can excommunicate disobedient Kivung followers, exclude them from the forthcoming distribution of the cargo or condemn them to death and hellfire leads to 'virtually complete conformity and subservience in even the most trying circumstances' (Valentine 1955a: 43). Thus Berger has been able, as Valentine writes (1955a: 52), 'to dictate virtually at will what relations the West Nakanai people will have with most of the individuals and institutions they come into contact with' and 'to lead the people in a successful eight-year-long campaign of passive resistance to all Administration policies', so that neither local government councils nor cooperatives promoted by the administration could be introduced.[30]

On the basis of the myth summarised above, and in fundamental continuity with ideas from the time of the Batari movement, the adherents of the Kivung pursued their goal 'phrased as living like Europeans and returning to the lost ancestral way of life in preparation for the millennium of Cargo' (Valentine 1955a: 31). According to Valentine, Christian commandments and prohibitions had to be observed, and a supposedly Western form of family living was propagated, with obedience to parents, a harmonious married life and regular meals and prayers. In each village there were two to six wooden houses, with corrugated iron roofs, tables and chairs – E.S. Sharp had mentioned small round houses (Chapter 1) – as well as an assembly hall used for discussions and designated as a storeroom for the expected cargo. The villages, and especially the cemeteries, were to be kept spotlessly clean, and at specified times certain signals would summon the adherents of the Kivung to eat, participate in communal work or attend church.

In addition, there is what Valentine calls the 'economic branch of the Movement', known as the 'Kampani', behind which Goodenough had early on suspected there to be 'something of a cultish movement'. After failed experiments in planting rice, cooperatively produced copra was sold to Frank Maynard, who ran the only plantation in the West Nakanai area, and who paid between one- and two-thirds of the legal price and sometimes distributed corrugated iron to individual villages for house-building. On one occasion, the adherents of the Kivung also received a shipload of industrially processed food, which Berger and Maynard announced as the 'first instalment of Cargo', but, since there was only a little for each family, it had merely led to general disappointment (Valentine 1955a: 36). Valentine (1955a: 36) states that, based on his observations, he is certain that Maynard 'has quite deliberately engaged in partnership with Fr. B. to exploit the Cargo belief to the greatest possible extent for his own gain'. In any case, the greatest part of the income obtained from the sale of the copra would go to Berger in the form of 'taxes'. According to Valentine (1955a: 34), he claimed he was sending this money to America in order bring the Americans, that is the ancestors, back to New Britain.

While the activities, commandments and prohibitions propagated within the Kivung were declared to be in compliance with Catholic teachings, Valentine (1955a: 31) sees them merely as a 'public façade' concealing the conviction shared by the initiated that all their efforts will eventually lead to the acquisition of the cargo. Within the hierarchy of the Kivung, the respective leaders hand down the individual elements of this 'secret doctrine' only to the extent that they 'feel its recipients can be trusted to keep it hidden from possible enemies of the Movement' (Valentine 1955a: 40). Valentine (1955a: 41) continues: 'Interwoven with this system of levels of secrecy and participation is a rather elaborate development of both oral and written double-talk.' At the Kivung assemblies, 'metaphorical language' and 'double meaning' would be pursued to such a degree that the meaning of an entire speech often remained hidden from anyone other than the initiated (Valentine 1955a: 42). According to Valentine, this created 'an atmosphere curiously compounded of varying degrees of secrecy, continuous rumours and not a little public confusion'. Thus a 'diffuse system' emerged that was able to sustain itself by compelling or inspiring people to believe in goals that were too vague to be checked. Moreover, Valentine (1955a: 42) writes, it became difficult for any outsider to determine responsibility, and Berger himself would be personally protected even if the 'secret doctrines' were to be revealed.

The only person who, in Valentine's view, 'has ever managed to deal a real blow to the Movement' was Fr. Franz Xaver Wagner, stationed at Sio in the interior, who, although certainly a colleague and compatriot of Berger's, rejected the latter's character and activities and had done everything in his power to oppose the Kivung.[31] However, since Wagner did not have much influence in the coastal area of the Hoskins Peninsula, Valentine (1955a: 45) sees the greatest threat to the Kivung in a combination of some of the Methodist inhabitants of Galilo, under the leadership of the same Boas referred to by E.S. Sharp (Chapter 1), and the Australian administration. In fact, most of the Kivung leaders had already been sentenced to at least one prison term, having been convicted for spreading 'false reports' following corresponding accusations from Boas and his followers (Valentine 1955a: 49). Because of the prescribed secrecy, however, the Kivung opponents had not been able to provide much more than rumours and either did not know Berger's role or did not dare to bring a charge against him. For Valentine (1955a: 50), court trials and imprisonments failed to fulfil the expectations of the administration and even had an opposite effect: '[T]hese experiences serve to confirm periodically and effectively not only the fundamental assumption that Europeans penalize all attempts to discover the Secret of the Cargo but also the necessity for hiding Kivung activities so long preached by Fr. B.'

According to Valentine (1955a: 44), at the time of his first field trip the Nakanai cargo movement counted more than 5,000 adherents from four different language groups, after having started originally as a 'highly secret cult' with only Berger and a few of the highest leaders as participants. For Valentine (1955a: 57), this growth had the potential to continue unimpeded in the future, since, like other cargo movements, the Kivung of the Nakanai was based on widespread ideas and embodied 'a consciously Pan-Melanesian ideal'. Encouraged by Berger, Valentine (1955a: 58) continues, 'the leaders and many of the followers of the Kivung consciously look forward to spreading their doctrine and organization over the whole of New Guinea and beyond'.

In the last version of his report to the colonial administration, completed after his second stay in Rapuri, Valentine does indeed write of the geographical spread of the cargo movement. He states, however, that while having maintained 'essentially the same character and organization' (1956a: 70) as at the beginning it had also lost some of its unity and was thus no longer able 'to act as a single body in the way that the West Nakanai Kivung does'.[32] At the same time, Valentine sees a gradually continuing process of 'partial disillusionment', which results from waiting in vain for 'miraculous events' to occur and which repeats or continues the disappointment over the first shipload of industrially processed food. By the end of 1956, there were only a few villages in which the signals for eating, communal work or church attendance could be heard daily, and the number of villages with the old functionaries of the movement still in power was even lower. According to Valentine (1956a: 74), the communal organisation had become more informal, and the slow decline of the Kivung's authority became obvious when the villagers became less willing to participate in the annual celebration of Berger's name day with dancing and donations. People still believed that the millennium would somehow be brought about by their movement, but they now had doubts whether they could achieve this by giving gifts to the priest or by performing dances (Valentine 1956a: 75).

In addition, after his second stay in Rapuri, Valentine (1956a: 73) states that Kivung and Kampani – closely interconnected as they had been in the past – were 'becoming increasingly disconnected'. While, on the side of the opposition, Boas and his followers were prospering economically, the people's own copra production had all but come to a standstill and the consequences were being felt. The Kampani had basically broken up into various groups, one of which was pursuing trade with a Chinese trader who had since replaced Maynard, while another one was placing its hopes in a new firm, founded at Berger's suggestion and named the 'West Nakanai Advance Society (Catholic Division)' (Valentine 1956a: 78–81). If, Valentine (1956a: 82) writes, the Kivung were to break up as an organisation, these groups might eventually develop into new centres of power.

Interpretation

Just as Valentine traces the Batari movement first and foremost back to Batari or to Masta Hitla, he also explains what in his view are the central elements of the Kivung, such as rejection of the colonial administration, a rigid hierarchy and pervasive secrecy, all through Berger's influence. When he mentions him for the first time, Valentine (1955a: 27) already attributes to Berger a 'predominantly paranoid orientation toward life', expressed in the fact that he believed himself to have long been persecuted by the administration and was seeking to get as much personal power as possible out of whatever situation he might find himself in. Accordingly, in the 'Postscript on the role of Fr. B.', one of the additions in the third version of his report (Chapter 1), Valentine (1956a: 88) writes: 'It is my opinion, as I have stated briefly in the body of this report, that Fr. B. is mentally abnormal. I believe this is the only possible explanation for his extra ordinary career among the Nakanai, and it is consistent with all that I saw of him during my stay there.'

At the time of Valentine's first and second stay in Rapuri, it was usual in the context of 'cargo research' not only to name phenomena like the Batari movement after individual persons but also to place these persons at the centre of interpretation.[33] In contrast to Valentine, however, Catholic functionaries refer not to Masta Hitla but to a Czech by the name of Zyganek, who had allegedly instructed Batari 'to form and drill native battalions, and then to wait for ships to bring firearms and ammunition'.[34]

Since, in the 1940s, colonial officials, missionaries and planters had already accused one another of causing cargo cults (Lindstrom 1993: 15–25), Valentine portrays Berger as a kind of white cargo cult leader, and in his field notes he even talks about 'the suffering and ignorance imposed on the people by Berger's cargo cult'.[35] Thus Valentine allows a picture to emerge that shows an authoritarian system of compulsion, with an autocrat, who at times recalls a character from a Joseph Conrad novel, using unrestricted power to rule over his followers, who, in their turn, appear as helplessly dependent and almost as puppets without a will of their own. Berger's followers become passive victims of the external influences breaking over them in the course of colonisation and missionisation. This corresponds to the Western understanding, already old by the start of the 1950s, of cargo cults as symptoms of a disturbance of equilibrium or health triggered by such external influences, and 'native cargo cult leaders' were often no less 'mentally abnormal' for colonial officials and missionaries than Berger is for Valentine.[36]

Although Valentine's interpretation shows him to be a 'child of his time', when viewed from the present-day perspective he is also, in many respects, ahead of his time. He writes that the Kivung unites members of different language groups and that it might spread further in the future, only a few years after Jean Guiart had described cargo cults as

'Forerunners of Melanesian nationalism' (1951b), and only a few years before Peter Worsley (1957: 228) listed as one of their main effects that they 'weld previously hostile and separate groups together into a new unity'.[37] Worsley was to defend cargo cults against the charge of irrationality that was implicit in the thesis of a disturbance of health. Adopting ideas from Tibor Bodrogi (1951: 282) and later influencing, among others, Wilhelm Emil Mühlmann (1961: 7), Worsley (1957: 227) saw cargo cults as a positive attempt to acquire Western goods in order to remove economic and political inequality in relation to the whites and thus to end one's own subjection.[38] At the same time, Worsley (1957: 231) believed that he could identify a general development 'away from apocalyptic mysticism towards secular political organisation, a trend from religious cult to political party and cooperative'.[39] Worsley's interpretation appears as, so to speak, a 'secular variant' of a model of explanation, which also emerged later and was formulated mainly by mission theologists who held cargo cults to be local forms of a universal *Search for salvation* (Strelan 1977; see also Schwarz 1980) common to all humanity; the expected redemption thus consists not in freedom from inequality and subjugation but in the return of a saviour.

However, while Worsley still sees the desired Western goods primarily under the aspect of their economic and political use, Valentine's understanding of cargo as a symbol of all the individual wants but does not know how to get already anticipates insights that Kennelm Burridge and Peter Lawrence were to formulate in the 1960s. In their 'classics' of 'cargo research', *Mambu* (Burridge 1960) and *Road belong cargo* (Lawrence 1964), they both understood Western goods as carriers of culturally specific meanings. Like Valentine, but in contrast to Worsley, on the basis of their own fieldwork they interpreted cargo cults primarily as an expression of equally specific orientation and value systems.[40]

Lawrence in particular describes a cargo movement as a succession of several attempts at explanation and action, following and building on one another. The much-acclaimed historical perspective[41] underlying this description can be found already in Valentine's account: while putting the figure of the missionary at the forefront, he certainly stresses convergences and continuities by picturing a coherent and uninterrupted process of development that begins before the First World War and ends in the mid-1950s.

Valentine's interpretation of cargo cults in general and the Kivung in particular was to change drastically after he stayed in Rapuri for a third time at the end of the 1970s. In a collection of articles on development and migration in what was now the independent state of Papua New Guinea, co-edited with his second wife, they describe the emergence of a colonial system of political and economic injustice exploiting the 'simple' villagers and depriving them of their rights. According to the Valentines (1979a: 65), however, this system is answered by a 'militant regional movement of protest' with the Kivung and the Kampani as its politico-religious and economic branches, the two constituting 'closely associated sides'. Yet, although the Kivung and Kampani initially succeeded in preventing the planned introduction of local government councils, in 1968 the Australian administration deployed an 'anti-riot force of police with rifles' against the five hundred to one thousand villagers who were demonstrating in Hoskins, and declared the controversial councils to be effective.[42] The Valentines (1979a: 69) summarise the consequences as follows: 'The historical movement organized by the villagers was set back severely and has not recovered its former vigor in the following decade.'

Here the adherents of the Kivung turn from being the victims of the unrestricted power of a white autocrat to being the victims of a capitalism introduced in the wake of colonisation, against which, however, they now act to defend themselves – accompanied by the intense sympathy of the same Valentine who had carried out research in the interests of the Australian administration in the 1950s and presented them with a report. As its adherents remain victims but become active in resisting the effects of colonisation, the Kivung changes, so to speak, from an authoritarian system of compulsion into a positive achievement, which 'supervised community social life, preserved both Christian and Melanesian sacred traditions, and organized local politics throughout a sizeable region' (Valentine and Valentine 1979a: 65). The Valentines (1979a: 65) even describe the combined movement of Kivung and Kampani as 'the main modern voice of local people' and in so doing explicitly decline to talk of a cargo cult: 'This movement is like many another action group of grassroots protest in the history of this country. As such it has been misunderstood and opposed by authorities and outsiders who call it mere traditionalism or senseless rebellion, often summed up wrongly in the label "cargo cult".'

In the concluding chapter of their edited volume, the Valentines thus place the Kivung in the context of social movements which had been used to protest against Western influences throughout Melanesia. While governments were correct in seeing such activities and organisations as 'forms of local and popular struggle', they had allegedly allowed themselves to be deceived by anthropologists and other 'experts from the outside world', and had designated these 'people's organizations' cargo cults, reacting to them with a mixture of contempt and fear (Valentine and Valentine 1979b: 99). The Valentines (1979b: 100) speak of a 'misapplied, over-used label "cargo cult"', which, in their view, is based on the fact that particular aspects of the respective movements 'have been exaggerated out of proportion by outsiders', thus making it easy for the opponents of such movements 'to dismiss them as primitive supernaturalism which must be suppressed'.

In his re-evaluation or reinterpretation of cargo cults in general and of the Kivung in particular, Valentine mainly seems to follow the explanatory model propagated by Worsley. From the present-day perspective, however, Valentine was again ahead of his time: by tracing the term 'cargo cult', which he himself had used earlier, back to the aims of colonial rule and by thus understanding this term first and foremost as a Western creation, he was already formulating an idea which only came to gain currency following a later 'self-reflexive turn' in 'cargo research': various interpretations of the phenomena labelled 'cargo cults' were seen as reducing them to only a few of their respective aspects in order then to turn these aspects into elements of Melanesian culture in general as a kind of 'cargo culture'. Thus it becomes possible to claim that, for example, economic undertakings, the foundation of Christian communities and political movements are all 'like cargo cults'.[43]

The reductions underlying these generalisations are all seen to refer to prevailing dispositions of Western culture itself. If cargo cults – as the name itself already suggests – are mainly about the acquisition of Western goods and if the corresponding theories are marked by economic metaphors, this might also be an expression of a predominant materialism on the part of the West, or of the fact that, in this context, as Ton Otto (1992b: 6) writes, 'the economy has become the primary locus of cultural innovation'. If, on the other hand, cargo cults are regarded as local forms of a universal desire for redemption, one does not feel surprised to find this view mainly among mission theologians. And, finally, it is most unlikely to be a mere coincidence to find that culture-specific orientation and value systems move to the forefront when the respective texts are authored by anthropologists.

Conflict

Success

Valentine describes his to some extent disastrous conflict with Berger (Chapter 1) in the last part of his report to the colonial administration under the heading of 'The author's relations with the present movement', and he justifies this as follows:

> Firstly, my assignment to investigate the Kivung as an anthropologist drew me willy nilly deeply into its affairs. Secondly, the experiences which my wife and I had as a result of this involvement help to reveal some important aspects of the Movement as it exists. And finally, our relations with the movement may have had some influence on its future.[44]

At the beginning of his time in Rapuri, Valentine, according to his account, experienced Berger as warm-hearted, cooperative and hospitable, as well as ready and willing to talk about the public façade of the Kivung.[45] Each time, however, that Valentine wanted to peer behind this façade,

Berger suddenly became evasive and denied knowing anything about any cargo movement or cargo belief among the Nakanai. 'He took some trouble', Valentine writes, 'to convince me that far from harbouring Cargo beliefs, Lima and the Kivung were the best possible antidote to the growth of such notions. When pressed he said that if there were any Cargo talk in the area it could only come from the anti-Kivung faction led by Boas.'

Yet Valentine obviously remained sceptical. He justified this scepticism by referring to the mistreatment of Weigl during the period of the Batari movement and, in particular after Goodenough's departure, saw his view as confirmed. I quote here the corresponding paragraph in its entirety, since it is the only one to have been systematically revised in the second version of Valentine's report:

> During the first four months of our work among the Nakanai, I received only vague hints of the secret doctrine and organization behind the Kivung's façade, which I studied intensively. By this time, however, I was convinced that there was more than met the eye, because the programme of good works exhibited to the public was carried out with a fervor difficult to attribute to Christian zeal in a people who only a few years previously had nearly murdered their priest *and had an active Cargo Cult in their immediate background. Dr. Goodenough felt that I had not addressed sufficient evidence to support my suspicions, which was indeed true at that time. So at the end of our first four months in the area, he left the field* with the impression that the Cargo Cult was dead among the Nakanai. *He made speeches in the Territory on his way home in which he expressed this opinion. By this time, however,* I had uncovered the fact that the Nakanai had paid large sums in taxes to Berger and that they expected some great but as yet unspecified reward for this sacrifice. *On the basis of this information Dr. Goodenough publicly accused* the mission of whom Berger was then the only representative in the area *of taking money from the natives on false pretenses or at least without correcting false impressions in the minds of the Nakanai.*[46]

While the news of Goodenough's statements – or, as the second version of the report has it, his supposed statements – did not reach the coastal villages of the Hoskins Peninsula for a month or more, Valentine learned the 'details of the Kivung secret'. Thus, Valentine assumes, Berger must have felt doubly threatened, and he reacted by telling the Nakanai that Goodenough had publicly accused them in Port Moresby of pursuing a cargo cult and that Valentine would do the same if people were to betray more to him. This would certainly be the end of all hopes of the cargo arriving.

Following this, Valentine in turn saw himself compelled to react, if only, as he writes, 'to clear Dr. Goodenough's name of the Father's slander' (1955a: 66). Valentine told the adherents of the Kivung that some of Berger's statements were untrue and only made to deceive them for the benefit of others. Berger responded with an order that no one must speak any further with Valentine about the affairs of the Kivung. When this made his research increasingly difficult, Valentine began what, in his account (1955a: 68), he calls 'a kind of campaign of limited reeducation': he visited most villages at least once in order to make people cooperate with the Australian administration and, more or less openly, to take his, Valentine's, side in the conflict caused by Berger. Thus Valentine hoped to find witnesses for his report to the administration, as well as to obtain sufficient information to continue his research (1955a: 67–68).

According to his own account, Valentine succeeded in making it clear to the adherents of the Kivung that Berger had deceived and exploited them in various ways and that in reality Western goods were made by humans. Berger responded again, this time by imposing an 'absolute tabu' against visiting Valentine's house or talking to him at all (Valentine 1955a: 72). When, one Sunday, Valentine refused to comply with Berger's prohibition on entering the church, Berger interrupted the service and immediately went to the station of the colonial administration in order to accuse Valentine of trespassing.[47] This, however, had no success, as Valentine writes (1955a: 72), and towards the end of his first stay eight men joined him in order to support his account of the Kivung to the colonial officer in charge.

According to the third version of his report to the administration, Valentine returned to Rapuri in 1956 and found Berger continuing in his attempts to deter the villagers from cooperation with him. In doing so, Berger was joined by his colleague and compatriot Fr. Georg Munzlinger.[48] Thus the conflict with Berger remained decisive, and Valentine assumed that should Berger come back to the West Nakanai after his home leave, which would probably begin at the end of 1956, the organisation of the Kivung was likely to survive with a few changes. If, however, Berger was replaced by a missionary 'who was willing and able to practice forcefully the official opposition of his Church to Cargo Beliefs, it seemed most unlikely that the Kivung organization could long survive in its present form' (Valentine 1956a: 77). Valentine did not want to imply that the social and economic conditions underlying the movement would lose their effect and that the resulting motivation or the attraction of the 'Cargo doctrine' would disappear as well. Nonetheless, he continued, 'it cannot be gainsaid that the whole situation would be greatly improved for all parties (including, in the long run, the Mission) if the influence of Fr. B. were removed'.[49]

All in all, Valentine's report to the colonial administration can be seen as virtually continuing his conflict with Berger. In portraying his opponent as a paranoid autocrat, Valentine seems to have sought relief from heartfelt rage and anger. At the same time, he obviously wanted to make the colonial administration take action against Berger by presenting him as the instigator of sustained passive resistance against all official policies and by explicitly referring to the spread and thus also to the relevance of the Kivung.

In the third version of his report, and corresponding to the experiences of his return to Rapuri, Valentine describes a tendency for the Kivung to become less important. In so doing, however, he attempts not to stress this tendency to a point that would render superfluous research into the causes of the Kivung or the struggle against its 'organizing genius'. The cargo movement loses some of its unity, but continues to spread geographically. There is 'partial disillusionment' and people feel the consequences of failed copra production, but, if Berger retains his power, it should be possible to resolve economic problems sufficiently 'to relegate them to second place once more in the concerns of Kivung members' (Valentine 1956a: 82). The authority of the Kivung is slowly declining, but although 'the remaining hierarchy of powerful men no longer functions as smoothly as it did before' this is not having any 'significant effect on the loyalty to the Movement of rank-and-file members'.[50]

Failure

The way Valentine describes his conflict with Berger in his report to the administration differs markedly from the picture that emerges from his field notes. According to an entry from 21 August 1954, he initially complained about not getting sufficient information on the Kivung, which he had also conveyed to Lima (CV 21 August 1954a: 2). Lima, in turn, reacted by visiting him over the next two days and by telling him for the first time that Berger had promised the imminent arrival of the cargo.[51] Yet two weeks later, on 7 September, Valentine confronted Lima again, now because he had allegedly accused some of Valentine's interlocutors of having betrayed too much to Valentine (CV 7 September 1954: 1). On 9 September, Valentine wrote the following with reference to a meeting at which several adherents of the Kivung complained about still not having been paid yet for earlier copra deliveries: 'Taking off from this point, I gave them quite a lecture on the deceit and real motives of brother Berger and Maynard, the fact that I know they are hiding from me, Manus, the U.N., etc. They evidence great interest in these ideas and express generalized agreement with and approval of them' (CV 9 September 1954: 3).

While in Valentine's report his conflict with Berger is caused by the latter's attack on Goodenough, in his field notes Valentine thus becomes the instigator himself because he wants to overcome the secrecy that he believes is shown to him by the adherents of the Kivung who have been deceived and misdirected by Berger. On 14 September, Valentine therefore delivered a speech to some fifty people in Rapuri.[52] Although this speech is not mentioned in Valentine's report, according to his notes it was to alter the course of his first field trip.

In it, he constructs an opposition between Berger and himself in which Berger, characterised as mean and often sick, stands for stultification and exploitation, while he himself, always generous and healthy, represents education and support. Thus Berger is allegedly lying to and intimidating the adherents of the Kivung merely to strengthen his own power and to enrich himself, whereas he, Valentine, would be following the best of intentions: 'I come to help you, to straighten out your thoughts and to enlighten.'[53] However, Valentine states a condition: '[Y]es, I can help you. But first you must tell us everything ... If you don't behave properly to us, we cannot behave properly to you.'[54] In any case, the opposition between the two rivals – at one point, Valentine (CV 14 September 1954: 3) speaks of 'Berger's way' and 'my way' – ultimately culminates in Valentine emphatically appealing to the people to side with him, while Berger should be brought before the court and expelled from the land of the Nakanai.

At first, however, this appeal seems to have found no particular resonance because, in Valentine's words, the audience reacted with 'nearly half an hour in almost complete silence' (CV 14 September 1954: 5), and by and large even his request that people should feel free to contradict or to question him remained unsuccessful.

In the days that followed, Valentine began to ask for support in the neighbouring villages, and he developed what, in his report, he calls 'a kind of campaign of limited reeducation' (1955a: 50). The reactions were again polite but reserved, and people said that, although Valentine was certainly right, nothing could be done, or that discussions would have to be held first before any decision could be made. At the same time, however, Valentine saw the inhabitants of Rapuri as increasingly dissociating themselves from him. On 24 September, that is, a bare two weeks after his speech, Valentine wrote that on the one hand they would like to act as if nothing had happened, while on the other they showed themselves to be concerned or ashamed and were no longer visiting him as often as before:

> For some days now only kids, a few of the young men who are secretly on our side, Kaavelevele, and people who smokes or medicine [*sic*] have come to our house. Many of those who have come even for these purposes have come only secretly, waiting til [*sic*] after dark, crawling about under the house, dodging the sections of ground lit up by our lamps, etc. (CV 24 September 1954)

On 1 October, Valentine even spoke of a 'campaign to keep people away from our house' (CV 1 October 1954). On 4 October, he mentioned a threat from Berger, according to which whoever spoke with him, Valentine, would receive no or only very little cargo,[55] and on 6 October, he reported a conversation with Laili, one of his main interlocutors:

This morning we had a long talk with Laili about the present situation here. He says that at present the main thing that is holding people back from joining us and getting rid of Berger is fear of a future without guidance. He says amny [*sic*] people have said to him that everything we tell them is true, but if they get rid of the Fr. and then we go away, who will lead them and guide them then? What road can they follow then, what wok can they kirap then? What white man will be there to steer them? ... Our answer to Laili was that in the immediate future they could do what I have told them over and over: sell their copra ... for twice or more the price they've been getting, campaign vigorously for a decent government school here, preserve the constructive aspects of the Kivung, and through all these means gradually educate themselves to the point where they can competantly [*sic*] manage more and more of their own affairs and not be at the mercies of whatever self-seeking or otherwise phoney 'guidance' is offered them by the nearest European ... I repeated that I would work hard to get help for them through the Government, the UN, or any other agency that might send me back here, provide money for some of them to travel a little, possible [*sic*] set up a school or even a development project here, etc. (CV 6 October 1954: 1)

At this point, Valentine was already quite sceptical about the results of his 'campaign of limited reeducation', because, in the context of the very same entry, he stated that the adherents of the Kivung would want an 'infallible leader' as well as 'glittering promises for a utopian future', and he assumed that this desire 'may yet defeat our efforts to get rid of Berger and help these people toward the point where they can deal more rationally with their problems' (CV 6 October 1954: 2).

Whereas Valentine concludes his report to the colonial administration by referring to the support he received from individual villagers and thus by portraying himself as having been successful, his field notes create, rather, an impression of failure. They become considerably less frequent as the end of Valentine's first field trip draws near, and on 8 October, under the heading 'Reign of terror', he stated that apart from Laili no one came to him any more, and that people hardly even greeted him any longer, or only in an unfriendly manner (CV 8 October 1954). By 21 October, Valentine's defeat seemed total. He reported the following: 'Lima convened a kivung in each place and told them all that he personally had killed the court, there would be no more proceedings against Berger, that Berger is now truly the boss of all Nakanai, and that no master is enough to rouse the Father' (CV 21 October 1954). Finally, the very last entry, written on 24 October, refers to a speech made by Munzlinger in the church at Vavua, according to which no one who had helped Valentine could still remain Catholic in the future (CV 24 October 1954).

Effects

Just as, according to his field notes, Valentine largely failed to persuade his audience to side with him, his attempt to make the colonial administration take action against Berger seems to have fallen on barren ground. Thus District Officer John Murphy welcomed Valentine's departure and wrote the following: 'I am sure that his presence, particularly towards the end of his sojourn, and his open and violent disagreements with Fr. Berger only served to exacerbate an already uneasy native situation.'[56]

The leader of his expedition and his designated doctoral supervisor, Goodenough, was not very pleased by Valentine's struggle with Berger either, having already considered the suspicion that there were cargo ideas behind the Kivung's 'public façade' as insufficiently proved. Goodenough (30 November 2001) recalls that he wrote Valentine 'a rather sharp letter telling him that he was out of order and this was not the kind of thing you did when you were doing anthropological fieldwork and so he never had anything to do with me again thereafter'. In addition, he assured me that Valentine had not fallen out of favour with Berger because of what he, Goodenough, had said, but 'because of his efforts to undermine Berger's influence with the cultists ... His claim that his motivation was to defend me is, I would say, an after the fact attempt to justify the hot water he got into by trying to compete with Berger for influence.'[57]

Accordingly, the way in which Valentine describes his conflict with Berger in his report to the colonial administration appears not to be free from of an occasional undertone of justification, as if he wants to defend himself in the face of criticism. This impression is strengthened when, in the third version of his text, Valentine not only claims to have checked all important statements many times, but also adds the assertion that he had 'integrated' his observations 'with the information given by informants' and that he had 'considered the opinion of all European [*sic*] in the area who were not directly associated with the Movement and who would discuss its activities' (1956a: 86).

After concealing, in the second version of his report, a difference of opinion with Goodenough and after he had in a sense protected him by no longer talking about his statements but about statements attributed to him, Valentine even distanced himself explicitly from fighting against Berger, although he was, in the end, to continue his struggle. Thus, before returning to Rapuri, he wrote to his designated doctoral supervisor: 'We have had quite enough of the controversy, however, and we feel strongly that nothing would be gained by or for anyone if further friction and conflict were to develop while we are in New Britain.'[58]

However, despite this concession – and regardless of who actually did not want to have anything to do with whom – there must have been a falling out: Valentine wrote his dissertation, submitted in 1958 and entitled 'An introduction to the history of the changing ways of life on the island of New Britain', under the supervision not of Goodenough, but of Alfred I. Hallowell, and not on the West Nakanai in particular but on the general history of New Britain from first contacts with whites into the 1950s.[59] With some very rare exceptions, Valentine refrains here from making any references to the Batari movement or the Kivung. Obviously he had planned their presentation and interpretation for a second part of his work, since there is a corresponding table of contents, though without page references, in an appendix. As far as I could find out, however, this second part was never written.

Even after submitting his dissertation, Valentine was to let the opportunity slip to utilise his data in any account focused on the original topic of his fieldwork. Instead, he used this material basically to illustrate historical considerations, for example, when he describes how, among the West Nakanai, a 'tripartite religious system' emerges out of 'tradition', Christianity and 'cargo components' (1959). He also refers to this 'system' in the context of his later attempts to reconstruct individual aspects of traditional culture such as masked dances (1961a), concepts of personhood (1963a) and beliefs linked to transcendent beings (1965, n.d.). Other historical considerations refer to the combination of written sources and oral tradition (Valentine 1960a; see also 1961b), as well as to the different reactions of Melanesians, Polynesians and Micronesians to the impacts of colonisation and missionisation.[60]

Thus Valentine's report to the colonial administration is the only place where he writes extensively about the Batari movement and the Kivung. Subsequently this theme retreats further and further into the background, until Valentine takes it up again – though in a much reduced form, as well as with an altered assessment and interpretation – in the volume he edited with his second wife Bettylou. However, neither here nor in any of his other texts does Valentine refer to his aforementioned report, and his conflict with Berger, too, is never again touched on with a single word.[61]

Until the end of the 1960s, Valentine found temporary employment in various universities in Kansas, Seattle and St Louis. Unlike his former fellow students, Chowning, Swindler and also Schwartz, he increasingly moved away first from Melanesia as his regional focus and then from anthropology in general. He engaged intensively with the concept of the 'culture of poverty' (1968) and between 1968 and 1973 lived with Bettylou in what they describe as a 'black ghetto' in a North American city,[62] while also becoming involved in the American civil rights movement. In an essay of 1975, the two Valentines speak of a 'mutual alienation between ourselves and our onetime colleagues or sometime comrades' (1975: 117n1). After his third stay in Rapuri – to some extent an interruption of his turning away from Melanesia and from anthropology – and following an invitation from the government there, Valentine worked as an English teacher in China for a year and a half, beginning in autumn 1982.[63] Towards the end of the 1980s visits to El Salvador and Nicaragua followed; then, on 17 June 1990, Valentine died of a heart attack in Seattle (Gilliam 1990).

Against the background of his later career, the course of Valentine's first stay in Rapuri, as this emerges from his field notes, could be described as a drama in which an anthropologist, although full of the best intentions, gradually but almost inexorably manoeuvres himself into a situation that isolates him from his hosts and informants, leads to a falling out with his designated doctoral supervisor, and accordingly prevents him from obtaining his due recognition within the academic community. The term 'drama', however, seems to be somewhat dramatic itself, and, all empathy aside, one should not neglect what is exemplary for the sake of the personal. In Chapter 6 of the present work, I shall therefore examine the question of how far Valentine's behaviour resulted from his pre-existing ideas and expectations, and if, on this basis, it is possible to make more general statements about anthropological perceptions of Other and Self.

Notes

1. See especially Powell (1884), Wichmann (1909, 1910, 1912), Friederici (1912) and Müller (1932).
2. On 'labour recruitment' in neighbouring regions, see Scarr (1970) and Corris (1973). Corris (1973: 26–27) shows that, in the Solomon Islands, people were lured on board ships with Western goods, taken away by force or, if they resisted, murdered in large numbers. Firth (1973: 14) describes the late 1870s as the 'golden age of German commerce in the Pacific'. Hanseatic trading companies like Hernsheim & Co. or Godeffroy & Son – renamed Deutsche Handels- und Plantagengesellschaft in 1887 – maintained settlements in the Gazelle Peninsula during this period. Even before missionaries, traders or representatives of the colonial administration had opened their first stations, however, whalers had appeared on the north-east coast of the Gazelle Peninsula (Gray 1999). According to Gray (1999: 24), their number reached a peak in 1840 and remained constant until 1870 before declining dramatically in the 1880s.
3. Rascher describes his activity as an interpreter and his travels to the area of Lolobau island in a volume published posthumously by members of his order (Missionare vom hlst. Herzen Jesu 1909: 202–29, 354–55). Friederici (1912: 14), who in 1908 travelled on a ship chartered by the colonial government to recruit workers, stresses the difficulties involved in carrying out academic research under such conditions: 'Everyone also knows that it is impossible to deal seriously with a native about anything if something is going on around him that diverts his attention. For example, it is out of the question to do any language recording with Melanesians when other Europeans in the neighbourhood are buying artefacts [or] taking photographs, let alone begin to check the huts occupied by women and girls for their contents. In such circumstances, I have always moved to a remote corner, preferably to my cabin on the ship, where the natives could not see anyone else.'
4. See Anonymous (1904a, 1904b, 1904c, 1904d, 1904e) for contemporary publications of the colonial government; F.D. (1904), Linckens (1904, 1905), Dicks (1905) and Schwester Brigitta (1905) for contemporary publications of the Catholic Church; Missionare vom hlst. Herzen Jesu (1909: 419–60), Linckens (1921: 49–58, 1922: 46–47), Bley (1925: 35–37), P.C. Janssen (1929), Kleintitschen (1929), Mertens (1932), Schmidt (1947), Waldersee (1995: 504–10) and Dunn (2004) for later mission histories; Hempenstall (1978: 147–50, 211, 1987: 109), Firth (1982: 143–44) and Hiery (1995a:

139–40, 178, 245) for later colonial histories; and Fajans (1985: 15–16) and Rohatynskyj (2000: 184) for later ethnographic presentations. In addition, the fairly extensive account of Jaspers (1979) tends to go beyond the above categories, in so far as they refer to the present.

5. See Jaspers (1979: 17–20).

6. Linckens (1904: 502). In his reports, published not long after the 'bloodbath' or 'massacre', Linckens goes only gradually into the charges laid against the missionaries. First he writes that 'some slanderous rumours [were] spread into the whole wide world as reasons' (1904: 502) and later he refers to the claim that To Maria 'was beaten up' before the deed, by claiming that this was a matter of 'pure invention' (1905: 360). Dicks (1905: 111) uses the term 'invention' with respect to newspaper reports in which Rascher is said to have whipped To Maria. Although, according to Dicks (1905: 112), 'corporal punishment for labourers' certainly existed in the colony, this was regulated by 'an ordinance of 20 June 1900'.

7. On the relationship between the Baining and the Tolai, see also Panoff (1987).

8. The first report on the murder of the missionaries that appeared in the Order's journal, the *Monatshefte zu Ehren Unserer Lieben Frau vom hlst. Herzen Jesu*, already refers to 'blood witnesses of Christ' ('Blutzeugen Christi', F.D. 1904: 452) and 'martyrdom' ('Martyrium', F.D. 1904: 454). In the following decades, the terms 'martyrdom' and 'martyr' were to be used regularly in church publications. Dunn (2004: 2), however, has recently put them in inverted commas in order to make it clear that none of the deceased 'has yet been designated as a "Martyr" in the ecclesiastical meaning of the term' and that many Baining who died at that time or in the context of later missionisation belonged with them. Dunn's volume was initiated by a church ceremony held in New Britain on the centenary of the 'martyrdom'. In fact, the deaths of many Baining had already been mentioned in the *Deutsche Kolonialzeitung* of 15 September 1904: 'the police troop ... has shot 15 of the guilty and captured 21. According to an official announcement of the governor, Dr Hahl, peace has been fully restored in the Baining Hills' (Anonymous 1904a). A no less laconic tone is used in an account apparently written by Fr. Bernhard Bley and published together with texts by Rascher: 'How many Baining fell on this occasion can hardly be said with any accuracy, but it is clear that none of the murderers or their accomplices escaped' (Missionare vom hlst. Herzen Jesu 1909: 435). In a contemporary report, Schwester Brigitta (1905: 66) describes the police troop's 'punitive expedition' as a 'wild hunt ... since every one of the murderers who came into view was shot down'. According to Jaspers (1979: 10n29), 'one [speaks] ... of more than 100 Baining who fell victim to the hunt'.

9. Hempenstall (1978: 218), who carried out his archival research during the last years of Australian colonial rule in an intellectual climate in which 'interpretations that ascribed agency to Papua New Guineans and indicted the colonizers had much currency' (Neumann 1998: 34–35), notes with regard to New Guinea, Micronesia and Samoa in general that 'the Germans never gained absolute control over the politics of their Island populations'. The works of Hiery (1995a, 1995b, 2001b) can also be read as a plea against exaggerating German influence. Hiery claims that there was no anti-colonial resistance in New Guinea partly because the German colonial government, compared with the mission, proceeded 'much more carefully, patiently, gently, even considerately' (1995a: 247) and because individual officials appeared 'frequently not as opponents but as mediators, partners and advisers' (1995a: 266). This thesis, however, must be seen as odd. Neumann (1998: 35) rightly accuses Hiery of an attempt 'to rehabilitate German colonial rule in the Pacific', while, in referring to a 'handbook' edited by Hiery (2001c), Senft (2002: 300) speaks of chauvinism, as well as of a mentality similar to that of the 'German colonialists' around the end of the nineteenth century. Neumann (1998: 35) continues: 'Like other German historians writing against the backdrop of the reunification of Germany in 1990, Hiery seemed intent on rejecting the idea that Germany could be blamed for its past''

10. On the Hamburg South Seas Expedition, see also Hefele (1927), Reche (1954) and Fischer (1981). A link between this expedition and the 'bloodbath in the Baining Hills', already mentioned, emerges from an entry in the log for 13 April 1909, making reference to a visit to the mission station at Vunamarita: 'With the help of a Brother from Wuna Marita, Reche managed to obtain three skulls of the natives who had then murdered a number of St Paul's missionaries' (Hellwig 1927: 135). According to Reche (1954: 41) himself, however, 'the exhumed skeletons of three of the executed Baining murderers' had been 'salvaged' by Rudolf Pöch for 'scientific purposes'.

11. Richard Parkinson (1907: 202) uses the term 'argonauts' for these Tolai, a full fifteen years before Malinowski (1922). According to Hempenstall (1978: 123), towards the end of the 1880s these journeys were often financed by the whites, since the Tolai had demanded to be paid for their services in *tambu*.

12. PRN 1929-N/60/29: 4. A perhaps somewhat less friendly explanation, but one equally related to the Tolai, is mentioned by Johnston: 'Elias and Sherwin, however, claim that the early Tolai traders in the East Nakanai region nicknamed the people *na kanai* after the fish-stealing seagull which the Tolais call by that name, because goods were often stolen from their trading canoes' (1980a: 18; italics in the original). Johnston is referring here to R.M. Elias and R.M. Sherwin, 'Origins of tambu shell currency', *Journal of the Papua New Guinea Society* 4(2): 69–76 (1970). According to Burgmann (1961: 930), on the other hand, 'nakanai' is an 'adverb of place' in Tolai (which he calls the 'Gunantuna language') meaning 'down there at the side'. Powell (1884: 178), one of the earliest travellers, merely states his belief that the members of the 'eastern tribes' of the Gazelle Peninsula 'give this name to any place they know nothing about'.

13. With reference to the Tolai, who in July 1897 accompanied Hahl and himself on their journey along the north-east coast of New Britain, Rascher writes as follows about the Nakanai and their homeland: 'Unnatural vices, unknown to either the natives of the related tribes of New Guinea or the inhabitants of Gazelle, occur here in full daylight and without any shame. I have been assured not only that marital relations with the closest blood relatives are the custom here, but also that such ties even occur between siblings and are permitted. I certainly did not want to believe these statements, but my informants from Vuna Márlta, to whom I owe these insights, stood by their claim' (Missionare vom hlst. Herzen Jesu 1909: 212).

14. This text bears the date of 25 October 1912. In it, Hees (1913a: 104) mentions the journey undertaken by Rascher in 1897 and then continues as follows: 'Since then our Reverend Lord Bishop has visited the coastal tribes three times on the mission steamer, and last year he succeeded in obtaining some boys from the Nakanai people.' According to Linckens (1922: 126), the station referred to by Hees had been founded in 1900, while Schmidlin (1913: 180) gives 1903 as the date of 'setting up a steam sawmill on the river Toriu'.

15. In the first of these reports (1913a), Hees describes how the 'boys' react to their new environment, referring to their attempts to explain their observations as the 'results of their researches' (1913a: 105). The second report (1913b) deals with Nakanai ideas of spirits, the afterlife and law, and it includes, in particular, explanations of war, vengeance and witchcraft. In the third report (1914a), Hees first pictures the immediate surroundings of the mission station and gives an account of common river journeys, in order then to thematise his 'charges" observations of nature and hunting methods. The focus of the fourth report (1914b), finally, is education, or the manner in which fishing, hunting, cultivation and the manufacture of ornaments are taught and learned among the Nakanai.

16. Chowning (1958: xv) writes that she has used the English-language translation of this collection. The 'legends and tales' presented by Hees consist of a total of thirty-nine texts, thirty-five of which come from three of the five 'boys' born in the area of Mount Pago. Hees reproduces all the texts in Nakanai together with an interlinear German translation, and he arranges them according to his own categories, to each of which he gives a German heading. The collection is introduced with descriptions in which Hees

(1915/16: 36), in his own words, seeks 'to provide the references that appeared to me to be useful in understanding or illustrating the Nakanai legends and tales'. He quotes one of his informants as follows: 'Those from the "X" (name of a recruiting ship), they are bad. They make bad the Nakanai. They fight us with the rifle (*la malakéta*), they go into the bush, they seize us, seize our pigs and carry them on to the boat, they seize the women, they seize the taro. They dig up the taro and dig up the taro, eat our pigs, they set fire to our houses, so that we burn in the fire. They (the Nakanai taken away) sit on the steamer, go over to the farmstead of the whites and never come back again, never' (1915/16: 45n1).

17. After an interval of some months Hees records the same stories several times without noting 'any essential alteration, whether in structure ... or in individual expressions' (1915/16: 50; see also 1914b: 213), and he writes that it should 'not be overlooked' that, if the Tolai travellers 'could easily be tempted to paint their "golden land" in the blackest of colours, the present-day informants must rather be inclined to the opposite' (1915/16: 36).

18. When later a report arrived of an eruption of Mount Pago, those who came from the area made what Hees (1913b: 344) calls 'a second, equally unsuccessful attempt to escape ... with the laudable intention of standing by their hunger-stricken people'.

19. Hees (1915/16: 38). Rascher, perhaps influenced by the Tolai who accompanied him, also formulated an, as it were, aesthetically based critique of the Nakanai by attributing to them 'a very unappetising exterior' (Missionare vom hlst. Herzen Jesu 1909: 210) and by reporting the sight of 'natives with the faces of rogues and thieves' (1909: 218).

20. Goodenough has summarised the results of his reconnaissance trip in a report (1952). He told me in an interview (30 November 2001) of his being accompanied by a white trader. In the University of Pennsylvania Museum Archives, there are nineteen pictures that Goodenough took in Koimumu, showing mostly canoes, shields and houses.

21. Goodenough (1952: 8; italics in original). In his foreword to Daris Swindler's dissertation, published in 1962, Goodenough also writes that New Britain had been selected because although there were admittedly many publications on the inhabitants of the Gazelle Peninsula, 'to all intents and purposes the rest of New Britain was ethnographic *terra incognita*' (1962: vii; italics in original). Goodenough (30 November 2001) has since repeated this phrase to me.

22. This becomes clear from Goodenough's journal, deposited in the University of Pennsylvania Museum Archives in the file marked '12 Methodology'.

23. Goodenough's journal, p. 5.

24. According to a letter that Bettylou Valentine wrote to me on 2 October 2004, the family arrived in Rapuri in April 1977, then moved to the University of Papua New Guinea and finally returned to Rapuri, remaining there until May 1979. Charles and Bettylou had married in 1963 (Gilliam 1990). In a joint publication, Bettylou is introduced as a 'Black American' (C. Valentine and B. Valentine 1979c: 106).

25. In this letter, Valentine (n.d.) writes: 'Recently a nativistic movement of the so-called "Cargo Cult" type has grown up. A prophesy [*sic*] has been made that a divine power will send a ship laden with great amounts of precious Europeans [*sic*] cargo to the native people. Following this, native and white will have equal statuses or the Europeans will be driven out. Aside from a few details this is all that is known, but it is enough to indicate that they will be an extremely interesting group to study.' The letter is not dated but must be from 1952, since Valentine states that Goodenough's reconnaissance trip of 1951 had taken place the previous year. With reference to the West Nakanai, Valentine states: 'They have not been studied before, but Goodenough picked up some preliminary information on a survey visit to their district last year.'

26. Valentine (1955a: 13). For the account of the Batari movement, paraphrased below, see Valentine (1955a: 14–23).

27. For the account of the Kivung, paraphrased below, see Valentine (1955a: 23–58).

28. Here and in what follows, Valentine no longer speaks of 'mythology' but of 'myth'.

29. Valentine (1955a: 28). Valentine uses the terms 'Cargo Movement', 'Cargo Cult' and 'Kivung' interchangeably.

30. The declared aim of Berger's campaign of passive resistance to all the administration's policies was, according to Valentine, to remove the Australian administration in a supernatural manner. Concomitantly, Berger had urged the villagers to avoid the administration as much as possible and to resist both the forms of economy it had introduced and the government schools.

31. In Silanga, near Sio, a settlement was created on Wagner's initiative, which in principle was based on a similar conception to the station of St Paul and which, according to Valentine (1956a: 83), had almost 1,200 people between 1955 and 1956. For further information on this settlement, see F.X. Wagner himself (1960, 1996), van Rijswijck (1966) and Taschner (1985).

32. Valentine (1956a: 71) writes further: 'Thus as the Movement extends itself further it becomes a less coherent organization.'

33. A similar tendency can be seen with reference to the murder of Rascher and his fellow-missionaries when contemporary church publications talk about a leading role played by To Maria. I have dealt with the history of 'cargo research' in greater detail elsewhere (Jebens 2004a) and will return to it in Chapter 6 of the present work.

34. Scharmach (1953: 60). See also Laufer (1955: 175) and Weigl (1955: 196).

35. CV 16 October 1954. The corresponding tensions between the colonial administration and the Catholic Church become obvious when, for example, in a patrol report, J.K. McCarthy complains that the West Nakanai have had the misfortune 'to have a succession of stupid and narrow-minded missionaries foisted upon them' and that, during the Batari movement, Weigl had been mistreated because of his own 'stupidity' (PRT 1952/53-7). On this 'mistreatment', see also Weigl himself (1955) and Scharmach (1960: 22, 235–38).

36. For example, the *Manuale missionariorum*, a handbook written for the instruction of missionaries, contains a chapter entitled 'Cargo madness', in which Scharmach (1953: 64) states the following: 'Like real insanity, Cargo madness is very hard to be treated in its acute state.' On the thesis of disturbed equilibrium or health, see, among others, Williams (1934: 377), Eckert (1940: 26) and Guiart (1951a: 229).

37. The statement that Valentine was ahead of his time could also be made with reference to Hees, in the sense that, although writing in the 1910s, he already allows his informants to speak for themselves, and he adopts their view that he is taking turns with them in being teacher and pupil.

38. Cargo cults thus become anti-colonial movements of protest or resistance. See Hempenstall (1978) and Hempenstall and Rutherford (1984), as well as Lanternari (1963).

39. See also Bodrogi (1951: 278). Similarly, Lommel (1953: 20–21) assumed a 'transformation from primitive magical to modern rational thought', and Uplegger and Mühlmann (1961: 187) identified 'an increasing "secularisation"'.

40. See Lindstrom (1999) on Burridge, and Jebens (2001b) on Lawrence.

41. See Harding (1967: 1), Schiefflin and Gewertz (1985: 5n1), Hiatt (1988: 1) and Kempf (1996: 42).

42. Johnston (1973: 79) mentions 'confrontations with police such as those which occurred in 1968 over the non-payment of taxes', and he claims that afterwards the leaders of the Kivung were quite careful not to repeat such encounters.

43. Accordingly, Lindstrom (1993: 42) writes: 'What used to be Melanesian culture becomes cargo cult writ large.'

44. Valentine (1955a: 62). In the third version of Valentine's report (1956a), this description becomes the last section of the chapter entitled 'The post-war Kivung, 1947–54'.

45. In his field notes, Valentine cites Lima as saying that he had been told by Berger to work together with Valentine (CV 27 August 1954a: 2).

46. Valentine (1955a: 62). I have put in italics the passages that were revised subsequently. In the second version of his report, Valentine writes: 'I was convinced that there was more than met the eye, because the programme of good works exhibited to the public was carried out with a fervor difficult to attribute to Christian zeal in a people who only

a few years previously had nearly murdered their priest in pursuing the Cargo ideal. Since he had no more evidence to go on than this, Dr. Goodenough left the field with the impression that the Cargo Cult was dead among the Nakanai. According to accounts published in the Australian and Papua-New Guinea [*sic*] press, he expressed this opinion publicly in the Territory on his way home. By the time he left, however, I had uncovered the fact that the Nakanai had paid large sums in taxes to Fr. B. and that they expected some great but as yet unspecified reward for this sacrifice. In this connection the press quoted Dr. Goodenough as saying that the mission of which B. was then the only representative in the area had taken large sums of money from the natives without explaining what would be done with the money. Finally, the press also attributed to Dr. Goodenough statements that the natives felt for various reasons that they were being exploited by Europeans. (See South Pacific Post, Port Moresby, 28 July–1 August 1954)' (1955b: 47–48; underlining in original). An interlinear translation of these two newspaper reports into Tok Pisin can be found in Valentine's field notes. In the paragraph cited here from the second version, Valentine conceals a difference of opinion with Goodenough with reference to his own initial suspicion that there was more behind the 'public façade' than could be seen from the outside. Moreover, Valentine also in a sense protects Goodenough by talking no longer about Goodenough's statements but about statements attributed to Goodenough. This is repeated in the third version of the report, when Valentine to some extent distorts Goodenough but also decidedly consents to him: 'I could not but agree with Dr. Goodenough at the time, however that it was impossible at that stage to adduce sufficient evidence to support my suspicion that Cargo Beliefs were somehow involved in the situation' (1956a: 62). (According to the first version of the report, Goodenough had not said that it had been impossible to collect enough evidence, but that Valentine had not done so.) However, Goodenough's own recollections concur only in part with Valentine's account. He wrote to me: 'I was interviewed on my way out of Papua New Guinea by a reporter who distorted things I said in order to make the administration look bad and be sensational. I had to apologize to officials the next day. They said not to worry, the reporter was notorious for that sort of thing. I believe I told him there was an active cargo cult among the Nakanai, as indeed there was' (email, Goodenough to Jebens, 1 February 2003).

47. Valentine describes this event in his field notes under the heading of 'Another fracas with Berger' (CV 19 September 1954a: 1–4). In his report to the colonial administration, Valentine (1955a: 72) calls this the 'only open challenge which the Father has offered', and he claims to have managed not to give way and thus to convince many people. Valentine's field notes, however, contain no references to the fact that he had later made another attempt to attend services.

48. Valentine (1956a: 76). In 1954, Munzlinger had, at his own wish, been transferred to Vavua, where he wanted to pursue the canonisation of the missionaries murdered at St Paul in 1904. Thus Fr. Dahmen (1955) writes the following after travelling through the region in June 1954: 'The triumvirate of Berger, Munzlinger and Wagner rules over the Nakanai area. I met the three fathers at the station at Valoka. Berger, the Nakanai missionary of long experience, has the Nakanai people, previously rebellious as they were, entirely under his influence again … Fr. Munzlinger looks after Vavua, a substation of Fr. Berger's. He himself had wanted to go to a quiet place where he would be able to work undisturbed on the history of the Baining martyrs while still providing some pastoral care. A year ago, Br. Grewe built a small house for him, suitable for a substation.' In the first version of his report to the colonial administration Valentine (1955a: 41) still writes that it is unclear whether Munzlinger knows about 'Fr. B's true role', whereas in the third version he claims that Munzlinger had accused the villagers of not being true Catholics and of 'returning to the principle of the Batari Cult'. According to to Valentine (1956a: 76), this was leading to an 'atmosphere of rumor and suspicion which threatens the unity of the Movement', and thus to the 'potentiality of a split in the Kivung membership'.

49. Valentine (1956a: 78). The baptism books kept in Valoka show that Berger actually remained there until 1958, when he was succeeded by Fr. Bruno Stapelmann.
50. Valentine (1956a: 74). In this context, Valentine writes that three of the eight men who had made a statement before the colonial officer in 1954 had since resigned from their leading positions within the Kivung (1956a: 73), thus implicitly claiming that the slow decline of its authority was at least partly due to his own activities.
51. CV 22 August 1954: 1–10. See Figure 2 and CV 23 August 1954b.
52. The corresponding entry in Valentine's notes begins with a summary, which he calls a 'considerably condensed version' (CV 14 September 1954: 5). In the two subsequent paragraphs, Valentine repeats a very tentatively formulated response from his audience (CV 14 September 1954: 6) in order then to spend more than two pages paraphrasing his attempt to refute this response (CV 14 September 1954: 6–8). Although Valentine writes that he has given the same speech before (CV 14 September 1954: 8; see also CV 15 September 1954: 1), there are no entries in his notes that would confirm such a claim.
53. 'M km l hlpm yp, l strm tgtg bl yp, na l kliaim het bl yp' (CV 14 September 1954: 1).
54. '[Y]es, mi inap long helpim yupela. Tasol yupela mas autim olgeta samting long mipela pastaim … Sapos yupela i no stret long mipela, mipela no ken stret long yupela' (CV 14 September 1954: 3).
55. Valentine wrote, with reference to Berger: 'He has been telling them that anyone who talks with me will get no cargo, or only very little, when the Kivung "breaks"' (CV 4 October 1954). According to Valentine's report to the colonial administration, however, Berger had already banned the villagers from speaking to him before he began his 'campaign of limited reeducation'.
56. PRT 1954/55-11. A more implicit allusion to Valentine can be detected in many reports of the administration later claiming that the 'native situation' among the Nakanai had already caused much sensation and that much had already been written about it.
57. Email, Goodenough to Jebens, 1 February 2003.
58. Letter, Valentine to Goodenough, 23 February 1956.
59. 'When Valentine wrote his dissertation,' Goodenough (email, 1 February 2003) told me, 'he never consulted with me about it at all … We had already fallen out, but I was still technically carried as his dissertation supervisor. I was, of course, an official reader of his dissertation.' From a present-day perspective, the exact timing of the breaking-off can only be calculated with difficulty, for even after completing his dissertation Valentine still wrote letters to Goodenough in which he addressed him in a quite friendly manner (letters, Valentine to Goodenough, 24 August 1959 and 8 November 1959).
60. Valentine (1963b). Moreover, Valentine concerned himself with 'health and health problems' among the West Nakanai in a book-length, unpublished manuscript (1956b: 1).
61. In this sense, there is a perhaps an extraordinarily large discrepancy between Valentine's field notes and his publications.
62. See Valentine's introduction (1978) to the monograph in which Bettylou (B. Valentine 1978) presents the results of this stay.
63. Bettylou Valentine told me about this appointment (letter, B. Valentine to Jebens, 11 March 2003).

3

Present-day memories

Fieldwork

Beginning

In April 1996, I travelled along the coast of the Hoskins Peninsula looking for a region suitable for future fieldwork, just as Goodenough had done forty-five years earlier. Greg Mongi, a public servant from the north of the Willaumez Peninsula, told me about a charismatic movement called 'Rosa Mystica' that had spread within the Catholic Church. Its adherents were being accused of merely wanting to seduce women and engage in a cargo cult.[1] With respect to Koimumu, which I had not yet visited, Greg said that it was a 'big traditional village' which, in earlier times, had provided building materials for the surrounding area, that it had served as a 'junction' in trading with people from Tarobi and Talasea and that its inhabitants still had initiation ceremonies as well as a *haus boi*.

Angie Dimas, the person running the Papalaba guest house in Kassia and thus my first host, also mentioned Koimumu. She recommended that I go there or to Tarobi, because in both villages people had respect[2] for visitors. When I asked her what she meant by this, she replied that people would not steal, quarrel with me or constantly demand things from me. I did not know it at the time, but, in mentioning 'respect', Angie was referring to one of the values that are of central importance to the image of one's own traditional culture.

Unlike Greg and Angie, some Big Men in Kassia complained that the entire Peninsula had already changed too much, since everyone had a television set and many children were growing up outside the village. During a joint visit to Tarobi, a member of Greg's staff made a similar comment in saying that there, but also in Rapuri, Koimumu and other places, the old way of life now only existed in people's heads and that one would have to go into the interior or into the mountains in order to find more *kastom*.

However, traditional culture, whether still intact or having already declined, and oppositions based on religion were not the only topics of conversation. I was also referred to cargo cults and – just as in the case of Goodenough – this happened even before my actual fieldwork had begun. Gerry Thomas (18 April 1996), the person in charge of a Talasea-based development project supported by the European Union, stated that there had been such movements in the area before, but hastened to add that nowadays people were tired of waiting for ships. In contrast, Fr. Klaus Eppmann, who had been stationed in Valoka as a Catholic priest since 1994, reminded me of the accusations that, according to Greg Mongi, were directed against the adherents of the Rosa Mystica. Eppmann partly made these accusations his own by describing the Rosa Mystica as 'nonsense' and as expressing a widespread 'cargo cult mentality'. Such a mentality, he added, was quite persistent and could not be overcome, especially since Batari, the cargo cult leader, had been born in the area.[3]

I visited Koimumu for the first time for a few hours on 25 April 1996, a Thursday, and I still remember vividly how I left the car provided for me by Greg Mongi. In the glaring light of the afternoon sun, I wandered somewhat hesitantly through the almost empty Malebulu (Chapter 1). At that moment, most of the villagers must have been in their gardens or oil palm blocks, since I only saw a few men sitting in the shade under their houses. They watched me closely but did not react until I took the initiative and greeted them. Thus I received an impression of indifference or even reserve, which unsettled me somewhat, having had entirely different experiences in my earlier fieldwork in the Southern Highlands of Papua New Guinea.[4] When I reported my impression to Angie Dimas, she replied that this behaviour was simply an expression of the respect she had already mentioned and that it in no way indicated that people were angry (*kros*) with me.[5]

On 27 April, I returned to Koimumu to stay there overnight for the first two times and to introduce myself and my intentions to the villagers (Chapter 1). My host, Joe Sogi (Figure 11), told me that in Valentine's time there had been a lot of *kastom* and the Big Men had still been alive.[6] In Koimumu, Rapuri and Vavua, however, feasts (*singsing*), slit gongs (*garamut*) and the masked dances called *tumbuan* (Tok Pisin) or *valuku* (Nakanai) were still as widespread as before. At present, Joe continued, life was hard, since one's own fathers had not planted any coconut palms because, in Valentine's time, they were in a cargo cult. But at least people nowadays plant coconut palms.

On the occasion of this visit, I discussed with Joe the possibility of my using a relatively new and empty house, which, originally built for teachers, stood on the edge of the school grounds and thus on the boundary of the village itself (Map 2). If I was living there, Joe said, my rent would go to the whole community, and it would also be of advantage that no one was permitted to enter the school grounds at night. In case anyone wanted to visit me, he would have to be accompanied by a member of the school board. While in other respects I had the impression that Koimumu was entirely suitable as a site for fieldwork, this situation struck me as a possible obstacle to my research. I conveyed my concerns to Joe, but, during a third visit from 3 May to 4 May 1996, he assured me that anyone could come and see me, day or night. If, however, anyone was uncertain because of the school regulations, he could ask a member of the school board to join him. I thus decided to move in; on 22 May 1996, Joe picked me up in Hoskins, and the first of my two periods of fieldwork in Koimumu began (Chapter 1).

Relations

I had lived in Koimumu for just two days when Paul Gar (24 May 1996), whom, people said, I definitely had to meet as the leading Big Man (Chapter 1), told me that people regarded me as the son of Joe Sogi. Peter Mape, who joined us, added that whoever wanted to come and see me could ask Joe beforehand and then come with him. This confirmed my initial concerns, and while I considered the attempt to fit in or appropriate my person understandable and unproblematic – later people also described me as an inhabitant of Guria (Chapter 1) and as a member of the Bualali clan – I was afraid that, in Joe's case and in view of my living in the school grounds, this attempt might unduly restrict my chances of making contacts.[7] Thus, only three days later, and in the context of a community meeting, I gave a speech and said that it was important for my work that I should be allowed to enter the houses of all the villagers, and that all the villagers, in turn, should be allowed to enter my house.[8] Accordingly, I concluded, I did not want to receive food from just one man but from everyone. People reacted with general agreement and immediately made a plan according to which every evening one family would bring me a meal, the village sections alternating from week to week.

These evening visits offered a welcome opportunity to meet men, women and children of different ages and belonging to different kin groups and sections of Koimumu, whereas otherwise, during the first third of my first field trip, my contacts were mostly restricted to the village authorities, such as Alphonse Mape, George Tautigi, Lawrence Olpitarea and Paul Gar (Chapter 1). Although I generally tried to encourage my interlocutors to speak as freely and extensively as possible about topics they themselves had chosen, the first few evening meetings in my house often seemed somewhat formal or even forced. As I learned only gradually, people were obviously doing their best to follow certain regulations. Thus one of my visitors, John Bubu (5 June 1996), told me that he had heard that one should not simply bring me food and then leave immediately, while another, Lawrence Olpitarea (6 June 1996) said that people should not stay with me for more than half an hour.

In addition, I soon had to realise that, apart from those who were in a sense officially obliged to do so, hardly anyone came to my house of his own volition. Apparently, some of the villagers addressed this issue themselves when they asked me from time to time if the Big Men had already visited me in order to tell me stories. When I had to answer in the negative, I was often referred to the value of *rispekt*, already mentioned by Angie Dimas. Roy Mou (22 June 1996), for example, explained that this value would make it impossible to enter my house or that of another man just like that or to call me over (*singautim*) without due cause whenever I was passing by.[9] As another reason, people mentioned the fact that my house stood in the school grounds. According to Francisca Paliavu (17 June 1996), entering this area was prohibited, and similarly Regina Kaue (18 August 1996) said that anyone who crossed the boundary without authorisation would be afraid of being punished.[10]

Evidently, it had not been of much use to convey my concerns about living on the school grounds to Joe Sogi, and my attempt to encourage the villagers to feel free to visit me had not been altogether successful. Some three weeks after my speech Paul Gar (18 June 1996) was still telling me quite openly that Joe was considered to be my father (*papa*) because I had gone to him first. Moreover, Paul added, people could not come to me in order to monopolise me, but had to speak to Joe first.

After my fieldwork had begun in, so to speak, spatial and social isolation, its course could be described as a process in which the corresponding distance was gradually reduced. During the first third of my first field trip, I initially extended my activities beyond the school grounds to the whole of Koimumu by collecting basic ethnographic data. I drew a plan of the settlement and recorded the names of the inhabitants of all the houses, as well as genealogies of the different clans. Little by little, I then increased the number of interviews, mostly asking questions on the economy and on history, and making use of the contacts that had developed during my evening meals or while collecting basic ethnographic data. During the second third of my first field trip, I started to accompany individual villagers to their nearby gardens and oil palm plots, as well as to the river Kapeuru, where they were making sago, and to Pokili in order to collect wildfowl eggs. Moreover, I visited the neighbouring villages of Rapuri, Vavua and Galilo.[11]

All in all, people seemed particularly impressed by the fact that I was both willing and in a position to participate in a night-long *singsing* in Rapuri as well as in several expeditions hunting wild pigs, each one lasting from morning to evening. When talking to the inhabitants of other villages, people sometimes referred to me as a 'boy from Koimumu' (*manki bilong Koimumu*) and added, not without a tone of pride, that I would usually chew betel nut and that I could already speak a little Nakanai.[12]

In extending my activities first to the whole of Koimumu and then to the surrounding area, I inevitably succeeded in overcoming not only the spatial but also the social isolation of the beginning of my fieldwork. The inhabitants of Koimumu obviously became more used to my presence and to my participation in village life, and soon evening meals seemed less tense. Some of my visitors began to invite me to their own houses, and with some of my acquaintances I developed increasingly friendly relations. In particular, I was soon meeting Alphonse Mape, the president of the Pulabe Local Government Council, several times a week. Our interviews and conversations became longer, and at the end of my first field trip he accompanied me to Port Moresby for a week.

During my second field trip to Koimumu, too, I increased the number of interviews only little by little. New contacts emerged, and at the same time some of the older relationships continued to intensify. Here, the fact that I had returned may, in itself, have helped in building or confirming trust by creating the impression that my intentions were honest.

Among the special events in village life during my second field trip were a death, elections to the national parliament, the preparation of dances for the farewell to Fr. Father Alois Hartmann, stationed in Vavua, and for a school festival in Hoskins (3 to 5 September 1997), and a land dispute with an oil palm company that eventually led to a court case in Kimbe.[13] In addition, I was able to extend my research further by witnessing the manufacture and performance of *tumbuan* not only in Koimumu and Vavua, but also in Makasili and Karapi.[14] This went back to the end of my first field trip, when some of the older men of Koimumu had, of their own volition, prepared various *tumbuan* and showed them during my farewell party (see cover illustration), because, as they said, I had to see this aspect of *kastom*, too, before I left.[15] In one of the speeches that were as obligatory as the meal that followed, Otto Puli, a Big Man from Vavua, said that on this occasion there had not been enough time really to show me anything, but on my next visit several villages should perform different types of *tumbuan*, one after the other. I welcomed this suggestion wholeheartedly, not only because I had been impressed by what I had already seen, but also because demonstrating their *tumbuan* appeared to be quite important to the people themselves.

When Otto's suggestion was put into practice after I returned, people often explicitly welcomed the fact that I was joining them when they collected the materials needed for the *tumbuan*, and that I sometimes tried my hand at painting a mask myself. As I also noticed, when I started to participate in the training sessions and Sunday matches of one of Koimumu's soccer teams during my second field trip, it did make a fundamental difference to my hosts and informants whether I was merely present as an observer or conversational partner, or whether I involved myself, so to speak, not only verbally but also bodily. In this sense, the level of practical action seemed to be particularly important.[16]

It is perhaps one of the paradoxes of anthropological fieldwork that, when some doors open, others close. During my second field trip, for example, I was returning from one of my visits to Vavua, which had become more frequent, when a young man remarked that I might as well move there.[17] In drawing closer to Alphonse Mape, I distanced myself from Joe Sogi, who was rather sceptical of Alphonse, or even rejected him because he believed he knew more about *kastom* and therefore was better qualified for a leadership position. At the same time, however, I did not break with Joe – he accompanied me when I visited Kapeuru and Pokili – and he himself held on to the view that, as I had come to him first, he was watching over me like a father and that everyone spoke of me as his child.[18] Yet the fact that people often saw me with Alphonse might ultimately have contributed more than any of my own statements to qualify my being assigned to or appropriated by Joe, and this certainly helped to overcome the concomitant restrictions. In August 1996, Paul Gar was still describing Joe as my father, but then continued as follows: 'He does not rule over you. He only ruled over you when you were still new.'[19]

First references

Although, just like Goodenough forty-five years earlier, I had already been referred to cargo cults prior to my actual fieldwork, I was to realise that – irrespective of how my relations with them developed – the inhabitants of Koimumu and neighbouring villages hardly ever mentioned the beliefs and practices described by Valentine of their own volition, and that they only very rarely used the term 'kago' in this context.

Joe Sogi, who, on the occasion of my first overnight stays in Koimumu, had talked about a cargo cult having been performed in Valentine's time, was an exception. When I asked him whether he could still remember any of the earlier missionaries, he gave me some names and said, with reference to Berger, that people had hidden him during the war and that he had begun with the 'Kivung family', which, however, then turned into a cargo cult and ended just like that (*pinis nating*).[20] I wanted to know whether such a thing had happened here as well, and Joe replied that here the Kivung had been *strong*. Then he continued as follows:

> People wanted to know something about the 'way of the whites' (*sindaun bilong waitman*) and about 'our way' (*sindaun bilong mipela*). Perhaps the reason is that during the war many things came up just like that, and then failed to appear after the war. Moreover, the whites must have said something too.[21] However, it didn't work. Fr. Berger had talked to Lima and encouraged him (*strongim*), but Lima, who had then talked to all the people, didn't have any knowledge (*save*) and was confused (*longlong*) ... Then the whites introduced local government councils and quarrels emerged because the Kivung opposed them and the paying of taxes. Some adherents of the Kivung went to prison, and the *council* won.[22]

In subsequent weeks, this was to remain the only time that anyone felt prompted to talk about the Kivung.[23] The term 'cargo cult', however, came up just a few days later. While we were having dinner, Albert Lowa (5 June 1996), a neighbour of Alphonse Mape's, said:

After Valentine had been here and Papua New Guinea had become independent, there was a cargo cult here. A man from Ubae called Paga, who sometimes comes here, had been collecting taxes (*takis*) here, as well as in other villages. Many men from here had given him money and had gone with him. In one house he had filled money from one bag into another, and he said that there would be more. He alone entered the house.

I thus felt encouraged to ask the first questions which included the word 'Kivung' as well as the name of Batari, whom I had already heard about from Klaus Eppmann before I had visited Koimumu. Albert's answer was relatively brief, but he said that the adherents of the Kivung had been opposed to the planting of coconut palms and had owned a big store. Batari, Albert continued laughingly, had seen a box labelled 'National Battery', had thought that it was for him, and had announced that a ship with goods for him would come, because, as Albert explained, earlier people had believed that the goods would be manufactured by the ancestors.

Compared with Joe Sogi and Albert Lowa, Paul Gar expressed himself in greater detail. On one occasion, I remarked in passing that I had read in the Patrol Reports that earlier people had a *family Kivung*. I did not know what that meant, I added, but would want to ask about it later at some point. Paul reacted spontaneously as well as with a heightened degree of agitation:

The government repeatedly took us to court (*kotim*) about this and so we stopped it. Lima and his people have changed it (*tanim*). It was brought up by Berger. We did what Berger told us to do. It was good. Later Berger went away and we stopped. We didn't do any cargo cult. Cargo cults have been done by others, like the people in Bali, Gloucester and Arawe. There was no *family Kivung* there. This existed only in Talasea and Bialla. There were no cargo cults among the Western Nakanai. The government repeatedly accused us of doing cargo cults, but we did not. Others were against us and they blamed us without reason. 'Cargo cult' means to bring food to the cemetery, to get money from the cemetery and cargo from the ancestors. This was done not by us but by others. We were just worshipping. We were against premarital intercourse, sorcery (*poisen*) and theft. We built new houses for people who were newly married, we built a store and a big house in Vavua. Encouraged by Father Berger we planted coconut palms, we sold copra and we received cargo from Rabaul … We did just that and it was good. Cargo cults are bullshit. Money and cargo do not derive from the ancestors, money derives solely from sweat (*tuhat*). Berger said that, too.[24]

In agreement with Joe Sogi, Paul mentioned here Berger's leading role, the change in the Kivung and the fact that its ending had been accompanied by conflicts, and he added that the adherents of the Kivung had only been pursuing Christian and economic goals. Thus, Paul already named the basic elements, most of which were to be repeated later – albeit in different forms, but with reliable regularity – almost every time the Kivung was talked about. Taken together, these elements form what can be called a collective 'Kivung story'.

Since my referring to possible future questions on the Kivung had been sufficient for Paul to assure me explicitly that the Kivung had not been a cargo cult, it became obvious that the term 'cargo cult' was considered quite negatively, and therefore I decided not to use it myself for the time being. Instead, I continued merely to state that I had heard about the Kivung, or just asked in general if anything was known about it.

I conducted my first interview focused on the Kivung on 4 July 1996 with Titus Mou, who, as a former public servant, was living in Vavua and had been introduced to me by Alphonse Mape (Chapter 1). While we had been sitting in Alphonse's car, on a drive from Koimumu to Kimbe, he had pointed to some houses with corrugated iron roofs along the road which had belonged to Lima and had been built with the money earned in his time. Then, just like Joe Sogi, of his own volition he had added:

> The Kivung began by taking care of family life (*lukautim family*), but along the line it turned into a cargo cult. Fr. Berger had performed conjuring tricks; people believed that he had returned from the dead and they were waiting to receive cargo from the ancestors. In addition people had captured Fr. Schweiger in Valoka because they thought it was his fault that the cargo was not coming. The leaders were first Batari and then, after the war, Lima.[25]

At this, I had invited Titus to visit me whenever it suited him, in order to tell me more about the Kivung. When he did, he repeated the thesis – previously formulated only by Joe Sogi – that the Kivung had changed into a cargo cult. Moreover, he situated the Kivung in a historical context by developing the story of a single continuous movement in which Batari, Kivung and Paga merely represent different stages that succeed one another but in principle are based on the same beliefs and needs. Moreover, in each of these stages, the group of followers largely remains the same.

I reacted by expressing my desire to learn more about this movement, and in the weeks that followed, Titus arranged numerous interviews with some of its former adherents and opponents living in Rapuri, Vavua and Galilo. When I left it to him to ask most of the questions, I found it interesting to see that, in the role of the anthropologist, Titus, too, avoided the term 'cargo cult' and only asked people to talk about the Kivung or Lima, and preferably to begin with how Berger had arrived in the Nakanai area after the war.[26]

In and around Koimumu, most of the relevant interviews and conversations took place during my second field trip. In conducting them, I followed the example set by Titus and began with rather general formulations. Later, I used the help of selected interlocutors to check particular information that I had collected in the course of time, and I sought to obtain further insights on specific topics, such as the capture of a Father mentioned by Titus.

'Surface'

Christian and economic goals

From among the various basic elements of their 'Kivung story', the inhabitants of Koimumu and neighbouring villages mostly chose the pursuit of Christian and economic goals whenever they talked about the Kivung in conversations and interviews.

The activities, commandments and prohibitions of Catholic Christianity, described as a 'public façade' by Valentine (1955a: 31), consisted in particular of the 'taking care of family life' mentioned by Titus. According to him, Berger had demanded that the family should behave decently (*stap gut*), that people should pray, practise all the good customs and help the old and sick, and that all the young girls should marry in church.[27] The building of houses for newly-weds mentioned by Paul Gar also refers to the 'taking care of family life'. In such houses, as I heard in Vavua, people sat down and taught their children, of whom it was said that in those times they still obeyed their parents and learnt (*stadi*), rather than running around everywhere like today, when things were completely run down (*dirty olgeta*).[28] John Bubu (5 June 1996) said that, when people heard the bell signal in the evening, they would go around and check that all the families were in their houses.

Like Valentine, who wrote of the goal being 'phrased as living like Europeans and returning to the lost ancestral way of life' (1955a: 31), Ludwig Gar, from Makasili, made a link with the whites and one's own ancestors. Having come to Koimumu because of a death in the family, Ludwig explained Berger's intentions to me as follows: 'He wanted the families to stay together so that the children would not run off elsewhere, because then they would quarrel and there would be conflicts between the parents. This rule is a good one: the ancestors had it and that's also how it is with you whites.'[29]

People in and around Koimumu repeatedly stressed that the 'decent behaviour' demanded by Berger included the giving up of *poisen*. Peter Tautigi (2 September 1997), for example, who like John Bubu belonged to the older generation, explicitly recalled the request to think of the church and discard all the substances used for witchcraft.[30] The 'soldiers' of the

Kivung had searched through all the houses, and if they found any such substances had thrown them into the sea. While previously, as Ludwig Gar (18 April 1997) assured me, all children had died because of witchcraft and people only had one or two children, there were now a lot of people, they were all well, and this was to the credit of Fr. Berger, who had said that one should give up everything, that is, all types of witchcraft.

The pursuit of economic goals – or, in Valentine's words, the 'economic branch of the Movement', known as the 'Kampani' (1955a: 35) – was referred to, first by Albert Lowa and Paul Gar, and then by many others when they talked about the existence of one or more stores.[31] People just as regularly mentioned rice cultivation, the sale of copra and the delivery of cargo from Rabaul.[32] For example, Joe Kaveu, employed temporarily as a driver by Alphonse Mape, recalled that, when a ship arrived in return for the copra sent to Rabaul, the Triton's trumpet (*tavur*) was blown and people ran from all the villages onto the beach. He himself saw as a child how the goods were unloaded and taken to the different stores.[33] Moreover, I heard about the 'taxes' which, according to Valentine, were paid to Berger. Some of my interlocutors talked about a daily collection, others described a single large meeting at which all the villages 'up to Hoskins' had collected a lot of money and then sent it to the Bishop in Vunapope with a request for help.[34]

Here, too, Ludwig Gar made a link with the whites by referring to the underlying intentions of the missionary. According to Paul Gar, Berger had said that 'money derives solely from sweat'. According to Ludwig, his wish was 'that we become like the whites, since, as Fr. Berger said, if they don't have something, they work hard day and night and then they get it. Fr. Berger wanted us to develop ourselves (*mipela i kirapim yet*). We should become members of a society that we run ourselves and, depending on our investments, we should get money.'[35]

Berger

When Ludwig Gar traces the Christian and economic goals and activities of the Kivung back to Berger's intentions or instructions, this not only corresponds to the general statements of Joe Sogi and Paul Gar – namely that Berger 'had begun with the "Kivung family"', that 'it was brought up by Berger' or that people just did what Berger said – but also confirms Valentine's picture of Berger as the 'organizing genius' behind the Kivung (Chapter 2).

However, whereas in his report to the colonial administration Valentine only briefly mentions that in 1946 Berger had been transferred first to Vavua and then to Valoka, some two months after the beginning of my first field trip, Fred Golumu (21 July 1996) told me about Berger's prior experiences during the war: the Japanese captured him and wanted him to be killed by bombs or machine-gun fire, but instead they were to suffer themselves and the Father survived (*ol Japan bagarap, Pater i stap*).[36] Without any food, he walked through the bush to Ramale, a place on the Gazelle

Peninsula, where the Catholic missionaries were interned during the war.[37] There, Fred continued, people were surprised to see Berger. They said that God had come,[38] and they gave him food until he recovered.

During my second trip, I was to hear in more detail about what had allegedly happened to Berger before he arrived in Vavua and Valoka. According to Peter Tautigi, the Japanese tied Berger to a ship, and when he survived an air attack nonetheless, they called him 'Christo' and released him. In Peter's version, the subsequent march through the bush – as Peter stressed, no one but Berger would have been able to persevere – ended not in Ramale but in Vunapope, where Berger was taken to be Jesus by a Catholic sister.[39]

In my penultimate interview, Paul Gar (18 September 1997), too, recounted that Berger had survived an air raid, that he was addressed as 'Christo' by the Japanese and that after his march through the bush – sketched much more explicitly and vividly – a sister saw him as Jesus. However, according to Paul, he introduced himself as Fr. Berger. Everyone, including the Bishop, came along, and Berger said that, while being beaten by the Japanese and running through the bush, he had thought only of God and of himself now having the same experiences as Jesus. Unlike Fred and Peter, however, Paul often interrupted his version of Berger's story by emphatically assuring me that it had come from Berger himself: 'Holger, he really did tell us about this … I cannot lie to you, Holger, I really do have this story from his mouth, he really did tell us about this, it was not any ordinary man who told us, it was the Father himself who told us.'[40]

At all events, after the war had ended, and after Berger had gone to Valoka and Vavua, he is said to have appointed two men as 'Kivung officials' in every village, 'up to the Bileki at Hoskins'.[41] Barth Sesega, the catechist of Koimumu, told me that at first Berger had wanted to transfer the leading role to Joe Kaveu's father, who, however, did not feel up to the task. Thus Berger continued to search until his choice finally fell on Lima from Rapuri.[42]

Ending

The basic elements of the 'Kivung story' include not only the pursuit of Christian and economic goals and Berger's leading role, but also the conflictual ending of the Kivung. This ending had already been referred to at the start of my first field trip, when Joe Sogi told me that the adherents of the Kivung opposed the introduction of local government councils and the paying of taxes, but that 'the *council* won'.

Titus Mou (4 July 1996), who was about forty-five years old, attributed the rejection of local government councils to the common rejection of the whites in general and the Australians in particular, as well as to the desire to come into possession of the cargo 'just like that', i.e. without working. However, as a representative of the older generation, Otto Puli (21 July

1996) stated that people did not want local government councils because they already had money, knew about the Kivung and possessed a large 'Kampani'.[43] While the councils were certainly seen as superfluous, according to Peter Tautigi (2 September 1997) it was also said that as soon as people could no longer pay the corresponding taxes their women would be forced into prostitution. 'We don't want councils,' Lima had declared, 'and we don't want taxes. We can live like the ancestors, for our own good way of life, back to the ancestors, will be sufficient for us … The law of the government comes in and forces the councils upon us, and later we will not be fine and the women will come to harm.'[44]

From their point of view, the adherents of the Kivung had good reason to mistrust the local government councils, as well as the intentions of the colonial government in general. After the accusations of and convictions for the spreading of 'false reports', mentioned by Valentine, they believed that for a long time they had already been persecuted by the colonial administration or by its supporters, led by Boas and coming from Galilo. Yet, in Koimumu, Paul Gar, Ambrose Bai, Peter Tautigi and others – mostly members of the clans from 'out of the bush' – started to join their former adversaries and to support the introduction of the controversial local government councils, whereas the Big Men of the time continued to hold fast to the Kivung.[45]

Thus the opposition between Kivung and council was brought inside the village, and there were continuous quarrels, with some declaring that only they would receive anything from the expected cargo, while others claimed that only they were entitled to plant coconut palms and sell copra.[46] Paul Gar recalled:

> We split up, and the group of the council went to one side and the group of the Kivung to the other … We pursued the work of the council, and they pursued the work of the Kivung, and whenever we heard anything about the Kivung, we came down on them, and whenever they heard anything about these councils, they descended on us. We fought continually.[47]

As such different groups have emerged in the past, different reasons are now given for the ending of the Kivung. On the one hand, Joe Ilo claimed that people no longer wanted to wait for what the Kivung had spoken of.[48] This recalls not only the process of 'partial disillusionment' mentioned by Valentine (Chapter 1), but also Garry Thomas and his statement, already made before my first visit to Koimumu, that nowadays people would be weary of waiting for ships.[49] On the other hand, Paul Gar (18 September 1997) told me that, after a major court case, the government had passed a law to end the Kivung, while Valentine also reports that the resistance to the local government councils had collapsed.[50] In Vavua, Otto Puli (21 July 1996) thought that Lima had been tricked (*trikim*), and that therefore people had finally accepted the councils.

Since the ending of the Kivung is traced back partly to disappointment and partly to a law or a 'trick', in some recollections the negative consequences of the Kivung or of the conflict between Kivung and council predominate, whereas in others criticism focuses rather on local government councils. Tomuga Bobore (28 July 1996), as a brother of Lima a very old man today, described the government's promise that the councils would 'put things in order' in the village (*bai wokim samting i stret long ples*). This, however, had been a lie. He himself, Tomuga added regretfully, had said at the time that people shouldn't ease up on the Kivung, and today he thinks that it would have been better to try it out for a bit longer (*bambai yumi traim pastaim na i go longpela moa liklik*).

Change

Reserve

As opposed to the pursuit of Christian and economic goals, Berger's leading role and the conflictual ending of the Kivung, its change over time was talked about only with the greatest reserve and in a very inexplicit manner. Mostly, my interlocutors restricted themselves to the statement that the things promoted by Berger had later been 'distorted', 'exaggerated' or continued 'a little differently'.[51]

The fact that, already at the start of my first field trip, Joe Sogi and Titus Mou spoke of the Kivung having changed into a cargo cult thus proved to be an exception. Yet I recalled these statements after my return to Koimumu when – certainly on the basis of a relationship of increased trust – Barth Sesega (27 May 1997a) and Paul Gar (18 September 1997) told me that 'the cargo cult' had 'come back in again' (*kago kalt i go insait gen*) and that the Big Men had 'put things back to the work of the cargo cult'.[52]

A hint made by Fred Golumu from Vavua points in the same direction. He said that the Bileki in the Valoka area had brought a 'part of the teaching' (*hap tok*) of Batari into the Kivung and wanted to continue in accordance with it. With unusual explicitness, Titus Mou asked whether the Kivung had later become a cargo cult, and Fred replied that this was precisely what he meant.[53]

Further, more paraphrased enquiries were necessary to shed light on what, according to people's present-day memories, had actually been thought and done when the Kivung was changing, that is, what beliefs and practices are constitutive for *kago*, i.e. the indigenous understanding of the term 'cargo cult'. Before summarising any results of these enquiries, however, I shall first go into the Batari movement in order to sketch the historical model to which, at least according to some accounts, the adherents of the Kivung later returned.

The 'Batari story'

As with the Kivung, in the case of the Batari movement I was gradually able to identify certain topics in the statements of my interlocutors that returned with varying degrees of frequency and elaboration. These topics or – as could be said in analogy to the Kivung – elements of a collective 'Batari story' include the organisation, spread and ending of the Batari movement, all of which were already mentioned at my very first interview in Koimumu. Ambrose Bai (26 June 1996) had just followed my invitation to talk about his experiences as a carrier during the Second World War when he surprisingly continued as follows:

> Before the war there was Batari. Then the Japanese came, then the Americans. Meetings were arranged, and all the men up to Ubae assembled. The whites heard about it and were afraid ... Batari was Number One (*nambawan*), the King. In every village he had appointed a Number Two (*nambatu*) and a Number Three (*nambatri*). In his home village of Vovosi the Number Two was Taukomo; in Koimumu it was Gume, who has already died. With Batari – sorry! (*sori*) – we young people were not allowed to fool around. You ended up straight away in prison, whether child or woman. People knew about the law of the prison from Australia. 'With the teaching of Batari you may not be disobedient (*bikhet*).' The teaching of Batari extended to all the villages. People said that a white man had appeared to him in Rabaul and given him this teaching. He had told him that he should go, no longer work, and do this thing (*wokim dispela samting*): 'Then you will be fine.'[54] Batari attracted all the people in all the villages ... The soldiers marched into the villages in formation, and the *nambatu* said that one should give taro, eggs and pigs to them. The Big Men believed all of this and they said that it was true. The people in the south of the Nakanai area did not accept it ... nor did the people in Galilo, but everyone up to Hoskins did.

Barth Sesega, who was brought up as a child by Gume and thus by Batari's alleged *nambatu*, followed Ambrose and Valentine (1955a: 16–18) in describing the grading of the different office-holders in the Batari movement. He spoke of 'Lance Corporals', 'Sergeants' and 'Sergeant-Majors', and he added that Batari himself – who, according to Ambrose and Valentine (1955a: 16), was made 'King' – had been carried around as 'Governor General' on a litter (*bet*).[55] The 'soldiers' of the Batari movement who had not belonged to the higher ranks are said to have worn red armbands and waistcloths (*laplap*) or waistcloths and shirts with red marks (*namba*) thought to be the insignia of the Japanese occupation forces.[56]

While Ambrose Bai said that the spread of the Batari movement stopped at the gates of Galilo, virtually no one in Koimumu, Rapuri and

Vavua remembered this as causing conflicts like the quarrels associated with the ending of the Kivung.[57] Only in Galilo did I hear about a visit by Batari's followers, who wanted to spear all those who defied them and whom, because of their great numbers, people could not beat up.[58]

The spread of the Batari movement reached a climax when its followers walked through the bush to Arawe on the south coast of New Britain, obviously to spread their 'teaching' there too.[59] The hosts answered this with a return visit, but then – as Valentine describes – the Japanese occupiers put a sudden end to the Batari movement.[60] According to Ambrose Bai (26 June 1996), they burnt the insignia of Batari's 'soldiers', thrashed him and said that he was lying so that 'it' was no longer continued. Later, Ambrose (28 May 1997) provided a somewhat more detailed version of this account:

> They captured him ... took a cord, tied him up and beat him until the blood ran. They burned all the marks of all the men up to Ubae ... and we all ran away. They thrashed him and said that he had to stop this. 'You are really lying, you are doing harm to all the villages ... You must stop this thing ... This thing is not true, it is doing harm to everyone, to all the villages.[61] We haven't seen your children or parents. This is not true. That man there [Batari] is lying and doing harm to all your villages with his lie.'

As a result, Ambrose explained, the whole thing was called a 'cargo cult', and correspondingly this term is also mentioned in the demand with which, according to Titus Mou, the Japanese had ended the Batari movement: 'Stop it! You may not do this cargo cult any longer! It is not true. It, it is a lie.'[62]

In my interview with him, Ambrose himself had decided to move from talking about his experiences as a carrier during the Second World War to a description of the organisation, spread and ending of the Batari movement. Yet he left rather open what Batari's 'teaching' or 'lie' actually consisted of, or what exactly 'this thing' was that the white man who had appeared to Batari in Rabaul had told him to do and what should be stopped on the orders of the Japanese occupiers. Even in response to my enquiries, Ambrose (26 June 1996) at first merely spoke of 'all possible statements' (*olgeta kainkain toktok*) before gradually giving up his initial reserve and explaining that Batari had heard from the white man that the cargo would be produced by one's own ancestors and soon delivered to all the villagers in a large ship.

The same explanation for the origin of Western goods and the same expectation of their imminent arrival were also described by Titus Mou, a man who was much younger than Ambrose. However, in contrast to either Ambrose or Valentine, he gave as the 'source' not an encounter with a white man but a dream Batari had had.[63] Like Valentine (1955a: 13), but unlike Ambrose, Titus also added that people had believed that the Australians had up to now prevented the promised delivery of goods in order to enrich themselves illegitimately at the expense of the villagers.

While the explanation and expectation of Western goods stands at the beginning of both Titus Mou's and Valentine's accounts, and while people in Galilo immediately answered my question about 'Batari's teaching' by saying that the cargo would arrive 'just like that',[64] Ambrose Bai's initial reserve corresponded far more to the 'Batari story' common in Koimumu, Rapuri and Vavua: in general, my interlocutors only addressed the beliefs promoted by Batari comparatively rarely and inexplicitly.

In contrast, and apart from the organisation, spread and ending of the Batari movement, another element of the respective 'story' was the conclusion of new marriages. Although not mentioned by Ambrose and only referred to by Valentine in the context of the 'rejection and destruction of certain aspects of the existing culture' (1955a: 14), these marriages were often mentioned first when my interlocutors talked about the 'times of Batari'.

According to Titus Mou, Batari lined up the young men and women in two rows and decided who should be married to whom.[65] Even in the case of young girls whose breasts had not yet formed (*susu i no kamap yet*), people were not allowed to disagree, Titus (4 July 1996) continued, and therefore many villagers preferred to go to Rabaul as contract workers so that their daughters could grow up in peace. When, during my second field trip, I sat together with a group of some elderly women, I asked if it was really true that in the past people had been forced to marry in accordance with 'Batari's teaching', and one of the women replied that this had been the case for herself.[66] As if to confirm this, Barth Sesega (27 May 1997b) later told me that even today, in the course of a marriage row, a wife can sometimes point out to her husband that, after all, it had not been her who wanted the marriage, but Batari.

All in all, and apart from references to marching soldiers and newly concluded marriages, the inhabitants of Koimumu, Rapuri and Vavua talked of their own volition as rarely and as inexplicitly about the practical activities of Batari's followers as about the corresponding beliefs. Here, too, however, Titus Mou constituted an exception in that he was the first to tell me that Batari's 'soldiers' had captured a missionary. In referring to this event, Titus (4 July 1996) assigned the 'role of the victim' first to Schweiger and then, in agreement with Valentine (1955a: 19), to Weigl:

People thought that the cargo would not come because many whites were still there (*planti waitman i stap yet*). People wanted to do something and kill Fr. Weigl ... Many men from all areas up to Talasea met in Vovosi, and Batari sent them to capture the Father ... They stripped him, beat him, tied him up and laid him down on a platform that they had built earlier. Under it they kindled a fire with wet coconuts and they really smoked him. His tears dropped on to the fire, and they said: 'I think he wants to pee (*pispis*) on the fire in order to put it out.' Some climbed on to the platform and beat the

Father. He was naked. They chased his catechist, his name was Tobakaki, into the bush and violated his wife.[67]

This account was confirmed during the course of my second field trip. Ambrose Bai, for example, who had initially not mentioned Weigl's capture at all, now went specifically into the sexual component of his mistreatment, referred to by Titus in the statement that the victim had been stripped.[68] In contrast, Klaus Eppmann (9 August 1997), the resident priest of Valoka, said that he had merely heard that Batari's 'soldiers' had captured Weigl and 'kept an eye on him'.[69] According to Barth Sesega, people took the clothing and books of the mistreated missionary in order to use them in conducting their own masses.[70] One of the brothers of Gume, who had participated at the time, is reputed still to get drunk sometimes and say, 'Come on, let's do a mass.'[71]

Just like Titus, but unlike Ambrose and Barth, Peter Tautigi (2 September 1997) saw a connection between the described event and the desire for cargo, that is, the lifestyle of the whites. Thus he attributed the following statement to Batari:

If you are holding on to Christianity, then you stop. You are preventing everything from coming to you ... You have to follow me, you can live like the whites ... Do you think the whites habitually work? The whites do not habitually work. They are just living; God gives them everything. Food emerges just like that. They don't, don't have the hard life that we have, because we are following the missions, we are putting great efforts into worship. This how we are blocking all the roads that lead to this. God will not give this thing to us.[72]

Among the practices ascribed to the Batari movement, nocturnal visits to the cemetery were spoken about in an even more reserved manner than the capture and mistreatment of a missionary or the holding of one's own masses. Titus Mou did not mention these visits at all, and it was only an old woman by the name of Kaose who told me that the men had designated two girls to bring food for the dead to the cemetery and to wait for the money and cargo to appear.[73] However, this had led to nothing (*tasol i go samting nating*), people were bitten by mosquitoes and felt cold to no avail, and, Kaose continued, they stole the food that had been left for the dead and consumed it themselves.

From Kivung to cargo cult

In Koimumu and surrounding villages, people seem to see precisely those beliefs and practices as essential, indeed as emblematic, for the Batari movement, and thus also for the term 'cargo cult' in general, that are mentioned less frequently and less explicitly than other elements of the 'Batari story'.

When I asked my interlocutors what exactly they meant by talking about a change in the Kivung in the sense that it 'went back to' the Batari movement or 'became a cargo cult', or when I asked them what exactly had been thought and done in the course of such a change, they replied by referring to both the expectation of goods produced by one's own ancestors and the visiting of cemeteries. Thus I heard, for example, that people had met so that the dead or the cargo would come, and the idea was mentioned that the cargo could arrive 'just like that'. Moreover, the adherents of the Kivung were said to have completely distorted (*tanim nambaut pinis*) the words of Fr. Berger, who had merely talked about the sale of copra in order then to claim that the dead would send the cargo.[74] According to Peter Tautigi, the hope of cargo was also linked to the 'taxes' already mentioned, and people thought that, for a little money (*liklik wanshilling*), they would obtain not a little but a lot of cargo, and very quickly. In Peter's words, Lima had announced the following:

> This thing there must come to you, lots and lots of it. Your village will be full of cargo, your village must be full of everything ... You will live like ... the whites now. Look, the whites do not work with much money, with a bit of money they can have an order placed, you see something comes, that's not child's play, a ship comes, full of your cargo ... We are like ripe bananas, they are ripe, they all fall down, fall down, fall down, fall down, fall down, fall down, fall down, only one, two remain, you will live well, something must happen, you will live well.[75]

Titus Mou even sketched a succession of several expectations, repeatedly disappointed, yet repeatedly renewed, while describing one of them in more detail:

> Once, in the year 1965, an eclipse of the sun was expected, and the Father had explained this earlier and said that then one should not look directly at the sun with bare eyes. At a meeting, people said that the Father was lying and that it would be dark not for a short time but for a whole week. In this darkness a ship would come and unload cargo in front of every house. Because of this, the darkness would last seven days without a break. A week before the date set, people met and instructed all the women to get enough water for seven days and harvest enough food. At this time I was in grade five. When I came home, my mother told me about this. She said that during the darkness, when we were hiding inside, our dead brothers and grandparents would come and put the cargo down in front of our house door ...
> I had a white with the name of Clive Johnson as a teacher. In the classroom Clive always told us: 'There is nothing. Tell them that they are wasting their time.'[76] I told my parents: 'My white man says that

the cargo cannot come.' They hit me on the ears and blood came because I had contradicted the Kivung. I told the teacher that my mother and all the women of the village were preparing everything and that they were storing everything in the houses, and that I would not be able to come to school the next day because I would be helping my mother. The teacher came to look at everything, and the old men said that a spy is coming who will make sure that no cargo will arrive and that he should disappear. They said to him, 'Masta, go away!'[77] He obeyed and went away. In the houses, people made holes to urinate in and repaired the walls, since it was forbidden to look out, because if one were to see the dead, the cargo would disappear just like that. Strict rules were laid down.

When the day came, people in the whole village felt like during a great feast, very excited. The eclipse came and went – nothing happened. The sun set and rose again. Everyone was completely frustrated at that. People held a meeting for a whole week, and the women were busy supplying food ... People came to say that (*ol i painim toktok*) the ship had been too big for the bay and the captain had turned and gone back to Australia. Everyone was very angry (*kros nogut tru*) and people asked themselves how they could enlarge the bay.[78]

Still in the context of the same interview, Titus not only confirmed my intentionally provocative statement, that the adherents of the Kivung had cleaned the cemeteries, but also answered in the affirmative when I asked him if, in addition, food had been laid out. Moreover, during my second field trip, Peter Tautigi (2 September 1997) told me that one night he had, together with some other men, checked a Big Man buried in the cemetery in order to see if, as Gume had claimed, there was any money there.[79]

All this, however – as Paul Gar (18 September 1997), the leading Big Man of Koimumu, assured me – only occurred in Batari's time, and even then only in Rapuri. Lima had only spoken about the dead sending the cargo at a later point, and, Paul continued, this had been precisely the reason for him leaving the Kivung and joining the supporters of the council.[80]

Yet in Rapuri I heard from Otto Puli, another Big Man, that there 'people had stayed strictly within the Kivung system',[81] and that changes had only come from the Bileki, who had been linked to Batari earlier and were living in the north. In the 'system of Batari' one had married on his instructions and not in the church, but people in Rapuri were observing Christianity.[82] In addition, I was told in Rapuri that Batari had neither a Kampani nor money and that he had merely waited for the cargo without doing anything (*wokim nating long wetim kago*). In the Kivung, however, unlike in the Batari movement or a cargo cult, goods were ordered with money.

Whereas Paul Gar firmly rejected the idea that people in Koimumu in general or during the time of the Kivung in particular had ever visited the cemeteries as in the time of Batari, and whereas Otto Puli opposed the

Kivung to the Batari movement or cargo cult and wanted to speak about a 'return to Batari' only with respect to the Bileki, in Galilo my general request to talk about the Kivung was already sufficient to elicit the following answer:

> This thing, you want know about, this thing is called 'cargo cult' (*dispela samting ol i kolim 'kago kalt'*) ... One thing they did was to wait at the cemetery for the mothers and fathers who had died already. They [the adherents of the Kivung] thought that they [the dead] would give them money and some kind of food like cargo (*sampela kaikai olsem kago*) ... At night they went to the cemetery, looked at the graves and spoke into the graves, but the dead did not answer. People believed this just like that (*tingting nating*). They told them [the dead] that they should give them money and cargo. They waited at the cemetery for nothing. They said that something would come to the cemetery today, but nothing came ... Lima had brought this up.[83]

Whenever or wherever the expectation of goods produced by one's own ancestors may have emerged or emerged again, it must have led to the idea that the production and sale of copra were superfluous, and this, in turn, is likely to have caused the opposition to the planting of coconut palms, which Joe Sogi and Albert Lowa had already mentioned at the beginning of my first field trip. At all events, I heard that coconut palms had been reviled as 'food for crows' or cockatoos, and Titus Mou (4 July 1996) reported that the whites were believed to have simply promoted them in order to feed the coconuts to their pigs.[84] Accordingly, Titus continued, people had beaten up anyone who wanted to start a coconut plantation. When I asked if at least rice had been cultivated, he answered in the affirmative, but added that this was only done under pressure from the colonial officials and, owing to the cargo cult, without much conviction (*tingting bilong dispela i no strong tumas*).

The decision not to produce or sell copra any longer obviously went along with the loss of the already accumulated capital, because the stores were given up, and the money earned or saved was, as I heard, 'misappropriated', 'finished off' or returned to the Big Men of various villages.[85] At first sight, the alleged rejection of coconut palms hardly fits with the economic goals of the Kivung, but many of my interlocutors resolved this contradiction by assuming a process of change. Thus Fred Golumu (21 July 1996) replied to my question as to whether coconut palms had really been described as 'food for crows' by saying: 'First we wanted to plant them, and then some distorted the talk of the Father and said what you said, and therefore we did not plant much.'[86]

My interlocutors certainly agreed with Valentine in considering Berger an important person. However, whereas Valentine portrays him as a kind of white cargo cult leader (Chapter 2), in the Koimumu area I heard that, if there had been a cargo cult at all, this could only have happened without Berger's knowledge or even against his will. Titus Mou (4 July 1996) claimed that Berger was surprised when the Kivung 'turned into a cargo cult', but that the other Fathers accused him of having brought about this change himself. According to Ludwig Gar (29 April 1997), Berger was so angry about 'Batari's teaching being brought in' (*pulim toktok bilong Batari*) that he finally left the Nakanai area and went to Rabaul, where he later died.

For Klaus Eppmann (9 August 1997), the last of Berger's successors in Valoka up to now, Berger had planned the Kivung from the start as an answer to Batari or as a countermovement. Similarly Titus thought that Berger had told Lima that he could not do 'that', not realising, though, that, as a former member of the Batari movement, Lima was still 'thinking about cargo'.[87]

Although, in the Koimumu area, Berger was by and large 'acquitted' of Valentine's accusation that he had led a cargo cult, some of my interlocutors also attributed statements to him that rather recall ideas otherwise mentioned in the context of the Batari movement. Ambrose Bai and Joe Kaveu, for example, claimed that Berger had talked about the existence of a secret – just as in Batari's time the Australians were said to intercept the expected goods. Moreover, this secret proves to be linked to the assimilation to the whites which, at least in Ludwig Gar's view, ultimately lies behind the Christian and economic goals and activities of the Kivung:

AB: He [Berger] said, he wanted to plan it like this ... the whites have a secret from us in respect to the way of life. 'God himself has created us, and what you have, we must have, too.' Fr. Berger said that ... 'I can achieve that for you too.'

JK: The whites keep things secret from us. Soon we will be like the whites.

AB: Everything belongs to us all.[88]

In the context of the same interview, Ambrose and Joe also told me that Berger had wanted to send Lima to the place where one's own ancestors were manufacturing all the goods. Out of fear, however, Lima did not go, and as a result people live in exactly the same way now as they have done in the past.[89]

Notes

1. Conversation with Greg Mongi (18 April 1996).
2. *Rispekt* (Tok Pisin), *latilogo* (Nakanai).
3. Conversation with Klaus Eppmann (19 April 1996).
4. See Jebens (1995, 1997a, 1997b, 2000).
5. Conversation with Angie Dimas (29 April 1996).
6. Joe Sogi, about fifty years old, belongs to the Ilalao clan and lives in Lakuba (house no. 31). He was George Tautigi's predecessor as Koimumu's representative in the local government, he has been elected chairman of the school board, and he is regarded as a leading man, not of all the villagers but at least of the Ilalao. Accordingly, he enjoys a slightly lower reputation than Paul Gar, but nonetheless he equalled Paul in rarely missing an opportunity to stress his own importance and his expertise with respect to *kastom*. I go further into my personal relations with Joe later in this chapter.
7. Peter, Hermann and Simon Mape told me, more or less jokingly, that, if I were to play in one of the football teams attached to the different sections of the village, I would belong to Guria (4 June 1996). Paul Gar and Casimir Tauvato assured me that in their view I was a Bualali. Given the general predominance of matrilineal descent, this corresponded to the role ascribed to me as Joe's son, since his wife belonged to the same clan.
8. 'Mi mas go free long olgeta haus bilong olgeta man na ol i mas go free long haus bilong mi.'
9. Accordingly, Peter Mape (23 July 1996) said that people would not come to my house out of *rispekt*, but he also added that they certainly would come if I had been black. Joe Sakim (1 August 1996), a man from Silanga, told me that there my house would always be full, but in Koimumu people would keep to themselves because they had a lot of *rispekt*. This association of *rispekt* with distance not only reminded me of the impressions I had during my first visit to Koimumu but was also confirmed in the first weeks of my fieldwork, when I walked through the village and occasionally heard mothers telling their children to show some *rispekt* and not approach me too closely. Accordingly, Leoba Olipitarea (18 July 1996) recalled the following: 'When I was still small, white geologists came to Koimumu once and slept in a tent. We were told not to go near them. We were only to go if they needed help.'
10. In at least partial agreement with Joe Sogi, John Bubu (5 June 1996) said that one had to leave the school grounds by ten o'clock at night and could not go there at night.
11. Towards the end of my first field trip, I also went to more distant villages such as Gavutu, Karapi and Rikau.
12. However, for the most part all my conversations and interviews took place in Tok Pisin, the lingua franca also used widely by the inhabitants of Koimumu and neighbouring villages when talking among themselves (Chapter 1).
13. Pius Magelau died on 17 April 1997. He was buried the same day, followed by gatherings of people mourning on 19 April, 20 April and 17 May, and the seclusion of the widow from 28 April to 16 May. In Koimumu the votes were collected on 16 June 1997, following campaigns by representatives of different parties. In general, the voting, which was covered on the radio, stretched over several weeks.
14. See Figures 15–20. In Koimumu and Vavua, there were two performances each. While in Vavua the same men wore different masks at the two events (19 June to 21 June, 25 June to 26 June), in Koimumu I saw first villagers coming from there (12 June to 15 June) and then migrants from Tarobi (15 July to 16 July, 30 July).
15. For more details, see Jebens (2001c, 2003b), as well as Chapter 5 of the present work.
16. Accordingly, it becomes understandable that my participation in a night-long *singsing* as well as in hunting expeditions made an impression and that, when talking to the inhabitants of other villages, people did not, for example, paraphrase any of my statements but instead stressed the fact that I would usually chew betel nut. When it came to playing soccer, I avoided being identified with any of the four village sections by joining a team formed from the older players from all parts of Koimumu. After people

had initially regarded me as especially qualified because, as everyone knew, Germany had formerly won the world championship, my first efforts were met with the advice that in future I should smoke less.

17. Conversation with Robert Boko (8 June 1997).
18. Conversation with Joe Sogi (9 July 1996). In contrast, Alphonse (20 July 1996) declared that he had not heard anyone refer to me in such a manner.
19. 'Em i no bosim you. Em i bosim yu taim yu nupela tasol' (interview with Paul Gar, 7 August 1996).
20. Conversation with Joe Sogi (26 May 1996).
21. Here Joe used the term 'masta' and answered my intervening question as to whether he was referring to soldiers in the affirmative.
22. Similarly, the colonial officer R. Tobia indicated that one half of the population of Koimumu was in favour of local government councils, but that they had been rejected by the other half (PR Hoskins 1967/68-15).
23. Even later, people restricted themselves to short statements, unless I enquired myself or encouraged them to go into greater detail. At the end of June 1996, for example, I heard from a man hitherto unknown to me that there had been the Kivung earlier. Also during my first field trip, Dominique Mape (13 April 1997) and Joe Ilo (8 May 1997) told me that Valentine had been here during the time of the Kivung. Joe Ilo, who like Joe Sogi is about fifty years old, belongs to the Kabilimosi clan and like Lawrence Olpitarea lives in Taivel (Tailabolo, house no. 48). Compared with, for example, Paul Gar and Joe Sogi, Joe Ilo seemed much more reserved, and I would assess his influence outside his own clan as rather limited. During my second field trip, he became an important informant for the allegedly final chapter of the history of the Batari movement and the Kivung. See Chapter 4 of the present work.
24. Paul said this in the context of an interview in which I had first asked Joe Ilo about the genealogy of the Kabilimosi (19 June 1996).
25. Conversation with Titus Mou (28 June 1996).
26. Even when, for example, Tomuga Bobore, a brother of Lima's, was recounting his life history and had just said that he had returned to his home village after a journey, Titus merely asked whether 'Lima's Kivung' had already started at this time (interview with Tomuga Bobore, 28 July 1996).
27. '[F]amily i mas stap gut, yu mas prea, wokim olgeta gutpela pasin, halpim ol lapun, halpim ol sikman, olgeta yangpela meri mas marit gut long haus lotu' (interview with Titus Mou, 4 July 1996).
28. Conversation with Joe Ilo (8 May 1997). Fred Golumu spoke of the teaching of children (21 July 1996).
29. Interview with Ludwig Gar (29 April 1997). Another link to the world of the whites is implied in Joe Sogi's statement that, in the context of the Kivung, people wanted to know 'something about the "way of the whites" and about "our way"'.
30. See also appendices: 'Tok Pisin texts'.
31. Fred Golumu (21 July 1996), Otto Puli (21 July 1996) and others mentioned a single store. As this store became bigger, according to Titus Mou (4 July 1996), it was divided up and branches were opened in different places. Accordingly, Tomuga Bobore (28 July 1996) talked about the existence of several stores. In addition, John Bubu (5 June 1996) and Alphonse Mape claimed that several cars had been owned (interview with Titus Mou, 4 July 1996).
32. Interview with Otto Puli (21 July 1996). In addition, John Bubu (5 June 1996) spoke of the cultivation of rice and the delivery of cargo, while Fred Golumu (21 July 1996) mentioned the sale of copra and also the delivery of cargo.
33. Joe Kaveu said this in the context of an interview with Ambrose Bai (28 May 1997). Joe was about thirty-five years old, belongs to the Gararua clan and lives in Malebulu (house no. 85). I initially became acquainted with him in the course of occasional trips to Kimbe, and then I also visited him when he was no longer working as a driver. Like Joe Kaveu, Ambrose Bai (Figure 14) is a member of the Gararua clan, but being about sixty-

five years old he belongs to the older generation. Living in Kovia (house no. 59), he is regarded as a Big Man, but, as in the case of Joe Sogi, his influence seems to be restricted to his own clan. People in and around Koimumu know Ambrose for the story of his encounter with a mysterious white man, to which I shall return in Chapter 4. I valued Ambrose as an interesting and animated interlocutor who had much to say, particularly about the Batari movement.

34. Titus Mou (4 July 1996) spoke of a daily collection, Otto Puli (21 July 1996) of a single one. According to Fred Golumu (21 July 1996), money was collected from individual families, but according to Joe Kaveu (interview with Ambrose Bai, 28 May 1997), it came from whole villages.

35. Interview with Ludwig Gar (29 April 1997).

36. I also heard briefer descriptions along the same lines during my second field trip from Ludwig Gar (29 April 1997) and Pius Geloa (31 August 1997).

37. Leo Scharmach (1960) describes life in the internment camp.

38. 'Em God nau ya.'

39. Interview with Peter Tautigi (2 September 1997).

40. 'Holger, em i stori tru long mipela ya ... mi no ken giamanim yu, Holger, em dispela tok, mi kisim tru long maus bilong em, em i stori tru long mipela, i no wanpela man nating i stori, em Pater yet i stori' (interview with Paul Gar, 18 September 1997).

41. According to Fred Golumu (21 July 1996) and Paul Gar (18 September 1997), Berger himself had wanted to be transferred to Valoka or Vavua. The formulation 'up to the Bileki at Hoskins' comes from Otto Puli (21 July 1996).

42. Conversation with Barth Sesega (27 May 1997a). According to Ambrose Bai (28 May 1997), Joe Kaveu's father did not properly understand the task formulated by Berger.

43. Similarly, and emphatically, Peter Tautigi (2 September 1997) expressed the point of view of the adherents of the Kivung as follows: 'We have had enough' (*mipela inap*).

44. 'Mipela i no laikim kaunsel, na mipela i no laik long takis, mipela i ken sindaun olsem tumbuna, long wanem, bai gutpela sindaun bilong mipela inap tumbuna inap nau ... Lo bilong gavman i kam insait na pushim kaunsel i go i kam insait na bihain sindaun bilong mipela bai nogut i bagarapim meri' (interview with Peter Tautigi, 2 September 1997).

45. According to Peter Tautigi (2 September 1997) and Maternus Mape (17 September 1997), Peter Mou had a decisive influence on the introduction of the local government councils. He was later to become the first Councillor and, as Peter Tautigi (2 September 1997) stressed, he received a car from the government. With respect to the clan membership of the adherents of the Kivung and the council, however, there is certainly a contradiction here, because only the clans of Peter Mou (Kabilimosi), Paul Gar (Kevemuki) and Peter Tautigi (Vavaha) are allocated to the 'bush', whereas the clan of Ambrose Bai (Gararua) is said to have come 'from the coast' (Chapter 1). Peter Tautigi (2 September 1997) and Joe Ilo (8 May 1997) also counted a man called Tomuga among the opponents of the Kivung. According to Peter Tautigi (2 September 1997), he was one of Lima's brothers, and thus he is in all likelihood identical to the 'Bobare (Tomiga), younger brother to Lima', of whom Valentine (1956a: 84) writes that, after long experience as a policeman, he had 'a greater potentiality for constructive, pro-Administration leadership than any other native in this area' and had already rejected 'practically all aspects of the Kivung'. 'If he is allowed to remain at home and supported by the Administration,' Valentine (1956a: 85) assumed at the time, 'he will be a potent source of opposition to the Movement.'

46. The first claim was reproduced by Sophia Dodo (19 July 1996), the second by Paul Gar (18 September 1997).

47. 'Mipela i bruk na ol lain bilong kaunsil i go long narapela hap, ol lain bilong Kivung i go long narapela hap ... Mipela i ranim wok bilong kaunsil na ol i ranim wok bilong Kivung, na mipela i harim wanpela tok bilong Kivung, mipela i go antap long ol, na ol i harim wanpela tok bilong dispela ol kaunsil, ol i kalap antap long mipela. Mipela i wok long pait' (interview with Paul Gar, 18 September 1997). However, as Paul assured me in response to my corresponding question, people fought only 'by mouth' (*long maus*), not 'by hand' (*long han*).

48. Joe Ilo (8 May 1997) also assured me that the colonial officials had said that the Kivung was good, but it should not fight with the government.
49. A feeling of disappointment was also referred to implicitly by Loko, a Big Man from Galilo. In an interview organised by Titus Mou, he explained his own rejection of the Kivung as follows: 'We in Galilo didn't believe this, because we know that something like this is not mentioned in Christianity. When the whites came earlier, they didn't tell us that later our parents would meet and give us money, and so we didn't believe it ... Later Boas prevented us from this ... He said that we must plant ... and he was right. We planted ... harvested ... sold and got money ... Lima's people saw that and began to leave him and do the same. Thus we outdid them because of what they have said, because of their false way of thinking (*giaman tingting*). They gave it up because they didn't see that there was anything in it. More and more people left him, and so it came to an end' (interview with Loko, 26 July 1996).
50. Valentine also mentions the deployment of an 'anti-riot force of police with rifles' in Hoskins (Chapter 2), and similarly Otto Puli (21 July 1996) and Joe Kaveu (interview with Ambrose Bai, 28 May 1997) said that the court case mentioned by Paul Gar took place just there and that it had been monitored by many policemen.
51. The formulation 'a little differently' (*narakain liklik*) comes from Peter Sarere (6 June 1997), the catechist of Vavua. Paul Gar (18 September 1997) and an old man, introduced to me as a former catechist of Berger's (interview with Anonymous, 28 July 1997), used the word 'exaggeration' (*ovaim*). Paul Gar (18 September 1997) also talked about 'distorting', as did Otto Puli (21 July 1996) and Maternus Mape (17 September 1997).
52. The corresponding sentence of Paul Gar's runs in its entirety: 'Ol bigman bilong mipela ol i no ranim gut, long wanem, ol i go ranim kranki gen ya ... ol i putim gen long wok long kago kalt ya.'
53. Literally, Fred's words were the following: 'Em ya, mi toktok long en ya' and 'Ol i laik ranim olsem tok bilong Batari gen' (interview with Fred Golumu, 21 July 1996). Ludwig Gar expressed himself similarly, but at a much later point, when he stated that people from Valoka had put in Batari's 'teaching' (*pulim toktok bilong Batari*, 29 April 1997). Berger's former catechist at first said that people returned to what they had done previously (*ol i go gen long nambawan samting ol i mekim*; Anonymous, 28 July 1996). Then Titus Mou asked him if he was referring to Batari, and he answered in the affirmative. According to Valentine, this 'return to Batari' was what the villagers had been explicitly accused of by Munzlinger (Chapter 2).
54. 'Em bai yupela sindaun gut.'
55. Conversation with Barth Sesega (27 May 1997a). Gume is the same man who, according to his field notes, later became one of Valentine's most important informants.
56. Cosmos Gar (interview with Paul Gar, 18 September 1997) mentioned the red armbands, Ambrose Bai (28 May 1997) the red waistcloths, Peter Tautigi (2 September 1997) the waistcloths with red marks, and Berger's former catechist (Anonymous, 28 July 1996) the shirts with red marks.
57. The spread of the Batari movement was later confirmed by Titus Mou (4 July 1996).
58. Interview with Varago (26 July 1996). Goodenough (30 November 2001) had obviously heard about this visit too, because in November 2001 he still mentioned three armed men from Galilo who had allegedly opposed Batari's followers there and forced them to retire. In Koimumu, only Ludwig Gar (29 April 1997) mentioned conflicts between the adherents and opponents of Batari, which had taken place in Galilo as well as in a part of Vovosi. However, Ludwig hailed from Makasili, as already noted, and did not spend much time in Koimumu.
59. This excursion was described by Ambrose Bai (26 June 1996, 28 May 1997) and Paul Gar (18 September 1997), but is not mentioned by Valentine.
60. According to Paul Gar (18 September 1997) and Barth Sesega (27 May 1997a), a man by the name of Avra – who had, so to speak, been converted to Batari – also participated in this return visit of the people from Arawe.
61. 'Yu giaman tru, yu bagarapim olgeta ples ... Yu mas pinisim dispela samting ... Dispela samting i no tru, i bagarapim olgeta, olgeta ples.'

62. 'Yu go daun! Yu no ken wokim moa dispela kago kalt ya! Em i no tru. Em, em giaman' (interview with Titus Mou, 4 July 1996). In the view of some of my interlocutors Batari's punishment extended beyond his death. Thus Barth Sesega (27 May 1997a), Joe Kaveu (interview with Ambrose Bai, 28 May 1997) and Peter Tautigi (2 September 1997) told me that, when Batari was about to be buried, rain fell so heavily that it completely flooded the grave that had been dug for him. Barth (27 May 1997a) described this as 'not good', and Michael Kautu (interview with Peter Tautigi, 2 September 1997) spoke of 'God's penalty'.

63. According to Titus (4 July 1996), Batari had reported this dream as follows: 'I see many men, some of whom I know, some I don't, and some of whom have died already, like my father and my brothers. I ask them what they are doing, and they say, they are like in a prison, and the more serious the crimes or the sins that they have committed in life, the longer they have to stay there, and when God is satisfied, they will go to heaven. I ask whether that is the place that the Father calls purgatory, and they agree. I ask what they are doing there, and they show me everything: planes, cars, big, big factories and many machines. I ask whether things are being sent to us too, and they agree. I say that nothing arrives with us, though, and they say that the fault must lie with the Australians who do not take down the names of the recipients properly. My father says that he always writes "Batari".' The confusion indicated here between 'Batari' and 'battery', also mentioned by Lucy Mair, Peter Worsley, Andrew Lattas (Chapter 1) and Albert Lowa, is briefly referred to by Valentine (1955a: 10) when he writes that Batari had 'seen his name (Battery) inscribed on a shipment of cargo consigned to a European'.

64. Interview with Varago (26 July 1996).

65. Peter Tautigi (2 September 1997) said that in Koimumu these instructions came not from Batari, but from Gume as his *nambatu*.

66. Conversation with Antonia Dumu (15 May 1997).

67. On 28 June 1996, however, Titus had spoken of Schweiger as the victim.

68. Unlike Titus, Ambrose did not name anyone, but he said the following: 'People in Valoka captured the Father. All our Big Men went there as well ... One Big Man, I think he came from Porapora, said: "You say this is a sin, eh?" This Big Man took hold of the Father's penis (*kok*) and tore off his clothing. "Sin, you say? This is no sin. With this, you are deceiving us" (*Em yu trikim mipela*). People beat him ... People made a fire and he was completely wrecked (*bagarap*) because of the smoke rising from the fire. He asked for water, and he was given water that had been peed in before. We were all there. The church was broken into. The catechists were beaten up ... the wives of the catechists were beaten up, badly pursued (*ranim nogut*) and their clothes were ripped up' (interview with Ambrose Bai, 28 May 1997).

69. When I told Eppmann that, according to my informants, Weigl had been tormented with smoke, he replied that he knew nothing about this. He himself, Eppmann continued, had only heard that Weigl had been tied to a tree, which was still standing.

70. For Barth (27 May 1997a), the victim was not Schweiger or Weigl, but Berger.

71. I heard this from Cosmas Gar in the context of an interview with Paul Gar (18 September 1997).

72. 'Sapos yu holim lotu, em yu stop. Yu stopim olgeta samting i no ken kam long yu ... Yu mas bihainim mi, yu ken sindaun olsem ol masta ... Yu ting masta i save wok? Ol waitman i no save wok. Ol i sindaun tasol; big man i givim ol long samting. Kaikai i kamap nating. Ol i, i no hat olsem yumi, long wanem, yumi bihainim ol misin, yumi wokim bikpela lotu. Em yumi stopim olgeta rot bilong samting ya. God i no inap long givim yumi long dispela samting'.

73. Kaose said this in the context of a conversation with Barth Sesega (27 May 1997b).

74. Paul Gar (18 September 1997) said the latter. The arrival of the dead or the cargo was mentioned, among others, by Barth Sesega and Fred Golumu. Their statements ran literally as follows: '[O]l i tok long bai kago ken i kam, kamap nating' (conversation with Barth Sesega, 27 May 1997a), and 'Mipela kivung bambai ol man i dai i kamap' (interview with Fred Golumu, 21 July 1997).

75. 'Dispela samting ya i mas kam long yu, moa moa yet. Ples bilong yu bai bagarap long kago, ples bilong yu i mas bagarap long olgeta samting … Bai yu sindaun olsem … ol waitman nau. Lukim, ol waitman i no wok long bikpela moni, liklik wanshilling, ol i ken wokim na oda i go, yu lukim samting i kamap, i no pilai, sip i kam, pulap long kago bilong yu … Yumi olsem banana mau, ol i mau, olgeta i go pundaun, pundaun, pundaun, pundaun, pundaun, pundaun, pundaun, wanpela, tupela tasol i stap, bai yu sindaun gut, samting mas kamap, bai yu sindaun gut' (interview with Peter Tautigi, 2 September 1997).
76. 'There's nating, tokim ol they're wasting their time.'
77. 'Masta, yu klia!'
78. Titus (4 July 1996) continued that when, some years later, a ship actually did arrive and when all the people of Koimumu were full of anticipation and assembled on the beach, they were forced to realise in disappointment that it was only a mission ship. Thus all the adherents of the Kivung felt very ashamed.
79. Titus Mou spoke of the attempt to enter into direct contact with the dead. In addition, food had been brought to the cemetery in the evening and had disappeared by morning. However, Titus continued, it was soon said that this food had secretly been consumed by people wanting to play a trick on others.
80. Following a description of the economic activities of the Kivung, Paul Gar continued as follows: '[B]ut they didn't do things well … the dead came into it, and we decided, we left them, because of this lie now' ('[T]asol ol i no ranim gut … long man i dai i kam insait, na mipela i kamap, mipela i lusim ol, em long giaman toktok nau'; 18 September 1997).
81. 'Ol i stap long sistem bilong Kivung stret' (interview with Otto Puli, 21 July 1996).
82. 'Mipela i bihainim lotu.'
83. Interview with Loko (26 July 1996).
84. The phrase 'food for crows' (*kaikai bilong kotkot*) was used by Loko (26 July 1996), while Peter Tautigi (2 September 1997) spoke of 'food for cockatoos' (*kaikai bilong koki*).
85. John Bubu (5 June 1996) spoke of 'misappropriating', Peter Sarere (6 June 1997) of 'finishing off' and Fred Golumu (21 July 1996) of 'returning'.
86. Similarly, Maternus Mape (17 September 1997) told me that people first sold copra and later said that a ship would come and that one should stop selling it.
87. Titus quoted Berger's demand to Lima as follows: 'You can't do that. We must build a new group' ('You can't do that. Yumi mas wokim nupela grup'; 4 July 1996). When I asked Barth Sesega whether people had gone to the cemeteries in Berger's time, he answered in the negative, and a young man by the name of John Kaveu explained that this had only happened with Batari, but that Berger had put a stop to it ('Berger i stopim ya'; conversation with Barth Sesega, 27 May 1997b). This corresponds to Dahmen's statement that Berger had 'the Nakanai people, previously rebellious as they were, entirely under his influence again' (Chapter 2).
88. Interview with Ambrose Bai (28 May 1997). In the original, the corresponding passage runs as follows:
    AB: 'Tok bilong en olsem, em i laik plenim olsem … ol masta i save haitim mipela long sindaun. "Em big man yet kamapim yumi na yupela i stap long en na mipela i mas stap." Em tok bilong Pater Berger … "Mi ken wokim dispela tu bilong yupela".'
    JK: 'Ol waitman i save haitim ol samting bilong yumi. Bai yumi tu olsem ol waitman.'
    AB: 'Olgeta samting, em bilong yumi.'
89. Joe and Ambrose said in detail:
    JK: 'He [Berger] told Lima that he should appoint his soldiers. "Soon you may go and there you will see the reason for things"' ('Bai yupela i ken wokabaut bai lukim as bilong samting long ples').
    AB: 'You will see how everything works, how it comes up from under the earth to the surface. You will come back again, and we will see. You will come back like the mothers and fathers, and people will see how you will come from there fully loaded'

('Bai yupela lukim raun bilong samting i raun daun long graun i go antap. Bai yupela i kam bek nau bai mipela i lukim. Yupela i kam bek olsem mama olsem papa bai ol i lukim yupela i pulimap olgeta i kam long hap').

JK: 'This means, they say that the whites do not make things like radios and things, the dead make them, that's it. This is what they believe' ('Dispela ya, ol i tok olsem, ol waitman i no save wokim ol samting olsem radio na ol samting, em ol man i dai pinis, em nau. Em bilip bilong ol').

AB: 'When you come back, the road has been smoothed, and they can come and you can go, soon things will be for you as they are for us now. Soon we can have just the same way of life' ('Bai yupela sindaun olsem mipela nau. Bai yumi ken wanpela sindaun tasol').

JK: 'This thing, the Father did it for a very long time, and it became very strong, but the man [Lima] was scared and therefore he came back' ('Dispela samting ya, em i Pater i wokim ya i go i go i strong olgeta, tasol man ya yet i pret na olsem na i kam bek').

AB: 'And because of this we were thrown back onto our present-day way of life' ('Olsem na mipela i kam bek gen olsem sindaun gen olsem').

4

Indigenous interpretation

Comparison

Batari movement and Kivung

In and around Koimumu, no one adopted Valentine's historical perspective with respect to older beliefs, the Batari movement and the Kivung (Chapter 2) as explicitly as Titus Mou. Apparently without knowing anything of Valentine's report to the colonial administration, he, too, stressed that, if the adherents of the Batari movement and the Kivung had not been the same people, they had at least been guided by the same beliefs and needs.[1] Following his description of the Batari movement, for example, Titus continued as follows: 'and on, and on, the cargo cult did not die ... it still remained strong. People thought that the war should end soon and we would soon get our cargo. This idea did not die.'

With the exception of Titus, however, my interlocutors refrained from attempting to see the Batari movement and the Kivung as part of a larger context, and they were not even much interested in discussing the relationship between the two phenomena. Accordingly, the change of the Kivung over time or its 'return to Batari' belonged to the elements of the 'Kivung story' that were talked about least, and least explicitly (Chapter 3). Yet people did sometimes allude to an underlying continuity, which, after all, accords with the statement that within the Kivung older beliefs and practices had been picked up. Thus I heard that each and every one of the Big Men who had 'stood with Batari' later joined the followers of Berger and that people 'kept on' after the Batari movement.[2] In addition, Lima was seen as a former member of the Batari movement by Titus (Chapter 3), and even as a Batari's committee (*komiti*) or 'Number Two' by others.[3]

In a manner recalling not only the past quarrels between the adherents of the Kivung and the local government councils, but also the different reasons given for the ending of the Kivung (Chapter 3), the idea of an underlying continuity is today shared by many, but rejected by some, at least as far as their own villages are concerned. Otto Puli, for example, opposed the Batari movement to the Kivung in relation to religion and economy, or marriage and the possession of money, and Paul Gar (18 September 1997) even denied a continuity on the personal level by claiming that, at the time of the Batari movement, Lima had still been too small and insignificant (*bun nating*) to participate. Similarly, a young man by the name of Michael Kautu first assured me that Lima had 'broken up Batari's entourage' (*brukim ol lain bilong Batari*) and 'removed this cargo cult' (*rausim dispela kago kalt*), and then answered decisively in the negative when I asked if Lima had not in fact been a follower of Batari.[4]

Valentine, Berger and Munzlinger

While present-day memories at least partly correspond to Valentine's report with respect to the relationship between the Batari movement and the Kivung, there is a far greater discrepancy when it comes to the course of Valentine's first stay in Rapuri and his conflict with Berger. Important or even fateful as this conflict may have been for Valentine himself, none of my hosts and informants ever felt inclined to bring it up when talking with me. Throughout neither of my field trips did I ever hear anything about Valentine's speech, so extensively documented in his field notes, his 'campaign of limited reeducation' or his statement made before the colonial officer in order to confirm his account of the Kivung (Chapter 2).

On the occasion of a visit to Rapuri I repeatedly and explicitly asked Henry Laili, one of Valentine's main interlocutors (Chapter 2), whether he knew anything about a conflict between Valentine and Berger. Henry's answer always began with the claim that he had told the Father that he did not want to become involved because the Father and Valentine had the same white skin, whereas he was black.[5] Towards the end of our conversation, however, Henry, just like Alphonse Mape later, said that Valentine had angered Berger because of his behaviour during a Sunday mass. According to Henry he took photographs, while according to Alphonse he took notes, and this led to the service being interrupted, as is also mentioned by Valentine (Chapter 2), as well as to Berger no longer wanting to see Valentine in the church.[6] Moreover, Alphonse was the first and, apart from Titus Mou, the only one of the villagers I spoke with who mentioned dissent in relation to one's own *kastom*: Berger and Munzlinger had asked the people to give it up completely, but, Alphonse continued, Valentine and Chowning believed that this would be regretted later and thus opposed Berger and Munzlinger. Titus added that Valentine had said that Berger would lie, and that in his, Valentine's, country it was forbidden to ask the people to destroy their *tumbuan*.[7]

Henry, Alphonse and Titus certainly did not confirm the versions Valentine gives of his conflict with Berger in his report and his field notes, but when asked they at least agreed that such a conflict did exist. Yet the great majority of my hosts and informants saw the relationship between Valentine and Berger has having been entirely free from tensions. Fred Golumu, for example, did not hesitate when I tried to provoke him by saying that people had told me that in many respects Valentine had disagreed with the 'Kivung family' and had therefore quarrelled with Berger: 'No,' he replied curtly: 'people have been lying to you about this.'[8]

It fits with the supposed harmony between the anthropologist and the missionary that they are both thought to have shared the interests of the people, that is, to have taken the side of the inhabitants of Koimumu and neighbouring villages. Thus the Kivung, with its alleged aim of improving current living conditions by means of Christian and economic goals and activities, is traced back to Berger, and is also said to have enjoyed the support of Valentine.[9] People in Rapuri, for example, stated almost literally that he was in favour of the Kivung because its adherents had worked with money and not merely waited for cargo, and that he himself had seen this.[10]

When Valentine returned to Rapuri in the 1970s (Chapter 1), he is reported to have expressed astonishment because he had thought that things would have changed during his long absence, but he found them to be exactly the same as before. Joe Kaveu paraphrased Valentine's words correspondingly, but added that people did not understand their real meaning:

'In what ways have you become independent? Your way of life is the same as before, and it has not changed a little bit. I think we don't know whose fault this is now. Whether or not it is the fault of your government, we might not know.' But we, we don't know what he is talking about ... What kind of talk is this now? We don't know. That was Vali's talk.[11]

According to Joe, Valentine had also said that there existed a great pathway, but that it was hard to find, and that, if he, Valentine, were to open it up (*sapos mi wokim*), he would be brought before the court.[12]

The statement that one's way of life 'has not changed a little bit' only implicitly alludes to a critique of or an opposition to the government. Yet Titus Mou expressed himself more clearly when he reported that Valentine had written about the Nakanai being disadvantaged vis-à-vis migrant settlers working on leased oil palm plots, and that, as a consequence, he had to leave the country while his books and notes were burnt.[13] Taking the side of the inhabitants of Koimumu and neighbouring villages obviously means confronting the government, regardless of whether this refers to the colonial past or the independent Papua New Guinea of the present day.[14]

In contrast to Valentine and Berger, Fr. Georg Munzlinger, who was transferred to Vavua in 1954, was sharply criticised by my hosts and informants when they repeated some of the accusations that are already mentioned in Valentine's field notes. After an initial meeting, Valentine first wrote that he saw Munzlinger as 'the most nearly normal priest we have seen here', but this impression soon faded, and he stated that Munzlinger was regarded as a 'man of anger' (*man bilong kros*) and that people were cross with him because he beat the schoolchildren and accused the community of not singing hymns properly.[15] Even before Valentine represented Munzlinger as a supporter of Berger in his report to the colonial administration (Chapter 2), his wife Edith stated: 'On the whole the attitude of the people toward Munzlinger, at first one of fear, is now gradually turning into one of ridicule' (EV 6 September 1954: 3).

Although my interlocutors did not talk about Munzlinger being laughed at, they also used the expression 'man bilong kros' and they described repeatedly and impressively the beatings that people received, for example, for looking around or chatting during services and for having a *singsing* during Holy Week.[16]

When I talked with the catechist of Koimumu, Barth Sesega, on the occasion of such a *singsing*, he pointed around and said: 'Look at all these men; their backsides were fodder for Fr. Munzlinger.'[17] He has certainly gone to hell, not to heaven, people stated, shaking their heads.[18] Not even his successors in office appear to see Munzlinger in a particularly positive light. They mainly accuse him of having forced the villagers to do 'slave work' in order to construct the church building in Vavua and to reshape the associated plot of land.[19] Fr. Alois Hartmann (19 April 1997), the resident priest of Vavua, found that 'today his way of treating the people cannot be ... appreciated any longer ... This is not on, it is not on any longer now and it was not really on then either.'

According to people's present-day memories, Munzlinger directed his anger as a *man bilong kros* against Valentine too, whether because Valentine had said that he knew nothing of God, because Munzlinger had believed that Valentine wanted to import a new church or because Munzlinger was opposed to Valentine's support for the Kivung.[20]

Otto Puli (21 July 1996), one of the Big Men of Vavua, claimed that Munzlinger had warned Valentine not to give to the people the 'good knowledge' (*gutpela save*) about how the whites lived, because, once they had learned everything from him, they would later kill him. For Otto and for other Big Men like Fred Golumu and Paul Gar, it was not Berger, as in Valentine's report to the colonial administration, but Berger's 'negative opposition', Munzlinger, who had prohibited the people from continuing to speak with Valentine.[21]

Correspondence and discrepancy

As much as present-day memories and Valentine's accounts may differ, the people of the Koimumu area did tell Valentine and myself about the same individuals, such as Batari, Lima or Berger, and, all in all, they described the same beliefs and practices. The activities, commandments and prohibitions of Catholic Christianity, for example, are placed in the foreground today, as they were earlier, since Valentine describes them as the 'public façade' of the Kivung. In contrast, Valentine saw the expectation of goods produced by one's ancestors and the visiting of cemeteries as lying behind this 'façade', and correspondingly my own interlocutors referred to these things merely as a result of changes that had only taken place elsewhere.

Such changes, however, had already been a topic of discussion in the 1950s. In Valentine's field notes, the same Gume, for example, who has been mentioned to me as well is cited with the statement: 'Batari's teaching belongs to the past, but people are almost bringing it back into the Kivung.'[22] During the same conversation, Gume reported that a colonial officer had told him that the Kivung was good, as he had heard, but that it was getting 'distorted' (*tanim nambaut*; CV 12 August 1954: 3).

The same is said to have happened already to the Batari movement, since, according to Valentine, people thought 'that Batari had perverted the true teaching of Master Hitler' (Chapter 2). Valentine quotes Gume as follows: 'Masta Hitla made a good speech, but Batari took it and turned it round, and he caused all kinds of things to happen.'[23] Another interlocutor of Valentine's, who, like Gume and Batari, was also believed to have met with 'Masta Hitla', referred to the latter's words as follows: 'This talk came to the people, but some [people] made it out to be bad, and these things that were bad went up, and things that were good went down.'[24]

However, not everything that Valentine had noted was brought up again by my hosts and informants. Much seems to have fallen into oblivion, particularly with respect to the time before the Kivung. Thus I heard nothing either of a Masta Hitla or of any differentiation between 'evil Australians' and 'good Americans', with the former appropriating the cargo sent by the ancestors and thus ultimately causing the Nakanai's relative poverty, and the latter representing, as it were, the hopes for a better future (Chapter 2).

Valentine partly traces the Batari movement back to the idea that the ancestors already had possession of the cargo, and he writes that, by the end of the Second World War, this idea had developed into an equation between the old way of life on the one hand and the Western, i.e. the desired way, of life on the other. This equation, in turn, came to my mind only once throughout either of my field trips, namely when Ludwig Gar claimed that family life was regulated by the ancestors in the same way as it is by the whites (Chapter 3).

Although individual elements of Valentine's account were not mentioned by my interlocutors, I would speak not of a loss of diversity but rather of a gradual process of shifting, in which some themes lose importance while others simultaneously gain it. Berger's experiences during the Second World War, for example, are now part of the regularly repeated basic elements of the 'Kivung story', whereas, in his report to the colonial administration, Valentine merely mentions Berger's arrival in Vavua and Valoka, and in his field notes only at one point does he write that the Japanese had 'imprisoned and badly beaten up' Berger.[25] The abolition of *poisen*, too, is treated rather cursorily by Valentine, while my interlocutors repeatedly stressed that, as followers of the Kivung, they had been required to discard all the relevant substances.

Irrespective of all correspondences and shifts, when the people in and around Koimumu show considerable reserve in talking about the Kivung, let alone its change over time, and when, in this context, they avoid or reject the term 'cargo cult' with equally considerable emphasis, they are doubtlessly reacting to the experience, still present in their memories, that they have been persecuted as alleged cargo cultists by the colonial administration or its supporters from Galilo, and that they have been condemned and imprisoned for spreading 'false reports'.

In Valentine's time, this experience seems to have led to a climate of threat and fear. Accordingly, Valentine's field notes repeatedly refer to unjustified accusations:

> The people from Galilo put us before the court. And they say that the Kivung is all about cargo. They say that people meet in order to get their cargo. But we tell the colonial officer that there is no cargo. We just want to put our village in order and live. No cargo will come. It is sufficient for us to eat taro.[26]

Here, persecution and imprisonment obviously contributed much to the writing down and thus to the objectification of one's own beliefs, since Valentine often mentions transcriptions of addresses by Lima, which the latter would show to the colonial officer 'all the time' in order to defend himself and to convince his opponent of the 'nature' of the Kivung.[27]

The term 'cargo cult'

Openness

Although the inhabitants of Koimumu and neighbouring villages certainly used the word 'kago' when talking to Valentine and me, the question as to what exactly they meant or mean by it cannot easily be answered because, as a medium for the 'Kivung story' too, their lingua franca, Tok Pisin, is largely distinguished, at least from the Western point of view, by its limited degree of precision or, to put it more positively, by its high degree of openness.

This becomes apparent when people articulate their expectations or describe beliefs and practices from the past. The term 'this thing' (*dispela samting*), for example, used for what Lima said must happen, as well as for what Batari should do according to Masta Hitla and stop doing according to the Japanese (Chapter 3), seems to be understood rather generally. The same applies to the promises attributed to Lima and the colonial administration that the adherents of the Kivung would soon 'live well' or that the introduction of councils would 'put things in order' in the village, as well as to the description of the Kivung's change over time as a 'distortion' or 'exaggeration' of what Berger had promoted (Chapter 3).

Because of its openness and rich imagery, Tok Pisin is particularly suitable for a rather oblique, indirect way of talking that plays with allusions.[28] This, however, is not a restriction forced upon the Nakanai by the characteristics of their lingua franca, but a specific element of their culture that they themselves objectify as such. During a stay in Port Moresby, for example, Maternus Mape explained to me that controversial points in particular should not be mentioned straightaway. Rather, one should first sit down and then gradually circle round them (*raunim*).[29] Without in the least wanting to mystify matters, this way of 'circling', paraphrasing or alluding to things sometimes created in me, as a Western observer, the impression that 'a residue of the unsaid' remained and that there existed something like an 'aura of mystery'.

Definition and evaluation

In the course of my two field trips, Paul Gar was the first to formulate a substantial definition of the term 'cargo cult', i.e. 'kago kalt', when he tried to reject the alleged accusations of others by saying: '"Cargo cult" means to bring food to the cemetery, to get money from the cemetery and cargo from the ancestors' (Chapter 3). Correspondingly, Titus Mou (4 July 1996) answered my question as to what he understood by a 'cargo cult' with the statement that the colonial officials and teachers had talked about people without resources who were dreaming that the cargo would come from the dead 'just like that' (*ol man i stap nating drimanim kako bai kamap nating long ol man i dai*). Loko (26 July 1996), one of my interlocutors in Galilo, thought that people had called the Kivung a 'cargo cult' and that its followers had not only gone to the cemetery but had also waited for the dead to 'give them money and some kind of food like cargo'.[30]

The expectation of goods sent from one's ancestors as well as the visits to cemeteries is obviously of central importance to the substantial definitions formulated in the Koimumu area. Thus, in their efforts to avoid the term 'cargo cult' itself, people take precisely these two elements and push them into the background, or merely refer to them as a result of the change of the Kivung, so that, in general, the expectation of goods and the visits to cemeteries are mentioned much less frequently or explicitly than, for example, the pursuit of Christian and economic goals, Fr. Berger's leading role or the conflictual ending of the Kivung.

The same degree of reserve becomes evident with respect to the Batari movement, for which the term 'cargo cult' is regarded as entirely applicable, since for most people the change of the Kivung 'into a cargo cult' and the 'return to Batari' are basically synonymous (Chapter 3). Accordingly, in the context of the 'Batari story', my interlocutors were not too inclined to address the beliefs promoted by Batari, and among the practical activities of Batari's followers, the visits to cemeteries were talked about even more rarely than the capture and mistreatment of a missionary (Chapter 3).

By avoiding the term 'cargo cult', its substantial definition is confirmed. Yet people also define the term relationally when they not only reject but also oppose it to the very beliefs and practices that they claim for themselves. Thus my informants in Koimumu, Rapuri and Galilo assured me, with respect to the Batari movement or to cargo cults in general, that they had not done 'any such thing', but had followed Christianity and planted coconut palms or pursued economic undertakings (*bisnis*), instead of believing in goods coming from the ancestors.[31]

At least in Valentine's time, the difference between *bisnis* and 'cargo cult' was perhaps mainly seen in the fact that the colonial government responded to the former with support and to the latter with prison sentences. At all events, this impression is created by a story repeated in Valentine's field notes that Gume had allegedly heard before the Second World War in Rabaul from people from Manus.[32] It begins with a woman receiving a paper with instructions from her dead sister. Her son follows these instructions and builds a ship that he sells to the government. According to Gume, a 'government official tells him that this would be OK, if he worked like that he would have *bisnis*, and he would be entitled to do well'.[33] Later the son repeats the white's view in a speech as follows: 'Listen to me! If we work like this, we will have money later. And this thing, that the cargo comes just like that, that is bad. Because in the past we have suffered too much from being imprisoned.'[34] Correspondingly, in another part of his field notes Valentine cites Gume as saying that, if someone was dead and were to send him something, he, Gume, would be brought before the court.[35]

For Valentine's interlocutors, 'kago' was everything that 'the authorities' persecuted, but, conversely, everything that was persecuted could also be 'kago'.[36] In this respect, not much seems to have changed. Cargo cult followers are still, by definition so to speak, opposed to the representatives of colonisation and missionisation, and thus 'cargo cult' becomes a term of exclusion: 'cargo cult' is not Christianity, *bisnis* or council. Obviously, the inhabitants of Koimumu and neighbouring villages define the term both relationally and negatively. If, however, cargo cult followers primarily distinguish themselves by what they do not believe or practise, the same connotation of passivity emerges that is alluded to in substantive definitions when people talk about merely waiting to get the cargo 'just like that', i.e. without having to work for it.[37]

The negative definition of the term 'cargo cult' corresponds to its negative evaluation, perhaps articulated most succinctly by Paul Gar's dictum that 'cargo cults are bullshit' (Chapter 3). Undoubtedly, this is to a large extent still influenced by the experience of having been persecuted by the colonial administration, if not by the memory of having 'suffered too much from being imprisoned', as Gume's story has it. At the same time, the negative definition of the term explains why the change of the Kivung 'into a cargo cult' is pictured as a 'distortion', an 'exaggeration', and thus ultimately as a deterioration. To claim that, at least in one's own village, the Kivung has not been a cargo cult or that it demonstrates no continuity with the Batari movement thus means putting the Kivung in a positive light retrospectively. Accordingly, Sophia Dodo (19 July 1997), a member of the older generation, told me the following, using an expression that, because of its openness, seems to be quite typical of the local lingua franca: 'If the people had done what the Father had said, something proper (*samting tru*) would have happened.'

Usage

In and around Koimumu, the term 'cargo cult' is nowadays not only avoided, rejected or applied with reference to the Batari movement and the Kivung, i.e. to the past, it also serves as a label for negatively evaluated beliefs and practices of the present. As in Valentine's time, such beliefs and practices may belong to the areas of religion, economy and politics.

Even prior to my actual fieldwork, I had already heard that the adherents of a charismatic movement by the name of 'Rosa Mystica' would be accused of doing a cargo cult. After Klaus Eppmann had spoken about a widespread 'cargo cult mentality' (Chapter 3), on the very next day and in the same context, in Koimumu Joe Kaveu (16 June 1996) replied to my question as to what he thought of the 'Rosa Mystica' by casually and in a derogatory fashion uttering the words: 'cargo cult'.[38]

Before the elections to the National Parliament in 1997, politicians from different political parties used the term 'cargo cult' in order to distance themselves from their opponents. In a speech given in the *haus boi* in Koimumu on 17 May 1997, Andrew Talingapore, who stood for the National Party, said about another candidate that he would promise to replace all the grass roofs in one village with corrugated iron and that he would probably want to do a cargo cult. This was met with general laughter. At another election meeting, held in Koimumu on 12 June 1997, Brown Bai, the candidate for the Pangu Party, mentioned 'some people' who claimed that Papua New Guinea would have to become communist if its national debts could not be paid. However, Brown continued, such ideas represented a 'cargo cult mentality'. Shortly afterwards, as I was sitting one evening with some villagers on the beach, I heard a rumour that Joe Vilei, an old supporter of the Pangu Party, had reputedly spread: if someone was to show one of Brown Bai's business cards (Figure 3), which had been distributed in the election campaign, anywhere, that person would be given 5,000 Kina and more in return.[39] At this, Michael Kautu (14 June 1997), who was much younger than Joe Vilei, replied spontaneously: 'Hey, this is now a cargo cult!'[40]

In using the term 'cargo cult', people never refer to their own beliefs and practices. In this sense, 'cargo cult' excludes Christianity, *bisnis* and council as well as people: cargo cultists are always the others. The same pattern becomes evident in the attempt to reject the term with reference to the Kivung. Paul Gar had declared, 'We didn't do any cargo cult. Cargo cults have been done by others.' Correspondingly, for Paul a change of the Kivung 'into a cargo cult' took place in Rapuri. There, however, Otto Puli ascribed such a change to the Bileki living in the north, whereas people in Galilo maintained their old accusation or equation of Kivung and cargo cult (Chapter 3). According to Valentine's report to the colonial administration, Berger had turned this accusation round by claiming that 'if there were any Cargo talk in the area it could only come from the anti-Kivung faction led by Boas' (Chapter 2).

Continuation and the present

Paga as a cargo cult leader

After the Kivung had ended, Papua New Guinea had become an independent state and Valentine's last field trip already belonged to the past, the activities of Paga from Ubae, who was first mentioned to me by Albert Lowa (Chapter 3), began to spread. For Titus Mou, these activities make up a further and, for the time being, the last chapter in the history of the Batari movement and the Kivung, so that, in a sense, Paga succeeded first Batari and then Lima.[41]

Like the Kivung, the beliefs and practices associated with Paga were also accompanied by conflicts. Correspondingly, Titus's memories differ in central aspects from those of Joe Ilo, who, unlike Titus, was not an adversary of Paga but one of his adherents. The conflicting descriptions and interpretations can serve as examples of the ways in which the people of the Koimumu area define and use the term 'cargo cult'.

When compared with the Batari movement and the Kivung, Paga's activities must certainly be regarded as less important. Yet, in their context, or in talking about them, the same explanations and expectations, the same ideas about the relationship between the whites and one's own way of life emerge that people otherwise associate with 'cargo cults' and thus reject. As will become apparent, however, these ideas may continue to be expressed today.

Just like Albert Lowa, Titus Mou (4 July 1996) first told me that Paga had collected money in many villages. In addition, he described Paga's 'teaching' as very enticing (*swit tru*) since, according to it, people should marry two or three women and then the cargo would come. Even Paga himself had married three times, his first wife having been a daughter of Batari.

Paga's 'career' proper, like Batari's, began in Rabaul. There, Titus said, Paga visited a settlement of Nakanai employed as contract workers, hid fifteen cartons of beer under his bed and collected payments of ten Kina from a lot of people for which everyone would later receive 10,000 Kina in return. Then Paga's departure from Rabaul approached. His last evening was described by Titus as follows:

> He said that he only had twenty Kina, and so people bought a crate of beer and drank the lot. When the crate was empty, he replaced it with a full one from under his bed. He repeated this often, and so it looked like he had performed a miracle (*i luk olsem man i wokim miracle ya*). He said: 'My vision has told me to do all this. What I say, you must follow.'[42] When the fifteen cartons were empty and everybody was drunk, people said that he was a proper man (*man tru*) and that it had been a real miracle just like Jesus had performed ... This story went around and everybody heard it. Now the movement grew, it became very large.[43] Everyone, including the old, little girls and young men, gave ten Kina.

Having returned to Ubae, Paga changed his money into coins and filled twenty new money bags with them, which he numbered consecutively and kept in his house. 'In front of the house,' Titus continued:

> there were tables. He took the first bag from the house and his *komiti* counted the money ... Then he fetched the second bag. The bags that had been counted he threw back into his house. In the evening he said that one would continue the next day. Things went on like that for the next two days. At night he wrote new numbers on the bags, so that the same money in the same bags was counted over and over again. Thus things went on, for nearly a week ... He asked the people from Ubae to slaughter pigs for his *komiti*, who came from almost all the villages in the area. People did that because they thought that they would be rewarded for it later. They built a house and fornicated with women (*wokim pasin pamuk*). At that time there was no money, no cash crops, nothing. People were completely stupid (*longlong nambaut*). Thus they did not take care of their daughters but sent them to the Big Men.

At this point Titus stressed that he had almost allowed himself to be convinced by Paga and that, had he been younger, he also might well have followed him. After the experiences with Lima, however, he thought that Paga's story could not be true or that one should first prove it. Thus he sent two young men, Phidelius and Mape, to Paga with ten Kina each in order to have things checked. According to Titus, Phidelius became Paga's secretary and so could approach his house, even though it was forbidden to enter the room in which Paga kept the money. Nonetheless, Phidelius was able to fulfil his task of checking things:

He secretly marked a money bag, noted down the sum when it was counted and saw that at the next round of counting a different total was produced for the same money bag. Phidelius heard how Paga handled the coins inside the room. He looked through a hole in the wall and thus realised Paga's trick.[44] Phidelius told me about it and said that people wanted to go on counting until the next day and on Monday give everyone his 10,000 Kina.

As a consequence, Titus said, he himself had prevented many people from giving ten Kina to Paga. On the day on which everyone was to receive his 10,000 Kina, people danced (*samsam*) in the road between Koimumu and Vavua with a large bag which was said to contain the promised money. When the bag was opened, however, there were only forms and not more than 5,000 Kina. According to Titus, people started looking for Paga, but could not find him and, when they came to Ubae, he had already run away.

Titus concluded by stating that today Paga lives in Ubae as a man completely without means (*wanpela rabis man stret*). He does not own an oil palm plot and his three wives left him after the money had dried up. My question as to whether Paga had been brought before the court was answered in the negative by Titus; and Alphonse Mape, who was also present, explained that the people were ashamed of having spent money for a 'cargo cult custom' (*kago kalt pasin*).

The internal perspective

Some ten months after Titus Mou told me about Paga's activities from the point of view of an adversary or sceptic (and without mentioning Paga's first name), Joe Ilo (8 May 1997) described these activities from an internal perspective while we were sitting in front of his house and having dinner.

Peter Paga from Ubae, he began of his own accord, belonged, like him, to the Kabilimosi clan and was a maternal relative (*kandere*). Frequently smiling or even laughing, Joe continued by saying that he himself had collected money in Koimumu, ten Toea per person. Then he was brought before the court following an accusation by the people from Vavua, but he told the judge, with the agreement of Paga, that he had only followed the latter's instructions. As a result Paga went to prison, and the people claimed that he was doing a cargo cult. Without going into details about the reasons for this verdict or for the collecting of money, Joe stressed that he had once said to Paga that he would not believe him too much. At this Paga took a bag of coins from a room in his house and replied that no one must enter the room and that the coins were just for him. Joe also added that, before the court, Paga had declared that his deceased mother had come to him in a dream to give him power (*paua*) and to tell him what to do. However, out of mercy (*marimari*), he, Paga, wanted everyone to benefit.

I asked Joe whether he could also tell me about Paga in the context of an interview, that is, with a cassette recorder running, and he was ready to do so on two occasions: the first a bare three weeks later, and then, after I had inadvertently taped over the recording, again in the last month of my second field trip.[45] In both cases Joe talked in a somewhat melancholy tone, smiling regretfully about the fact that the efforts described had been unsuccessful, and he repeated his initial account with much more detail, but without adding anything substantially new.

Nonetheless, it struck me that Joe did not repeat the term 'cargo cult' even once, that he referred to a 'work' (*wok*) done by or for Paga in a manner which seemed to become more and more general and unspecific every time, and that he increasingly put his own scepticism in the foreground.[46] Thus it always took specific questions to make Joe mention Paga's promise of a multiplication of money, and he repeatedly stressed that the coins that Paga had taken from his house might have been the same that people had collected earlier.

At our second and last interview, Joe decided on a chronological account; that is, he began with the 'revelation' on which Paga's activities were to be based:

> When he was sick, he was sick, and he lay down on the bank of a river and there he was. Well, he was sleeping and he thought ... he said, that his mother appeared to him ... And she appeared to him and she gave him a story, she said: 'Peter Paga, you must get up and take this book, it has power, you will take it, bring it to the village and do something for me.' Well, he took it and then went to the village, went to the village now ... He stayed there and thought about this talk, that his mother, as he said, had given to him, and he began with a small – something like a society of his, a sort of group ... Well, he started and got a couple of men who were in Ubae itself ... from his clan and from his married relatives, they cooperated in this work, which, which he was starting now. Well, he did it and did it and did it.[47]

Later, Joe continued, Paga came to see him once in Koimumu. He told Joe to visit him in Ubae and to take part in his activities. As he said, Joe followed this request and worked in Koimumu. According to Joe, many people joined Paga, but at the same time they were having doubts or were not too convinced. At any rate, for Joe it had been a mistake on Paga's part to divulge too much to others:

> Regarding this work, his mother had given him power, this power was just for him, but he spoiled it and gave it to us, all the people, and so on, he did it, he did it and did it and did it, it went totally wrong, it didn't go well any more, because he invited too many people, from the oil palm settlers up to the Ulamona area we all joined him, with this work of his, this story of his, that he did.[48]

When, finally, Paga fetched money from Ubae and when people were dancing in the road with many of his adherents from various villages, he was arrested by the police in Rapuri, brought before the court twice, and also imprisoned. In Joe's view, the last sentence should have a lasting impact: 'At this time he went to prison now and I believe he was a little bit afraid of the government and so he stopped this work of his.'[49]

I responded with the question as to what exactly Paga had been accused of. According to the government, Joe explained, Paga should have kept his 'little power' to himself. Moreover, it had not been too good to oppose the government or to talk badly about it. If, however, one had cooperated, there would have been no problem.[50] When I said that I did not quite understand where the money promised by Paga was supposed to have come from, Joe laughingly replied that Paga probably thought that it would come from the dead, but he, Joe, did not really know.[51] With similar reserve, Joe answered my question as to what had been said about Paga later and whether people had been angry (*belhat*) with him. People had been afraid because of Paga's prison sentence; he, Joe, did not know what every single person was thinking, but nobody had been too angry because nobody had really lost too much money with Paga's collections.

Finally, our second and last interview ended with Joe's supposition that, if Paga had not told everything to everyone, economic success might well have been the result since before coming to Koimumu, Paga had already started his 'work' in Ubae and he had run a store at which people could buy goods and beer.

Titus Mou, as an adversary of Paga, and Joe Ilo, as an adherent, hardly seem to be remembering the same events. The correspondences between what they said are basically restricted to the statement that money was collected, that Paga promised future profits and that people had danced in the road together. Nevertheless, each of the two accounts omits precisely those elements that stand at the centre of the other. Thus, unlike Titus, Joe did not say that, through various tricks, Paga had faked the increase in beer in Rabaul or money in Ubae, that he had demanded to marry two or three women or that people had sent their daughters to the Big Men, i.e. to Paga's *komiti*. On the other hand, unlike Joe, Titus did not trace the activities of Paga back to a contact with his deceased mother, and for Titus, unlike for Joe, these activities were not ended through persecution by the authorities, that is, more or less violently.

The interpretations of Titus and Joe prove to differ just as much as their descriptions. Titus sees the beliefs and practices promoted by Paga as a continuation of the history of the Batari movement and the Kivung, and he calls them a cargo cult – in opposition to Joe, but in agreement with Albert Lowa, Joe Sogi and Alphonse Mape.[52] In accordance with the negative definition and evaluation of the term, Titus stresses the violation of Christian commandments when he states that, as in the times of Batari, polygamous marriages were conducted and when he talks about fornication. Moreover, he ultimately depicts Paga's adherents as the victims of their own gullibility or stupidity. In this sense, it would have been understandable if, as Alphonse claims, people were to remember their participation in Paga's activities with shame.[53] Yet to attribute deceitful intentions to Paga himself means assessing him differently from his 'predecessors', since, at least in and around Koimumu, no such accusation was made against either Batari or Lima, and certainly not against Berger.

Joe Ilo only used the term 'cargo cult' when he first mentioned Paga's imprisonment, and then only to repeat the charge against Paga. Although he did not explicitly reject this term, his increasingly general and unspecific reference to 'work' done by or for Paga does appear to be an attempt at least to avoid it.

At the same time, and without making any links himself between Paga's activities, the Kivung and the Batari movement,[54] Joe inadvertently hinted at certain parallels: if Paga was responsible for his efforts having gone 'totally wrong' because he told others about what had been entrusted to him, this corresponds to the statement that the Bileki had caused the 'distortion' of the Kivung (Chapter 3) and also to the idea that 'Batari had perverted the true teaching of Master Hitler' (Chapter 2). Moreover, Paga's activities had been ended as violently for Joe as the Kivung or the Batari movement had been for many of my other interlocutors, and Joe's account appeared to be influenced by the same feeling of regret with which Tomuga had said that it would have been better to try out the Kivung 'a bit longer' (Chapter 3). Thus, Joe in no way struck me as a shamed victim of gullibility, stupidity or – to cite Paul Gar again – 'bullshit'. Rather, when he vividly described, for example, how people had danced together, he seemed to express the view that, despite the ultimate lack of success, he had still taken part in a period that, by and large, was evaluated quite positively.

Ancestors, goods and the whites

The expectation of goods sent by one's own ancestors is a central aspect of a 'kago kalt' or 'cargo cult', and thus people reject it decisively along with the term itself: 'Money and cargo do not derive from the ancestors, money derives solely from sweat' (Chapter 3). Yet some of my hosts and informants were still convinced that the dead were indeed able to help them in achieving economic success. Just as, in Gume's story, the instructions of a dead sister form the basis for *bisnis*, according to Joe Ilo, Paga began his 'work' in Ubae by running a store. For Joe as well as for his daughter Mathilda Ragi, Paga had almost profited even more from being in contact with his deceased mother. When Joe spoke about Paga for the first time, Mathilda, a young woman who appeared to have enjoyed a longer school education, stressed that what Paga had received had only been intended for him. If he had not divulged it (*tokaut*), therefore, it would certainly have 'become true'.[55]

In order to illustrate the potentially negative consequences of not keeping encounters with the dead to oneself, Mathilda then told me about a woman who received no money from her husband for her children and who met a white man in the market who looked exactly like one of her deceased *kandere*. She described her situation to him and he gave her money, but, when her husband forced her with beatings to tell him where the money came from, the deceased *kandere* did not return. By way of explanation, Mathilda added:

> Here, things like that do not happen too frequently, but in Popondetta the dead often return as whites. Here, the dead often hold out money to us in a dream, and the Big Men say that we could get it if we were only to hold out our hands long enough. That doesn't work, however, or at least it doesn't work here.

The link that Mathilda made between one's own ancestors, the whites and their money was confirmed by Joe Sogi with respect to their goods when I told him that, in the Southern Highlands of Papua New Guinea, I had heard of the notion that the dead would assume a white skin, would live beneath the earth and would, for example, produce bush knives for their descendants. 'People think that here, too,' Joe replied, 'and people did think that in the context of the Kivung. However, they do not say it openly because they have no evidence for it.'[56]

Another man, whom Joe Sogi had already told me about just two weeks after my moving into Koimumu, allegedly had an encounter which was at least as unusual as those of Peter Paga or of the woman in Mathilda Ragi's story. The man, Joe said, met a white person in the bush on several consecutive days, and each time he asked this person to talk to him or to give him something, but without success.[57] Although Joe did not mention any name, it soon became clear that he was talking about Ambrose Bai, since during my very first interview in Koimumu, even before he discussed the Second World War and the Batari movement, Ambrose (26 June 1996) described in the first person the events outlined by Joe.[58]

The war was long past, Ambrose began, but the colonial period had not yet ended when he was making sago near the Kapeuru and heard someone clapping his hands. He followed the noise, drew nearer and saw a large man with a white skin. He was not afraid, Ambrose stressed, and he addressed the white man with the following words:

> Two *kandere* of mine have died ... I think you are one of my *kandere* ... You summon me to give me some money or whatever you will ... You feel pity for me and thus you clap your hands ... Your trouser pockets are completely filled with your power, with which you go around ... I want something ... that you will give to me.[59] If you give it to me, it will remain between the two of us. I will not say

anything to my wife, to my father, to my sister or to the young people in the village.

Ambrose repeated this promise of secrecy when he met the white man again on the following days, and in so doing he was doubtlessly referring to the persecution and punishment of alleged cargo cult adherents by the colonial administration:

> I want to find good power and something good with you. If you give it to me, I will tell no one. It will remain between the two of us. If something happens on my side, I will go to the government and say that I have found something, that I became rich as a result and that those people should not be listened to who want to bring me before the court. It belongs to me alone: I have found it.[60]

In the course of their last encounter, Ambrose finally expressed his anger that the white man had refused him an answer, and also an idea, which, according to Titus Mou, had earlier been formulated by Batari, namely, that the ancestors were producing 'planes, cars, big, big factories and many machines' in purgatory (Chapter 3). Ambrose quoted his corresponding statement as follows:

> I think you're a mechanic, I have recognised you already ... Your time on this earth was over, you went to our father, and our father saw you. I think you have committed a great sin, you don't live well in, in this place there ... from where he has removed Adam and Eve ... You're a mechanic, our father has made you that, you're a mechanic in, in this place of his, in his big workshop. If we do something wrong or if we might kill someone or whoever, then we go to this workshop. I reckon that's what happened to you.[61]

Ambrose concluded by stating that people everywhere had already heard about his story and had regretted that the white man had refused to give an answer. 'This man ... in the last village,' Ambrose's listeners would say about him, 'if anything had happened on his side, he would have become rich.'[62]

The fact that the inhabitants of Koimumu and neighbouring villages firmly reject the term 'cargo cult' obviously does not prevent them from continuing to construct a link between ancestors, whites and Western goods. Even the idea, described by Valentine for the period between 1944 and 1946, that some whites had been killed before they could bring the advantages of their old or of the Western way of life to the Nakanai (Chapter 2) is still expressed in a similar form.

On one evening, for example, people were sitting in the *haus boi* of Guria and talking about the fact that the night before, John Bubu, a member of the older generation, had asked me whether Jesus had ever been to Australia and where he had been murdered. People like John,

Peter Mape explained to me, wanted to find out the 'true core' (*as tru*) of Christianity. Then Peter stood up and turned to the others:

> Jesus wanted to visit all countries, the whole world, but the whites – you know how the whites are[63] – have killed him so that he cannot go everywhere. Had he come to Papua New Guinea, we too would be able to build factories. We are just like the whites, they are just like us. Why, why, I ask, do they know how to build factories and we don't? I think it is just because of this reason.[64]

Peter concluded these words with the remark that he had just made a 'little joke' (*liklik tok funny*), and some days later Alphonse Mape (28 June 1996) stated that Peter had wanted to make fun of the Big Men, who would seriously believe what he had said. When I had reported the contents of Peter's 'little joke' to Barth Sesega, he expressed the view that nowadays such ideas could still be found among the older but not any more among the younger generation.[65]

As if to confirm this, Joe Sogi (9 July 1996), himself one of the Big Men referred to by Alphonse, told me the following when we were discussing the causes of the differences between people: Jesus had first punished Adam and Eve, then he began to give back their earlier lives to everyone, but he was killed by the whites before he could go everywhere.[66] However, in contrast to Barth Sesega's view, 'such ideas' do not at all appear to be restricted to the members of the older generation, as I noticed during a conversation in which Peter Mape asked me why, unlike the people of the Koimumu area, whites have everything but do not give anything to the poor. When I replied with a question about how people would explain this themselves, it was a young man, Peter's brother Hermann (1 April 1997), who spontaneously said: 'You have killed Jesus.'

Notes

1. Chapter 3. I believe that Titus did not know about Valentine's report because in one of our conversations he assumed that Valentine had not written anything about the Kivung.
2. John and Joe Kaveu said this in an interview I conducted with Ambrose Bai (28 May 1997). A connection between the Kivung and the Batari movement can perhaps also be inferred from the fact that people sometimes used the term 'Kivung of Batari', that is, 'Kivung te Batari' in Nakanai (conversation with Barth Sesega, 27 May 1997a) and 'Kivung bilong Batari' in Tok Pisin (interview with Ambrose Bai, 28 May 1997; interview with Paul Gar, 18 September 1997). In contrast, Titus Mou (4 July 1996) had explained to me that the Batari movement would only be called 'cargo cult', not 'Kivung'.
3. I heard this from Fred Golumu (21 July 1996) and Loko, whom I consulted at Galilo (26 July 1996).
4. Michael Kautu said this in the context of an interview with Peter Tautigi (2 September 1997), who agreed with him no less decisively. Apparently, the opposing groups of the past cannot be correlated directly with the positions assumed today with respect to the relationship between the Kivung and the Batari movement. While the rejection of any

continuity on the part of Otto Puli and Peter Tautigi as earlier adherents of the Kivung is perhaps to be expected, it surprised me to hear such a rejection coming from Paul Gar, a former 'convert' to the supporters of local government councils.

5. Conversation with Henry Laili (1 June 1996).
6. Alphonse said this in the context of a conversation with Titus Mou (28 June 1996).
7. Interview with Titus Mou (4 July 1996).
8. 'Nogat. Em ol i giamanim yu long dispela' (interview with Fred Golumu, 21 July 1996).
9. Joe Ilo (8 May 1997) said this when I asked him how Valentine had assessed the Kivung. He was later confirmed by Peter Sarere (6 June 1997). In contrast, Ludwig Gar proved to be the only one of my interlocutors to claim that Valentine may have thought that 'Batari's teaching' had come back in and that he therefore did not like the Kivung.
10. Interview with Otto Puli (21 July 1996). The formulation, used in the context of the same interview, that Valentine had backed up the people and 'explained everything to them' (*kliarim ol samting long ol*) may refer to his 'campaign of limited reeducation', but this was the first and only time I ever heard of any 'explanations' given by Valentine.
11. Joe said the following during an interview with Ambrose Bai: '"Yupela i independens olsem wanem? Sindaun bilong yupela olsem bipo yet i no gat senis liklik. Ating yumi no save rong bilong husat nau. Rong bilong gavman bilong yupela o yumi no ken save." Tasol mipela, em mipela i no save wanem samting em i toktok long en ... Em wanem tok nau ya? Mipela i no save. Em toktok bilong Vali' (28 May 1997).
12. People did not know, Joe continued, what sort of pathway that was, but many whites who had come here would say the same. At this point, one of the women present added that, according to these whites, it was hard to tell the villagers about this pathway. The danger of being brought before the court, supposedly voiced by Valentine, was also, according to his field notes, expressed by a white soldier. Valentine cites a man by the name of Uboro with the claim that, while talking with him, this soldier had mentioned the arrival of more whites and then continued: 'I may not speak about them, because later we will both be accused' ('Mi no kn tktk l ol, l wnm, bhn mitup gt kot'; CV 17 August 1954a).
13. Interview with Titus Mou (4 July 1996). I also heard about Valentine's expulsion in Makasili. Here, however, one young man gave as the reason the fact that Valentine had falsified (*paulim*) and written about things in such a way that one had to believe that the people were *longlong*.
14. Valentine had condemned Berger's alleged opposition to the government by accusing him of a 'successful eight-year-long campaign of passive resistance to all Administration policies' (Chapter 2).
15. See CV 14 June 1954, CV 27 July 1954, CV 16 August 1954.
16. I heard the expression 'man bilong kros' from Peter Sarere (6 June 1997). Christoph Bubu (24 June 1996) spoke of the beatings for 'wrong' behaviour during services, while the prohibition on having a *singsing* during Holy Week was mentioned by Titus Mou (22 July 1996).
17. 'Yu lukim disela olgeta man, as bilong ol i kaikai bilong Father Munzlinger' (conversation with Barth Sesega 19 July 1996). The accusation of using violence was also made by colonial officials against Matthäus Rascher (Chapter 2), as well as by Batari against Sebastian Schweiger (Chapter 1), and it would have been justified to raise it against Friedrich Hees (Chapter 2). On 11 July 1960, after a journey through New Britain, the provincial superior, Fr. Johannes Kordt (1960), still felt impelled to note down the following recommendation: 'In preparing them for mission life, the brothers or young fathers can usefully be advised that the natives, too, should not be treated with violence, and that they should not allow themselves to be driven to scuffles, particularly not against adults and teachers. In this respect, the Kanakas have a very delicate sense of honour. Beatings should never be a part of pastoral care or mission, however impatient the missionary may become, alone and in the middle of nothing but "ignoramuses".'
18. This was said by George Tautigi (6 April 1997) and Ambrose Bai (28 May 1997).
19. Conversation with Klaus Eppmann (9 August 1997).

20. Fred Golumu (26 May 1996) mentioned the first of these reasons, Paul Gar (interview with Joe Ilo, 19 June 1996) the second and Otto Puli (21 July 1996) the third. In the field notes, Edith Valentine, too, hints at a disagreement between Munzlinger and her husband. After Munzlinger had threatened the catechists that he would take them to the cemetery if they did not teach the children properly, and after a subsequent conversation with Valentine, Lima is supposed to have told the people that if they felt weak they could go to Valentine, 'and he would straighten them out' (EV 6 September 1954: 1). Correspondingly, Titus Mou (22 July 1996) stated that the people had been afraid that Munzlinger would 'say a prayer against them' (*wokim prea long ol*) and then they would die.

21. Conversation with Fred Golumu (26 May 1996). Paul Gar said this in the context of an interview I conducted with Joe Ilo (19 June 1996).

22. 'Tk bl Batari i smtg bl bipo, tsl oli lk wkm i kam l Ki gen' (CV 12 August 1954: 4).

23. 'Mst Hitla mkm gutp tk, tsl Batari i ksm na tantanim, mkm plt kain kain kmp' (CV 14 August 1954a: 4). Apparently, Gume accused Batari above all of having concluded new marriages, since on another occasion he said: 'But Batari came and made mischief, mischief only in relation to women. This manner of his was not right' ('Tsl Batari km, i mkm hgbk, hgbk l mri tsl, em kain bl em i no str'; CV 9 August 1954: 9).

24. 'Dp tk i km l ol, tsl smp i tanim i ngut na dp i ngut igo atp, na gutp i go dn' (CV 8 August 1954a: 4). Here Valentine is citing a man by the name of Kaveu who lived in Karapi.

25. In doing so, however, Valentine states, with reference to a man named Bubu, that he 'spoke with great emotion of Father Berger's plight during the Jap occupation' (CV 8 June 1954: 1). Titus Mou, whose accounts generally corresponded much more to Valentine's than those of my other interlocutors, did not mention Berger's wartime experiences at all.

26. This quotation from Gume runs in the original: 'Ola Galilo ktm mip. Na oli tk, Ki bl kako. Oli tk, oli ki l kako bl ol. Tsl mip tkm kiap, tk, ingt kako. Mip lk strt pls bl mip tsl, na mip sdn. Ngt kako i kmp. Inp l mip kk tro' (CV 12 August 1954: 2). Labu, like Gume from Koimumu, told Valentine the following: 'We are always going to prison because of cargo, because of the lie of cargo … Cargo does not come out of our mouths … We are always brought before the court because of cargo. It is not because of anything else, it is only because of cargo' ('Mip oltm kal l kako, l gm bl kako … Kako ino kmp l maus bl mip … Oltm mip kal l kako tsl. Ino wnp samt, l kako tsl'; CV 20 August 1954a: 1). In this context, Barth Sesega told me about the hard work which those who had been imprisoned because of 'Batari's teaching' had to perform from morning to night. According to Barth, there was not even a lunch break and, if anyone interrupted his work, he was beaten by policemen.

27. CV 8 June 1954: 1. Copies of the transcripts can be found at various places in Valentine's field notes (CV 7 June 1954: 2–5, CV 11 June 1954: 2–5).

28. An example of such an indirect way of talking is Joe Ilo's claim that people no longer wanted to wait for what the Kivung had spoken of, and similarly Fred Golumu's answer to my question as to whether coconut palms had really been described as 'food for crows' included the words: 'some … said what you said' (Chapter 3).

29. Peter Mape (16 September 1997) also spoke of 'raunim' while telling me about a conversation with Joe Sogi:

    PM: 'He asked me what people would say about him wanting to run for the local government council. I did not think properly, I did not react properly, and I replied directly by telling him that he should rather resign from his candidature. After that he did not say much anymore and soon went away.'

    HJ: 'That [what you did] does not correspond to your custom' ('I no pasin bilong yupela').

    PM: 'First you must circle round it' ('Yu mas raunim pastaim').

30. See also Chapter 3.

31. In Koimumu I heard this from Paul Gar (during an interview with Joe Ilo on 19 June 1996), in Rapuri from Martin Gar (during an interview with Otto Puli on 21 July 1996) and in Galilo from Loko (26 July 1996).

32. Valentine took down this story under the heading, 'Cargo brought by the dead to pre-war Manus' (CV 12 September 1954a: 1–5).
33. '[K]p i tkm, o, y wk ols y gt bsns, y kn gutp' (CV 12 September 1954b: 4).
34. 'Yp hrm tk bl m, sps ym wk ols, bhn ym gt mni. Na dp smtg, kko i kmp ntg, ingut. L wnm, bpo ym pen tms l kal' (CV 12 September 1954b: 4).
35. This statement was part of an attempt by Gume to clarify the distinction between *bisnis* and 'cargo cult' by referring to Paliau from the island of Manus, after whom the Paliau movement has been named (Chapter 1): 'Paliau, that is *bisnis* ... Now we Nakanai hear that the people on Manus are doing well, they have shoes, clothing, that is *bisnis*, that is *bisnis*, work ... If I don't have a good education and I'm completely stupid, I'm confused, then I live like the ancestors. With Paliau it is like this, he does not point at anyone who is sending the cargo, no. This comes from his own ideas, his power. If someone has died and sends something to me, I will be brought before the court. It is not like this. And with Paliau, it's just like *bisnis*' ('Paliau, em bsns ... Nau mp Nakanai hrm em ol Manus i sdn gut, oli gt su, kls, em i bisnis, em i bisnis, wk ... Sps m nogt gutp skl, na m lglg pns, m krnki nbt, m sdn ols tbna. Em Paliau i ols, em ino mkm hst i slm kko, ngt. Tgtg bl em yt, strg bl em. Ols mn i dai pns, na i slm smtg l m, m gt kt, ingt. Na em Paliau i ols bsns tsl'; CV 19 September 1954b: 1). On the relationship between *bisnis* and 'cargo cult', see also Allen (1976) and Schindlbeck (1984).
36. Correspondingly, there was no certainty at all in Valentine's time about the point to which the prohibitions of the colonial administration might extend, and Valentine attributes to Lima the statement that, when people had received their first corrugated iron, they were afraid that this might be banned ('oli prt i gt kal l en'; CV 13 August 1954a: 3).
37. For Varago, this was the main content of 'Batari's teaching' (Chapter 3).
38. The accusation of merely wanting to seduce women, also mentioned by Greg Mongi (Chapter 3), was brought up again when, during a pig-hunting excursion, Hermann Mape (15 August 1996) told me that the adherents of the 'Rosa Mystica' had organised a prayer meeting with unmarried people in the bush and had, on this occasion, slept with one another. People would certainly pray in the 'Rosa Mystica', but within themselves, Hermann added, they were still full of bad thoughts (*tingting nogut*).
39. The Kina is the official national currency of Papua New Guinea. One Kina equals 100 Toea and had roughly the same value as one Euro at the end of the 1980s.
40. 'Em kago kalt nau ya!' Previously, Joe Vilei himself had not only told me that Brown Bai had already been in Rome several times, as well as in all the places named in the Bible, and that money comes out from him (*moni i kamap long en*; 3 April 1997), but had also whispered to me in a conspiratorial tone that Brown Bai had spoken with the Pope in Rome, but that no one knew what the Pope had said (9 May 1997).
41. See Chapter 3. Shortly after the corresponding conversation with Albert Lowa, I said to Joe Sogi that I had heard of a man from Ubae who had collected money in Koimumu. Joe laughed, confirmed this and told me that the man had shown some forms to the people and claimed that these forms were money (6 June 1996). This, Joe continued, had been a cargo cult. About a month later, Titus Mou spoke first of the Batari movement, then of the Kivung and finally of a man who sought to 'revive this movement' (*traim long kirapim dispela muvment gen*; 4 July 1996). I replied that this must have been Paga, and as a result Titus felt prompted to give the account reproduced in this chapter.
42. 'Mi wok wanem, yupela i mas bihainim.'
43. 'Movement i grow nau, i go bikpela nogut tru.'
44. It only occurred to me later that Titus's account does not seem to be entirely free of contradiction, since, having said earlier that 'the same money in the same bags was counted over and over again', he now hinted at what Albert Lowa had stated, namely that Paga 'had filled money from one bag into another' (Chapter 3).
45. Interviews with Joe Ilo (26 May 1997, 4 September 1997).
46. While otherwise I am inclined to think that the frankness of my interlocutors tended to increase with the duration of fieldwork, there might thus have been a reverse process

of a growing reserve in my relationship with Joe. Yet, at least in my view, our relationship was always untroubled.

47. 'Taim em i sik, em i sik na i go slip long wanpela arere bilong wara na em i stap long en. Orait, em i slip i stap na em i ting … em i tok olsem, mama bilong en i kamap long en … Na em i kamap long en na em i givim em long wanpela stori, i tok olsem: "Peter Paga, yu mas kirap na yu kisim dispela buk, em paua i stap long en, bai yu kisim, karim i go long ples na yu wokim wanpela samting bilong mi". Orait, em i kisim na em i kirap i go long ples nau … Em i stap na i tingim dispela toktok, mama bilong en i, em i tok, i bin givim na i statim wanpela liklik – olsem society bilong en, olsem grup … Orait, em i statim i go na i kisim sampela ol man i stap insait long Ubae yet … bisnis bilong en na tambu bilong en, ol i go wantaim long dispela wok, em i, em i bin statim nau. Orait, em i wokim i go i go i go.' See also appendices: 'Tok Pisin texts'.

48. 'Em dispela wok mama bilong em i givim em long paua, dispela paua em bilong em yet, tasol em i go bagarapim na i givim mipela olgeta man, na i go, wokim, wokim i go i go, samting i go bagarap olgeta, i no moa kamap gut, long wanem, em i kisim planti man tumas, insait long ol blokman na i go long hap bilong Ulamona, mipela olgeta i kam insait long en ya, dispela wok bilong en ya, stori bilong en, em i bin wokim.' See also appendices: 'Tok Pisin texts'.

49. 'Em taim em i go kalabus nau, na ating i pretim gavman liklik na olsem em i lusim dispela wok bilong en.'

50. 'Sapos i wok wantaim, em, i no gat samting.'

51. A few minutes later, I again asked whether Paga had said that the dead would take care of the appearance of the money, and Joe replied: 'Yes, that was it in his view' ('Ahh, long tingting bilong em olsem').

52. This designation was also formulated by others. When, for example, immediately after my first interview with Joe, I answered Regina Kaue's question as to what Joe had talked about with the words 'Peter Paga from Ubae', she said in her turn, 'cargo cult' (26 May 1997).

53. According to Titus, the adherents of the Kivung reacted with the same feeling when they were forced to realise that they had assembled full of anticipation at the arrival of a ship that had not been sent by the ancestors, but by the church (Chapter 3).

54. Unlike Titus, Joe never talked about the Batari movement, and mentioned the Kivung only once, namely when he told me about Paga for the first time. However, he appears to have seen the Batari movement and the Kivung as separate phenomena having nothing to do with each other.

55. Although he clearly differed diametrically from Mathilda in terms of age, gender and school education, Joe Vilei (9 May 1997) expressed himself quite similarly when he heard Paga's name mentioned: 'Many were also against him. He made the mistake of divulging what only belonged to him.'

56. Conversation with Joe Sogi (9 July 1996). While Mathilda did express her own beliefs, Albert Lowa and Philibert Mape spoke only of a link between their own ancestors and the whites in relation to the past. Albert said that the whites or the missionaries had earlier been taken for the dead returned, and Philibert reported that as a child he had heard that one's skin would assume a white colour after death (Albert Lowa, 19 August 1997). For many of my interlocutors, this also happens in the case of illness. Thus, John Bubu (6 July 1997) said of Paul Uboro that he did not look healthy and that his skin was very white. Conversely, I heard about Paul Gar that he had recovered well from having been sick and that his skin was quite black.

57. According to Joe (6 June 1996), the man was so angry that the white had not said anything to him and refused him a gift that, when he saw him the last time, he wanted to kill him.

58. See also appendices: 'Tok Pisin texts'.

59. 'Tupela kandere bilong mi i dai pinis … ating yu wanpela kandere bilong mi … Yu singautim mi bilong givim mi sampela o moni o wanem samting yu laikim … Yu sori long mi olsem yu paitim han … Pocket trausis bilong yu ya i pulap tru long paua bilong

yu, yu wokabaut long en ... Mi laikim wanpela samting ... bai yu givim mi.' See also appendices: 'Tok Pisin texts'.

60. 'Em bilong mi yet, mi painim.'
61. 'Ating yu wanpela mekanik, mi lukim yu pinis ... Yu pinis long dispela graun, yu go long papa bilong yumi na papa bilong yumi lukim yu, ating yu gat traipela sin, yu no stap gut long, em ples ya ... em i rausim Adam tupela Eve ... Yu mekanik, papa bilong yumi putim yu, yu mekanik long, long ples bilong en, long bikpela woksop bilong en. Sapos yumi rong o yumi ken kilim man in dai o husat, em yumi go long dispela woksop. Ating yu olsem.' See also appendices: 'Tok Pisin texts'. When hearing these words, I remembered that Joe Sogi had told me that the man who had met the white person had wanted to kill him. Thus I asked Ambrose if he did not wish to beat the white man. Ambrose confirmed that he had been angry about the white man not saying anything, and laughingly repeated the various curses he had inflicted on him. Two days later, however, Alphonse Mape, Titus Mou and Joe Kaveu reported to me that Ambrose frequently entertains people with the story as outlined, and that, in so doing, he always mentions his desire to spear the white man (Titus Mou, 28 June 1996).
62. 'Man ya ... long las ples, sapos samting i kamap long en, em bai rich bihain.'
63. 'Yu save long pasin bilong ol waitman.'
64. 'Ating long dispela as tasol.' – This statement was made on 23 June 1997.
65. Conversation with Barth Sesega (19 July 1996). Barth (19 August 1997) also said that he had believed this himself before he had been trained as a catechist, and about a year later Albert Lowa and Philibert Mape told me, unprompted, that the Big Men still believe that the murder of Jesus by the whites was the reason for the whites being white and the blacks being black and without knowledge.
66. The idea of a 'giving back' of earlier lives recalls the equation between the old and the Western ways of life, which, in turn, corresponds to a link between one's own ancestors and the whites and which, according to Valentine, underlay the Batari movement. Yet this equation was otherwise only formulated in my presence when Ludwig Gar talked about the Christian goals of the Kivung (Chapter 3). Joe continued that Jesus had taught his disciples in his work, but that his words had been distorted by them. In this sense the disciples are doing to Jesus what Batari had done to Masta Hilla, what the Bileki had done to Fr. Berger and – if one interprets 'distorting' as 'spoiling' – what Peter Paga had done to his deceased mother.

5

Indigenous perceptions
of other and self

Kago

Oppositions

When the people in the Koimumu area speak about the Kivung or the Batari movement, they are ultimately referring to an attempt to overcome the differences between the Western and ancestral ways of life, whether through Christian and economic activities or through the acquisition of Western goods. As constructions of *kago*, therefore, these accounts offer a medium through which cultural perceptions of the Other in particular are given expression. At the same time, however, the formulation of the corresponding ideas is by no means restricted to the context of cult movements.

For the Nakanai as a whole, white missionaries, colonial officials, 'blackbirders' and travellers must have initially distinguished themselves above all by their superior power, which in the end allowed them to introduce and, seemingly, to establish their forms of religion, economy and political organisation. This power was believed by Ambrose Bai to be in the trouser pockets of the mysterious white man he met near the Kapeuru (Chapter 4), and for the contemporaries of the Batari movement it must have manifested itself most clearly in the goods imported by the representatives of colonisation and missionisation, whereas today people like Peter Mape refer instead to the fact that the whites know 'how to build factories'.[1]

All in all, however, the cultural perception of the Other in the Koimumu area appears to be ambivalent: The whites reputedly grow faster and better, but they are said to be weaker, and their skin colour can even be seen as a sign of sickness.[2] The Western power which allows factories to be built and planes to fly is positively evaluated and also sought after, but, since people fled from the whites at the start of colonisation and missionisation and since they have spoken of being mistreated by 'blackbirders' (Chapter 2), they are now formulating a critique that is rather religiously based. Francis Mou (20 June 1996), for example, commented as follows when I told him that in my country I would have to leave my apartment if I could no longer pay the rent:

> This is against Christianity and this will later lead to a punishment. The whites think too much about life on this earth and too little about what will happen to them after death. The whites think too little about Christianity. You have a lot of knowledge and you don't think any more of God. We always think of God first.[3]

As for the adherents of the Batari movement, the whites have illegitimately appropriated the shiploads sent by the local people's ancestors, and as they have allegedly murdered Jesus, they are now believed to lie to the villagers by forcing them to give away their mineral resources cheaply and then to pay a lot for the products produced with these resources.[4] George Tautigi (29 June 1996), Koimumu's representative in the local government (Chapter 1), saw another form of 'lying' in the fact that, when people start working oil palm plots, the whites first grant them credits but later insist on the money being paid back.

Accordingly, many of my interlocutors developed an opposition between their own generosity on the one hand and the greed of the whites and their dependence on money on the other: while people in Koimumu share with others, or let the people from Ubae, Lavege, Rapuri and Galilo collect wildfowl eggs at Pokili freely and without demanding anything in return, the whites – just like the Tolai – even have to pay for the food they receive from their own parents.[5] In agreement with Peter Mape (Chapter 4), George Tautigi (2 June 1996) stated that the whites give nothing to the poor, but unlike Peter, he continued to explain this by saying that they don't own any land and that therefore they only obtain something to eat when they have work and earn money.[6]

While George's words may be seen to express a certain degree of empathy, in view of the opposition between 'indigenous generosity' and 'foreign greed' it was not intended as a compliment when Alphonse Mape (5 April 1997) said of the politician Brown Bai that he only thinks of his own family and that he is in essence a white person. People like him, Alphonse added, who bring the 'custom of the city' into the village and who isolate themselves there, are only black on the outside and white within.[7]

Next to their own generosity, the inhabitants of Koimumu and neighbouring villages found their own peacefulness and harmony particularly worth mentioning. Already on the second day after I had moved in, Peter Mape (24 May 1996) assured me that there were no quarrels between different clans in Koimumu – if there were, the leaders would tell people to end them, and then they would end them straight away. Later, too, I heard repeatedly that there are no disputes among the

Nakanai and that this would fit with the inhabitants of the coastal regions of Papua New Guinea in general, who distinguish themselves through their modesty and friendliness.[8] Casimir Tauvato (11 June 1996) claimed, 'We obey the leaders ... Our behaviour was good in the times of the Big Men [of the past] and it is still good today.'[9] Similarly, Peter Mape (24 May 1996) identified the young criminals (*raskals*) who are said to cause various problems at present as settlers from the Highlands of Papua New Guinea. For George Tautigi (3 May 1996), they merely imitated what they had seen previously on video films or what they had heard about the whites.

Francis Mou linked peacefulness and harmony with obedience not to 'the leaders' but to the colonial officials, as well as with *latilogo*, that is, respect as the value which people in the Koimumu area had referred to in order to explain the initial distance in their relationship with me (Chapter 3). In a tone of utter conviction, Francis (12 June 1996) stated the following:

Earlier there was no fighting. You could walk up to Talasea and sleep on the road. People did not kill you but invited you to their house and fed you. We obey and the Big Men of the past, too, obeyed and did whatever the colonial officials told them to do. We always had respect for our neighbour (*rispekt long man*).

Moreover, the striving for peacefulness and harmony, together with the feeling of shame, contributes to the rather oblique and indirect way of talking for which Tok Pisin is particularly suitable.[10] Whereas Alphonse Mape (9 August 1996) described the whites as 'so straightforward' with respect to 'the toilet or something like flatulency', and whereas, in his view, they have no fear in saying anything, people in the Koimumu area strongly disapprove of letting others know about their own physical functions, like the breaking of wind (*kapupu*), of explicitly asking for anything or of expressing oneself openly about someone else's body.[11]

Shame and respect are certainly highly valued and praised, but at the same time denounced as a factor that causes confrontations to be avoided, even when they might in fact be necessary. Thus, just like the perception of the Other, the perception of the Self, too, seems to be ambivalent. For example, Alphonse Mape and William Padio, the candidate of the People's Resources Awareness Party, complained that – in contrast to the highly successful inhabitants of the Highlands or the Sepik region of Papua New Guinea – the Nakanai would simply sit around and smile all the time, feeling ashamed without reason (*sem nating*) and not saying anything, instead of fighting for their own rights. One should, Alphonse and William added, rather be ready to attack others if necessary and, in the case of problems, not just hope that they will disappear by themselves.[12]

Differentiation

At first sight, the villagers construct a dichotomy between 'white' and 'black' in which power, in the form of goods or factories, confronts a lack of power, greed or dependence on money confronts generosity, and straightforwardness or shamelessness confronts shame. Apart from their skin colour, therefore, each of the two groups is characterised precisely by what the other lacks when they are contrasted with one another. At the same time, however, they each appear as coherent only in being opposed; when viewed on its own, each group proves to be subject to differences.

Although, unlike in Valentine's time, 'evil Australians' who appropriate the cargo sent by the ancestors and 'good Americans' who represent the hopes for a better future are no longer spoken of today, people do share the general conviction that, as adherents of the Kivung, they were persecuted by the Australian colonial administration. According to Titus Mou, the rejection of the local government councils was partly due to the rejection of the whites in general and the Australians in particular.[13]

When Titus (4 July 1996) remembered his work for the colonial administration in the early 1970s, he particularly stressed that, unlike his white colleagues, he was not allowed to drink beer, that he had to stay outside when they were having their 'social nights' and that, while on patrol, officers of different skin colour had to sleep in separate houses, regardless of their rank.[14]

This separation had also been mentioned to Valentine, especially since it apparently contrasted with his own hospitality. 'You know no bad behaviour,' Valentine quotes one of his interlocutors, who then refers to the Australians as follows: 'We are more ashamed of them. It is not possible that they take us into their house, like you do here, because we are afraid of them. They are men of anger, and it is not possible that we go there and have a cup of tea with them.'[15] According to Valentine's field notes, he often heard that the Australians had told the American soldiers that the villagers had 'tails like dogs'.[16] This claim, which is said to have been reported by the Americans, supposedly caused particular indignation because people interpreted it as an attempt to deny them their humanity.[17]

In and around Koimumu, 'the Japanese' are viewed just as negatively as 'the Australians'. This is not so much because they ended the Batari movement (Chapters 2 and 3) or because, according to Ambrose Bai (30 July 1996), they were running around 'almost naked', whereas the Australians had at least been well dressed; rather, it is because of the accusation, regularly repeated in the context of the Second World War memories, that they mistreated the villagers and stole from them.[18] Such mistreatment and cases of theft were already talked about in Valentine's time, though unlike me he also heard of individual Japanese occupiers who had given food and clothing to the people.[19]

The widespread condemnation of 'the Australians' and 'the Japanese' on the one hand appears to be diametrically opposed to the equally widespread positive view of 'the Americans' and 'the Germans' on the other. Correspondingly, Valentine writes in his field notes that his interlocutors 'have become more outspoken about their dislike for Australians and preference for Americans' (CV 16 May 1954).

At the same time, Valentine himself must have been regarded as embodying the hospitable and generous American, and people certainly interpreted the entire research group to which he belonged as confirming their expectations. Thus Goodenough notes the following: 'There has been much talk since our arrival that we are the advance group of a large body of Americans who are going to come and settle here and usher in the "golden age". We are constantly being asked when the Americans are coming.'[20]

Paul Gar, considered to be the leading Big Man of Koimumu, told me that the Americans had acted in exactly the same way as my ancestors, the Germans: 'They have helped us well, they did not argue with us, they said that we are matrilateral relatives ... They gave us things for nothing.'[21] For Ludwig Gar, who belonged roughly to the same generation as Paul, people would still be badly off had the Germans never come. If, however, the Germans had stayed longer, Ludwig (29 April 1997) continued, then today the villagers and their inhabitants would look completely different (*narakain olgeta*), since under the Germans – as Valentine's interlocutors also claimed – one still received everything without payment, and the Germans used to reward contract work far more generously than the Australians.[22] Moreover, according to Ludwig, cars and bicycles, for example, not only were better and lasted longer in the times of the Germans but also cost less than in the period of the Australians or today.[23]

Like the group of the 'whites', on closer inspection that of the 'blacks' also proves to be divided into different subgroups. Here, people first distinguish between their own homeland, the coastal region, and the Highlands of Papua New Guinea by opposing the characteristics of peacefulness and obedience they claim for themselves to the alleged aggression and stubbornness of the Highlanders.[24] Moreover, Peter Mape (30 June 1996) stated that no women from the coast would allow herself to be seduced by a man from the Highlands, since there the magical practices used for that purpose were as cold as the climate so that they do not work.[25]

Within New Britain, if not the whole coastal region of Papua New Guinea, the area around Talasea is supposed to correspond most closely to the Highlands. When, during the electoral campaigns a man from Talasea gave a speech in Koimumu, and when I commented that in its speed and expressiveness his way of talking reminded me of what I had become acquainted with in the Highlands, my interlocutors confirmed this impression and stated that people from Talasea were indeed similar to Highlanders. Accordingly, the activities of *raskals* – generally identified as settlers from the Highlands – are said to be particularly widespread in Talasea and to contribute to the dreadful state of affairs there.[26]

My hosts and informants claimed that, as Nakanai, they would distinguish themselves not only from the people from Talasea, but also from the 'Kaulong' and the Tolai. According to Alphonse and Otto Mape, the term 'Kaulong' describes the inhabitants of the south coast of New Britain, as well as the Mamusi living in the interior of the island and thus those who are 'not yet properly civilised' (*i no civilised gut yet*) or who have not yet changed very much. I reacted by saying that I did not quite understand this statement, and Otto explained that the Kaulong did not yet know much and that they were still 'in the dark'. Alphonse added that their traditional culture was 'still strong', which Otto confirmed with the assertion, referring to magical practices, that the Mamusi still had possession of their 'full power' (*full paua*) and that everything the people in and around Koimumu own in terms of the relevant knowledge and substances would derive from them.[27]

The wealth of magical practices attributed to the Kaulong also allegedly characterises the Tolai,[28] though, unlike the Kaulong, they are almost equated with the whites when it comes to the dichotomy between indigenous generosity and foreign greed or dependence on money. If the Tolai once represented themselves 'as better and more complete humans' in comparison with the Nakanai (Chapter 2), the same is now, to some extent, true of the reverse, because the Nakanai say that the Tolai even have to pay for the food they receive from their parents, corresponding to their *pasin* not to return gifts. Moreover, they may surpass the people from Koimumu with respect to *bisnis*, but unlike them the Tolai have no land and do not help their affinal relatives. All this, my interlocutors concluded, could only be described as being greedy or *atetu*.[29]

Assimilation

People often picture the desired overcoming of the differences or oppositions between their own and the Western way of life as achieving assimilation with the whites. Gume, for example, seemed to have nothing else in mind when, according to Valentine's field notes, he spoke of 'a good education' without which one would remain 'completely stupid' and 'confused' or live 'like the ancestors' (Chapter 4). This 'good education' is supposed, so to speak, to bring light into the darkness, which, at least for some of my interlocutors, primarily results from a lack of factories.

Lawrence Olpitarea (8 June 1996), the headmaster of the school in Koimumu, explained to me that, although people did not possess as much *poisen* today as earlier, one would still have to reckon with diseases caused by it. Large parts of the bush have disappeared, Lawrence continued, but a few spots still existed.

Here, assimilation to the whites is represented, not as a change in culture, but basically as its emergence, since, when primary forest is replaced by areas which have been cleared and indeed cultivated, culture has spread where there was nature before. In the image of clearing, of eradicating uncontrolled growth, education and enlightenment turn into domestication and taming. It therefore seems consistent that those who have not yet been subjected to such a procedure, but who because of a defect of pigment have the same skin colour as Westerners, are called 'untamed', i.e. 'wild whites' (*welmasta*) in Tok Pisin.

My interlocutors projected the diachronic change in or emergence of culture into space by linking the various phases of this process with different groups living at different places. Thus a kind of contemporaneity of the uncontemporary results and the Kaulong, who are allegedly 'not yet properly civilised' or who 'have not yet changed very much', appear as the representatives of one's own past, whereas the Tolai, who are equated with the whites, embody the future.[30]

Education and enlightenment, or domestication and taming, start out from the way of life of one's own ancestors and then run unilineally, as it were, towards the way of life of the whites. This direction, however, can also be reversed when the oppositions collapse into one another, that is, when people believe, for example, that their own ancestors have already been in possession of cargo (Chapter 2).

As if to confirm this idea, the inhabitants of Koimumu and neighbouring villages reported to Valentine that they had been asked by the Americans where they had left their shirts and trousers (CV 18 August 1954: 2), and that the Americans had told them that their waistcloths were not their traditional dress.[31] Valentine, too, is claimed to have pointed to the waistcloths of the men and to have stated that they did not correspond to their own tradition. Then he reportedly pointed to his own trousers and said: 'This is for you.'[32]

If, however, the oppositions collapse into one another and if the family life of the whites corresponds to that of the ancestors (Chapter 3), the turning towards the Other becomes a turning back towards the Self, and the aim of 'living like Europeans and returning to the lost ancestral way of life' (Chapter 2), attributed to the adherents of the Kivung, consists of two basically identical aspects.[33] Simultaneously, the future becomes a repetition of the past, and the past an anticipation of the future.

For many of my interlocutors, the process of a change in or emergence of culture begins with contact with the whites, since they were the ones who have imported or brought back Western goods and – more or less as a means of achieving them – Western forms of religion, economy and political organisation. Moreover, whites are also said to have instructed Batari and 'begun' the Kivung. The impetus for change thus comes 'from the outside', and the dichotomy between 'black' and 'white' turns into an opposition between indigenous passivity and foreign activity. Here, a hitherto unaltered tradition is exposed to the intrusion of a dynamic modernity.[34]

To participate in the Kivung or in its Christian and economic activities means participating in the imported change and subjecting oneself to the corresponding process of domestication and taming.[35] Yet the hitherto unaltered tradition is also referred to as an alternative when Valentine quotes Lima with the statement that he could leave the Kivung for some time and live like the ancestors ('sidaun olosem tubuna'; CV 5 October 1954: 1) and when, according to Peter Tautigi, Lima hints at the possibility of such a life in giving voice to his rejection of councils.[36]

In addition, the beliefs and practices addressed as 'cargo cults' can be interpreted as an attempt to withdraw entirely from the demands associated with the imported change, since cargo cultists are by definition opposed to the representatives of colonisation and missionisation and do not engage in what is promoted in the context of Christianity, *bisnis* or council.[37] Moreover, in light of the inactive waiting implied by indigenous understandings of the term, taking part in cargo cults could appear as an activity, or better a 'non-activity', that corresponds to one's own tradition in so far as this tradition allegedly distinguishes itself by immobility and passivity.

Kastom

Complaints

During my field trips to Koimumu and neighbouring villages, constructions of *kastom* manifested themselves in the form of both verbally expressed ideas and observable actions, that is, in the performance of masked dances and in complaints about the decline of one's own traditional culture.

After I had already heard, prior to the beginning of my actual fieldwork, that the old way of life only existed in people's heads throughout the Hoskins Peninsula, Joe Sogi later told me that in Valentine's time there had been a lot of *kastom*, thus implying that this is no longer the case today (Chapter 3). My other interlocutors, too, especially when we talked for the first time or didn't know each other well, repeatedly referred to the disappearance of particular institutions, practices or values. 'Earlier it was good,' a young man by the name of Andrew Dao (4 June 1996) claimed, with an expression of regret: 'People beat the slit gong and sang in the men's house at moonlight. Today, however, people sleep at night. They think only about money and want to be with the women. Earlier, masked dances were often performed and feasts were often hosted. Today these things do not happen any more.'

Alphonse Mape, who as the president of the Pulabe Local Government Council belongs to the authorities of Koimumu, linked the rejection of *poisen*, promoted in the context of the Kivung (Chapter 3), to the loss of obedience. Earlier, Alphonse (27 July 1996) said, people had followed the Big Men out of fear of otherwise being killed through magical practices, but the decline of such practices had allowed the power of the Big Men to decrease and the insubordination of the younger generation to increase.[38] Corresponding to the connections made between obedience, peacefulness and harmony, this is generally believed to be leading to criminality, allegedly unknown in the past, as well as to the fact that today things are completely run down, i.e. that the children are running around everywhere, whereas in the times of the Kivung they still obeyed their parents and learnt (Chapter 3). In addition, I heard that the food taboos of individual clans were not observed any longer and that people nowadays would marry according to their own personal inclinations instead of complying with the traditional prescriptions.[39]

The members of the younger generation are said to be no longer obedient, and no longer to possess the knowledge necessary, for example, to prepare and host a feast. Moreover, they have allegedly become so accustomed to Tok Pisin and English that they can hardly understand or use their mother tongue any more.[40] While John Kikei (16 August 1996), who comes from the south coast of New Britain and is therefore classified as a Kaulong, traced this loss of knowledge back to the fact that in Koimumu, unlike in his home region, there was no longer a *haus boi* and thus no longer a place for the transmission of stories, Alphonse Mape (13 July 1996) thought that when young people graduate from school they believe that they have sufficient education and that the elders are no longer in a position to tell them anything.[41]

Young people themselves, however, accuse the Big Men of being unable or unwilling to impart their knowledge.[42] Ambrose Bai joined in this complaint but, already belonging to the group of elder men himself, passed it on, as it were, to the previous generation. 'When the time for stories comes,' Ambrose (30 July 1996) said, 'we feel confused (*puul nambaut*), since our parents have not told us everything well.'[43]

My general question as to what had changed in and around Koimumu since Valentine's time was frequently answered with a no less general reference to the change of generations or with the statement that many large men (*bikpela man*) or Big Men who were still well versed in *kastom* had since died.[44] In view of one's allegedly disobedient and ignorant offspring, this implies that one's own traditional culture is in decline. Yet the phrase 'death of the Big Men' also has a quite literal meaning, since I often heard that people today no longer are as big, stay as healthy or live as long as in the past. Thus the disappearance of particular institutions, practices or values corresponds, so to speak, to a disappearance of vital force, a biological degeneration. As the cause of this, my interlocutors listed the consumption of food that counted as Western, such as tinned meat and rice, but also the fact mentioned by Andrew Dao, namely that people today 'want to be with the women', i.e. that, unlike in the pre-colonial period, men marry and no longer sleep in the *haus boi* while they are still young.[45]

Alphonse Mape (9 August 1996) confirmed the idea, also expressed by Andrew, that people 'only think about money' today, when he said that in the past they had obtained their food from the garden, bush and sea and that, although they may have sold something now and then, they had not systematically sought for ways to earn money, whereas now they were spending more and more time in doing precisely that.[46] While money had appeared 'just now' (*nau tasol*), it was becoming 'stronger and stronger', and accordingly the inhabitants of Koimumu and neighbouring villages repeatedly and emphatically referred to a rapid rise in the marriage payments demanded.[47] As a consequence, assimilation to the whites obviously means not only striving for their power but also adopting their much criticised dependence on money. Conversely, their earlier freedom from this dependence contributes to the past often being described as a 'good time' (*gut taim*), in which, according to Alphonse Mape (9 August 1996), people did not possess many things but were much more satisfied with their lives.[48] Moreover, Alphonse added, no disturbances in, for example, the form of 'interference' by government officials or whatever group (*husat ol lain*) had intruded into the small community of villagers.[49]

Masked dances

The masked dances of the villagers consist in a variety of different types of masks, which can be grouped into three large categories: the *biriri*, the 'small' *valuku* (*valuku bisisi*) and the 'big' *valuku* (*valuku ururu*). The *biriri* ideally appear first. Intended as a means of frightening and disciplining the spectators, they are only shown together at the beginning, and later they accompany – or, as people say, 'protect' – the 'small' and the 'big' *valuku*. The category of *valuku bisisi* includes types of masks described as 'funny' but also as 'evil' (*barabara*). Some of them re-enact scenes from daily life, while others embody particular animals. After the *valuku bisisi*, the *valuku ururu* represent the crowning conclusion. Described as the 'government of the *valuku*', they are considered to be especially 'heavy' and, unlike the mask types of the other categories, they may only be painted by a small number of suitable specialists.[50]

I heard that previously the masked dances had been performed annually prior to the start of the rainy season and during the ripening of the almond-like canarium nuts (*galip*). Starting out from the north of the Hoskins Peninsula, each village had to have made and presented all types of masks from the *biriri* to the *valuku ururu* before it was the turn of the next village to the south.[51] Thus the *tumbuan* or *valuku* moved along the coast, until they came to an end in Koimumu as the 'last village' (Chapter 1) and started again the following year in the north.

Obviously, the villagers did not allow themselves to be too impressed by the rejection of the Catholic Church, which at times can still be expressed today. In a manuscript, undated but presumably from the start of the last century, P. August Kleintitschen described the *tumbuan* as a 'bulwark of heathenism' (n.d.: 12) and as the 'mission's greatest enemy' (n.d.: 13), while Fr. Alois Hartmann (7 July 1996), the priest stationed in Vavua, seemed to be forgetting his advanced age when he assured me that he would beat 'such people' if they dared to enter the church premises.[52]

After the idea to demonstrate their own *tumbuan* or *valuku* to me had come from some of the older men from Koimumu, as well as from Otto Puli from Vavua, my attempt to document the fate of the masks, from the collection of the materials required up to their performance, was basically welcomed.[53] All in all, my hosts and informants were willing to talk about the *tumbuan* in general or about individual mask types in particular, and they often and emphatically pointed to the beauty of the *tumbuan* as well as to the degree to which some of them resembled the animals they represented.[54] Peter Mape (14 June 1997) thought that previously people had respected the *tumbuan* 'like their god',[55] and similarly one of the older men from Vavua expressed himself as follows: 'If we talk about going back to the ways of *kastom*, we will have to start with the law of the *tumbuan*, since formerly only the *tumbuan* came first.'[56]

My interlocutors in Koimumu, Vavua, Makasili and Karapi shared the same general appreciation of the *tumbuan* or *valuku*; yet, in nearly every village they claimed that it was precisely there that people had the greatest competence and that the masks made elsewhere were of inferior quality.[57] Thus, apart from a few exceptions, villagers who had long been living in Koimumu did not criticise the masks I had seen there, whereas Michael Maito and Joe Tali, who both come from different regions of East New Britain, declared that in their home areas, unlike in Koimumu, one still used colours taken 'from the bush' and not those bought in stores.[58] In Karapi, people expressed their appreciation of their *tumbuan* by telling me that they had once been asked by 'Father Klaus' (Eppmann) to give him a particular mask called 'Pakasa'.[59] Moreover, when, shortly before the conclusion of a performance in Karapi, I asked a group of masked dancers to stand still for a last photograph, they surprised me by taking off their masks while still in the road, obviously in order to be immortalised not only as the embodiments of particular types of *tumbuan* or *valuku* but also with their own faces (Figure 19).

Although I certainly saw individual men and women, mostly younger ones, who did not seem to have any particular interest in them as objects of value and pride, the *tumbuan* or *valuku* were for the most part made with joy and eagerness and, during the performances, watched with enthusiasm.

When the masked dancers, their bodies concealed with palm-leaf coverings, solemnly paraded from village to village humming loudly or wildly jumped around as individuals, the reactions of onlookers ranged from silent and almost reverent astonishment to a mixture of fear and fun accompanied by shouting and laughing (Figure 18). Thus, during the parade of masks that was held in Koimumu towards the end of my first field trip (Chapter 3), I had already noted how babies began to cry, how small children ran away and how one woman fled into her house on stilts, pulling up the ladder behind her. All this was treated with the same amusement with which the Big Men had earlier rejected the attempts of some boys to come near and catch a glimpse of the men who were in the act of putting on their masks. As a relatively untrained observer, I could not help but be impressed by the unique fascination that stemmed from the *tumbuan* or *valuku*, who, when I saw them lining up on the beach of Koimumu, seemed almost like visitors from another planet (see cover illustration).

The *tumbuan* or *valuku* are believed to have come originally from the area of Mai. There, as John Mataligi (10 July 1997), one of the Big Men of Makasili, told me, two ancestors had secretly watched several spiritual beings, so-called 'men from the bush' (*tahalolorivo*), while they were making masks. Then the two men had told the people in the village to imitate what they had seen and, in the process, particular mask types were allocated to particular clans.[60] According to many of my interlocutors, the Big Men of the past had said that since that time humans and the *tahalolorivo* perform their masked dances simultaneously so that, in relation to a masked dancer, one can never be sure whether he is a man from the village or from the bush, i.e. a human or a spirit being.[61] Moreover, an encounter with the *tahalolorivo* is seen as a chance to adopt new, previously unknown mask types. As I also heard frequently, in their company people feel so strong when wearing a mask that they can go without fear to far-off villages, even at night, and even if someone has died there beforehand.[62]

My interlocutors repeatedly referred to the fact that the making and performing of masks were earlier regulated by strict commandments and prohibitions which could not be violated without running the risk of being punished by the *tahalolorivo* or the Big Men. As long as the masked dancers were still in the village, for example, everyone had to lay down his firewood almost without making a noise, no man could beat his wife and the children could not cry.[63] People interrupted their meals and did not resume eating until the masked dancers had left. Even when someone died at the time of the *tumbuan*, the burial involved only the deceased's closest circle and took place without much mourning.[64] In addition, women and small children are still completely excluded from the making of the masks, and, as was stressed in Vavua, should a man participate who had just had sexual intercourse, his attempts would fail, the other men would lose interest and, at least in that village or in that year, all the masked dances would be broken off early and ingloriously.[65]

The general appreciation of the *tumbuan* or *valuku* notwithstanding, some of the younger men in particular also expressed a certain distance, either by explicitly talking about the ideas and practices of the past, or by accompanying their statements about the *tahalolorivo* or commandments and prohibitions with a certain smile, if not with laughter.[66] Similarly, I sometimes heard that the masked dances had not been performed in their entirety for a long time or that they had even been given up altogether in recent years. Complaints about the decline of the traditional culture or about the loss of obedience and knowledge thus do not stop at the *tumbuan* or *valuku*. Here, the loss of obedience, that is, the violation of commandments and prohibitions, is allegedly causing the masked dances to be broken off, so that they do not even reach Koimumu.[67] The loss of knowledge, on the other hand, is not attributed to different generations simultaneously, but solely traced back to the fact that the old Big Men had died without handing down sufficient instructions to their successors beforehand.[68] 'Those who really know are lying there,' one young man in Vavua told me, pointing to the cemetery.[69] All in all, I therefore assume that most of the inhabitants of Koimumu, Vavua, Makasili and Karapi must have thought like Fred Golumu (21 July 1996), who, already during my first field trip, had offered a rather gloomy prediction: 'In twenty years, everything about *kastom* will be lost, and there will be no more *tumbuan*.'

Valentine

Complaints about the decline of the traditional culture are by no means new. Thus the field notes of the research expedition led by Ward Goodenough already include the following entry: 'Tovili came in today and began, as usual, to mourn for the past and the customs of the ancestors which have been forgotten now.'[70]

Moreover, the present claim that the commandments and prohibitions for the performance of masked dances are being observed less and less can also be found in the old field notes. Referring to an interlocutor from Galilo, Goodenough writes that the young men had previously not participated in the *tumbuan* to avoid being killed by sorcery if they did something wrong, but today, Goodenough continues, 'there is hardly anyone left who knows how to make these poisens, so even young boys of twelve or thirteen are initiated into the tumbuan'.[71]

Valentine himself paraphrases the statements of various inhabitants of Koimumu, according to whom people had possessed books, pencils and typewriters in the past, and could also write themselves. Since then, however, 'their writings no longer go into a book. People write on canoes and shields, because they are completely stupid.'[72] This recalls the idea that the ancestral way of life was no different from the Western one, and the loss of knowledge converges with the loss of cargo.

The accusations made today that 'our parents have not told us everything well' and that the Big Men had kept their knowledge secret were already being formulated in Valentine's time, too, but were complemented with the claim that the 'custom of the ancestors' – or of the whites – had also been given up out of fear of being punished by the Australians.[73]

Goodenough started out from the assumption that because New Britain was for the most part a *terra incognita* one had to fill in 'white spots' on the ethnographic map (Chapter 2). Accordingly, in 1954, the *tumbuan* or *valuku* counted as an important research topic: Valentine devoted a brief but richly illustrated monograph to them, entitled *Masks and men in a Melanesian society* (1961a), the University of Pennsylvania Museum stores a few masks collected by Goodenough and Valentine, and File 78 ('Religious practices') of the old field notes contains numerous entries on the manufacture and performance of the *tumbuan* or *valuku*.[74]

Valentine begins his monograph with some comments about masks in general and about the 'changing culture' of the villagers. Then he first describes an ideal-typical series of mask types, arranged into the categories of 'vertical', 'simple horizontal', 'special' and 'complex horizontal',[75] and subsequently gives accounts of the commandments and prohibitions associated with the masked dances and of the corresponding beliefs. This is followed by a definition of functions according to which the *tumbuan* or *valuku* symbolise the 'status of manhood more generally' and help 'to maintain ties between villages' (C. Valentine 1961a: 47). Valentine considers the masked dances as an 'aesthetic spectacle' (1961a: 47) that belongs to the 'most colorful and dramatic aspects' of village life, and also hints at having participated in them himself.[76] Finally, and without using the term, Valentine refers to an ambivalent attitude vis-à-vis the masks. Thus, though he assumes that there is a certain 'mystification' surrounding them which allegedly adds to an 'atmosphere of secrecy', as well as to a 'sense of the uncanny', he makes clear that the spectators are fully aware of what they are seeing: 'Here is mystery and yet no mystery, effective illusion together with artful drama recognized and appreciated as such, seriousness and even sanctity combined with a carnival atmosphere of playful pageantry' (1961a: 48).

At the time of my field trips to Koimumu, Vavua, Makasili and Karapi, *Masks and men in a Melanesian society* seemed to be completely unknown, since no one mentioned the book of his own volition and, when I showed an unbound copy to my interlocutors, they said that they were seeing it for the first time.[77] Apparently less interested in the text itself or even in its title, people went straight to the illustrations, identified some of the mask types and villagers shown, and immediately criticised Valentine for having listed only the names of the mask types and not those of the individual persons who had made the masks or who had been photographed.

In contrast to the inhabitants of Koimumu and neighbouring villages, who today complain about the loss of *kastom* and the *tumbuan* and who, in 1954, said that the 'customs of the ancestors' had been forgotten and that the commandments and prohibitions for the performance of masked dances were observed less and less, Valentine assumes not a decline but a continuation of traditional culture when he describes the emergence of a 'tripartite religious system' consisting of 'tradition', Christianity and 'cargo components' (Chapter 2) and when he refers to the West Nakanai as 'a people of three distinguishable but closely interrelated religions' (1961a: 13). Accordingly, for Valentine the *tumbuan* or *valuku* change, but they do not disappear.[78]

Here, however, Valentine contradicts not only his (and my) interlocutors but also many other anthropologists. Ann Chowning sees the end of the complex mask types as imminent, and A.L. Epstein (1998: 25–26) writes, with reference to the Tolai, in the last paragraph of an article published posthumously, that it is 'hard to escape the conclusion that the sands of time are running out for the tubuan'.[79] Finally, Wolfgang Laade (1999: 71–72) finds similar ideas already in the field notes of Felix Speiser dating from 1938, and at the same time revives these ideas himself when he states that, while the masks still exist in south-east New Britain, many of their aspects 'are gradually waning'.[80]

Interpretation

Mutual influence

At first sight, the constructions of *kago* and *kastom* expressed in the Koimumu area appear to be diametrically opposed. Whereas accounts of the Kivung and the Batari movement refer to past events aimed at overcoming intercultural differences and thus directed towards the future, the newly performed masked dances can be seen as currently observable practical actions that point to the past, since they refer to the ancestral rather than the Western way of life.

On the other hand, cultural perceptions of Other and Self cannot really be separated. They influence one another mutually because ideas of 'blacks' and 'whites' are never formed independently, regardless of whether one develops oppositions between power and powerlessness, greed and generosity, or whether one dissolves such oppositions with the idea that one's own ancestors have already been in the possession of cargo.[81] Thus perceptions of the Self are also articulated in constructions of *kago* and perceptions of the Other in constructions of *kastom*. Here, however, a negative evaluation predominates when people represent Western influences as an 'interference' or as a cause of cultural loss and biological degeneration.

To contrast or to equate Other and Self means referring the former to the latter, that is, understanding the Other, so to speak, according to the pattern or model of the Self. At the same time, the appropriation of the Other seems to entail an alienation on the part of the Self. When, for example, Peter Mape said that previously people had respected the *tumbuan* 'like their god', he was implicitly claiming that worship of the Christian god as promoted by the missionaries did not really represent anything new, and he simultaneously subjected the *tumbuan* to a sort of 'retrospective Christianisation'. Titus Mou (4 July 1996) interpreted the old transcendental authorities in a similar way when he answered my question regarding their names as follows: 'The god of the Nakanai, from our own area … is called Tamalegaike, this means "father of Gaike".

Gaike is Jesus. We also have the Holy Spirit, but unfortunately we don't have his name. Valentine told me he is Pipisa. God is the father of Gaike ... Jesus is Gaike. The Holy Spirit is Pipisa.'[82]

Ambivalence

However different or even oppositional the ideas of 'whites' and 'blacks' might be in the context of *kago* and *kastom*, regarded in and of themselves they are no less ambivalent than the process of change or assimilation that supposedly mediates them.

In and around Koimumu, the representatives of Western culture stand for a future in which one participates in their superior power, equals them in commanding allegedly unbounded wealth and, above all, knows how to build factories. When viewed vis-à-vis this future, one's own past seems like an obstacle to be overcome – for example, through the giving up of *poisen* – and accordingly people say that, like the Kaulong, their ancestors were 'in the dark' and, being 'stupid' and 'confused' (Chapter 4), they had to work with stone blades instead of the steel ones brought by the Germans.

However, just as the promise of heaven is closely linked to the threat of hell in the Christianity imported by the missionaries, so the future appears to be seen in terms of not only the positive but also the negative characteristics attributed to the whites and to the Tolai, who are equated with them. In view not of power, wealth and knowledge but of greed, dependence on money and shamelessness, one's own past turns from an obstacle into a 'good time' in which one was perhaps 'not yet properly civilised' but at least less disturbed and much more satisfied than today. The statement that, for example, a particular custom 'belongs to tradition' can thus give expression to the demand that it should be retained as a part of one's own identity or, conversely, that it should be given up as something antiquated.

Whether as a turning towards the Other or as a returning to the Self, the overcoming of the differences between Western and ancestral ways of life is on the one hand striven for as a change in or even the very emergence of culture and on the other deplored as its decline.[83] Here, my interlocutors traced the biological degeneration that is allegedly linked to the disappearance of particular institutions, practices or values partly to industrially processed foods such as tinned meat or rice, and thus to the very same Western goods which initially must have appeared as the most obvious materialisation of the superior power of the white missionaries, colonial officials, 'blackbirders' and travellers.

Practice

Although constructions of *kago* and *kastom* equally manifest themselves in the form of both verbally expressed ideas and observable actions, I often had the impression that my hosts and informants regarded the practical side of their lives as particularly important. Thus it obviously made a difference whether I remained in the role of an observer or conversational partner, or whether I actively participated in a night-long *singsing*, in expeditions for hunting wild pigs or in the painting of *tumbuan* (Chapter 3), and Titus stressed not the research interests or publications of Valentine, but the fact that he 'took part in many feasts' and 'danced himself'.[84] Similarly, present-day memories of the Batari movement tend to focus on its organisation, spread and ending, rather than on the underlying web of explanations and expectations (Chapter 3), and, while people were quite ready to make, perform and describe different mask types, they had much less interest in classifying them or in speculating over their origins or functions. Moreover, the hosting of a feast is referred to as 'wokim kastom', i.e. the 'making' of traditional culture (Chapter 1), whereas an analogous expression that would depict *kastom* as something to be thought or believed is not known in Tok Pisin.

In and around Koimumu the cultural perception of the Other appears ambivalent. Accordingly, the ways in which it has been and is being translated into practice vary considerably. Since the first missionaries, colonial officials, 'blackbirders' and travellers initially counted as harbingers of power, wealth and knowledge, it is reasonable that people should have attempted, for example by way of the Christian and economic activities of the Kivung, to participate in the process of change and assimilation that the foreigners had allegedly imported, that is, to reduce the distance between Self and Other. In the context of 'cargo research', many scholars have spoken of an 'imitation' of individual aspects of Western culture, and indeed this seems to be the case when, for example, the adherents of the Batari movement held their own masses or organised themselves in a manner described by Valentine as symbolic Europeanism.[85]

The fact that, like one of the first catechists, Valentine has been made a Suara (Chapter 1) can be seen as indicating that people also wanted to reduce cultural distance in their relations with him. At the same time, the statement that Valentine 'took part in many feasts' and 'danced himself' or that I chew betel nut (Chapter 3) gives expression not only to a widespread appreciation but also to the idea that the anthropologists, too, are interested in 'imitating' what is foreign to them.[86]

Just as, in the course of my fieldwork, some doors opened and others closed (Chapter 3), the reduction of distance goes along with its increase. Just as the image of the whites is valued not only positively but also negatively, the villagers have supported the allegedly imported process of change and yet have also tried to oppose it with the concept of an unaltered tradition and to withdraw from the demands associated with change and assimilation through the beliefs and practices addressed as 'cargo cults'.[87]

It may be due to the values of shame and respect, as well as to the correspondingly oblique and indirect way of talking, that negative images of the Other can influence one's behaviour, but are talked about not at all or only in retrospect. While I was participating in the making of *tumbuan* in Makasili, for example, a young man from Talasea suddenly came and sat down beside me. Unknown in Makasili, and employed in road construction nearby, he asked me a rapid series of very explicitly formulated questions concerning my work, my homeland and the length of my stay in Papua New Guinea. I answered, and noted simultaneously how the bright and lively atmosphere seemed to become noticeably cooler, until my interlocutors were no longer chatting and joking, but continuing their work seriously and quietly, now sitting even further away from me. Then the uninvited guest quickly left and the general mood lightened up again. I said that the man had asked too many questions (*askim planti kwestin tumas*), and in confirmation I was told that this was what the people were like in Talasea (*kain bilong ol*) and that these people were bad (*ol man nogut*).

In and around Koimumu, the cultural perception of the Self generally appears to be no less ambivalent than the perception of the Other, and accordingly it is also articulated in the form of various actions, some of which appear as a reduction of distance, others as its increase. Thus I observed the *tumbuan* and *valuku* being made and performed again, but at the same time the younger men explicitly talked about ideas and practices of the past and smiled or laughed when referring to spirit beings or commandments and prohibitions.

The distance expressed in this manner only vaguely recalls the 'rejection and destruction of certain elements of the existing culture' mentioned by Valentine concerning the Batari movement (Chapter 2) or the complete giving up of one's own *kastom* as allegedly demanded by Berger and Munzlinger (Chapter 4). Yet it can also be seen as a result of the alienation of the Self and thus, so to speak, as the reverse side of the appropriation of the Other.[88]

Without a certain distance vis-à-vis the Self, the villagers would perhaps not objectify individual aspects of their traditional culture at all, since they only talked, for example, about food taboos and marriage prescriptions at the moment when they regarded them as being violated and thus as becoming problematic. Conversely, the fact that in Koimumu everyone seemed to be able to place everyone else in a network of kin relations (Chapter 1) impressed me at first, but was obviously far too self-evident for my interlocutors to find it worth mentioning.[89] In this sense, the levels of verbally expressed ideas and observable actions can diverge in different ways. This is true for cultural perceptions not only of the Other but also of the Self.[90]

Notes

1. See Chapter 4. In a similar vein, Francis Mou (5 July 1996), one of the villagers who visited me in the evenings at the beginning of my first field trip (Chapter 3), complained that, in contrast to the whites, people did not own any factories and that accordingly they were still living in the dark. Francis's brother Jack Koro laughingly commented that this would probably correspond to one's skin colour (*ating ... bihainim skin*).
2. See Chapter 4. Christoph Bubu explained that, in contrast to one's own skin, the skin of the whites is not *strong* (conversation with Hermann Mape, 15 August 1996). Francis Mou (12 June 1996) thought that the whites would 'grow gut', because, unlike the Nakanai, as children they did not have to work already, and also because they receive money from the government even when they don't work. In Carolyn Bole's view, whites can be tall but still young (30 May 1996).
3. Otto Mape (17 April 1997) expressed a similar view when I told him that, among white people, often only a few family members would attend a burial: 'With you it is bad. You do not respect death. You forget that we are all the children of God and that Mary is our mother. That's all ("Em tasol")'.
4. See Chapters 2 (appropriation of shiploads) and 3 (Jesus's murder). Peter Mape (20 June 1996) spoke of the sale of goods produced with one's own mineral resources.
5. Conversation with Francis Mou (12 June 1996). Jack Koro mentioned people's own readiness to share, in the context of an interview I conducted with Francis (5 July 1996). Generosity with respect to wildfowl eggs was referred to by John Bubu (1 July 1996). When Leo Mape asked me if the female teacher married to a Tolai and living next to me on the school grounds would sometimes invite me over, I answered in the negative, and Leo remarked that such behaviour was called 'greedy', or 'atetu' in Nakanai (20 July 1996). I reacted with the question as to whether this could be seen as typical of the Tolai and Paul Bubu's wife, who was also present, spontaneously answered in the affirmative.
6. Hermann Mape (15 August 1996) stressed that, unlike the whites, one would not even be concerned if one had work and was made redundant because there is always food in one's own garden. Peter Mape listed the lack of land on the part of the whites as the reason for the fact that earlier they had to invent many things (conversation with Hermann Mape, 1 April 1997) and that now they are forced to pay for everything (Peter Mape, 19 May 1997).
7. Hermann Mape (9 June 1997) described Brown Bai as 'in essence a white person'. In a conversation with Albert Lowa (16 June 1997), I had just mentioned the wire fence that surrounded the house of Joe Tauvasa, the candidate of the People's Progress Party, when Albert referred to Tauvasa with an expression of disdain and said: 'We call him a white man.'
8. In a similar vein, Alphonse Mape (19 July 1997) claimed that the Nakanai were gentle (*isi*), and, according to Peter Mape (7 July 1996), they did not quarrel but merely seduced women (*paulim meri*). The inhabitants of the coastal regions were described as 'humble' by Lawrence Olpitarea (27 May 1996) and as 'friendly' by Sabina Mape (28 May 1996). The importance of friendliness or of peacefulness and harmony may also be reflected in the fact that my interlocutors initially pictured the relationship between Valentine and Berger as having been free of conflicts (Chapter 4).
9. Like Peter Mape, Casimir was about thirty-five years old.
10. See Chapter 4. The indigenous terms for 'shame' are 'sem' (Tok Pisin) and 'lamahela' (Nakanai). When, in a conversation with Leoba Olpitarea, I stated that in the Highlands one could easily tell whether someone was angry, Leoba's husband Lawrence answered that the inhabitants of the coastal regions were not direct and that, if they wanted to take revenge, they could wait for many years (10 August 1996). People say, Lawrence continued, that the sun and moon each have their own periods and that, when they meet, times become bad (*taim nogut*).

11. When I told Alphonse that I would be ashamed to ask anyone to wash my dishes, he replied laughingly: 'Some whites do not feel ashamed. We feel ashamed, too. Perhaps you have adopted the local way of thinking' (Alphonse Mape, 1 April 1997). The necessity of concealing physical functions was talked about by Otto Puli and others (8 June 1997). In the context of this conversation, Titus Mou remarked, to general laughter, that in earlier times people would have died of constipation rather than consult a nurse or doctor.

12. Conversation with Alphonse Mape (22 May 1997). Similarly, during a community meeting in Koimumu I heard that there, unlike in Silanga, for example, people would not shame electoral candidates after their speeches by getting to the bottom of things (*digim stret*), but instead just remain on the surface (*autsait tasol*) and make sure that everyone is happy. Albert Lowa (16 June 1997) expressed this perception of Self somewhat more negatively when he described 'one's own custom' (*pasin*) as follows: 'When the candidates come, we talk nicely to them, and when they have gone, we talk badly of them (*tok baksait*).' The ambivalence of cultural perceptions of Other and Self is also referred to by Ira Bashkow when he writes, in the context of so-called 'whiteness studies', that the 'Orokaiva construction of whiteness is charged with ambiguities that invert the virtues and vices that Orokaiva see in themselves' (Chapter 1).

13. See Chapters 3 (rejection of whites and Australians, persecution by the Australian colonial administration) and 4 ('evil Australians' and 'good Americans').

14. Similarly, in Vavua two young men told me that the Australians always kept to themselves (*bilong ol yet*) and that, even when working together, one not only had to eat and sleep separately but also to travel by ship, whereas the Australians would take a plane.

15. 'Yu no sv ngut … mip moa sem l ol. Na ino inp b oli ksm mip i km inst l hs ols hia nau. L wnm, mip prt ol. Ola mn bl krs. Na ino inp b mip km drng kap ti l ol' (CV 21 August 1954b: 1). Similarly, in Valentine's field notes, Gume is recorded reproducing a conversation with Masta Hitla, in which the latter asks whether people would be eating together with the Australians. At this, Gume replies: '[N]o, they say that we black people smell' ('[I]ngt, em oli tk mip blkmn sting'; CV 5 August 1954: 2). In addition, Gume claims that communal meals would be punished with a prison sentence of seven months.

16. CV 8 August 1954b: 4, CV 17 August 1954b, CV 18 August 1954: 2, CV 31 August 1954a, CV 3 September 1954. Thus, under the heading of 'Complaints against Australians', Valentine lists statements about much work, little payment and unjust treatment, as well as a 'Story of Ast. telling Americans natives have tails like dogs' (CV 5 September 1954). Already at the end of the nineteenth century, Powell (1884: 250) reported that, on the Gazelle Peninsula, he had heard 'stories of humans with tails'. Powell also assumed 'that at some time a family had been living with such an appendage', which earned him an accusation by Rascher (Missionare vom hlst. Herzen Jesu 1909: 217) that 'he had the naivety to believe in people with tails'.

17. Apart from the Americans, Masta Hitla was another source. According to Valentine's field notes, Gume quoted him as follows: 'Well, he [Masta Hitla] says that the Australians are lying to us, he tells us, you have tails like pigs and dogs, you have ears like pigs and dogs. Now I have seen you, you are just good people. You are all good men as soldiers, good men for fighting' ('O, em i tk, Ast i gmn mip, em i tkm mip, yup gt tel ols pig na dog, yup gt ia ols pig ols dog. Nau mi lkm yup pns, yup gutp mn tsl. Olg yu gtpl mn bl soldia, gtp mn bl pait'; CV 5 August 1954: 2).

18. Paul Gar (7 August 1996) spoke of mistreatment, Ambrose Bai (26 June 1996) of thefts.

19. The corresponding paragraph in Valentine's field notes runs as follows: 'The Japanese are rembered [*sic*] as almost universally overbearing & cruel. It is said that they wantonly destroyed much property & that they took any food, animals, etc that struck their fancy without any compensation, much less permission. The only reason many women were not raped is that they all fled to the bush. Men were constantly being beaten for little or no reason, & and some were cruelly tortured. [new paragraph] A few

of the Japanese are said to have been kind & understanding. In most cases these were the few individuals who knew or learned Pidgin. These few talked with the Nakanai & sometimes gave them food, clothing etc. The vast majority of the troops & officers knew little or no Pidgin, & none of them learned Nakanai' (CV 22 June 1954).

20. WHG 19 May 1954: 1. In addition, Goodenough (30 November 2001) told me that he was also asked when the cargo would come, so that he felt like John the Baptist or a 'precursor of the coming of the kingdom of God on earth'. Regarding the assessment of various groups of whites, the people who have attached themselves to the Batari movement and the Kivung obviously do not think any differently from the inhabitants of Galilo, since Ann Chowning reports that the latter have also praised the Americans and criticised the Australians and Japanese (AC 31 May 1954).

21. 'Ol i helpim mipela gut, ol i no save krosim mipela, ol i tok, yumi kandere ... Ol i givim mipela nating long samting' (Paul Gar, 7 August 1996.). The fact that Heinrich Berger, too, had German nationality would have fitted with this 'praising of the Germans', but was not mentioned by my interlocutors. The same, however, could be said of Georg Munzlinger, Berger's 'negative opposition' (Chapter 4).

22. He handed me a couple of old stone blades with the request to report in Germany that in the past one had to work with them. On this occasion he told me that, at a later point, the Germans had distributed steel blades and had told the people to throw away their stone tools. In his field notes Valentine often refers to indigenous praise of the Germans (CV 13 August 1954b: 1, CV 1 September 1954b), and he quotes Gume with the statement that the Germans had promised his father that they would return in the future and give him even more things for nothing (CV 14 August 1954b: 1). I never heard of any such promise in and around Koimumu.

23. Hiery (1995b: 311) refers to similar statements about the German colonial period and, in his attempt 'to rehabilitate German colonial rule in the Pacific' (Chapter 2), he sees them as being based on 'concrete historical experiences'.

24. Lawrence Olpitarea (6 June 1996) said that stubbornness actually comes from the Highlands, while Titus Mou (4 July 1996) ascribed a 'careless attitude' to the Highlanders and depicted them as 'very aggressive' and as capable of doing anything.

25. With respect to magical practices that could make a person invisible or evoke the aggression appropriate to fighting, Philibert Mape (5 July 1996) similarly asserted that there were far more of them in Koimumu and neighbouring villages than in the Highlands.

26. Conversation with Philibert Mape (5 July 1996). He characterised Talasea as 'the very worst place' (*wanpela worst ples stret*), because there people would murder each other when in a fit of rage.

27. Conversation with Alphonse Mape (14 July 1996). Otto and Alphonse said of the Kaulong: 'Pasin bilong ol i strong yet' and, 'Ol i no klia gut, ol i stap long tudak yet.' Both Alphonse and Otto claimed, like Titus Mou (4 July 1996), that people from the Highlands are also called Kaulong. Certainly the connotations of backwardness or even primitiveness associated with the term would correspond to the predominantly negative evaluation of the Highlanders; yet no one in and around Koimumu attested to them that their traditional culture was 'still strong'.

28. According to Hermann Mape (1 May 1997), the Tolai, or, to be precise, the people from Rabaul, can transform themselves into pigs, dogs or snakes, while Tomarum (16 May 1997) claimed that there is a lot of *poisen* in Rabaul and that the corresponding substances owned by him have come from there.

29. Conversation with Leoba Olpitarea (6 September 1997). Dominique Mape (26 June 1997) mentioned the failure to return gifts, Francis Ave (29 July 1997) the 'backwardness' of the Nakanai with reference to *bisnis*. In Valentine's time, people attributed a generally more advanced economic development to the Tolai as well as greater social differentiation. Thus Valentine noted with reference to Lima: 'Stresses individual enterprise of Tolai. Those that are strg [strong] have kars etc. and kapa – but those that aren't have nothing' (CV 31 August 1954b: 4).

30. Since the Western influence noted in and around Koimumu originally proceeded from the Gazelle Peninsula and thus from the homeland of the Tolai (Chapter 2), people seem to assume that, with increasing propinquity to the whites, assimilation increases as well. The linking of different groups living at different places with different phases of a diachronic process basically appears as a connection of space and time which is similarly at the root of indigenous concepts of history. Thus Meinhard Schuster (1990: 18) writes, with reference to corresponding ideas of the Aibom (West Sepik Province): '[W]e may consider Aibom history, understood as the Aibom picture of history, basically as a spatial system; the order in time is given as the sequence of localities associated with events, and even genealogy has its temporal aspect – already contained in the sequence of persons – enhanced by the association of persons with events in designated places.'

31. Valentine notes, with reference to Tovili, Sogi and Vuaroa from Koimumu: 'They talked about this waistcloth here, and said: "This waistcloth is not yours"' ('Tk l dp lplp hia, tk dp lplp np bl yup'; CV 17 August 1954b: 5).

32. Conversation with Martin Gar (31 May 1997). Then, Martin continued, Valentine said to the people that the Father had not told them everything; certainly, there was a core of Christianity ('Bun bilong lotu i stap'), but the Father was keeping it to himself.

33. From this point of view, not assimilating to the whites properly means the same as not realising traditional values properly. Accordingly, it is understandable why, when I visited Galilo (22 July 1996), elderly women told the children who closely surrounded me to show respect, and also reprimanded them as 'Kaulong'.

34. On the other hand, people also attributed activity to themselves when they believed that, by attempting to return, their ancestors had caused the Americans to appear towards the end of the Second World War (Chapter 2).

35. Thus Valentine cites two of his interlocutors as follows: 'The Bola and the Bulu have not yet received it [the Kivung], they are still disobedient' ('Ol Bola na Bulu, oli no ksm yet, bikhet yet'; CV 20 July 1954).

36. See Chapter 3. The colonial officer R. Allmark (PR Hoskins 1965/66-2) refers to the antagonistic attitude implied here by attesting to the Nakanai 'an inbuilt resistance to change – even in the manner of patrolling'. At the same time, if there had been no change, as Valentine had stated according to Joe Kaveu (Chapter 4), this can be taken as a reason for the alleged fact that, as Francis Mou thought, people were still in the dark.

37. See Chapter 4. According to Titus Mou (4 July 1996), the villagers were similarly abused as 'lazy people' or even as 'lazy bastards' by colonial officials, businessmen, missionaries and teachers. Indeed, a patrol report of 1956/57 claims that the Nakanai are 'a contradictory people; quick, intelligent and lazy' as well as 'spoilt by the very fertility of their soil' (PRT 1956/57-6). In a patrol report of 1965/66, R. Allmark describes their general attitude towards the whites as 'apathetic' (PRH 1965/66-2: 4).

38. Such an increase in insubordination appears to contradict the idea that the change in or emergence of culture as a process of domestication and taming goes along with an overcoming of *bikhet*. My interlocutors, however, did not note or talk about this contradiction.

39. Albert Lowa (26 June 1996) spoke of food taboos, Leoba Olpitarea (10 August 1996) of marriage prescriptions. She complained that today even people would get married who, for example, being the children of cousins, were actually close kin. In Kassia, some Big Men similarly thought that in the future people would perhaps marry entirely at random, i.e. in utter confusion.

40. Accordingly, I heard that, for example, the address term 'tilala' was today increasingly being replaced by 'mama'.

41. As Alphonse Mape (9 August 1996) added on a later occasion, the young would even disparage the elders (*daunim*). With reference to the statement that people are hearing the calls of deceased women, encountering the dead or curing sicknesses with particular magical practices less and less frequently, Joe Sogi (6 June 1996) thought that,

when the children go to school, they no longer want to hear any stories from the past. At the same time, however, the young are also accused of not thinking about school education (Leoba Olpitarea, 30 May 1996), of being lazy (Alphonse Mape, 14 July 1996) and of only wanting to be provided for by others (Lawrence Olpitarea, 27 May 1996).

42. George Tautigi (2 June 1996) supposed that the parents would be told by the teachers not to talk about *kastom* so that the children could concentrate on school.

43. According to Titus Mou (4 July 1996), much knowledge had been lost because previously people had worked for many years away from the village on plantations. As a result, Titus continued – in an unusual reversal of the idea that otherwise predominates with respect to the relation between the generations – the young would know more about *kastom* than the old.

44. While the term 'Big Men' is only used for particularly influential men, in a more inclusive sense all those who have lived earlier are seen as 'bikpela man' (large men). With reference to the past, all Big Men are thus also 'large men', but not all 'large men' have necessarily also been Big Men. John Bubu (5 June 1996) referred to the death of 'large men', Alphonse Mape (22 May 1996) and George Tautigi (2 June 1996) to the death of Big Men. In so doing, George continued as follows: 'Much has been lost for ever (*lus pinis*) and thus is difficult to get back again (*hat long rewinim*).'

45. Robert Boko (28 June 1996) mentioned early marriages, and Joe Sogi (27 June 1996) talked about young men no longer sleeping in the *haus boi*. In addition, Joe continued, even while women are menstruating they give food to the men, which was prohibited in the past. Leoba Olpitarea (30 May 1996) and Alphonse Mape (9 August 1996) referred to the damaging effects of tinned meat and rice. Camillus Kautu (21 July 1996) thought that people today would mix their own food with that of the whites, and that in addition they had to work harder now than previously.

46. On the other hand, Leoba Olpitarea (18 July 1996) thought that many of the feasts required by *kastom* amounted to a waste of money and should therefore gradually be given up.

47. John Bubu (5 June 1996) said that in the past one did not need any money, but had married with shells. The statement that money had appeared 'just now' but is becoming 'stronger and stronger' was formulated by Otto Mape (30 May 1996) and others.

48. Similarly and curtly, Leoba Olpitarea (10 August 1996) stated that 'earlier things were good and today they are bad, since today people think too much of business. That was not the case in the past.' According to Valentine, the phrase 'good time' ('gut tm') was also used by Gume with reference to the period before the Second World War (CV 19 August 1954: 11).

49. Here Alphonse is sharing the desire, expressed in the form of cargo cults, to withdraw from the demands associated with imported change, although as a government officer he himself represents this change to a certain extent.

50. The phrase 'government of the *valuku*' was Otto Mape's (19 August 1996). All in all, my interlocutors were not of their own accord particularly interested in attaching their mask types to different categories. I developed the corresponding classification myself, relying on numerous statements, some of which, however, were not very specific or were even contradictory. Thus, for example, particular mask types were described sometimes as *biriri* and sometimes as *valuku bisisi*, and people disagreed over whether the *biriri* were *valuku* at all, or whether they merely accompanied them. Some of my interlocutors grouped the *valuku barabara* with the *valuka bisisi*, while others treated them as a kind of separate category.

51. According to Otto Mape (19 August 1996), the first performances took place in Talasea, Mai, Buluma and Kassia. Conversely, Augustin Sande and Titus Mou named the area of the Garua and the village of Dage respectively (Augustin Sande 22 June 1997).

52. The statement ascribed to Valentine, that in his country it was forbidden to ask the people to destroy their *tumbuan* (Chapter 4), also hints at the oppositional attitude of the Catholic Church.

53. See Chapter 3. In Nakanai the individual performance is called 'sibi', the place where the masks are made 'lalomaloma' and the collection of the materials required to make them 'kuruloto'.

54. Pius Paga (26 April 1997) spoke of beauty, Joe Ilo (26 May 1997) of resemblance. Moreover, Otto Mape (14 June 1996) and Paul Gar (11 August 1996) had already praised the beauty of the *tumbuan* during my first field trip, that is, at a time when the suggestion that they be shown to me still lay in the future.

55. In total, this statement also contains a reference to the threat of punishment through magical practices: 'That was, it was like this, the people respected them like their god. If they had not respected them, then many people would have got problems ... the Big Men who lived in the village, they also possessed sorcery' ('Dispela em, em i olsem, em ol i save rispektim ya, olsem God bilong ol ya. Sapos ol i no rispektim, em bai planti man bai kisim taim ya ... ol big man i stap long ples ya, ol i stap wantaim ol poisen tu ya'). Some young men from Tarobi also spoke of a godlike worship of the *tumbuan*, but added that the belief of the people was what had turned the *tumbuan* into something real.

56. 'Sapos yumi toktok long go bek long pasin kastom, bai yumi mas stat bek long lo bilong tumbuan, long wanem, bipo em tumbuan tasol i go pas' (conversation with Otto Puli, 8 June 1997).

57. Moreover, in Koimumu I heard that the type of *tumbuan* or *valuku* called 'Matematevuva' belonged there (Dominique Mape, 26 June 1997), whereas people in Vavua performed Matematevuva (Figure 16), while claiming that the inhabitants of Koimumu would not be able to do so.

58. Conversation with Michael Maito (6 May 1997). According to Michael and Joe, the general rules surrounding the *tumbuan* or *valuku* were followed more strictly in their home areas than in Koimumu. In addition, Tarobi-born Francis Ave said on several occasions that people in Koimumu did not really know how to make the *tumbuan* (6 July 1997, 15 July 1997, 30 July 1997). The only critics who had been resident in Koimumu for a long time were Hedwig Mape (15 June 1997), Andrew Dao (16 June 1997) and Dominique Mape (22 June 1997), who described the masks shown there as 'too small' (Hedwig), 'rough' (Andrew) and 'not good' (Dominique).

59. Conversation with Thaddäus Tubu (23 August 1997).

60. See also appendices: 'Tok Pisin texts'. Another link with the sphere of the transcendent emerges from the thesis formulated by Titus Mou that in the past people tried to use the masked dances to push the 'bush spirits of the canarium nuts' (*masalai bilong galip*) – that is, the epidemics of colds that occurred during the ripening of these nuts – along the coast and then into the sea, or to keep them away from their own villages (conversation with Augustin Sande, 22 June 1997; see also appendices: 'Tok Pisin texts'). It was believed, Titus added, that without the *tumbuan*, many people would not have remained healthy. Thaddäus Tubu described them as 'like medicine' (*olsem marasin*; 27 August 1997), and similarly Ann Chowning (1958: 65–66) wrote that 'an occasional informant asserts that the masks frighten away contagious diseases that might otherwise cause epidemics'. Augustin Sande and Titus Mou did not speak of 'men from the bush' but of '*valuku* from the bush' (*valukulorivo*; Augustin Sande, 22 June 1996), and I also heard the expression 'spirits of the *valuku*' (*saveilevaluku*; George Tautigi, 13 June 1997).

61. Among these interlocutors were Titus Mou (1 June 1997), Otto Puli (8 June 1997) and Augustin Sande (22 June 1997).

62. Conversations with Peter Mape (7 July 1996), Pius Paga (26 April 1997) and George Tautigi (13 June 1997). The chance to adopt new mask types was mentioned by Ambrose Bai (26 June 1996) and Otto Puli (8 June 1997).

63. Conversation with Otto Puli (8 June 1997). Just as Peter Mape linked the statement that people would have had problems for not respecting the *tumbuan* with a reference to the Big Men's sorcery, Otto Puli (8 June 1997), Thomas Sauli (conversation with Peter

Mape, 14 June 1997) and Augustin Sande (22 June 1997) stated that those who proved
to be disobedient had immediately been killed by the Big Men through *poisen*.

64. Interview with Otto Mape (19 August 1996).

65. Conversation with Augustin Sande (19 June 1997). Being excluded from the making of
masks, women are obviously supposed to believe that, when they see the *tumbuan* or
valuku, they are being confronted not by dressed-up men but by spirits from the bush.
The women themselves, however, indicate with a wink that they know very well what
is expected of them.

66. While some of my interlocutors, like Peter Mape, referred to villagers who had lived in
the past and described the *tumbuan* as 'their god' (*God bilong ol*), others like Otto Mape
(19 August 1996) or Camillus Kautu (24 August 1996) used instead the phrase 'our god'
(*God bilong mipela*).

67. Fred Golumu (21 July 1996) and Peter Mape (7 July 1996) said this. Henry Laili and his
son Marcus Valentine complained that nowadays women would even watch the men
as they put on their masks (Henry Laili, 1 June 1996). Conversely, John Bubu (5 June
1996) criticised the men themselves: they would beat the women even when there
were *tumbuan* in the village and would disclose to them the identity of the persons
wearing particular masks.

68. Otto Puli, regarded as a Big Man himself, explained to me many times that previously
the Big Men had kept their knowledge secret and that, as a result, people had to steal all
the information they had about the *tumbuan* or *valuku* (8 June 1997, 21 June 1997).

69. In addition, Paul Gar (conversation with Peter Mape, 14 June 1997), Otto Mape (22
August 1996), Michael Vavala (21 August 1996) and others referred to the increasing
dependence on money by claiming that today people were forced to think too much
about *bisnis* to have sufficient time to perform masked dances.

70. This can be found in the file '62 Community', dated 27 April 1954, though without an
author's name.

71. WHG 13 May 1954: 1. The declining observance of commandments and prohibitions is
here referred to the relationship between the generations, not to the relationship
between the genders as today. In addition, Chowning reports the view that in the past
the children who were among the spectators had still been beaten properly by the men
dressed as *biriri* (AC 5 August 1954: 1).

72. '[O]l rait bl ol i no moa go l buk. Oli raitim knu na plang, l wnm, oli lglg pns' (CV 17
August 1954c: 1).

73. Referring to Tovili, Sogi and Vuaroa from Koimumu, Valentine writes: '[P]eople were
afraid of the whites ... and they gave up the custom of the ancestors. The Australians
beat the people and treated them badly' ('[O]li prt l ol wtmn ... na oli lusim psn bl ol
tubuna. Ol Ast i paitim nbt ol, oli mkm ngut ol'; CV 13 August 1954c: 3). The following
quotation from Valentine's field notes includes the accusation of secrecy: 'I think they
hid it from us. The ancestors hid it from us boys. They did not talk about it, that was
strictly prohibited. The ancestors strictly prohibited it to our fathers, and our fathers did
the same with us, and we have no knowledge any more. Father had it, but he didn't
want to give it to me' ('Ai tg oli haitm l mip. Ola tubuna oli haitm l mip manki hia. Oli no
sv tk aut l dp smtg, bgp tbu tru l en. Ola tubuna mkm bgp tbu moa l ola ppa bl mip, na
ola ppa tu i mkm ols l mip, na mip no moa sv. Em ppa i sv, tsl em i no lk lusim l mi'; CV
20 August 1954b: 5).

74. The University of Pennsylvania collection includes eight masks (Goodenough is noted
as having acquired seven of them, Valentine one), as well as seven pieces of painted
barkcloth, collected by Valentine, with which the frames of the masks had been
covered.

75. Valentine (1961a: 16). In the appendix ('Summary of the mask types described'),
Valentine (1961a: 50–52) lists the names of several mask types for each of these
categories, differentiating the Kasoso type further into three subtypes. If my categories
and those of Valentine were to be referred to each other, the 'vertical masks' would

correspond to the *biriri*, the 'simple horizontal masks' and the 'special masks' to the *valuku bisisi* and finally the 'complex horizontal masks' to the *valuku ururu*.

76. Valentine writes that he can confirm 'that an impulse to parade proudly up and down comes over one inside a *valuku* costume' (1961a: 48; italics in the original). He expresses himself in somewhat greater detail in a report on his fieldwork intended for the general public and published under the title 'We were adopted by the Lakalai ... K.U. anthropologist initiated into primitive tribe' in the *Topeka Capitol Journal*: 'Then came the season when men dress in masked costumes and playfully terrorize the women and children or parade through the villages to be admired by all. It was an exciting occasion one evening when I was first allowed to have the experience of marching through Rapuri, my head encased in a light yellow bark-cloth mask, the rest of my body clothed with a mantle of coconut fronds – hunting in the approved fashion as I went' (1960b: 142). The title of Valentine's fieldwork report refers to the fact that he had been made a Suara (Chapter 1). The *Topeka Capitol Journal* is a journal of Kansas University, where Valentine was employed temporarily after his second field trip to Rapuri. *Masks and men in a Melanesian society* was part of a book series published by this university.

77. See Figure 15. The only exception was Maternus Mape, who lives in Port Moresby. Entirely of his own volition, he told me that George Tautigi's father-in-law is depicted in one of Valentine's books with a mask type called 'Riau' (17 September 1997).

78. Valentine (1961a: 28), for example, refers to a 'crepe paper ball' used for a particular mask type as 'one of the few modern elements which have been incorporated into the mask design in recent years'. Accordingly, the objects in the University of Pennsylvania Museum include three pieces of linen painted in industrial colours (collected by Valentine), as well as two masks covered with linen and packing paper respectively (collected by Goodenough). In addition, Valentine (1961a: 31) states, with reference to the *tumbuan* or *valuku*, that 'the atmosphere of secrecy and exclusiveness has lessened somewhat'.

79. At the same time, however, Epstein (1998: 25) states that the masks have survived up to now because, as symbols of Tolai identity, they would create a link with the present and express 'some of the most fundamental of their traditional values'. In an article on indigenous painting, Chowning (1983: 103) writes the following: 'Missions' pressure against the masked ceremonies has always been heavy, and together with new demands on time, may be spelling the end of the more elaborate kinds of masks.' In her dissertation, she refers to the making and performing of *tumbuan* by claiming that 'interest in it is beginning to weaken. Men say that they are too busy to bother with it. It is nevertheless a flourishing institution' (1958: 62).

80. Already at the start of the last century, Kleintitschen (n.d.: 14) had referred to what he regarded as an observable loss of meaning when he mentioned missionary reports 'according to which the Tubuan ... has assumed the form of ordinary dances'.

81. Similarly Ira Bashkow has stressed the interrelation of cultural perceptions of Other and Self by stating that the Orokaiva are applying their ideas of 'white men' to 'criticizing their own moral failings and those of their society' (Chapter 1).

82. With reference to the Christian god, Valentine quotes Mou, Sogi and Vuaroa from Koimumu as follows: '[T]he Big Men say that he doesn't come from any other village, God comes from here, he belongs to us' ('[O]la bgp mn i tk, em i no bl nrp pls, em Deo i bl hia, i bl mp yet'; CV 1 September 1954a: 1).

83. In this sense, the thesis of a civilising process that has not yet proceeded very far among the Kaulong fits with the statement of Otto Mape that, in the form of the Mamusi, they still possess their 'full power'.

84. See Chapter 1. Similarly, Ursula Batari (23 June 1996) told me that Raymond Johnston's wife (Chapter 1) used to cultivate, cook and distribute taro like the other women, and a young man from Gloucester reported that a white woman who was working there as an anthropologist would roast tapioca in the fire and carry things on her head.

85. See Chapters 2 ('symbolic Europeanism') and 3 (conducting of masses) and, for the thesis of an 'imitation', among others Höltker (1941: 189), Pos (1950: 563), Allan (1951: 94), Guiart (1951c: 170), Worsley (1957: 11), Lawrence (1964: 144) and Steinbauer (1971: 37). The importance which, according to Valentine, people attributed to writing, i.e. to transcriptions of Lima's addresses, in the context of the Kivung (Chapter 4) can perhaps also be interpreted in this sense. Similarly, Joe Ilo referred to a book that Peter Paga had allegedly received from his deceased mother (Chapter 4). At the same time, when some of Valentine's interlocutors claim that people were already capable of writing in the pre-colonial period, this fits in with the equation of ancestral and Western ways of life.

86. On the verbal level, people express the reduction of distance in their relationship with Valentine by claiming that, just like Berger, he has taken their own side (Chapter 4). This, however, is restricted to Koimumu, Rapuri and Vavua, for in Makasili I heard that Valentine had stayed put in his own house (Chapter 1) and had written in such a way as to create the impression that the people were *longlong* (Chapter 4).

87. At the same time, the maintenance of intercultural distance is a major point of criticism in indigenous accounts of the Australians. When, on one occasion, Andrew Dao told me that people would warn their children against approaching neighbouring houses too closely, so as not to create the impression that they wanted to be fed there, I wondered if, paradoxically, hospitality might not also be a method of 'keeping guests at a distance'. Certainly, this cannot easily be transferred to people's attitude vis-à-vis the anthropologist, but, in retrospect, allocating me a house on the edge of the school grounds and thus on the boundary of the village itself (Chapter 3) may have been an attempt to integrate the Other while simultaneously making it controllable by not letting it come too close. In addition, the fact that the whites are also assessed negatively perhaps found its most drastic practical expression in the capture and mistreatment of Josef Weigl by the adherents of the Batari movement (Chapter 3).

88. When the concept of an unaltered tradition is opposed to the allegedly imported process of change, the increase in distance from the Other leads, conversely, to its reduction vis-à-vis the Self.

89. It may therefore point to an increase in the distance vis-à-vis *poisen* that its abolition was treated rather cursorily by Valentine, or in his time, but stressed much more often by my own interlocutors (Chapter 4).

90. This divergence also becomes obvious in relation to a 'custom' described as 'lavikuala', according to which, in the context of feasts hosted on the occasion of a girl's first menstruation, women are said to be entitled to beat the men. Although, particularly at the beginning of my time in Koimumu, Otto Mape (30 May 1996), Joe Sogi (26 May 1996), George Tautigi (2 June 1996), Roy Mou (3 June 1996), John Bubu (5 June 1996), Casimir Tauvato (11 June 1996) and others presented *lavikuala* as an aspect of their own *kastom* that continued to be important, no such event took place up to the end of my second field trip.

6

Anthropological perceptions of other and self

Criticising Valentine

Valentine in the field

When Charles Valentine arrived in Rapuri on 27 April 1954, he did so not only with the aim of studying the Kivung, but also assuming that there existed a cargo cult in the region. As he had already written in a letter to his parents in 1952, and also in accordance with the way his doctoral supervisor, Ward Goodenough, understood the term, the villagers were thought to expect ships full of Western goods and to believe that 'native and white will have equal statuses or the Europeans will be driven out'.[1] In the course of his first field trip, Valentine's interlocutors then expressed themselves in a manner which he documented faithfully in his field notes and which doubtless contributed to his impression of a prevailing atmosphere in Rapuri that was 'curiously compounded of varying degrees of secrecy, continuous rumours and not a little public confusion'.[2] However, Valentine viewed the indigenous way of talking not, so to speak, as a language- or culture-specific datum 'in its own right', but as an indication of a hidden substance, that is, as a symptom of a secrecy enforced by Berger. Ultimately, this interpretation appears to have caused the somewhat disastrous conflict which emerged during Valentine's first field trip, while the contents of the alleged secret, i.e. the promise of the arrival of Western goods, was in fact the central element in Goodenough's definition of the term 'cargo cult'.

I do not wish to claim that in Valentine's time people had not been hoping for a 'cargo ship' sent by the ancestors, especially since my own interlocutors, too, were partly convinced that the dead could help them in achieving economic success and that a link existed between ancestors, whites and Western goods (Chapter 4). Moreover, I can easily relate to the atmosphere described by Valentine because the way of talking I encountered in the course of my own fieldwork proved to be no less oblique, allusive and indirect than that documented in Valentine's field notes. Accordingly, I sometimes felt that 'a residue of the unsaid' remained and that there was an 'aura of mystery' present, but this does not mean that the villagers concealed anything from me, nor does it make them the passive victims of a paranoid and autocratic white missionary.[3]

If Valentine's interpretation shows him to be a 'child of his time' (Chapter 2), and if, in addition, it confirms the assumption he brought with him to Rapuri that there was a cargo cult in the region, in the sense of Goodenough's definition of the term, then in essence Valentine did not understand the Other very differently from the villagers, namely according to the pattern or model of the Self (Chapter 5), that is, according to the measure of his own preconceptions.[4]

By portraying Berger as a kind of white cargo cult leader and thus placing him in the position of the 'native prophet' whom Goodenough thought to be typical of cargo cults (Chapter 2), Valentine began by assuming that Western influence existed. At the same time, he himself contributed to making such influence real when, at least according to his field notes, he took the secrecy allegedly dictated by Berger as a reason to confront him publicly and when he developed his 'campaign of limited reeducation' in order to persuade as many villagers as possible to take his own side. In so doing, Valentine obviously saw himself not only as their advocate and spokesman, but also as a pioneer of autonomy and enlightenment. In his report to the colonial administration he stressed that he had succeeded in bringing some men to support his account of the Kivung (Chapter 2). Although his field notes create rather an impression of failure, and although his 'campaign' seems to have left no traces in present-day memories (Chapter 3), Valentine must have reproduced the negative definition and evaluation of the term 'cargo cult' (Chapter 4) by adopting the 'cargo accusation' with which the colonial officials had persecuted the villagers and by directing it against Berger.[5]

Valentine's influence on the villagers also manifests itself in the fact that he himself contributed to the uttering of statements that served to confirm his preconceptions. Thus it was certainly not by chance that, only a short time after he had complained about not obtaining sufficient information about the Kivung, Lima told him about Berger promising the imminent arrival of the cargo.[6] Moreover, Valentine interpreted the silence with which people often reacted to his appeals against Berger as indicating agreement or a lack of counter-arguments,[7] not as a culture-specific form of refusal that, precisely because of the emphasis on respect, shame and the striving for peacefulness and harmony, could not be expressed differently.[8]

Valentine may have welcomed Lima's statement about Berger's promise as a confirmation, whereas for Lima the opportunity to refer to

Berger was perhaps no less welcome, since it allowed him to articulate, corroborate and check the idea of the arriving cargo without having to take responsibility for it himself.[9] Lima thus used Berger as a sort of rhetorical figure. Likewise Gume was able to articulate the unusually explicit critique of Australian colonial rule documented in Valentine's field notes by claiming merely to be quoting Masta Hitla.[10] Some of the references to Berger reproduced by Valentine even create the impression that Valentine's interlocutors have provoked him somewhat or have tried to play him off against Berger or Chowning and Goodenough.[11] In this sense, the statements interpreted as confirmatory by Valentine express both the influence he exerted and the influence that was exerted on him, so that Valentine's descriptions and interpretations appear to be a product of the interaction between the ethnographer and the people he works with.

The influence exerted by Valentine seems to fit the paradigm, predominant in the early 1950s, which represented the villagers as the passive victims of the external influences that broke over them in the course of colonisation and missionisation (Chapter 2). In order to make the influence exerted on Valentine equally apparent, however, it would have been necessary to reverse this paradigm and to take Valentine's own ideas and expectations into account.

Despite the rich and multilayered nature of his ethnographic data and despite the fact that, in his interpretation, he was somewhat ahead of his time, when viewed from a present-day perspective Valentine's limited inclination towards self-reflexivity is striking. Whereas Friedrich Hees, as an 'ancestor of Nakanai research', openly describes his intentions as well as the way his interlocutors viewed their relationship with him (Chapter 2), Valentine almost completely excludes his own person from his texts, whether published or not, and even from his field notes.[12] Apart from the report intended for the general public and published in the *Topeka Capitol Journal* (Chapter 5), he consciously refers to the subject of research, i.e. to himself, only in the context of his conflict with Berger, while the corresponding report seems to serve his aim of defending himself in the face of criticism, or, in Goodenough's words, 'to justify the hot water he got into' (Chapter 2). However, neither in this report nor in his field notes does Valentine account to himself for the feelings he must have had when his hosts and informants increasingly avoided him in the course of his first field trip.[13]

Valentine reflected just as little on the fact that his interlocutors regarded him according to the measure of their ideas and expectations as on his own contribution to the emergence of the statements that served him as a confirmation. He cites Lima with the statement that he, Valentine, had initially been referred to Masta Hitla,[14] and, in his report to the colonial administration, he admits the possibility that the villagers might have understood his 'campaign of limited reeducation' as 'a new version of the Secret of Cargo' (1955a: 69). Yet, in contrast to Goodenough, Valentine does not record the idea that the members of the whole research group were seen as the harbingers of a 'golden age'. Thus, one can only infer from his field notes that Valentine must have counted as the embodiment of a hospitable and generous American (Chapter 5).

Lattas

The example of Andrew Lattas shows that, without increasing self-reflexivity, not even an altered theoretical approach necessarily helps to take the interaction between the ethnographer and the people he works with into account.[15]

Lattas stayed with the Kaliai between 1985 and 1996. In several articles (1991a, 1992a, 1992b) and in a monograph entitled *Cultures of secrecy* (1998), he examines present-day representations of a cargo cult that had taken place among them in the first half of the 1970s and that had originally become known through Hermann Janssen (1974), as well as through Dorothy and David Counts.[16]

For Lattas, the Kaliai are trying to bring the process of civilisation, which aims at their assimilation to the whites, under control by supporting it through making the imported Western institutions and discourses their own. In so doing, they are allegedly internalising the 'moral evaluations of their culture made by missionaries, kiaps and whites' (1992a: 74), thereby ultimately contributing to their own alienation and subjugation.[17] According to Lattas, the Kaliai situate themselves between past and future (1998: 267) or 'simultaneously inside and outside Western culture as well as inside and outside traditional bush Kaliai culture'.[18] Correspondingly, he identifies 'relations of mutual appropriation' through which both sides 'feed off each other's appropriations but also feed off each other's appropriations of each other's appropriations'.[19]

As a detailed analysis of his texts demonstrates, however, Lattas fails to transfer his idea of 'relations of mutual appropriation' to the relationship between himself and his interlocutors. Indeed, he excludes his own person hardly less than Valentine, and it is only in the preface to *Cultures of secrecy* that he makes some mention of his fieldwork. Here, Lattas (1998: xi) claims to have hosted and questioned visitors in his house and later to have lived in the houses of 'close informants'. Thus, he was allegedly able to win the trust of those who had been persecuted by missionaries and colonial officials as cargo cultists and who now believed they were finding 'tacit recognition and legitimacy from an outsider, a sympathetic white man' (1998: xii).

In his preface, Lattas (1998: xii) moves from the opposition between his interlocutors and their 'relatives and neighbours who assumed the overbearing attitudes of government officials and missionaries' to the New Tribes Mission (NTM), active among the Kaliai since 1984. As Lattas (1998: xiv) reports, the American missionaries representing the NTM told the villagers 'to get rid of me because I was encouraging them not to convert to the mission'.[20] Lattas (1998: xiv) even writes of the desire on the part of the NTM 'to demonize me', so that, just like Valentine, he apparently sees himself as a victim of persecution, which, however, emanates not from a single person but from an entire group.

When Lattas argues that the Kaliai are internalising a Western view and thereby contributing to their own alienation and subjugation, he is repeating a pattern which, in earlier publications, he had already applied to the relationship between Kaliai women and men (1989), between white men and Aborigines (1987, 1990, 1991b) and between the upper and lower classes in white Australia in the nineteenth century. As a result, the impression is created that Lattas's main motivation for hosting and questioning his visitors, as mentioned in the preface to *Cultures of secrecy*, was to have his preconceived ideas and expectations confirmed.

However, Lattas seems unable to imagine that he himself may have contributed to the emergence of the statements he recorded, or to consider that an influence may have been exerted on him – perhaps with the exception of his alleged persecution by the NTM. This is even more striking since Lattas has the same skin colour and the same nationality as the negatively assessed colonial officials, whom, according to one of his earlier articles, the Kaliai usually approach with 'trickery'.[21]

Although Lattas does not mention the objections that could be raised on the basis of the indigenous perception of his person, he seeks to refute these objections by claiming that he was able to win the trust of his interlocutors. Lattas's references to his fieldwork in the preface to *Cultures of secrecy* can thus be seen as revealing the same undertone of justification as Valentine's description of his conflict with Berger (Chapter 2).

Self-reflexivity and specificity

Valentine and Lattas wrote at different times and with different theoretical approaches, but they share the tendency not to acknowledge their own persons as part of the social reality they are examining. Neither of them talks about the various ideas and expectations with which he 'went to the field' or with which he was confronted there, and accordingly neither can take the influence exerted by him or on him into account.

However, Valentine's descriptions and interpretations differ from those of Lattas in that they obviously have a solid ethnographic basis and in particular his field notes allow conclusions to be drawn concerning how he contributed to the statements he documented in detail, and about the intentions of his interlocutors. Valentine shares this ethnographic specificity with his predecessor Friedrich Hees, who tries to illustrate his more general comments on Nakanai culture by extensively quoting his 'charges' and describing individual incidents from his living together with them (Chapter 2).

Lattas regards the relationship between indigenous and Western culture first and foremost as a relationship between pre-existing and introduced ideas, but he is not much interested in the way these ideas are translated into practice.[22] Accordingly, conversations and interviews appear to be no less important for Lattas than they had been for Valentine, and yet, unlike Valentine, Lattas offers virtually no information about their origin or context.

Moreover, Valentine does not reproduce indigenous statements verbally, but in indirect speech or in a paraphrase of his own, his translations having been characterised aptly as 'untenable' and 'inadequate' by Dorothy and David Counts.[23] Thus, Lattas not only reduces the possibility of understanding the influence exerted by and on him, but also makes himself a spokesman for the Kaliai or, in other words, he does not permit them to speak for themselves.[24]

At the same time, the differences between the genders, the generations and the denominations disappear, and the Kaliai tend to turn into an equally homogeneous and faceless mass, instead of also becoming visible as individuals, as, for example, Laili, Gume and Lima do in Valentine's field notes.[25]

Background

Dependence

When I compare Valentine's research with my own, I am struck by both similarities and differences. The results are the same and not the same, or, in other words, the story of predecessor and successor is marked by both continuity and change.

While I could emphasise differences and change and thus attempt to foreground the originality, if not the progressiveness of my position, it would make little sense to criticise Valentine for not having followed insights and demands that had still not played any role in the anthropological discourse of the 1950s.

The fact that Valentine had to depend on the theories of his day rather applies to myself too. This dependence constitutes, so to speak, a theoretical similarity that links predecessor and successor and can thus be seen as an element of continuity. Just as Valentine's interpretation shows him to be a 'child of his time', notwithstanding his being ahead of it in many respects (Chapter 2), my thesis – that the influence exerted by and on the anthropologist can be taken into account through self-reflexivity and can be made understandable through ethnographic specificity – relies on anthropological works on *kago* and *kastom* which, for the most part, have been published in recent years, i.e. 'in my time'.

'Cargo research'

In the history of 'cargo research', perceptions of Other and Self are closely linked to one another.[26] First, the idea that various interpretations of the phenomena labelled as 'cargo cults' can be traced back to certain dispositions not of the foreign but of one's own culture appears as an expression of the 'self-reflexive turn' (Chapter 2). The same applies to Lamont Lindstrom's understanding of articles and monographs on these phenomena – or, in his words, of 'cargoist literature' – as 'parables about our desire' (2004: 16), as well as to the attempt to use the term 'cargo cult' to describe the pursuit of material well-being in US American society, the Monday demonstrations in the former GDR or Western beliefs concerning UFOs.[27]

Then, as a kind of countermovement, an 'ethnographic turn' followed, which was based mainly on the objection that it does not suffice 'for an anthropological critique to focus only on Western discourses about cargo cults, without being concerned about the ethnographic reality to which these discourses refer'.[28]

Ultimately, however, the ethnographic reality causes the view to fall back again onto one's own culture, since not only the term 'cargo cult' but also the phenomena associated with it – understood by Dalton (2004: 205) as 'the Melanesian physical enactment of historical context, which is provided by Western colonial culture' – present the Western observer with a mirror, which he sometimes regards as 'accurate', sometimes as 'distorting'.[29] I believe that this is a major reason for the fact that the topic has continued to exert a considerable fascination in the West up until the present day (Chapter 1).

Given the insight into the close link between perceptions of Other and Self, earlier interpretations are superseded which, by seeking to explain cargo cults as a struggle for economic and political equality or as an expression of anti-hegemonic resistance (Chapter 2), still proceeded from a more or less strict separation between the agents of colonisation and missionisation on the one hand and their victims on the other.[30] In contrast, Dalton (2004: 199) opts for an understanding of Melanesian cultures 'that does not see them as separate from the European global domination and sees them as neither its victims nor its resistance'; Elfriede Hermann (2004: 53) stresses that 'the Western Self can in no way be divorced from the indigenous Other'; and Kathleen Stewart and Susan Harding describe the term 'cargo cult' as 'an artifact of entwined practices'.[31]

Just as the anthropological view oscillates between the cultures of Other and Self, some contemporary authors prefer to focus on the individual case encountered in fieldwork, whereas others see the examination of Western ideas as essential.[32] At the same time, Nancy McDowell (2000: 378) states a 'failure to do genuine comparison', after Roy Wagner had already suggested such a comparison in the 1970s (Chapter 1). McDowell accuses Western observers of having exaggerated differences and neglected similarities, thereby increasing intercultural distance while missing the opportunity 'to use the "other" to understand ourselves as well as to provide an impetus for our own cultural critique, so eloquently called for by Marcus & Fisher (1986)'.[33]

'Kastom *research*'

Since the beginning of the 1980s, the term 'kastom' has been used for cultural self-representations (Chapter 1). The inhabitants of the South Pacific, from village to state level, either rely on them in order to stress their own respective identities vis-à-vis another group, or conversely try to distance themselves from these self-representations, for example, in the context of the adoption of Christianity.[34] In both cases, specific ideas, practices or artefacts are often foregrounded as 'key symbols' (Howard 1990: 276) and seen as 'emblematic' (Thomas 1992: 215) of one's own culture.

Just like 'cargo research', the examination of cultural self-representations has by now largely parted company with the idea of a strict separation between 'us' and 'them', and, just like the term 'cargo cult', most authors have come to understand 'kastom', too, as 'an artifact of entwined practices'. Yet, while for Roger Keesing (1982b: 300), as for Jocelyn Linnekin and Lin Poyer (1990a: 14), the process of Western influence constitutes a kind of precondition for the objectification of one's own culture, Margaret Jolly and Nicholas Thomas (1992a: 241–42) start out from the assumption of an already existing awareness of cultural difference in the pre-colonial period, which, in their view, has merely been strengthened since.[35]

Keesing's thesis in particular, that cultural self-representations, as inventions in the sense of new creations (see Hobsbawm 1983: 2), sometimes differ considerably from the actual pre-colonial reality, has been met with severe criticism.[36] The claim implicitly made by Keesing, that as an anthropologist he has privileged access to this 'actual pre-colonial reality', was rejected by indigenous elites as a continuation of colonisation (Trask 1991) and by Jolly and Thomas (1992a: 244) with the argument that anthropological and indigenous notions or categories were in principle equivalent since they both had to be seen as constructions shaped by particular circumstances, perspectives and interests.[37]

Jolly and Thomas follow the approach of an interpretative or symbolic anthropology, which focuses not on the substance or authenticity of particular statements, even if they are intended as descriptions of reality, but on the genesis and contents of their meanings.[38] Accordingly, the protagonists of present-day '*kastom* research' do not understand 'tradition' or 'traditional culture' in an essentialist manner, as, for example, in the complaint about its decline. 'Tradition' or 'traditional culture' is here not a fixed ensemble of ideas, practices and artefacts that are handed down unaltered and constitute the identity of a group, but rather a model of the past that the members of this group are constantly developing and applying in accordance with their current needs.[39]

The anthropological works on *kago* and *kastom* that have been published in recent years agree in their view of the relationship between cultures, as well as in their conclusions. The demand for self-reflexivity, for example, raised within the context of 'cargo research', fits with the protagonists of '*kastom* research' asking about the significance of Western influence or realising the fact that anthropological ideas and categories always depend on particular circumstances, perspectives and interests. Ethnographic specificity, however, is targeted when authors claim that cultural self-representations have so far been 'homogenised', that they must be examined in their local polyphony and multilayeredness, and that in addition the way verbally expressed ideas are translated into practice should be taken into account.[40]

Continuity and change

Activity and passivity

As the cultures that encounter or collide with one another in the course of colonisation and missionisation are no longer regarded as being separate, and as the terms 'kago' and 'kastom' are understood as 'artifact[s] of entwined practices', i.e. as products of interaction, in relation to his interlocutors, the anthropologist appears simultaneously as the subject and object of influence. While the fact that their interpretations depend on the scientific discourses of their respective times links predecessor and successor in terms of theory, the corresponding interplay of activity and passivity can be seen as a more practical element of continuity. Just like Valentine, I, too, contributed to the emergence of the statements I recorded, and just like the people Valentine spoke with, my hosts and informants, too, were pursuing their own aims in delivering these statements.

Although I avoided the term 'cargo cult' in favour of rather general formulations, and although the idea to present their masked dances came from some of the older men from Koimumu as well as from Otto Puli from Vavua, without my presence people might have neither spoken about the Kivung and the Batari movement nor made and performed the *tumbuan* or *valuku*.[41] At the same time, my interlocutors rejected the accusation that they had participated in cargo cults by 'passing it on', as it were, to the inhabitants of Rapuri or to the Bileki, and they tried to surpass neighbouring villages by claiming that the masks manufactured there were only of inferior quality.[42]

Accordingly, constructions of *kastom* can also show an intracultural dimension and be directed against people who, unlike the representatives of colonisation and missionisation, do not have a different skin colour.[43] Up to now this intracultural dimension has not received sufficient attention, perhaps owing to what has been criticised in the context of '*kastom* research', namely the tendency towards 'homogenisation' and 'intellectualisation', i.e. the focus on indigenous elites and the neglect of the practical level.

As with the 'passing on' of the 'cargo accusation' and the criticisms of the masks of neighbouring villages, my interlocutors were also pursuing their own aims when they told me that Valentine had said that there existed a great but hard-to-find pathway, that waistcloths did not correspond to their tradition and that the Father was keeping the 'core of Christianity' to himself.[44] Here, the people of the Koimumu area used Valentine in conversations with me exactly as they had used Berger or Masta Hitla in conversations with him, namely as a sort of rhetorical figure that made it possible to articulate and to corroborate certain ideas and perhaps to check them by provoking a reaction.[45] In addition, by referring to Valentine, people also expressed expectations that were actually directed at me, since the claim that he only sat in this house or, by contrast, that he had been 'in every village' (Chapter 1) clearly meant nothing else than that I should, or alternatively should not, do exactly the same.[46]

On the practical level, the interplay of activity and passivity, i.e. the influence exerted by and on Valentine and me respectively, corresponds to the distance between ourselves and our respective interlocutors being simultaneously reduced and increased in the process of fieldwork. Valentine postulates such a reduction by claiming to have succeeded in learning the allegedly hidden 'details of the Kivung secret', while I represent the course of my two field trips as an overcoming of spatial and social isolation.[47] The increase in distance, conversely, expressed itself in Koimumu when my assignment to or appropriation by Joe Sogi was qualified or when Joe Ilo showed a growing reserve in talking about Peter Paga, while in Valentine's case it assumed the unusual form of him being increasingly avoided by the inhabitants of Rapuri.[48]

Approach

Regardless of the similarities that link me with my predecessor in terms of theory and practice, against the background of more recent research on *kago* and *kastom*, it has to be stressed that, unlike the representatives of a later interpretative and symbolic anthropology, Valentine was more interested in the substance and authenticity of the statements he recorded than in their meaning. He understood these statements primarily as verifiable references to particular phenomena and persons and less as expressions of people's own intentions. Thus, for example, he interpreted Lima's claim that Berger had promised the imminent arrival of the cargo as a confirmation and not as an attempt to exert influence. From the present-day point of view, Valentine's focus on substance and authenticity did not allow him to treat the indigenous definition, evaluation and usage of the term 'cargo cult' as an object of research, or to examine cultural self-representations as such.[49]

In agreement with the anthropological discourse of the 1950s, Valentine started out from the assumption that the superior power of the West would almost inexorably prevail. Yet, for him the corresponding assimilation to the whites did not at all lead to a loss of cultural difference, since, in contrast to other anthropologists, and in contrast to his (and my own) interlocutors, he did not believe in an impending end of the *tumbuan*, but postulated instead a simultaneity of 'tradition', Christianity and 'cargo components'.[50] Although Valentine abstained from complaining about decline, he shared the respective idea of 'traditional culture', which, from today's perspective, seems essentialist and which, in the context of recent '*kastom* research', has been replaced by the concept of a model of the past.[51]

In and around Koimumu, the history of the traditional culture, thus understood, equals the history of predecessor and successor in that it is characterised by both continuity and change. This history involves not only missionaries and colonial officials but also villagers, not only anthropologists but also the people with whom they work.[52] Accordingly, traditional and Western culture cannot be separated – they mutually influence each other just like the ideas of 'whites' and 'blacks' expressed in the context of indigenous perceptions of Other and Self.[53] On the one hand, villagers seek to take part in what they see as assimilation and change, while on the other hand they try to withdraw from the corresponding demands; on the one hand they seek to reduce intercultural distance, while on the other hand they try to increase it (Chapter 5). Without wanting to conceal the differences in power between the subjects and objects of colonisation and missionisation, the process of alienation and subjugation stressed by Lattas thus has to be opposed to at least an intentional strengthening and confirmation of the Self.[54]

Influence

When Valentine describes Berger as an autocratic ruler responsible for the central elements of the Kivung (Chapter 2), he is correct in so far as Berger may have followed his own intentions in making use of the beliefs and needs he met with after having been transferred to Vavua and Valoka.[55] Yet Valentine's interpretation overlooks part of the truth, since conversely the same beliefs and desires have also shaped the way in which Berger, for his part, came to be perceived by the villagers.[56]

Valentine's thesis that Berger was 'mentally abnormal' thus cannot be seen at all as 'the only possible explanation for his extraordinary career among the Nakanai' (Chapter 2). Although Valentine asked his interlocutors to differentiate between himself as a representative of education and support on the one hand and Berger as a representative of stultification and exploitation on the other (Chapter 2), from the present-day point of view, it is rather the similarities that predominate. In the field of tension characterised by mutual influence between traditional and Western culture, the two rivals equally appear as active subjects and passive objects and their individual personalities seem to be comparatively less important. Thus it would be rather pointless to go into the question of whether Valentine's characterisation of Berger was 'actually' correct or not.[57]

Similarly, I would also like to qualify my own significance, since the demand for self-reflexivity and ethnographic specificity should not create a temptation to take the figure of the anthropologist which has commonly been suppressed in the past, and to overemphasise it within a sort of countermovement. It is true that without my presence people might not have spoken about the Kivung and the Batari movement, or made and performed the *tumbuan* or *valuku*, yet the corresponding statements and practices gave expression to specific beliefs and needs that did not just come into being with my arrival in Koimumu, and that will certainly continue to exist even if Fred Golumu's prognosis that 'there will be no more *tumbuan*' (Chapter 5) should come true.

Notes

1. See Chapters 1 (Valentine's task) and 2 (Goodenough's understanding of the term; expulsion of Europeans).
2. See Chapters 1 (documentation in field notes) and 2 (atmosphere).
3. See Chapters 2 (passive victims) and 4 ('aura of mystery').
4. The colonial officer P.F. Sebise refers to prior expectations when, following Valentine's second field trip, he stated: 'The two American anthropologists Dr. and Mrs. Valentine finished their second six monthly visit to the area in November 1956 and I am afraid they were greatly disappointed that a full scale cargo cult did not break out during their stay' (PR Talasea 1956/57-6).
5. See Chapters 3 (no traces of Berger's 'campaign') and 4 (negative definition and evaluation). Valentine's representation of Berger as a white cargo cult leader may even be connected to the fact, mentioned by Titus Mou, that Berger was accused by his colleagues of having brought about the change of the Kivung 'into a cargo cult' himself (Chapter 3).
6. See Chapter 2. Titus Mou indicated another influence originating from Valentine when he explained to me that Valentine had told him that the Holy Spirit was identical with Pipisa (Chapter 5).
7. A corresponding passage in Valentine's field notes runs as follows: 'I gave Pakela a short lecture ... Pakela had no reply' (CV 27 September 1954).
8. See Chapter 5. When, however, the villagers explicitly contradicted him with the advice that he should not take one of Munzlinger's sermons as referring to himself, Valentine took this, too, as a confirmation of his idea of a prevailing subjugation: 'It was obvious that Fr. M. had heard what we said and sent them to spike it in this manner' (CV 12 September 1954b: 2).
9. The attempt to check certain ideas also becomes obvious when Valentine notes that, according to Reki from Gavutu, Berger had said that, if people did not miss any church services, a ship with cargo and men from all countries would come, as well as one's own ancestors. Then Valentine continues as follows: 'Reki appeals to me to know whether these things are true' (CV 11 September 1954a).

10. See especially CV 29 July 1954: 1–10. In addition, 'the Americans', too, appear as a sort of rhetorical figure when they confirm the conviction that one's own ancestors had already been in possession of the cargo by stating that waistcloths were not traditional dress (Chapter 5).

11. Thus Valentine writes: 'B. told them that he is wiser than any other whiteman ... Recently he told them that while Ward [Goodenough] and Ann [Chowning]'s savvy [knowledge] was not very great, mine was nearly as great as his and intimated that soon I might winim [supersede him]' (CV 11 September 1954b).

12. Even without having intended it, however, Valentine's field notes do give some information about his methods. In accordance with the thesis that he had only sat in his house (Chapter 1), he appears to have relied mainly on the interviews he conducted there. The headings of individual entries, partly supplied with additional explanations and noted down before recording the statements of the interlocutors, create the impression that Valentine usually knew in advance what a particular interview would be about. Generally, the entries consist of a longer text and a subsequent series – also in Tok Pisin shorthand – of questions and answers, as well as, from time to time, a brief concluding note on the surrounding circumstances or on the behaviour of the people with whom Valentine talked. It seems that, in the course of time, he increasingly conducted his interviews on the basis of an evolving list of questions. Often these questions are only noted down in the form of keywords or abbreviations, and in a later phase of his fieldwork he no longer documents the answers, but simply indicates their agreement with earlier entries: 'Repeats most of the stories recorded elsewhere' (CV 31 August 1954a). The shorthand writing was at times directly referred to by Valentine's informants, when, for example, they described and explained a noise as being like Valentine's typewriter (CV 17 August 1954d: 3).

13. Nevertheless, in the foreword to his dissertation, Valentine (1958: cxxi–cxxii) writes of the necessity 'that the scholar be as aware of and make as explicit as possible, to himself at least, the underlying presuppositions which condition his thought about human affairs'. As Valentine continues further, this basically involves 'an introspective exercise in the sharpening of self-awareness which should include at least the maximum possible insight into one's own personality, the greatest obtainable clarity of such matters as moral and political values'.

14. 'And when you came and spoke to us, we said in Nakanai: "I think this white man is like the one that, in the past, had come to Vunapope [Masta Hitla]"' ('Na tm yu kmp, na yu bin tk l mip, nau mip tkpls ols, ah, ai tg dp mst i ols dp i kmp pst l Vunapope bipo'; CV 13 August 1954a: 4).

15. Moreover, I also find Lattas to be of interest because – apart from the fact that he describes the spread of the 'Batari cult' in north-east New Britain (Chapter 1) – he is praised in a review as 'one of the foremost students of race and of the colonial and postcolonial dynamics of power in Melanesia' (Robbins 2000: 540) and can thus claim relevance for the examination of cultural perceptions of Other and Self.

16. See Dorothy Counts (1972, 1978) and David and Dorothy Counts (1976). If one attempts to bring together the information in Lattas's articles (e.g. 1991a: 251, 1992b: 52) – brief and not always free from contradiction as they are – with a reference in the foreword to his monograph (1998: xi), then he visited six to eight different villages in 1986 (twelve months), 1990 (nine months) and on five further occasions between 1990 and 1996 (altogether nine months). I have analysed *Cultures of secrecy* in more detail elsewhere (Jebens 2002), also taking into account publications by Lattas that do not concern the Kaliai. In addition to the review by Joel Robbins (2000), already mentioned, see also the critiques by Dorothy and David Counts (2000) and Todd Harple (2000).

17. Lattas (1998: 267) claims that the Western view had been 'internalized by people, producing alienated subjects who hated the past for that moment of its savagery that they read into themselves'. Thus he believes that he is able to identify a 'profound self-alienation that colonialism produces as a condition of its hegemony' (1991a: 251; see also 1998: xxxi–xxxii).

18. 'These forms of double incorporation and double alienation', Lattas (1998: xxiii) continues, 'encoded people's ambivalent attitudes towards both white-skins and their past.'

19. Lattas (1998: 311–12). In a similar vein, Lattas (1998: 312) also speaks of a 'specular relationship in which identity emerges not simply through the mirror of the other but also through appropriating and mirroring back the other's appropriation and mirrorings of oneself'. The same idea had already been expressed in an earlier article when Lattas (1992b: 37) wrote the following: 'Colonialism becomes a hall of mirrors where white and black are made into unstable reflections of each other and even of their own identities.'

20. While, as Lattas states in an earlier article, the NTM missionaries are trying to 'transform and eradicate not only the collective memories created by cargo cults' (1996b: 286), the Catholics, for their part, claim that 'the new missionaries are exploiting cargo cults, if not working a cargo cult of their own' (1996b: 301).

21. In this text, Lattas describes a 'pervasive culture of trickery' (1989: 467n5), in which 'trickery' is not only 'celebrated' but also practised against young men and children, as well as against 'people from other villages and government officials' (1989: 452).

22. Robbins (2000: 542) is thus correct in writing that *Cultures of secrecy* treats 'Bush Kaliai talk about cargo and cargo ritual without for the most part situating that talk in relation to action of either the "cultic" or the everyday sort'.

23. Dorothy and David Counts (2000: 327). The Counts (2000: 327) justify this judgement extensively, and, in so doing, they state the following: 'Rather than clarifying the contributions of his informants, his translation makes them more obscure.' I have also analysed various examples in order to criticise how Lattas deals with Tok Pisin (Jebens 2002: 196).

24. The readiness to make oneself a spokesman for one's interlocutors may very well be a consequence of one's identification with them and also becomes apparent in Valentine's case. Yet Lattas combines this identification with a distinct moral dualism, as well as with a corresponding claim to a position of superiority that permits him to distinguish, sharply and without doubts, between 'good' and 'evil', between the victims of alienation and subjection on the one hand and the agents of colonisation and missionisation on the other. Accordingly, in referring to one of his earlier articles, Steven Thiele (1993: 77) accuses Lattas of pursuing a 'moral sociology'. Robbins (1998: 45) refers to the 'idealization of whites' as a 'core aspect of contemporary social life' in many parts of Melanesia and correspondingly criticises 'Lattas' single-minded focus on the critical aspects of whites'. Indeed, Lattas (1998: xxiii) does ascribe a unanimous rejection of colonial officials and missionaries to the Kaliai, although, in agreement with my findings from Koimumu and neighbouring villages (Chapter 5), he also mentions an 'ambivalent attitude towards both white skins and their past'.

25. Accordingly, Harple (2000: 143) states, 'Lattas tends to promote a rather monolithic notion of Melanesian culture and cultural traits.' Lattas himself apparently unintentionally hints at the heterogeneity that he otherwise makes disappear when he writes that the message of the NTM had been 'eagerly accepted' by the younger generation especially (1993: 77n27), and when he refers to the opposition between his interlocutors and the followers of the colonial officials and missionaries, stating that the Catholics had accused the NTM of doing a cargo cult. In view of the Kaliai being portrayed as an equally homogeneous and faceless mass, one feels tempted to assume that, to put it somewhat sharply, they interested Lattas only as an element within his preconceived dichotomy between oppressors and oppressed, or only as a 'substitute' for, among others, the Aborigines who had previously occupied their place there. See Jebens (2002: 196).

26. On this link, see also Jebens and Kohl (1999).

27. Gerrit Huizer (1992: 126) refers to an 'obsessive pursuit of material accumulation' which took place in the USA during the presidency of Ronald Reagan and describes this as a 'cargo cult unleashed by the bourgeoisie and its charismatic leaders'. On the Monday

demonstrations, see Rutschky (1992); on ideas about UFOs, see R. Wagner (2000). The 'self-reflexive turn' in 'cargo research' is not without its historical model, since, in the 1940s, colonial officials, missionaries and planters had already accused one another of causing cargo cults (Chapter 2). With reference to this period, Doug Dalton (2000a: 351) states that 'explanatory emphasis shifted toward the West and away from the Rest'. See Jebens (2004a: 12n5).

28. Otto (2004: 209; see also 1999: 92–94). Accordingly, Joel Robbins (2004b: 246) states that the criticism of the work published so far would 'lead scholars to go back to the millenarian data'.

29. While Dalton (2004: 206) describes 'cargo cult' as 'an accurate mirror of the exploitative self-contradictory ideology of modern Western bourgeois culture', Karl-Heinz Kohl (2004: 90) speaks of a '"distorting mirror" in which we can recognize a familiar image of Western society, its hopes, desires, and fears projected on to foreign cultures'. According to Otto, however, this recognition has not yet been successful. He writes that 'the very word "cargo cult" has provided us with a mirror in which we have failed to recognize ourselves' (1992b: 5). A reflection is also referred to in Lattas's description of colonialism becoming a 'hall of mirrors'.

30. Thus, for example, Hempenstall and Rutherford (1984) turn against simple conflict models, but retain Hempenstall's earlier emphasis (1978) on resistance and protest. Conversely, Nils Bubandt (2004: 110) refers to the thesis formulated by Michael Brown (1996), according to which anthropologists ultimately soothe their own consciences by describing 'acts of resistance'.

31. Stewart and Harding (1999: 287). Otto and Lattas also refer to intercultural links: the former speaks 'of mutual attempts at interpretation between Melanesians and Westerners' (Otto 2004: 217), the latter of 'relations of mutual appropriation'. Here Lattas is arguing against the same separation he himself helps to maintain with his preconceived dichotomy between oppressors and oppressed.

32. Steven Leavitt (2004: 185), for example, makes a plea for basing one's interpretations on the statements specific persons make in no less specific situations, since, in his view, a 'more enhanced understanding can emerge from the more intimate features of cargo ideology as revealed in the personal narratives of individual actors'. According to Dalton (2000a: 352), however, 'the irrationality of the Western views Melanesians mimic in what appears to be "cargo cult" type behaviour' should be examined. Similarly, Roy Wagner (2000: 372) writes first that 'cargo cult has grown into something of a Loch Ness Monster', and then continues: 'It looks like we will never figure out what it is until we have made some progress in figuring out what we ourselves might be.'

33. McDowell (2000: 378). Here, she is referring to G. Marcus and M. Fisher 1986, *Anthropology as cultural critique: an experimental moment in the human sciences.* Chicago.

34. Robert Tonkinson (1982: 302) and others have referred to the significance of one's own identity: 'It is evident that *kastom* is intimately connected with identity at all levels, from individual to national.' See also Linnekin (1990: 150, 1992: 253) and Linnekin and Poyer (1990b). Thomas (1992: 216, 223) has coined the term 'inversion of tradition' for the rejection of 'one's own' in favour of its 'antithesis' or of what is seen as characteristic of the 'foreign'. See also Keesing (1982a: 371) and Linnekin (1990: 159).

35. See Thomas (1992: 214, 218). In addition, Jolly and Thomas (1992a: 244–45) see the specific conditions of colonial history as having been responsible for the emergence of different ideas of *kastom* in different regions.

36. Keesing writes that politicians who have grown up in cities and who have been raised in the West are proclaiming the advantages of a *kastom* they know nothing about (1982b: 299) and that, for example, in New Caledonia a common identity is being forged between groups whose ancestors have been at war with one another as members of completely different cultures (1989: 22). According to Keesing (1989: 30), Western influence causes people to 'edit out' everything that contradicts the values not of their own ancestors but, for example, of Christianity.

37. However, as Jolly and Thomas (1992a: 244) state, this also involves the danger of a general relativism, which might allow the anthropologist to avoid justifying his or her decision to prefer particular versions of the past to others. Linnekin (1992: 257–58, 260), Jolly (1992: 62–63) and others refer to the necessity of such decisions in the face of the multiplicity of local identities or traditions.
38. Jocelyn Linnekin in particular has explicitly invoked interpretative or symbolic anthropology (1990: 152, 1992: 256). See also Linnekin and Poyer (1990a: 4).
39. For Linnekin, 'tradition' is the 'contemporary interpretation of the past rather than something passively received' (1990: 152), as well as 'a selective representation of the past, fashioned in the present, responsive to the contemporary priorities and agendas, and politically instrumental' (1992: 251).
40. Apart from a few exceptions (e.g. Keck 1993), most descriptions of cultural self-representations tend to foreground the statements of indigenous elites; thus Jolly and Thomas (1992a: 246) rightly point to the necessity 'to attend further to the diversity of views within particular communities'. In addition, Ad Borsboom and Ton Otto draw attention to the neglect of the practical level. This neglect may seem surprising, given that, according to Linnekin and Poyer (1990a: 246), in many societies in Oceania, social identity is mainly manifested in the form of practical behaviour and actions (see Linnekin 1990: 155). Borsboom and Otto (1997: 8) write: 'The treatment of the formation of concepts like tradition often seems restricted to the intellectual sphere.'
41. See Chapter 3. It would not be at all unusual for a Western visitor to evoke masked dances. See Philip Dark (2001) with reference to West New Britain, and Wolfgang Laade (1999: 104–5) for East New Britain.
42. See Chapters 4 ('passing it on') and 5 (surpassing neighbouring villages).
43. Elsewhere I have shown that, in the context of the adoption of different forms of Christianity, constructions of *kastom* can even be applied against people belonging to the same settlement or kin group (Jebens 1997b).
44. See Chapters 4 (pathway) and 5 (waistcloths; 'core of Christianity').
45. Berger and Munzlinger were also used in the same way in conversations with me, as when Ambrose Bai and Joe Kaveu told me that Berger had talked about a secret of the whites and had wanted to send Lima to the place where the ancestors were manufacturing Western goods (Chapter 3), or when Otto Puli claimed that Munzlinger had warned Valentine not to give the people the 'good knowledge' about how the whites lived (Chapter 4).
46. Thus, when I initially resisted Joe Sogi's invitation to join him in getting drunk, he told me that Valentine had often bought beer for the people and had then, in the context of conviviality, learned about things that would otherwise have remained unspoken (9 July 1996).
47. See Chapters 2 (learning 'details') and 3 (overcoming of isolation).
48. See Chapters 2 (avoidance of Valentine), 3 (assignment or appropriation being qualified) and 4 (growing reserve). A reduction of and an increase in distance can also be identified in the case of Andrew Lattas, who claims that his interlocutors increasingly trusted him and were told by the New Tribes Mission 'to get rid' of him.
49. In Valentine's time, cultural self-representations were already being expressed in people's complaining about loss or decline when they made and performed their *tumbuan* or *valuku*, or when the concept of a hitherto unaltered tradition was referred to as an alternative to a supposedly imported change (Chapter 5). In addition, and again from the present-day point of view, one could list the 'community or educational centre', which, during Valentine's third field trip, the members of the younger generation had been promoting 'both to preserve and modernize custom'. As Valentine writes in the collection he later edited with his second wife (Chapter 2), this centre was intended to support the following developments: a change in the settlement pattern in favour of a 'more traditional loose cluster of hamlets', a return to older forms of house-building, and the increased usage of 'traditional dress' by 'more mature and even younger women' (C. and B. Valentine 1979a: 64).

50. See Chapter 5. Valentine's predecessor, Friedrich Hees (1914b: 217), had also referred to the contemporaneity of the uncontemporary when he first wrote that one could not ask the Nakanai to 'give up their earlier ideas and opinions almost completely', and then continued as follows: '[R]ather, there emerges a peaceful state of contradictory things existing next to and with one another.'

51. Valentine's rather essentialist understanding doubtless corresponds to Goodenough's declared aim to fill in 'white spots' on the ethnographic map, and it is also evident in his attempt to reconstruct individual aspects of traditional culture such as masked dances, concepts of personhood and beliefs linked to transcendent beings (Chapter 2).

52. This results in the terms 'kago' and 'kastom' each being an 'artifact of entwined practices'. The fact that there are correspondences and discrepancies between Valentine's accounts and present-day memories (Chapter 4), as well as between my results and those of Valentine – or between the masked dances performed in the 1950s and in the 1990s – correlates with the relationship between continuity and change.

53. See Chapter 5. Similarly, Otto and Lattas refer respectively to 'mutual attempts at interpretation' and 'relations of mutual appropriation', while Chris Gosden and Chantal Knowles (2001: xix) refer to 'a single social and cultural field of mutual influence' having emerged in the area under German colonial rule.

54. In this sense, Ira Bashkow describes the 'Orokaiva construction of whitemen' as 'a medium in which Orokaiva morality is perpetuated' (Chapter 1). Elsewhere, I have analysed the tension between alienation and strengthening, or between subjugation and confirmation, with reference to the idea that one's own ancestors were producing Western goods in purgatory (Chapter 3): the Self (ancestors) becomes part of the Other (purgatory), and simultaneously the Other (Western goods) turns into a product of the Self (ancestors; Jebens 2004c: 166).

55. Similarly, Goodenough (30 November 2001) expressed to me the view that Berger had used the already existing Kivung 'as a vehicle' for missionisation, and that, being asked by the villagers what they had to do in order to obtain the cargo, he had replied that they must become good Catholics. Valentine describes various meetings at which the adherents of the Kivung discussed the 'actual meaning' of some of Berger's communications. He writes that people were 'discouraged because Berger never spoke out clearly on the fundamental ideas of the movement', and that there was a 'lack of clarity on Berger's part' (CV 27 August 1954b: 5). In this respect, Berger may have consciously made use of the small degree of precision or high degree of openness of Tok Pisin. On the other hand, the 'real meaning' of some of Valentine's words was also said to be not clear (Chapter 4).

56. An indigenous reinterpretation of the figure of Berger becomes obvious when he is said to have returned from the dead or when, in the stories about his wartime experiences, he appears almost like a transcendent authority (Chapter 3). Yet, from the present-day point of view, it is hard to decide whether such a reinterpretation was what Berger himself had intended.

57. I therefore mention only in passing that Goodenough shared Valentine's view and that, referring to an evening meal with Berger, he said: 'I sort of sized him up as a somewhat paranoid personality' (30 November 2001). Theodore Schwartz (Chapter 1) similarly describes his impression 'that Berger was at least semi-mad' (letter, Schwartz to Jebens, 20 February 1997). In a letter to Fr. Alfred Völler, the provincial superior of the Missionaries of the Sacred Heart, Fr. Norbert Brinkmann (29 August 1986) sketches a somewhat more positive picture, and yet perhaps also hints at the accusations directed at Berger (Chapter 3): 'Fr. Berger was always a person somewhat shrouded in mystery and a loner. He had his own style, which no one could copy. But somehow he was successful with it among the Kanaks in Nakanai when, shortly after the war, the Cargocult [original spelling] spread there. He concentrated on pastoral care for the families. That was new here at the time. When that proved successful, naturally it provoked clerical envy among some of the brothers.' His colleagues, Klaus Eppmann (9 August 1997) and Norbert Empen (22 July 2003), described Berger as 'cunning' and

'shrewd' respectively. Fr. Hans Limburg (letter to Jebens, 18 May 2004) reported to me that he had asked Sr. M. Donia, who had been active in New Britain after the Second World War, whether she had known Berger and what he had been like then: '"Different!", was her reply, and she repeated this two or three times.'

7

Subjects and objects

Similarities

Demand

The cultures that encounter or collide with one another in the course of colonisation and missionisation may mutually influence each other (Chapter 6), and yet they do not dissolve but maintain their own respective identities while changing. I see this as a precondition for any comparison between indigenous and anthropological perceptions of Other and Self.[1]

In the context of cargo research, Nancy McDowell bemoans a 'failure to do genuine comparison' and claims that intercultural differences have been exaggerated and similarities neglected (Chapter 6). Her criticism suggests a need to do the opposite in the future: to direct one's attention to what connects rather than to what separates. Such a demand is certainly no less justified than the claim to equality articulated in the idea that the ancestors already had unrestricted access to cargo or in the statement made by the interlocutors of Hees that they would be 'faithfully taking turns' with him 'in being teacher and pupil' (Chapter 2).

Indeed, similarities seem to be obvious, since if cultures cannot be separated or are exerting mutual influences, then their representatives must be subjected to the same interplay of activity and passivity, and ethnographers as well as the people with whom they work with can be seen as both subjects and objects of a process of influence.[2]

Other and self

In the early 1960s, Leo Scharmach (1960: 227) still spoke of '[o]ur natives, who belong to the Stone Age people', while Keith McCarthy gave his memoirs the title of *Patrol into yesterday* (1963; see Chapter 1).

Scharmach and McCarthy regarded the inhabitants of present-day Papua New Guinea as the representatives of their own past, which is exactly how my interlocutors in and around Koimumu, in their turn, regarded not only the Kaulong, but also the whites who were associated with the ancestors.[3]

Like the people with whom they work, ethnographers apparently relate the Other to the Self by understanding the former according to the pattern or model of the latter. Thus, like Valentine and me, they prove to be shaped by the scientific discourses of their times and, like Valentine and Lattas, they ultimately find their preconceived ideas and expectations confirmed 'in the field'.[4] Moreover, 'on both sides' the appropriation of the Other goes along with an alienation of the Self, when masked dances are smilingly assigned to the past or when such disparate phenomena as the pursuit of material well-being in the USA, the Monday demonstrations in the former GDR or Western beliefs concerning UFOs are denoted with the term 'cargo cult'.[5]

The fact that cultural perceptions of Other and Self exert mutual influences on the part of both ethnographers and the people with whom they work corresponds to the mutual influences between the cultures that encounter or collide with one another in the course of colonisation and missionisation in general. In this hall of mirrors of Other and Self, what at first sight seems to be irreconcilable oppositions often gives way to evaluations that can only be described as quite ambivalent.[6]

The early colonial officials and missionaries considered themselves the bearers of civilisation and 'development' and when confronted with alleged cargo cultists tended to regard them as victims of a disturbed equilibrium of health (Chapter 2). Thus Hees writes about the Nakanai that their 'will, governed by unordered passions and malice, leaves no place for reason', while he simultaneously characterises them by referring to their capabilities, virtues and moral categories. The same ambivalence becomes obvious in the form of aesthetic evaluations, as when Hees admits to a 'repulsive impression' of the Nakanai and yet praises their 'large, powerful men and pretty, slim women'.[7]

Conversely, the people in the Koimumu area construct a dichotomy between 'black' and 'white', in which they characterise each of the two groups precisely by what the other lacks. At the same time, the overcoming of the respective differences is both striven for as a change in or even as the emergence of culture, and deplored as its decline (Chapter 5).

Goods, secrecy, persons

The intercultural similarities which certainly deserve attention include not only the interplay of activity and passivity and the mutual influences between perceptions of Other and Self but also a pronounced interest in the material culture of the respective Other. Thus missionaries, colonial officials, travellers and anthropologists have all appropriated ethnographic artefacts, from individual souvenirs to whole collections, while Western goods are already foregrounded in the very term 'cargo cult'. Moreover, according to at least earlier authors such as Bodrogi, Worsley and Mühlmann, they were supposed to remove economic and political inequality in relation to the whites and to help end the Melanesians' own subjugation.[8]

When, in Valentine's view, the promise of the arrival of Western goods is hidden behind the 'public façade' of the Kivung, and when Valentine complains to his interlocutors about not being given sufficient information on the Kivung, then Ambrose Bai and Joe Kaveu seem to be responding in kind when they state that the whites have a secret 'in respect to the way of life' or that they 'keep things secret'.[9]

Statements or complaints concerning secrecy have proved to be extraordinarily long-lasting 'on both sides', the more so since any objection can be interpreted as proving that the Other is not prepared 'to say it all'. Thus people in and around Koimumu could 'pass on' the accusation that there was a cargo cult beneath their Christian and economic activities, but they were unable to refute it effectively vis-à-vis the colonial administration.[10] When Joe Sogi (9 July 1996) told me that he wondered why all human beings did not have the same skin colour, way of life and knowledge, since, according to the Bible, they all came from the same mother and father, I had the impression that he was proceeding from the assumption of a secret cause. Yet I did not succeed in changing his opinion because he merely answered my attempt to sketch different historical developments with the supposition that obviously 'my people' had considered me too young and had therefore not instructed me fully.

According to Theodore Schwartz, Melanesians in general believe they are more or less helplessly at the mercy of powers which they perceive perhaps not as secret, but certainly as inscrutable and as belonging to a potentially hostile environment. In this context, Schwartz (1973: 155) speaks of a 'paranoid ethos', out of which, 'in the interplay of other forces and factors, the cargo cults are precipitated'.[11] If one wished to use the term 'paranoia' in this sense and apply it to the inhabitants of Koimumu and neighbouring villages, one would also have to include Berger, who believed he was being persecuted by the administration, as well as Valentine, who imagined himself to be subject to a 'reign of terror' created by his opponent (Chapter 2). Thus, Valentine's diagnosis that Berger had a 'predominantly paranoid orientation toward life' could equally be applied to himself.[12]

Whereas I have tended to qualify the personal significance of Berger, Valentine and myself, in the 1950s it was usual on the Western side to name phenomena like the Batari movement after individual persons and to interpret them, so to speak, as their creations.[13] In Ward Goodenough's definition of the term 'cargo cult' the figure of the 'native prophet' accordingly appears as essential, while Valentine explains what in his view are the central elements of the Kivung entirely with reference to

Berger's influence (Chapter 2). This perspective, focused on individual persons as it is, was shared by my interlocutors when they talked about what had been said and done 'under Batari' and when they traced the Christian and economic goals and activities of the Kivung back to Berger's intentions or instructions (Chapter 3).

Differences

Transference

Although the similarities between indigenous and anthropological ways of seeing Other and Self seem to be obvious, I would like to point out the danger that these similarities may, at least in part, exist only as a product of one's own perceptions.

If, as a Western visitor, one understands the Other according to the pattern or model of the Self, one might, by way of transference, observe exactly what one expects to observe.[14] Thus, Valentine believed that, in the form of the Kivung, he had found the same cargo cult that his designated doctoral supervisor had already thought existed, while Lattas imagined the Kaliai to be victims of the same process of alienation and subjugation that, in earlier publications, he had described for the Aborigines (Chapter 6).

My own statement that in and around Koimumu the *tumbuan* or *valuku* were made with joy and eagerness and, during the performances, watched with enthusiasm might be based on a rather emotional transference, since 'joy', 'eagerness' and 'enthusiasm' are in any case terms that characterise my own feelings in documenting the masked dances: I experienced the corresponding work as a success not least because it went along with an expansion and intensification of my relations with the inhabitants of different villages.[15]

Finally, the ethnographer's perceptions may also correspond to his expectations and sentiments because this is exactly what the people he works with intend. In their attempts to reduce intercultural difference (Chapter 5), they can just tell or show him what they think he wants to hear or see.[16]

The process of transference, which contributes to intercultural similarities, as it were, thus appears as an aspect of the mutual influence between the 'subjects' and 'objects' of ethnographic research. In view of more recent works on cargo and *kastom* one should attempt not to suppress this process but to make it conscious through self-reflexivity and discernible through ethnographic specificity.

Indigenous terms

The terms 'kago' and 'kastom' each have specific characteristics through which they can be distinguished from 'cargo' and 'custom' as their Western opposites, even though this may not be apparent at first sight.

For Elfriede Hermann (1992a: 67), 'kago kalt' describes an 'attitude of passivity coupled with an expectation of cargo materialising out of nothing', while academic definitions neither refer to people waiting for such an emergence 'just like that' nor 'directly incorporate the attributes of laziness, primitiveness and paganism'.[17] Hermann is referring to the inhabitants of Yali's home village, the man after whom the cargo movement examined in *Road belong cargo* was named.[18] They have allegedly 'internalised a series of negative constructions [belonging to the Western term "cargo cult"]' (Hermann 1995: 169), and they would 'in no way doubt the truth and existence of "cargo cult", but insist it should be ascribed to nonlocal Others'.[19] Cargo cultists are thus always the others, not only for my interlocutors, but for Hermann's, too.[20] In addition, Hermann (2004: 45) points out that, when villagers are 'passing on' the accusation of having participated in cargo cults, unlike the originators of Western discourses they do not rely on 'binary oppositions of civilized versus uncivilized, Christian versus heathen or rational versus irrational', they do not pursue any aims of conquering, missionising or civilising others and they still feel subordinate vis-à-vis the position of power out of which the 'cargo accusation' has been formulated in the first place.[21]

In and around Koimumu, too, 'kago kalt' and 'kago' are not the same as 'cargo cult' and 'cargo'. My hosts and informants shared Goodenough's view in that they considered the expectation of goods sent by the ancestors to be particularly important and, like the colonial officials, they applied the term only to others, and yet they defined it relationally and negatively, that is, by contrasting it to Christianity, *bisnis* and council (Chapter 4). This process of contrasting refers to an ambivalence which is often overlooked by anthropologists: if the corresponding beliefs and practices are opposed to an allegedly imported change, it makes sense to revile them, with Paul Gar, as 'bullshit', but at the same time they offer relief from the demands associated with colonisation and missionisation or the process of domestication and taming.[22]

For Lamont Lindstrom (1993: 147), the contents of the term mainly depend on against whom or with what purpose it is being put to use: 'When the task is to define oneself against non-Melanesians, Islanders may embrace cargo cult as their mother culture. When the task is to accentuate political, religious, regional, or other difference among themselves, however, Islanders can revile and denounce one another for being cargo cultists.'

In the first case, cargo cults – incidentally, in a manner that strongly recalls Valentine's interpretation from 1979 (Chapter 2) – appear as a form of anti-colonial resistance, as a contribution to 'development' or as evidence for an 'authentic Melanesian Christianity' (Lindstrom 1993: 149–50), and it is suggested to the citizens of the new nation states of the Pacific that they should 'both take pride in and profit from their genuine cargo-cult culture' (Lindstrom 1993: 151). If, however, 'the contested social boundaries are internal', then the term can serve the political elites in condemning whatever they see as a threat.[23] In this context, the relational and negative definition or evaluation of the term does not appear to differ much from the one that can be observed in and around Koimumu or in Yali's home village.

The idea, still widespread among missionaries and colonial officials in the 1960s, that in the inhabitants of present-day Papua New Guinea they were confronted with representatives of their own past is at first sight no less evolutionist than the construction, formulated by my interlocutors, of a process of change triggered by the whites and then running unilineally towards their way of life, its various phases being represented by different groups living in different places (Chapter 5). If I were to postulate an indigenous evolutionism, however, this would tend to be an evolutionist idea itself, because it would equate the concepts of culture and culture change that are widespread in and around Koimumu with an earlier period in the history of anthropological theory and thus, if I spoke as an anthropologist, with my own past.

The term 'kastom', closely linked to culture and culture change as it is, distinguishes itself from 'custom' through its ambivalence, just as 'kago' does with respect to 'cargo'. Thus, 'kastom' basically refers to a past way of life which appears sometimes as a starting point for change in, or even the emergence of, culture, and sometimes as a state of purity still untouched by a later degeneration – sometimes as an obstacle to be overcome, sometimes as a positively valued alternative to the present (Chapter 5).

In addition, the differences between 'kago' and 'kastom' on the one hand and 'cargo' and 'custom' on the other may also be due to the fact that the need for substantial definitions or – as Valentine (1965: 192) writes with respect to beliefs linked to transcendent beings – for 'precision or exact differentiation' is apparently more marked among ethnographers than among the people with whom they work.[24] Accordingly, my hosts and informants differed from Valentine and me in that they were not overly interested in attaching their mask types to different categories of their own accord.[25] Their inclination to foreground such categories or to develop largely coherent constructions that are free from contradictions could be caused by the fact that ethnographers primarily rely on interviews, like Valentine, or regard the relationship between indigenous and Western culture first and foremost as a relationship between pre-existing and introduced ideas, like Lattas, whereas the people of the Koimumu area consider the practical side of their lives as particularly important.[26]

'Cultural memory'

In light of how indigenous terms are applied, I would be sceptical about whether the constructions of *kago* and *kastom* documented in and around Koimumu can be analysed with the concept of 'cultural memory', which seems to be unknown in Melanesian anthropology so far (Chapter 1).

The term 'cultural memory' itself certainly represents a metaphor, since, as A. Assmann correctly states: 'Culture itself naturally does not "remember" anything at all, nor is it in a position to forget.'[27] In and around Koimumu, constructions of *kago* and *kastom* are indeed always expressed by individuals, even when they act in common, as in the making and performing of *tumbuan* or *valuku*. Similarly, J. Assmann (1991: 347) writes that '[t]he subject of memory and recollection always remains the individual human being'.[28]

Without explicitly mentioning the Assmanns, Cancik and Mohr (1990: 309) have objected that the 'examination of the social conditions of memory [cannot be based] on a metaphor of biology or individual psychology' and that 'the particular way in which the past is present in human culture and communication [would be] obscured by the extension of the metaphorical use of memory on to "society" or "culture"'.[29]

Referring to Cancik and Mohr, J. Assmann (1991: 350n3) does acknowledge a 'justified criticism ... of the metaphorical use of the term "memory"'. Yet, according to A. Assmann (1998: 132), a 'group memory' has 'no organic basis' and is therefore 'inconceivable in the literal sense', but at the same time, she argues, it should not be regarded as 'purely metaphorical [since] beyond the common symbols, the individual person takes part in a common memory and in a common identity'. Correspondingly, and after linking her distinction of 'functional' and 'storage memory' (Chapter 1) to the relationship of remembering and forgetting in individual memory, A. Assmann (2004: 48) continues as follows: 'NB: here we are using a structural comparison, not an animistic metaphor.'[30]

For the Assmanns, 'cultural memory' mainly has the function of constructing and perpetuating a collective identity by going back to the past (Chapter 1). Using the terms 'concreteness of identity' and 'group reference', J. Assmann (1988: 13) writes of a 'stock of knowledge' that is preserved or cultivated within 'cultural memory', that lends to the group 'a consciousness of its unity and uniqueness' and that is 'characterized by a sharp boundary separating members from non-members, i.e. Self from Other'.[31]

However, in the Koimumu area, 'unity' can only be recognised in a very restricted sense. There, instead of the more or less homogeneous groups that J. Assmann seems to have in mind as the bearers of 'cultural memory', one finds different parties, as it were, using the terms 'kago' and 'kastom' against each other by adopting accusations of participating in cargo cults, by contesting the introduction of local government councils and by claiming to have the greatest competence in the making and performing of *tumbuan* or *valuku*.[32]

In addition, the mirrorings and mutual influences that have been unfolded in the preceding chapters of the present work, together with the corresponding dialectic of the reduction and increase of distance (Chapter 5), show that the 'sharp boundary separating members from non-members, i.e. Self from Other' may in fact be much more permeable than J. Assmann's definition of 'concreteness of identity' and 'group reference' would suggest.[33] Against the background of the data collected in and around Koimumu, this very permeability or dialectic appears as a blind spot in the concept of 'cultural memory', which after all has been developed with reference to the written cultures of antiquity and the West.

Concluding remarks

Reversal

If one compares the masked dances performed in the 1950s and 1990s, the representations in Valentine's report to the colonial administration and the corresponding present-day memories, and the results of predecessor and successor or indigenous and anthropological perceptions of Other and Self, it is possible, at least on a rather general level, to describe similarities as well as differences. Accordingly, the demand, implicitly made in the context of more recent 'cargo research', that attention be paid to similarities appears to be in principle no less justified than the claim to equality expressed by the interlocutors of Hees and Valentine.

On the other hand, similarities may only exist as a product of one's own perceptions and obscure views of the difference, for example, between 'kago' and 'cargo' or 'kastom' and 'custom'. Yet this difference proves that the impact of anthropological notions on the society under study (Chapter 1) cannot be reduced to mere acceptance, since the relational definition and negative evaluation that are characteristic of 'kago' and 'kastom' testify to an indigenous influence rather than a Western one.

In the context of so-called 'whiteness studies', Ira Bashkow thus acknowledges similarities between the 'Orokaiva construction of whitemen' and the 'western conception of race', but, referring to the 'complexities of local racial dynamics', he also warns against overestimating the Western origin of indigenous discourses and against seeing them merely as a form of 'western hegemony' or as an example of 'counter-hegemonic resistance'.[34] Instead, for Bashkow the 'Orokaiva construction of whitemen' constitutes a medium in which the morality not of the whites but of the Orokaiva themselves is being perpetuated (Chapter 1).

To overestimate the Western origins of indigenous discourses or to start out from the assumption of a mere acceptance of anthropological terms means reducing the mutual influence between the cultures that encounter or collide with one another in the course of colonisation and missionisation to a solely Western one. This was done by colonial officials and missionaries in Valentine's time and it corresponds to the opposition between indigenous passivity and foreign activity, between an unaltered tradition and a dynamic modernity, constructed in the context of indigenous perceptions of Other and Self.[35] From a present-day perspective, however, the idea of an influence that comes only from the West appears to be outdated, not least because it tends to contribute to the very 'homogenisation' criticised in '*kastom* research' (Chapter 6), i.e. because it tends to make disappear precisely those differences which become obvious when the villagers use the terms 'kago' and 'kastom' against one another.

In the context of 'cargo research', it has been bemoaned that the exaggeration of differences and the neglect of similarities would lead to an increase in intercultural distance as well as to the omission of a critique of one's own culture (Chapter 6); and this entails the demand that in the future the focus should be on what connects rather than on what separates. Against the background of the preceding considerations, however, I would like to plead for attention to be directed not to similarities instead of differences but conversely to differences instead of similarities. It is precisely in the differences between indigenous and Western terms, or between indigenous and anthropological perceptions of Other and Self, that the 'cultural Self' articulates itself, which – to repeat a formulation from the introduction of this study – should be taken seriously, explicated and made fruitful for a critique of Western culture itself.

Critique

The aim of criticising one's own culture ultimately results from the 'self-reflexive turn' in 'cargo research'. Thus, for Ton Otto (1999: 96–97), the combination of 'cargo' and 'cult' constitutes 'a felicitous conceptual match', since – as he writes, in agreement with his assumption of a mirroring (Chapter 6) – it makes us think about our conventional separation between economy ('cargo') and religion ('cult') and allows us to sense that 'cargo cults concern also our image of ourselves'. Similarly, Doug Dalton sees an 'essential critical nature' emerging from the tension between 'cargo' and 'cult' (2004: 205), and he opposes the 'destruction of the category "cargo cult"' because this would preclude 'the critical self-reflection and examination of Western culture and social scientific rationalism that discussions which understand "cargo cult" to be a phenomenon emanating from the West necessitate'.[36]

Here Dalton is defending the 'category "cargo cult"' against attacks which, in the history of 'cargo research', have been based on the thesis that the phenomena thus described would actually not have much in common (Read 1958) and that therefore cargo cults do not exist as an analytically distinct category (McDowell 1988). In addition, and in accordance with Valentine's interpretation of 1979 (Chapter 2), Hempenstall and Rutherford (1984) point to the negative connotations of primitiveness and irrationality that are due to missionaries and colonial officials having used the term 'cargo cult' to devalue and persecute everything that seemed to contradict their intentions.[37]

For Hermann (2004), finally, the fact that individual aspects of cargo cults have been turned into elements of Melanesian culture in general as a kind of 'cargo culture' (Chapter 2) contributes to the frequently invoked tendency towards 'Othering', and thus – as in the complaint about the exaggeration of differences and the neglect of similarities – to an increase in intercultural distance. However, whereas Hermann, with reference to the term 'cargo cult', postulates 'a need to reconsider the advisability of its use at all' (1992a: 69) and suggests that, in future, it should only be written *sous nature*, i.e. crossed out (2004: 38, 54–55), Karl-Heinz Kohl (2004: 83) stresses that the tendency towards 'Othering' can also 'enable the so-called subjects of ethnographic research to see their own customs and behavior in a new light'.

As significant as dealing with cultural difference still remains in Melanesia (Chapter 1), to assume that, for example, the inhabitants of Koimumu and neighbouring villages necessarily share the interest in the West that has grown in the wake of increasing demands for self-reflexivity would mean becoming guilty of the same 'Western overestimation of oneself' through which colonial officials and missionaries have long assumed a solely Western influence. One should, as an ethnographer, maintain the aim of arriving at a critique of one's own culture by examining indigenous terms and by comparing them with their Western counterparts, but one should not, by way of transference, put this critique into the mouths of one's hosts and informants.[38]

Predecessor and successor

I have pleaded for attention to be directed not to similarities but to differences between indigenous and Western terms, or between indigenous and anthropological perceptions of Other and Self. If I were to emphasise the differences between predecessor and successor accordingly, I would have to point out again that, unlike myself, Valentine was more interested in the substance and authenticity of the statements he recorded than in their meaning, that he had a rather essentialist idea of 'traditional culture', and that he tended to place too much importance on the individual personality of his opponent Berger (Chapter 6). Thus, I could use the figure of the predecessor to distinguish myself, hereby taking up a certain tradition from the history of anthropology (Chapter1), and at the same time I could claim that I wanted to homogenise the group of ethnographers as little as the group of people with whom they work. Moreover, if, at a distance of some forty years, two Western visitors travelled to the Koimumu area with completely different ideas, but found basically the same constructions of *kago* and *kastom*, this would seem to confirm the indigenous opposition between an unaltered tradition and a dynamic modernity.

However, it would be no less justified to reverse this opposition. The fact that in present-day memories individual elements of Valentine's account lose or gain importance (Chapter 4) and that younger men in particular nowadays express a certain distance from the *tumbuan* or *valuku* (Chapter 5) speaks for a dynamic tradition, while modernity appears static in the sense that ethnographers continue to depend on the theories of their respective times (Chapter 6) and to appear simultaneously as the subjects and objects of influence vis-à-vis their interlocutors.[39]

At any rate, when I examine the relationship between indigenous and anthropological perceptions of Other and Self from a historical perspective, it is clear that I can only do so because of Valentine's research (Chapter 1). I hope that the present work will contribute to a similar opportunity being available in the future, too. It would have probably been a surprise for Valentine that in the mid-1990s people in and around Koimumu did not feel inclined to bring up his conflict with Berger, that they did not mention his 'campaign of limited reeducation', that they represented him as a supporter of the Kivung and that they wondered about the 'real meaning' of some of his statements (Chapter 4). I am therefore not inclined to risk any prediction as to how my interlocutors might remember me and my field trips in the future. If, however, another anthropologist should succeed me in going to Koimumu and neighbouring villages, I do consider it likely that the people he encounters will tell him about me, if only to articulate their own expectations. In this moment I would have replaced Valentine in the role not only of a predecessor but also of a rhetorical figure.

Notes

1. Gosden and Knowles (2001: 6) also refer to people retaining their own identity when they state that 'Melanesian and Euro-Asian cultures have maintained themselves as different', or that social and cultural change in the last 150 years 'has not made New Guineans more like Europeans than they were'.
2. Thus, Georges Devereux has argued that one should 'abandon – at least in a naive sense – the notion that the basic operation in behavioral science is the observation of a subject by an observer'. Instead, Devereux (1967: 274) continues, it is rather a matter of 'the analysis of the interaction between the two, in a situation where both are at once observers to themselves and subjects to the other'.
3. See Chapters 4 (whites) and 5 (Kaulong). Gosden and Knowles (2001: 8) have also noted this connection: 'New Guineans were inclined to see Europeans as their ancestors, especially on first meeting. Europeans saw New Guineans as their ancestors, in a more generalised sense'. In addition, they refer to McCarthy's memoirs, as well as to the monographs entitled *The technology of a stone age people in New Guinea* (B.M.

Blackwood 1950, Oxford) and *Adam with arrows* (C. Simpson 1954, Sydney). One might also mention an exhibition on the western half of New Guinea which took place in 1979 in the then Museum für Völkerkunde in Berlin under the title 'Steinzeit-heute' (The stone age today). See Koch (1979).

4. See Chapter 6. According to Andrew Lattas, the Kaliai, too, understand the Other in terms of the Self by finding models for thinking about intercultural differences in the gender relationship, as well as in the separation between the living and the dead (1991a, 1992b, 1998). See also Jebens (2002: 192–93).

5. See Chapters 5 (masked dances) and 6 (term 'cargo cult').

6. I adopt the term 'hall of mirrors' from Lattas (Chapter 6), but it also appears in the title of the article 'The hall of mirrors: orientalism, anthropology, and the other', in which William Sax (1998: 294), although not mentioning Lattas, supposes that the tendency to see the Self in the Other is a reason for ambivalent assessments: '[I] contend that difference making involves a double movement, where the Other is simultaneously emulated and repudiated, admired and despised, and that the source of this ambivalence is the recognition of the Self in the Other.'

7. See Chapter 2. My own perception of Hees appears to be no less ambivalent, since his assumption of 'taking turns in being teacher and pupil' can hardly be reconciled with the violence he used against his interlocutors (Chapter 2). As a whole, however, the Western assessment of the Nakanai must be described as generally negative. This begins with the accounts of the early Tolai traders (Chapter 2) and continues with the Batari movement and the Kivung, as Raymond Johnston states, not without reference to Valentine's report to the colonial administration: 'The pre-war reputation of the Nakanai people for cultism under Batari, as described in J.K. McCarthy's book Patrol Into Yesterday, has tended to unfairly stigmatize the Nakanai people in the post-war era up until the early 1970's. The popularity of the "Kivung" in the 1950's and '60s did not help reduce this reputation (Valentine 1955, 1956)' (Johnston 1980b: 134–35; underlining in the original). Similarly, in a patrol report dated 17 February 1962, the colonial officer Colin S. Booth still thinks that he must stress the friendliness of the villagers, before continuing: 'I was pleasantly surprised after hearing so many tales about the uncooperativeness of West Nakanai natives' (PR Talasea 1961/62–11: 6).

8. See Chapter 2. In addition, the striving for material possessions attributed to the alleged cargo cultists can certainly be seen as a central motivating force behind the emergence and development of colonialism itself. On the significance of material objects for intercultural relations in colonial New Guinea, see also Gosden and Knowles (2001: 24).

9. See Chapters 2 (hidden promise; Valentine's complaint) and 3 (secret of the whites). The selfsame secrecy may be what Valentine's informants accuse their own ancestors of (Chapter 5), but it can also be justified, for example, with the claim that Peter Paga would have been successful if only he had kept his encounter with his deceased mother to himself (Chapter 4). Similarly, Ambrose Bai assured the mysterious white man whom he allegedly met near the Kapeuru that he would not say anything to his relatives 'or to the young people in the village' (Chapter 4).

10. In fact, the officials involved, were they living in the present, would perhaps see this accusation as confirmed, since some of the inhabitants of Koimumu and neighbouring villages continue to believe in a link between their own ancestors, the whites and Western goods (Chapter 4). In addition, I was reminded not only of the Paliau movement (Chapter 1) and of the respective police and army camps in particular (Schwartz 1962; Otto 1991), but also of the settlements founded by Franz Xaver Wagner in Sio and by Matthäus Rascher in St Paul (Chapter 2), when Vincent Gelu (22 April 1997) told me about the plan to tear down Koimumu entirely and to rebuild it according to a strict raster, with all the houses having corrugated iron roofs and all the stores forming a coherent 'business centre' that would be fenced in and monitored on a shift basis.

11. Moreover, Schwartz (1973: 155–56) suggests the following: 'The paranoid ethos in Melanesia derived from the uncertainty of life, from the high mortality rate and short life span, from the many births and relatively few surviving children. It depended on the

uncertainty of the yield of productive activities even though technologies were ingeniously diversified within the limits of an evolutionary level. Perhaps more fundamentally for Melanesia, the paranoid ethos related to the extreme atomism of social and political life, to the constancy and omnidirectionality of war and raiding, to the uncertainty of alliances, and even to the uncertainty of village and clan cohesion.'

12. In addition, just like Berger, Valentine became the object of an explanatory approach that was focused on the individual personality. Thus, Schwartz (20 February 1997) wrote to me regarding Valentine's conflict with Berger: 'I have often been tempted and I understand the exasperation that led Valentine to do what he did. I think, however, that it related to something in himself and not simply from the objective situation.'

13. See Chapters 2 (phenomena as creations of individual persons) and 6 (personal significance).

14. Following Devereux, 'transference' would have to be replaced by 'counter-transference'. Devereux uses this term to characterise the totality of all the 'distortions' or 'disturbances' which, in his view, the data in the behavioural sciences (anxiety-creating as they are) cause in the perception and interpretation of the behavioural scientist. Here, according to Devereux, it is 'strictly a matter of convention that the relevant reactions of the informant or of the analysand are called "transference" and those of the fieldworker or analyst "countertransference"' (1967: 42). If, as a Western visitor, one observes what one expects to observe, this would similarly constitute a form of 'distortion' or 'disturbance', i.e. the result of an attempt to cope with anxiety. Yet, however commendable his intention may be 'to clarify the importance of the epistemology and methodology implicit in psychoanalytic work for behavioral science research in general' (1967: 318), in my view Devereux tends to render invisible the differences between the relation of analyst and analysand on the one hand and the relation of ethnographer and the people he works with on the other. In a similar vein, see especially Hartmut Zinser's critique of 'generalisations of psychoanalytical ideas and methods' (2000: 189). Yet it must be stated that Devereux opts to treat the 'distortions' and 'disturbances' on the part of the researcher 'as the most significant and characteristic data of behavioral science research' (1967: xvii). In this respect he anticipates the demands for self-reflexivity that have been voiced in various ways in the context of more recent works on cargo and *kastom* (Chapter 6) and that fit in with the development of 'research becoming increasingly reflexive', noted by Heike Kämpf (2005: 135, 138, 142).

15. See Chapters 3 (expansion and intensification of relations) and 5 (making and performing of *tumbuan* or *valuku*). Moreover, given the fact that my interlocutors hardly ever mentioned the beliefs and practices described by Valentine of their own volition (Chapter 3), the *tumbuan* or *valuku* seemed to be comparatively easier to examine.

16. In this context, it struck me that, when talking to Valentine and me, the villagers praised precisely those nationalities, 'the Americans' and 'the Germans', to which they knew we belonged (Chapter 5).

17. Correspondingly, Hermann also states the following: 'While the spectrum of meanings of the Tok Pisin term *kago kalt* and the anthropological term "cargo cult" do partly coincide, they are at loggerheads in respect of their evaluational connotations' (1992a: 67; italics in the original). In my view, Hermann deserves attention not least because she examined the indigenous use of the term 'cargo cult' relatively early in the history of 'cargo research'.

18. See Chapter 1. Hermann first gives the actual name of this village (1992a: 55, 1992b: 51), but later replaces it with the pseudonym of 'Yasaburing' (1995: 1, 1997: 88, 2004: 43).

19. Hermann (2004: 44). The thesis of an internalisation, which strongly recalls the pattern of interpretation suggested by Andrew Lattas (Chapter 6), is also formulated by Hermann elsewhere (1992b: 61, 1997: 90).

20. See Chapter 4. The same is true for the Catholics mentioned by Lattas, in so far as they accuse the NTM of 'working a cargo cult' (Chapter 6).

21. For Hermann (2004: 46), people in Yali's home village have the chance both 'to invoke the power of Western "cargo cult" statements ... to empower oneself against an indigenous Other', and to resist this power at the same time. Hermann (2004: 55) then seems to follow Hempenstall's emphasis on resistance and protest (Chapter 6) when she concludes that 'kago kalt' would play an 'important role in exercising indigenous counterhegemony'.

22. See Chapters 3 ('bullshit') and 5 (relief).

23. Lindstrom (1993: 157). Thus, Lindstrom (1993: 162) also states that '[a] wide range of oppositional or subversive behaviour and opinion can be explained away and contained as mere cargo cult'.

24. This corresponds to the openness and obliqueness of Tok Pisin (Chapter 4). Having stated, in his report to the colonial administration, that the language of the adherents of the Kivung was leading to 'not a little public confusion' (Chapter 2), in a later article Valentine (1965: 170) ascribes to the traditional religion he reconstructs a 'pervasive quality of ambiguity and ambivalence', and he writes that 'the presence of apparently clear, named concepts does not rule out inconsistency, ambiguity or a degree of confusion'. Whereas Valentine views the obliqueness of Tok Pisin as a symptom of secrecy in relation to the Kivung (Chapter 6), he thus treats it as a culture-specific datum in relation to 'traditional religion'.

25. See Chapter 5. The categories according to which Hees arranged the reproduction of 'legends and tales' were also his own and not those of his informants (Chapter 2).

26. See Chapters 5 (inhabitants of Koimumu and neighbouring villages) and 6 (Valentine; Lattas). However, the demand formulated in the context of '*kastom* research' to take into account the way verbally expressed ideas are translated into practice should not lead to a revival of images of the Other from the early period of colonisation, which represent 'the native as incapable of abstract thought and only conceptually capable of appreciating concrete phenomena like ceremony and ritual' (Lattas 1996b: 304n8). Here, Lattas is quoting Hubert Murray, who expresses himself as follows about 'the savage' in the *Annual Report for the Territory of Papua*: 'Religion to him is a matter of practice, not of theory – a thing, in other words, to live out rather than to think out (Murray 1919/20: 109).'

27. A. Assmann (2004: 48). In the context of a representation of different metaphors of memory, A. Assmann (1991: 13) states: 'The phenomenon of memory is obviously not accessible to direct description and presses itself into the metaphorical.' See also A. Assmann (1998: 149–78). Similarly, the terms and definitions that J. and A. Assmann have adopted in order to develop their concept of 'cultural memory' must be seen as metaphors as well. This is also true of Halbwachs's 'collective memory', Warburg's 'pictorial memory' or 'human memory' and Lotman's and Uspenskij's definition of culture as the 'non-heritable collective memory' (Chapter 1).

28. If there is no 'cultural' or 'collective memory' beyond the metaphorical, the same can be said of the 'collective unconscious'. See Zinser (2000: 197). According to Hubert Cancik and Hubert Mohr (1990: 308), the notion of a 'collective memory' derives from this concept. Moreover, the 'collective unconscious' had been rejected by Sigmund Freud, and apparently Lotman and Uspenskij wanted to distance themselves from it when they stated that 'collective memory', which for them constitutes culture, would be 'non-hereditary' (Chapter 2).

29. According to Cancik and Mohr (1990: 308–9), there are already sufficient appropriate and adequate descriptions available for the different aspects of so-called 'collective memory', including 'collective recollection', 'phylogenetic memory' and 'expressions from the lexical field of "history" and "image of history"'. The critique of a metaphorical use of the term has a long tradition, since in 1925, as J. Assmann (2000: 133) himself states, Marc Bloch had already accused the Durkheim school of 'simply adding the adjective "collective" to terms drawn from individual psychology such as "représentation", "conscience", "mentalité" and "mémoire"'.

30. Similarly, J. Assmann emphasises that he 'does *not* understand the terms "collective" and "cultural mnemonics" as metaphors' (1991: 359n3; emphasis in the original). In trying to reject any metaphorical terminology, he apparently arrives at contradictory statements. Thus, he first writes that Halbwachs coined 'terms like "group memory" and "memory of the nation", in which the term memory is transformed into the metaphorical' (1991: 347), and later claims that 'for Halbwachs the term collective memory is precisely *not* a metaphor, since he wants to prove that individual memories too are a social phenomenon' (2000: 47; emphasis in the original).

31. Later in the same text, J. Assmann again refers to a 'consciousness of unity and uniqueness' (Chapter 1).

32. See Chapters 3 (introduction of local government councils), 4 (accusation of participating in cargo cults) and 5 (greatest competence for *tumbuan* or *valuku*). For J. and A. Assmann, possible tensions exist less within the 'group' than between it or the 'social and political reality of a present' on the one hand and the 'space of memory' on the other (Chapter 1).

33. Although J. and A. Assmann see the connection between 'reference to the past', 'political imagination' and 'the formation of tradition' as flexible, and although they examine this connection in its development, it is no accident that A. Assmann refers to a 'crisis' of cultural memory with respect to the present (Chapter 1), since the latter can be characterised through processes of globalisation and medialisation, i.e. through the dissolution of old group boundaries.

34. See Chapter 1. This corresponds to the later formulation of Dalton, with which he opts for an understanding of Melanesian cultures 'that does not see them as separate from the European global domination and sees them as neither its victims nor its resistance' (Chapter 6).

35. See Chapters 2 (colonial officials and missionaries) and 5 (perceptions of Other and Self).

36. Dalton (2000a: 352). Lamont Lindstrom (2004: 19) expresses similar ideas, albeit a bit more concisely, when he writes that 'a combination of the words "cargo" and "cult" can make us prick up our ears'.

37. See also Martha Kaplan (1990, 1995).

38. Similarly, and correctly, Nils Bubandt (2004: 110) asks: 'In seeing cargo cults or other exotic phenomena as critiques of Western culture or bourgeois consumerism, whose critique are we really voicing?' According to Ira Bashkow (2000: 323), this critique is in any case not important to the Orokaiva: 'Whitemen are not constructed by the Orokaiva in a way that contributes to a global critique of white power and privilege: indeed, people are disinterested in participating in such a critique, since it is not useful locally.'

39. See Chapters 4 (elements lose or gain importance), 5 (distance vis-à-vis the *tumbuan* or *valuku*) and 6 (dependence; subjects and objects of influence).

Appendices

Maps

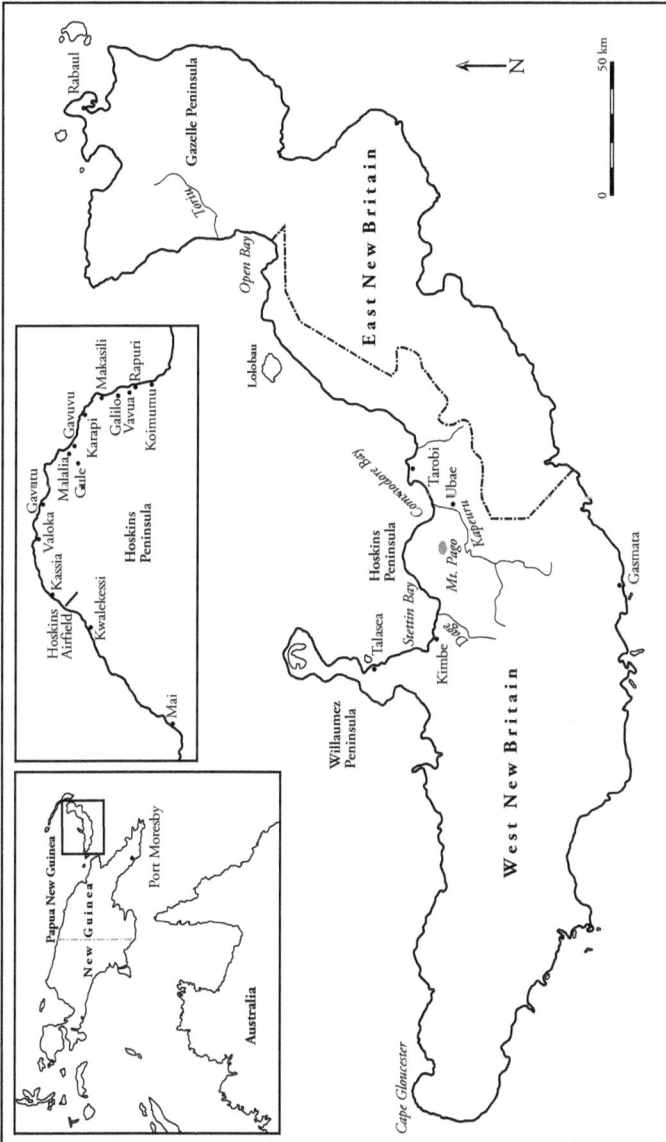

Map 1. New Britain

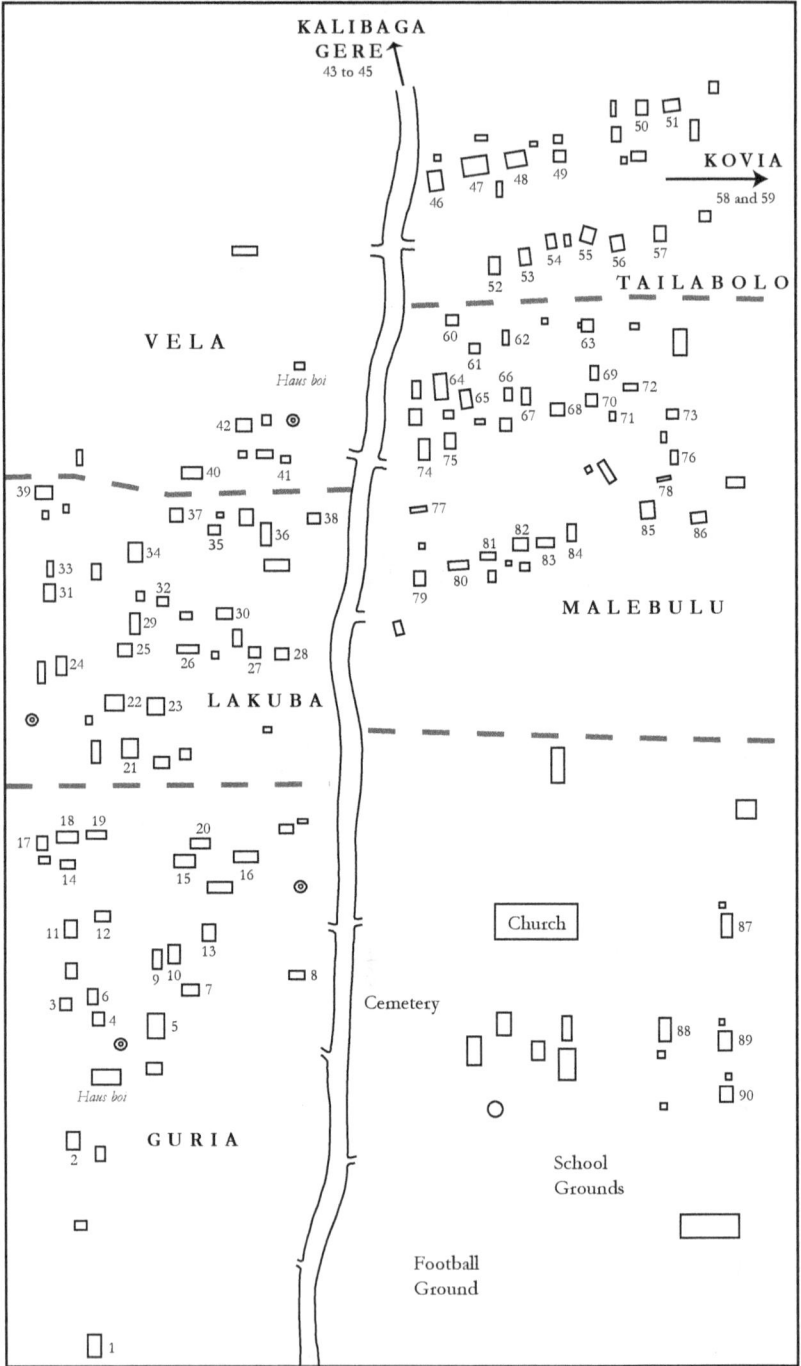

Map 2. Koimumu

Figures

1. Rapuri 1954: Ben Posoi, Edith Valentine, Charles Valentine (from left to right; photo: Theodore Schwartz, University of Pennsylvania Museum, Philadelphia. Neg. 60936)

668,795

668 Political movements   22 Aug 54   Lāma (CV)   Rapuri
795 Sects   W. Nakamai

Lāma Tells A;l (?) About the Kivung and Kabani

O, mitup stat gen. Nau mi st, na ..... Parava, lain bl Parava i wk pst.
O, oli wk pst, i go atp l ptr. Na mi lukm, mi lukm ol igo atp. O, oli km dn,
O, mimi go l Parava. Parava i lukm mi, na i tkm ole: mi askm Parava, yu wkm
wrm? Oh, mi lk wkm wnp smtg, Lāma. Mim tk, ah. Na bhm mi makm yu. O, dp tm
nau oli kmbk. Nau l Pode gen, oli km, oli go atp l ptr, oli tktk. O, oli kmbk,
na oli tkm mi nau: Lāma, mi mkm yu pns l ptr. O, ptr i krp, tk, l Pode yup kmbk.
O, l Pode, mip kmbk. Oli km kmp dn l ptr, mi go kmp. Mi go kmp, mi go wmtm l
oli, mi go atp l ptr. O, Batili nau i tktk, en i statm dp tktk bl en ole: ptr,
mip tkm yu, ai tg dp Tubioularoki bl yum, na oli lukm dp masin na dp sip. En
i kmp l en. O, na en sv lus l wrm? Olg smtg bl wk bl mip, en igo bk. En i go bk,
as bl en i ole: en bgp pamli bl kk, na en i kmp l dp masin na dp sip. O, olg mn
oli bung wmtm, na oli putm bgp ki l dp ola masin na ola kk bl olg kain gutp kk.
Nau oli laim tk l en, na belo, na oli krpm ola kk, na oli lk go l la malilo.
Tm bl dp kk l Pode oli putm, oli putm dp l Pode. O, na nau oli opim dp kk, na
wnp pk i stng. En i stng. O, na oli no moa kk, oli pem bk. Oli pem bk, ino rait.
Na ola masin na olg kako, oli krm sua l pls na krm i go bk l sip. Igo bk l sip.
Na ia bl ol mri na ol bo na ola mn, en i ms ps l krai bl masin. O, nau olg kk nau
en i bgrp nau, en i stng nau, na oli krs. Oli gt bgp krs l dp kk. O, na oli krpm
olg kks inst l pls tru, na pulimapm l sip. O, sip igo mg nau, i ksm i go bk nau
l Romo. O, na nau pls i bgrp olg. Ngt mn i st nau, oli brk nbt pns. Oli no moa
st nau. O, na ol mri, ola mn i go atp l sip, igo bk l sip. O, na oli go brgm
wnp mn, wnp mri. Oli go brgm l Laviu, en pls i st l dp tsin ptr i st l en....
Vunamarita. En. O, sip i rn igo, igo putm wnp l Manus, wnp mri, wnp mn. Igo
putm wnp l Buka, wnp mri, wnp mn. Na sip i wk l brgm oli go, na ol mn i st nau,
oli st yet, oli rn nbt. Smp i wk l sdn l weten yet, na smp igo l hap dn. O,
nau oli tktk, sri tms, yum b ols wrm? Pls bl yum bgrp pns. Na olg kk bl yum go
bk pns. Olg kk bl yum go pns, na b yum painim moa we? O, sip igo brgm ol dn
l Rom.... Romo, na sip i pulimpm smp bo moa, smp mri. Na oli sokm ol, yup
brgm ol, na yup arere we? Na sip i tk, mn bl sip i tk, oh, igo dn moa. Na nau
mip km ksm yup. O, oli wk l pulmpm sip i go bk, ola pk, ola dg, ola mri, ola
mrki. Na oli krp igo nau. Sip i wk l ol igo, igo i brgm nbt ol l olg bk l
olg pls i brgm wmp mri, wmp mn. O, igo km nau, igo kmp l Rom. Na i kapstm bok
olg kk. Bhn i km bk. Kmbk, pulmpm moa. Na ol bo hia l Tubisularoki, oli no moa
gt kk, oli no moa sdn gut. Oli no moa paim smtg bl wk. Pns olg. Na oli sri tsl
l minmuk on, l ola smtg bl wk. Olg maip bl wk, na olg maip bl wk, na olg so, na
ola smtg, en igo pns nau. Na olg kk i go, i st pns l Rom nau. O, na ol wnp wnp
wnp i st l pls. Nau oli sdn tgtg nbt l ola smtg bl wk. Na bgp hagri moa kmp
nau. L wrm, olg kk go pns. O, oli paim ola smtg bl wk nau. Na nau oli ksm dp
kina nau. Na oli ksm dp tamiok, oli soim Val l en, ston hia. O, nau oli wk l
en. Nau oli st. Na oli tgtg ols, dp kk i kmbk l Rom i km. Ngt. O, nau oli st,
no moa go. Nau oli tgm yet kk bl ol yet, sip ksm i go bk. Na oli sdn, oli tgtg
i st. Na dp ola pait, ola mn bl pait, na en krs, na l pulimmri, en poinim, en i
kmp l pls nau. Nau oli luklk l en, na tgtg bl en i strg l dp, na tg bl ol i no
moa ksm bk ol dp kk sip i brgm bk igo l Rom. Nau oli sdn l krs nau, l paut nau,
na oli ksm tup mri nau, na t tg bl ol i no moa ksm bk l dp sdn bl ol pst i gutp sdn
na kk i sv kmp l ol. I pns olg. Na het bl en i bgrp pns l smtg ngut. Na l paim
mri l bgp pe. Na bipo,mx tm bipo, gutp pls i gt masin, i sip, en i st, na ingt
krs l en. Na inogt pait, na ingt pisin, na ingt mn i sv mrtm 50 mri, 6p mri, 4p
mri, smtg ols. Ngt. Oli sdn l hsm tsl. Nau o, nau ola dp tgtg kmp l het bl e
na nau oli wk l tgtg bl mkm wk bl ol yet. Na oli putm plt wk moa nau. Bipo wm
wk tsl.

2. Valentine's field notes (University of Pennsylvania Museum,
Philadelphia)

CURRICULUM VITAE for Mr. Brown BAI, CBE.
- 1973-1996 Worked in Public Service.
- 1973-1975 Economist with National Planning Office.
- 1977-1979 Deputy Director of Planning Office.
- 1979-Sep.1981 Secretary - Dept. of West New Britain.
- 1981-1985 Secretary - Dept. of Primary Industry.
- 1986-1988 Secretary - Prime Minister's Department.
- 1988(Oct)-1990 PNG's Ambassador to Belgium, EEC, Italy, Netherlands, Luxemburg, UNESCO.
- 1991-1995 Secretary - Prime Minister's Department.
- 1995-1996 Managing Director - PNGBC.
- Voted PNG's most reputable Public Servant since Independence.
- Possesses vast wealth of experience in Government & Private Sector.
- Proven honesty, stability, leadership qualities, believes in Christian principles & formerly PNG National Soccer Representative (1972-1980).

Brown Bai CBE

P.O. Box 91, Port Moresby, NCD, PAPUA NEW GUINEA.

3. Brown Bai's business card (Collection Holger Jebens)

4. Malebulu (photos 4–20: Holger Jebens)

5. Beach at Guria

6. Bank of the Kapeuru

7. Children playing in Lakuba

8. Sunday service

9. Preparing taro

10. Producing copra

11. Joe Sogi

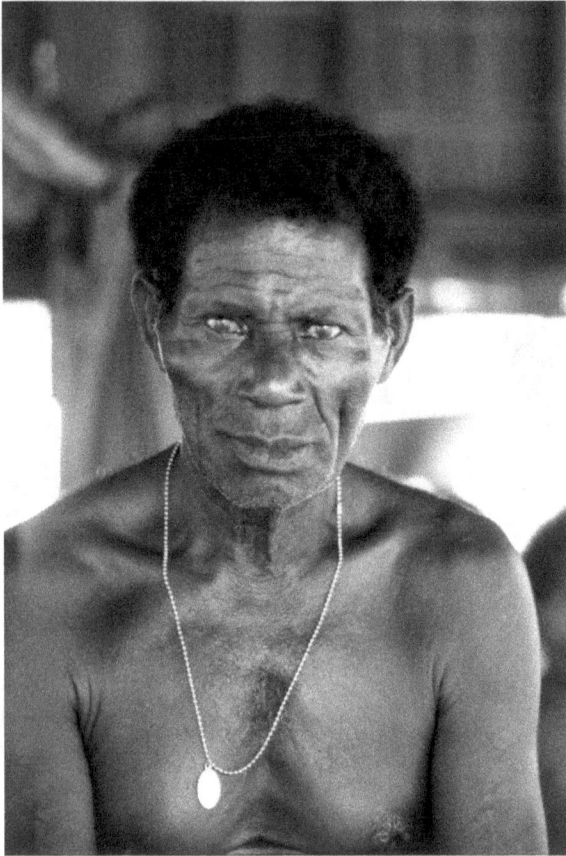

12. Paul Gar

13. Alphonse Mape

14. Ambrose Bai

15. Makasili *lomaloma*

16. Preparing for Matematevuva: John Puli, Otto Puli, Andrew Lailo, Martin Gar (from left to right)

17. Before putting on the mask: Blasius Puga

18. *Sibi* in Makasili

19. Masked dancers from Karapi: George Labiti, Alois Pui, Otto Puma
(from left to right)

20. Viewing the *tumbuan* on video

List of houses in Koimumu

The names of the inhabitants of each house are given in the order in which my interlocutors listed them to me. In the case of houses in which whole families live, usually the name of the father was given first, followed by the names of the mother and the children. The gender and, where known, the clan of each individual are given in parentheses.

1. Otto Valuku Mape (m., Ilalao), Maria Mata (f., Bobiso), Frieda Lomo (f., Bobiso), Leo Guviaro (m., Bualali), Carol Taukomo (m., Bobiso), Mosuku (f., Gararua), Bubu Russel (m., Gararua), Hermann Gelu (m., Bobiso), Ursula Talobubu (f., Bobiso), Chanel (m., Bobiso)
2. Hermann Mape (m., Ilalao), Gertrud Buso (f., Kurukuru), Justin Tiale Misili (m., Kurukuru)
3. Bernhard Lome (m., Bualali), Sophia Talobubu (f., Gararua), Cordula Kolisi (f., Gararua), Ida Kaiwa (f., Gararua), Joe Lome (m., Gararua), Doreen Roka (f., Gararua)
4. Albert Lowa (m., Ailili), Theodora Kalapoe (f., Gararua), Garfield Balive (m., Gararua), Theresa Kohogi (f., Ailili), Leonie Boige (f., Ailili), Alphonsa Kalapoe (f., Ailili)
5. Alphonse Ipa Mape (m., Kevemuki), Hedwig Tavilalili Mape (f., Bobiso), Loraine Mape (f., Bobiso), Victoria Mape (f., Bobiso), Simon Gar Mape (f., Kevemuki)
6. Ben Ubi (m., Kurukuru)
7. Helen Bibilo Mape (f., Kevemuki), Sabina Magelau Mape (f., Kevemuki), Francisca Mata Mape (f., Kevemuki), Philibert Batili Mape (m., Kevemuki), Alois Bubu (m., Kevemuki)
8. Robert Boko (m., Kevemuki), Adolpha Komo (f., Kabilimosi), Alois Galia (m., Kabilimosi)
9. Augustin Bauba (m., Gararua)
10. Katrin Galiki (f., Gararua), Jack Pigia Bauba (m., Gararua), Steven Ragi (m., Gararua), John Meki (m., Gararua), Ida Bai (f., Gararua), Josinta Dala (f., Gararua), Hedwig Kolisi (f., Gararua), Otto Bauba (f., Gararua), Gabriela Magelau (f., Kevemuki), Bitris Bai (f., Kevemuki), Ursula Bua (f., Kevemuki)
11. Michael Taumosi Mape (m., Ilalao), Sabina Gala (f., Ilalao), Margaret Gavuri (f., Kabilimosi), Martin Kobi (m., Kabilimosi), Samuel Boko (m., Kabilimosi), Paula Kale (f., Kabilimosi), Basil Sesega (m., Kabilimosi)

12. Leo Kalakulu Mape (m., Ilalao), Agatha Bai (f., Kabilimosi), Jonathan Pakela (m., Kabilimosi), Michael Vavala (m., Kabilimosi)
13. Christoph Bubu (m., Kevemuki), Magdalena Tovili (f., Baumunu), Ursula Bua (f., Kevemuki), Mathilda Malu (f., Kevemuki)
14. Boas Mera (m., Kurukuru), Relida Kamuta (f., Ilalao), Augustin Ragi (m., Ilalao), Gertrud Busu (f., Ilalao)
15. Kato (m., Kevemuki), Agnes Magelau Poe (f.,Vavaha), Magila (f., Vavaha), Tovili (m., Vavaha), Mataimi (m., Vavaha), John Baimo (m., Vavaha), Batari (f., Vavaha)
16. Alfred Gar Makelekele (m., Bualali), Antonia Dumu (f., Ugeuge), Grace Mosuku (f., Ugeuge), Konstantina Ubae (f., Ugeuge), Moses Paliavu (m., Ugeuge), Blasius Baimo (m., Ugeuge), Francis Xavier (m., Ugeuge), Polikap Magio (m., Ugeuge), Kevin Bubu (m., Bualali), Maria Meme (f., Bualali), Engelbert Tolouva (m., Bualali), Georgina Kauwe (f., Gararua), Sakias Gar (m., Gararua), Cyril Marike (m., Gararua), Hendrika Baba (f., Gararua)
17. Michael Magio (m., Ilalao), Maria Muki (f., Ugeuge), Susan Kaiwa (f., Ugeuge), Victor Ragi (m., Ugeuge)
18. Thomas Paliavu Bubu (m., Ugeuge), Lucia Tovo (f., Ilalao), William Tauabe (m., Ilalao), Cecilia Talobubu (f., Ilalao), Carolyn Bole (f., Ilalao), Greg Bauba (m., Ilalao), Hilda Sauli Paliavu (f., Ilalao), Sabina Gala (f., Ilalao), Brigitta Buso (f., Ilalao), Carola Adolpha (f., Ilalao)
19. Peter Mape (m., Ilalao), Susan Teni (f., Kurukuru), Scholly Mape (f., Kurukuru), Alex Mape (m., Kurukuru), Linda Motsi (f., Kurukuru), Vincent Galia (m., Kurukuru), Maria Tuka (f., Kurukuru), Peter Panda (m., Kurukuru), Cordula Yvonne (f., Kurukuru)
20. Kaose (f., Vavaha)
21. Andrew Dao (m., Bobiso), Dominika Bauba (f., Ilalao), Chris Marisa Dao (m., Ilalao), Max Gar (m., Ilalao), Otto Valuku (m., Ilalao), Prudence Sovei (f., Ilalao), Sylvester Dao (m., Ilalao), Edward Kapei (m., Ilalao), Anna Gar (f., Bobiso), Jeanette Ubala (f., Bobiso)
22. John Marerego Bubu (m., Bualali), Ursula Batari (f., Vavaha), Liane Boko (f., Vavaha), Agester Marerego (f., Vavaha), Roslyn Lagaia (f., Vavaha)
23. Roy Mou (m., Bobiso), Josepha Gar (f., Gararua), Eileen Puga (f., Gararua), Roy Mou (m., Gararua)
24. Paul Uboro (m., Ilalao), Monica Waba (f., Bobiso), Isidor Kadoka (m., Bobiso), Stephen Geloa (m., Bobiso), Martha Misili (f., Bobiso), Valentine Magelau Uboro (m., Bobiso), Stephania Gar Uboro (f., Bobiso), Augustina Lati (f., Bobiso), Olga Laga (f., Bobiso), Jack Bego (m., Bobiso), Helen Kavelevele (f., Bobiso), Janet Ubala (f., Bobiso)
25. Michael Labu (m., Gararua), Elisabeth Maiti (f., Kabilimosi), Andrew Mou (m., Kabilimosi), Christian Laga (m., Kabilimosi), Patricia Kua Labu (f., Kabilimosi), Engelbert Wilfred Kaiwa (m., Kabilimosi), Michaeline Kaula (f., Kabilimosi)

26. Pius Geloa (m., Bobiso), Muimui Nenamur (f., Ilalao), Niba Dovincent (f., Ilalao), Hedwig Sovei (f., Ilalao), Mathilda Pitil (f., Ilalao), Regina Alea Geloa (f., Ilalao)
27. Ben Kali (m., Kakea), Ida Kaula (f., Kabilimosi), Norbert Bubu Kali (m., Kabilimosi), Leonard Ilo Kali (m., Kabilimosi), Joe Misili (m., Kabilimosi), Lawrence Olpitarea (m., Kabilimosi), Jack Lailo (m., Kabilimosi)
28. Jack Lailo (m., Kabilimosi), Francisca Paliu (f., Gararua), Michael Maito (m., Gararua)
29. Zacharias Malaga (m., Kabilimosi), Cecilia Malu (f., Kevemuki), Alphonse Tulu (m., Kevemuki), Raphael Marerego Malaga (m., Kevemuki), William Kua (m., Kevemuki), Gervina Made (f., Kevemuki), Edmund Made (m., Kevemuki), Flora Gua (f., Kevemuki), Celestine Kato (f., Kevemuki), Priscilla Mauma (f., Kevemuki), Elsa Bubu (f., Kevemuki)
30. Michael Vavala (m., Kabilimosi), Elisabeth Magelau (f., Kakea), Brian Kaore (m., Kakea), Conrad Tovili (m., Kakea), Rosemary Laia (f., Kakea), Olga Karogo (f., Kakea), Gabriel Bola (m., Kakea), Lawrence Kosi (m., Kakea)
31. Joe Babo Sogi (m., Ilalao), Maria Gava (f., Bualali), Mocklin Voku (f., Bualali), Nick Polope (m., Bualali), Angelin Taivile (f., Bualali), Bernadette Puta (f., Bualali)
32. David Sesega (m., Kabilimosi), Evodia Kaose (f., Kevemuki), Jackary Lailo (m., Gararua)
33. Stephen Ragi Sogi (m., Bualali), Sam Sogi Aupas (m., Bualali)
34. Thaddäus Muma (m., Mamapa), Francisca Tovili (f., Bualali), Fredi Muma (m., Bualali), Jovita Magea (f., Bualali), Rufina Meme Muma (f., Bualali), Marian Muko (f., Bualali), Engelbert Tolouva (m., Bualali), Agesta Bubu (f., Bualali), Felix Morobule (m., Mararea)
35. John Tokile (m., Kurukuru), Regina Kua (f., Bobiso), Frank Galia (m., Bobiso), Terence Taumosi (m., Bobiso)
36. Caspar Mou (m., Bobiso), Susan Marisa (f., Kurukuru), Felicitas Variri Mou (f., Kurukuru), July Pate (f., Kurukuru), Benjamin Kaukia (m., Kurukuru), Jessy Reki (f., Kurukuru), Michael Kautu (m., Kurukuru), Evelyn Mata (f., Kurukuru), Prisca Lea (f., Kurukuru), Michael Kautu Tautigi (m., Kurukuru), Helen Kavelevele (f., Bobiso), Rayna Hugo (m., Bobiso)
37. Joe Sakim (m., Ilalao), Gabriele Pepe (f., Kevemuki), Alexia Koimu (f., Kevemuki), Walter Peduma (m., Kevemuki), Joanne Misili (f., Kevemuki), Augusta Leleme (f., Kevemuki), Christa Mosuku (f., Kevemuki)
38. Otto Rava (m., Kakea), Phidelma Baba (f., Gararua), Aloisa Tangole (f., Gararua), Felix Tautigi (m., Gararua), Max Mera (m., Gararua)
39. Peter Tobagili (m., Ababe), Roswitha Tobagili (f., Ilalao), Donald Moholi (m., Ilalao), Loreen Peau (f., Ilalao), Stephanie Gar (f., Bobiso)

40. Pius Magelau (m., Bualali), Meta Bubu (f., Kevemuki), Bernadette Mage (f., Kevemuki), Celina Talkibe (f., Kevemuki)
41. George Labu Tautigi (m., Kurukuru), Cecilia Sugupolo (f., Kabulubulu), Georginia Mape (f., Kabulubulu), Kevin Misili (m., Kabulubulu), Masalin Bubu (f., Kabulubulu), Joachim Leslie (m., Kabulubulu), Caspar Mou (m., Kabulubulu)
42. Ben Kautu (m., Bualali), Gabriella Luvi (f., Kurukuru), Gordon Peduma (m., Kurukuru), Madeleine Tuka (f., Kurukuru), Dominique Ubi (m., Kurukuru), Gabriel Peduma (m., Kevemuki), Antonia Lea (f., Kurukuru), James Variri (m., Kurukuru), Scholastica Reure (f., Kurukuru), Valentine Dumu Peduma (m., Kurukuru), Lawrencia Toku (f., Kurukuru), Columban Bubu (m., Bualali), Manuel Nele (m., Mararea)
43. Richard Malip (m., Bualali), Dorothee Gavuri (f., Kerakera), Toni Elvi (m., Kerakera)
44. Fabian Kiri (m., Kerakera), Josephine Magea (f., Bobiso), Justina Kua (f., Bobiso), Stephen Bai (m., Bobiso), Bartholomeus Raka (m., Bobiso), Regina Bai (f., Bobiso), William Kenso Tovo (m., Bobiso), John Tauluvu (m., Bobiso)
45. Theodor Taotola (m., Kevemuki), Gertrud Dala (f., Gararua), Calance Misili (m., Gararua), Chris Matabau (m., Gararua), George Sabubu (m., Gararua), Alexia Balauta (f., Gararua)
46. Lawrence Olpitarea (m., Bualali), Leoba Pago Olpitarea (f., Kevemuki), Colleen Olpitarea (f., Kevemuki), Owen Olpitarea (m., Kevemuki), Max Olpitarea (m., Bualali)
47. Michael Maito (m., Mararea), Regina Kaue (f., Bualali), Justina Maito (f., Bualali), Josephine Vitolo Maito (f., Bualali), Stephen Buku (m., Bualali)
48. Joe Ilo (m., Kabilimosi), Lucia Magelau (f., Bualali), Martina Gala (f., Bualali), Lea Scholly (f., Bualali), Regina Kaue (f., Bualali), John Marerego (m., Bualali), Andrew Boko (m., Ilalao), Vincent Ulo (m., Bualali), Boniface Ragi (m., Bualali)
49. Albert Garoka (m., Bualali), Mathilda Ragi (f., Ilalao), Clemencia Mulai (f., Ilalao), Silverius Sauala (m., Ilalao)
50. Camillus Kautu (m., Ugeuge), Regina Kobi (f., Bualali)
51. Paul Bubu (m., Boumumu), Bertha Vitolo (f., Bualali), Valentine Bubu (m., Bualali), Linda Gar Bubu (f., Bualali), Stephania Kolisi Bubu (f., Bualali), Nancy Bubu (f., Bualali), Edward Labu (m., Bualali), Bernadine Voku Bubu (f., Bualali), Sharon Bubu (f., Bualali), Madeleine Bubu (f., Bualali), Vincencia Bubu (f., Bualali)
52. Peter Magelau (m., Mararea), Marianne Bosa (f., Ilalao), Ben Kasila (m., Ilalao)
53. Coleman Tande (m., Mararea), Elisabeth Botola (f., Bualali), Felicitas Tore (f., Bualali), Emma Talo Tande (f., Bualali), Patricia Meme Tande (f., Bualali), Lucia Tomapa (f., Bualali), Stephen Lome (m., Bualali), Linus Ari (m., Bualali), Patrick Piakale (m., Bualali)

54. Peter Mou (m., Mararea)
55. Joe Vilei (m., Kevemuki), Sophia Dodo (m., Ugeuge), Jack Kautu (m., Ugeuge), Fredi Kulu (m., Ugeuge), Bertha Makaria (f., Ugeuge), Balbina Gar Vilei (f., Ugeuge), Elisabeth Ragi Vilei (f., Ugeuge), Samson Tovili (f., Ugeuge), Claudia Lome (f., Ugeuge)
56. Blasius Biku (m., Ugeuge), Petrolina Bili (f., Gararua), Genoveve Pui (f., Gararua), Pauline Rebecca (f., Gararua)
57. Ignes Vavala (m., Kevemuki), Clara Vavala (f., Ailili), Charles Vavala (m., Ailili), Justina Vavala (f., Ailili), Daina Vavala (f., Ailili), Joanne Togapu Vavala (f., Ailili), Jennifer Vavala (f., Ailili), Russel Vavala (m., Ailili), James Vavala (m., Ailili), Margaret Vavala (f., Ailili)
58. Camillus Tovili (m., Vavaha)
59. Ambrose Bai (m., Gararua), Anna Bai (f., Ugeuge), Daniel Bai (m., Kevemuki), Rita Bai (f.), Monica Bai (f.), Lucas Bai (m., Kevemuki), Sebastian Vulo (m., Ugeuge), Cletus Vavala (m., Ugeuge), Alois Ribi (m., Ugeuge), Susan Kaiwa (f., Ugeuge), Walter Bubu (m., Ugeuge), Cecilia Keve (f., Ugeuge), Francis Mare (m., Ugeuge), Ambrose Bai (m., Ugeuge)
60. Barth Kulu (m., Ugeuge), Gorethy Tele (f., Ilalao), Barth Raka (m., Bobiso), Angelica Magea (f., Ilalao), Cecilia Vitata Peau (f., Ilalao)
61. Albert Kaore (m., Ilalao), Benedicta Talkibe (f., Bualali), Edmund Baimo (m., Bualali)
62. Namno Nanis (m., Bualali), Vuluku Elisabeth (f., Ugeuge)
63. Christian Adam Sabubu (m., Kevemuki), Anastasia Vitata (f., Bobiso), Markus Vali (m., Bobiso), Dixon Palio (m., Bobiso), Philemon Sagali (m., Bobiso), Philip Gevia (m., Bobiso), Urban Tauloko (m., Bobiso), Erik Nari (m., Ugeuge), Bonita Ubala (f., Bobiso)
64. Kaliba (f., Mararea), Tovili (m., Ugeuge), Gar (m., Mararea)
65. Thomas Sauli (m., Ilalao), Agnes Pueta (f., Kurukuru), Calvin Kaore (m., Kurukuru), Smith Mayats (m., Kurukuru), Abraham Thomas (m., Kurukuru)
66. Thomas Taukomo (m., Bobiso), Martha Roro (f., Kevemuki), Mathilda Malu (f., Kevemuki), John Koma (m., Kevemuki), Theodore Kadoka Taukomo (m., Kevemuki)
67. George Tauviki (m., Kevemuki), Damaris Mata Moli (f., Baumono), Valentina Laogo (f., Baumono), Cina Nina Sou (f., Baumono), Brendan Veneki (m., Baumono), Alex Viula (m., Baumono)
68. Markus Lima (m., Kevemuki), Phidelma Pepe (f., Bualali), Geraldine Kaliba (f., Bualali), Nathaniel Makelekele (m., Bualali), Winfred Tokile (m., Bualali), Petra Magea (f., Bualali)
69. Sebastian Baimo (m., Ilalao), Hedwig Lome (f., Bualali), Stanis Mera (m., Bualali), Ida Sulu (f., Bualali)
70. Emil Avra Gar (m., Gararua), Joanne Kaiwa (f., Kabulubulu), Glen Felix (m., Kabulubulu), Bradlyn Waba (f., Kabulubulu), Madonna Vitata (f., Kabulubulu), Paul Gar (m., Kevemuki), Hedwig Bai Bauba (f., Gararua), Susan Mou (f., Gararua)

71. Augustin Kulu (m., Ugeuge), Christina Peau Kiri (f., Bobiso), Trancilla Muma (f., Bobiso), Barth Umari Sesega (m., Bobiso)
72. Pius Tiroro (m., Bualali), Emma Tovili (f., Bobiso), Marianne Kaose (f., Bobiso), Gledwyn Anki (m., Bobiso), Ingnasia Made (f., Bobiso), Jude Tiroro (m., Bobiso)
73. Albert Kosi (m., Kakea), Augustina Karutu (f., Ailili), Damian Sili (m., Ailili), Virginia Kuere (f., Ailili), Lucy Baba (f., Ailili), Manuel Kosi (m., Ailili)
74. Francis Mou (m., Mararea), Judith Mauma (f., Bualali), Joe Variri (m., Bualali), Justin Mape Mou (m., Bualali), Catharine Mou (f., Bualali), Lawrence Vitata (m., Bualali), Valentine Tauvilelo (m., Bualali)
75. Jack Koro (m., Mararea), Maria Maki (f., Bualali), Togapu (f., Mararea), Baela (f., Bualali), Kabe (m., Bualali), Tou (m., Bualali)
76. Jessica Gar Gaiva (f., Gararua), Francis Gelu Puloko (m., Kurukuru), Junior Gar Puloko (m., Gararua), Celesta Puloko (f., Gararua), Greg Vanag (m., Gararua), John Bosco (m., Gararua), Roy Magea (m., Gararua)
77. Casmir Kulu Tauvato (m., Ugeuge), Pauline Bai (f., Kakea), Philomena Bai (f., Kakea), Otto Rava (m., Kakea)
78. Jack Malauma (m., Gararua), Relida Balauta (f., Kabilimosi), Reu Victor (m., Kabilimosi), Apollonia Bubu (f., Kabilimosi), Eric Sakoe (m., Kabilimosi), Maria Baliae (f., Kabilimosi), Anna Kua (f., Gararua)
79. Vincent Wavo Gelu (m., Kurukuru), Maria Kaveu (f., Kevemuki), Josepha Gabulo Gelu (f., Kevemuki), Alice Bai (f., Kevemuki), Therry Babo (f., Kevemuki)
80. Julius Bauba (m., Ilalao), Agnes Kaiwa (f., Bualali), Geoffrey Kulu (m., Bualali), Christina Vitata (f., Bualali), Ben Ilo Bauba (m., Bualali), Joachim Taumosi Bauba (m., Bualali), Bibiana Vaila Bauba (f., Bualali), Annunciatha Tovili Bauba (f., Bualali), Clemencia Kuka (f., Bualali), Lucia Mauaga (f., Bualali), Hubert Batari (m., Bualali)
81. Simon Taukibe (m., Kurukuru), Barbara Valien (f., Ilalao), Conny Mou (m., Ilalao), Leonora Togapu (f., Ilalao), Andrew Kaseka (m., Kurukuru)
82. Pius Paga (m., Gararua), Brigitta Kuka (f., Kurukuru), Rachel Mataolo (f., Kurukuru), Richard Peau Paga (m., Kurukuru), Silvia Loua Paga (f., Kurukuru), Maristella Tagupi Paga (f., Kurukuru), Rex Gar (m., Kurukuru), Michaeline Paga Bubu (f., Kurukuru), Susan Mou (f., Kurukuru), Vincent Wavo (m., Kurukuru)
83. Peter Anki (m., Ugeuge), Lucia Misili (f., Bobiso), Paru (m., Ugeuge)
84. Peter Gar (m., Ilalao), Elisabeth Soke (f., Gararua), Oscar Magea (m., Gararua), Rose Buku (f., Kakea), Sebastian Muma (m., Gararua), Hubertina Bai (f., Gararua), Gervina Kua (f., Gararua), Cosmas Gar (m., Gararua), Gelinda Gulumele (f., Gararua), Emil Avra (m., Gararua), Pius Paga (m., Gararua), Patrick Muli (m., Bualali), George Dome (m., Kakea), Ben Kali (m., Kakea), Sebastiana Kaue (f., Kakea)

85. Joe Kaveu (m., Gararua), Gertrud Waba (f., Ugeuge), Jacklyn Kaveu (f., Ugeuge)
86. Sophie Bubu (f., Bobiso), Stephen Meta (m.), Hedwig Lili (f., Bobiso), Rose Lilo (f., Bobiso), Timothy Kailoka (m., Kakea), Carl Mohe (m., Bobiso), Barth Babe (m., Bobiso), Fabian Kiri (m., Bobiso)
87. Barth Umari Sesega (m., Bobiso), Petra Magea (f., Bualali), Eugene Kua (m., Bualali), Joyce Vaina (f., Bualali)
88. Gabriel Kaiwa (m., Bobiso), Thekla Kaiwa (f.,Vavaha), Brigitta Tagupi Kaiwa (f., Vavaha),
89. Patrick Gar (m., Vavaha), Cordula Gar (f.), Peter Choropwe (m.), Georgina Taliuru (f.), Rosemary Poilep (f.)
90. Holger Jebens (m.)

Tok Pisin texts

Ambrose Bai

Ambrose Bai tells of his encounter with a white man (Chapter 4), reproducing the words he had directed to him.

Mi mas kisim paua long yu. Mi save, i gat paua bilong yu i stap ya ... Mi save yu paitim han, yu singautim mi ... bai mitupela i toktok ... Mi laikim warɪpela samting long yu ... Mi laik askim yu olsem ... Tupela kandere bilong mi i dai pinis ... ating yu wanpela kandere bilong mi ... Yu singautim mi bilong givim mi sampela o moni o wanem samting yu laikim ... Mi laik bai yu toktok, maus bilong yu i no ken pas ... lukim skin bilong yu gutpela ya, yu masta ya ... Yu sori long mi olsem yu paitim han na yu gat samting ... Pocket trausis bilong yu ya i pulap tru long paua bilong yu, yu wokabaut long en ... Mi laikim wanpela samting ... bai yu givim mi ... Man, gutpela tru na mitupela tasol ya, mi laikim painim paua bilong yu. Lukim, taim mi wokabaut i kam olsem, yu no hangre, bilong wanem, yu gat paua ya. Yu laik wokabaut long wanem hap i go i go i go, yu laik hangre, yu sindaun gut tasol na bai yu wokim samting ya, traipela haus bilong yu i kamap, traipela tebol bilong yu, olgeta kap, olgeta samting, yu ken sinduan, yu kaikai, yu kaikai pinis, yu pulap, yu pulap nau, yu wokim tasol, bai putim long [inaudible] gen na bai yu wokabaut gen, na mi laikim dispela long trausis, long pocket trausis bilong yu, mi laikim bai yu givim mi, bai yu tokim mi gut long en ... Mi laik painim gutpela paua long yu na gutpela samting ... Em bilong mitupela tasol ...
　　Ating yu wanpela mekanik, mi lukim yu pinis ... Yu pinis long dispela graun, yu go long papa bilong yumi na papa bilong yumi lukim yu. Ating yu gat traipela sin, yu no stap gut long, em ples ya, em ya, redim yumi, mi go daun long en, em i rausim Adam tupela Eve na i no stap long dispela ples. Yu mekanik, papa bilong yumi putim yu, yu mekanik long, long ples bilong

en, long bikpela woksop bilong en. Sapos yumi rong o yumi ken kilim
man in dai o husat, em yumi go long dispela woksop. Ating yu olsem …
God i lukim yu na yu gat traipela sin … God i no kisim yu bai yu stap long
gutpela han bilong en, gutpela ples, lukim ol gris i pulap … Em tasol,
apinun bilong yu, gudnait bilong yu, moning bilong yu, bai mi go nau.

I must get your power. I know that your power exists … I know that you
clap your hands, that you summon me … we will speak to one another …
I want something from you … I want to ask you the following … Two
kandere of mine have died … I think you are one of my *kandere* … You
summon me to give me some money or whatever you will … I want you
to speak, your mouth must not be closed … Look at your skin, it's good,
you're a white man … You feel pity for me and thus you clap your hands
and you have something … Your trouser pockets are completely filled
with your power, with which you go around … I want something … that
you will give to me … Man, that's really good and it's only the two of us, I
want to find your power. See, when I came here like this, you were not
hungry because you have power. If you want to walk somewhere and
keep walking, if you're hungry, then you just sit down well and then do
something and then your big house emerges, your big table with all the
cups, all the things, you can sit down, you eat, you've finished eating,
you're full, you're full now, you just do it, you put it into [inaudible] again
and then you continue walking, and I want this from your trousers, from
your trouser pocket, I want you to give it to me, to tell me everything
about it … I want to find the good power and something good with you …
It will remain between the two of us …

I think you're a mechanic, I have recognised you already … Your time
on this earth was over, you went to our father, and our father saw you. I
think you have committed a great sin, you don't live well in, in this place
there, that he had prepared for us, to which I go, from where he has
removed Adam and Eve so that they do not live in this place. You're a
mechanic, our father has made you that, you're a mechanic in, in this
place of his, in his big workshop. If we do something wrong or if we might
kill someone or whoever, then we go to this workshop. I reckon that's
what happened to you … God saw you and you've committed a great sin
… God hasn't accepted you so that you're in his good hands, at a good
place, where one sees all the good things in abundance … That's all, I say
to you 'Good evening', 'Good night' and 'Good morning', and now I will go.

Joe Ilo

Joe Ilo talks about Peter Paga (Chapter 4).

Ah, orait, tede mi laik wokim wanpela liklik stori. Wanpela stori, mi bin
lukim na mi bin harim long ia bilong mi na mi go facim dispela stori tru
long Peter Paga long Ubae. Taim em i sik, em i sik na i go slip long

wanpela arere bilong wara na em i stap long en. Orait, em i slip i stap na em i ting … em i tok olsem, mama bilong en i kamap long en … Em mama bilong em i dai, i dai pinis. Na em i kamap long en na em i givim em long wanpela stori, i tok olsem: 'Peter Paga, yu mas kirap na yu kisim dispela buk, em paua i stap long en, bai yu kisim, karim i go long ples na yu wokim wanpela samting bilong mi.' Orait, em i kisim na em i kirap i go long ples nau, i go long ples nau na em i stap. Em i stap na i tingim dispela toktok, mama bilong en i, em i tok, i bin givim na i statim wanpela liklik olsem society bilong en, olsem grup. Mm, i statim nau … long Ubai yet. Orait, em i statim i go na i kisim sampela ol man i stap insait long Ubae yet. Mm, i no kisim planti man, i kisim olsem ol sait bilong em stret, olsem bisnis bilong en na tambu bilong en, ol i go wantaim long dispela wok, em i, em i bin statim nau. Orait, em i wokim i go i go i go.

Orait, wanpela taim em i kam, kam daun long nambis, i kam long ples bilong mipela long Koimumu, i go mitupela i stap, em i go kamap long mi, mi stap … Em kandere bilong mi. Olsem em i bin kam long Ubai na i kam stret long mi. Na mitupela i stap na em i toktok long mi nau long dispela liklik wok em i laik wokim. Na mi askim em: 'Olsem wanem tru kandere, dispela stori bilong yu olsem wanem?' Na em i stori long mi tok: 'Kandere, em dispela liklik stori, em olsem mi sik na mama i givim mi. Orait, nau mi laik wokim long toksave yu, bai yu brukim sampela lain man, bai ol i mas kam, kam wantaim yu na i kam long mi long Ubae.' Em, mi harim dispela toktok bilong em na mi wok nambaut nau insait long ples nau. Na mi toktok i go na mipela i sampela lain man ol i bihainim mi i go long Ubae mipela bai go aprovim dispela samting, stori bilong en. Na mipela i go nau, mipela i stap, mipela i lukim. Orait, i no longtaim na em i wok i go long hap bilong Amio, kisim sampela long Arawe. Ol i kam insait tu long dispela wok bilong en, long wanem, dispela stori em i bin tokim ol, i tok: 'Dispela, dispela wok nau mi wokim, bai yumi gat bikpela moni, bai ol i, ol i givim yumi.' Mhmh, tok bilong en. Orait, mipela i wok nau i go i go i go i go, wok wantaim em.

I go i go i go na wanpela taim mipela i go long haus bilong en, mi go stret long haus bilong en, mi stap na mi tokim em long ai bilong en, mi tok: 'Kandere, mi no bilip tumas long dispela wok yu bin wokim, mi no lukim tru long ai bilong mi.' Na wanpela taim, em i go karim wanpela hap bek, kik bek moni inap olsem na i kam autsait, i karim na i kam na mi kapsaitim nau [inaudible] mi lukim, mi no kauntim tu dispela moni, mi lukim tasol na mipela i putim bek insait long bag gen. Orait, em i karim bek i go insait. Orait, dispela mipela i kam, mipela i lukim pinis long ai bilong mipela. Mipela i kam bek gen, mipela i toktok nau long ples nau, tok: 'Ating dispela wok bilong en, ating tru ya.' Long wanem, mipela i bin i go na mipela lukim hap, hap moni, em bilong bek, em i karim i go autsait na mipela i lukim tru long ai bilong mipela … Long haus bilong en, long wanpela rum. Orait, em nau, olgeta man nambaut we ol i harim dispela …

Wanpela man i troimwe olsem long laik bilong en olsem ten Toea o twenty Toea. I no bikpela moni long tax i go long en, em tax bilong mipela olsem tasol. Mhmh, orait, i go i go i go, olgeta ples inap long blok, ol blok man tu i tax i kam i kam long Peter Paga. Wokim i go i go olgeta long Arawe tu i tax i kam, i kam long en. Na mi, mipela tu, mipela i no tingting tumas long dispela, ah, dispela wok em i bin wokim. Ating dispela moni tasol em, em mipela i save tax, em i go soim mipela long en – o nogat? Olsem mipela i i no bilip tumas long dispela wok tu, long wanem, mitupela yet, mi tingting olsem, long wanem, dispela moni bilong mipela yet em, em i bungim na i soim mipela long en, pastaim mi go lukim, long tingting bilong mi olsem, long dispela.

Em dispela wok mama bilong em i givim em long paua, dispela paua em bilong em yet, tasol em i go bagarapim na i givim mipela olgeta man, na i go, wokim, wokim i go i go, samting i go bagarap olgeta, i no moa kamap gut, long wanem, em i kisim planti man tumas, insait long ol blokman na i go long hap bilong Ulamona, mipela olgeta i kam insait long en ya, dispela wok bilong en ya, stori bilong en, em i bin wokim.

Orait, mipela i stap na wanpela taim em i tok, bai kisim moni ya i kam daun long hap bilong mipela nau, i kam long hap bilong mipela long nambis. Orait, em i bungim olgeta man, we olsem, ol Umua, Bereme … i go long hap bilong Amio … olgeta ples long hap bilong bus, ol i kam daun, ol i go i stap long Ubae, ol i bung long Ubae. Bihain ol i, ol i karim wantaim dispela moni i kam daun, nambis, wantaim em, wantaim Peter Paga. Orait, ol i kam, ol isi isi i kam, i kam long rot, i kam, i kam, i kam, ol i kisim mipela long Koimumu, mipela i go wantaim ol gen. Mipela i singsing wantaim ol i go long Vavua nau, mipela wokabaut long rot, singsing i go, amamas i go, i go, i go singaut nambaut i go, i go, i go, mipela i go stret long Rapuri nau. Mipela i laik lukluk i go, ol car bilong gavman i no pilai i kam, ol polis car. Man, mipela i stap nau, na mipela i sanap nau, dispela ol polis, car bilong polis ya i kam nau, stopim mipela olgeta nau, long rot. Man, olgeta man, we, long kaulong ya, olgeta i sut nambaut, ol i pretim polis nau. Ol i ranawe. Mipela i stap, em i singautim ol tok: 'Ey, yupela i no ken ranawe nambaut, i kam, bung wantaim, long wanem mipela i stat, dispela samting yupela i lusim ples pinis, yupela i kam daun, OK, sanap, bai ol polis i mas lukim yumi olgeta'. Mhmh, ol polis i kisim mipela i go, mipela i go bung long ples nau, long Rapuri ples nau. Mipela i go i stap, ol polis i toktok i go, i go, pinis, na Peter Paga tu i toktok, toktok i go, ol polis ya i harim pinis na ol polis i tok: 'OK, big man, kam long car'. Ol i putim em nau long car bilong ranim em i go … Ol polis i kisim em nau, i go, i go long sell nau, long Hoskins, i go i stap, i go, ol i go kot … i go kalabus.

Em i kalabus na i kam bek, mipela i wokim gen na mi-mipela i laik traim wokim gen na em i, kot i kisim mipela gen. Mi go long kot tu … Mi na papa bilong en ya, tambu ya, wanpela tambu bilong mi, mipela i go long kot, wanpela brata i dai pinis, Laia, na wanpela carpenter bilong misin, tupela, Reki na Kaumu, mipela i go wantaim long … Vavua, mipela i go kot, mipela i stap … em i tok: 'Olgeta samting, yupela sutim tasol long i kam long mi. Mi yet, mi givim yupela long dispela stori na yupela i bringim nambaut long ol ples.' Na mipela i go insait long kot nau, mipela i toktok i go antap long en tasol, givim em tasol, tasol dispela taim mipela i winim kot, mipela i kam long ples. Em taim em i go kalabus nau na ating i pretim gavman liklik na olsem em i lusim dispela wok bilong en.

Ah, well, today I'd like to tell a little story. A story I have seen and heard with my ears, and I really went and faced this story with Peter Paga from Ubae. When he was sick, he was sick, and he lay down on the bank of a river and there he was. Well, he was sleeping and he thought … he said, that his mother appeared to him … His mother was dead, she had already died. And she appeared to him and she gave him a story, she said: 'Peter Paga, you must get up and take this book, it has power, you will take it, bring it to the village and do something for me.' Well, he took it and then went to the village, went to the village now and stayed there. He stayed there and thought about this talk, that his mother, as he said, had given to him, and he began with a small – something like a society of his, a sort of group. Mm, he began with it now … in Ubae itself. Well, he started and got a couple of men who were in Ubae itself. Mm, he didn't get many men, he got them from his own people, like from his clan and from his married relatives, they cooperated in this work, which, which he was starting now. Well, he did it and did it and did it.

Well, at one time he came, he came to the coast, he came to our village, to Koimumu, then we were both together, he came to me, I was there … He's my *kandere*. That's why he came from Ubae and he came directly to me. And we were both together, and now he told me about this little work that he wanted to do. And I asked him, 'How is it really, *kandere*, how does this story of yours go?' And he told me the following, he said: '*Kandere*, this little story, it is that I was sick, and my mother gave me something. Well, now I'd like to explain it to you, you'll get a couple of men together, they must come, they must come with you and come with me to Ubae.' So, I heard this talk of his, and now I did some work in the village. And I talked and talked, and we were with some men, they followed me to Ubae, we were to go and confirm this matter, this story of his. And we went now, we were there, we looked around. Well, it didn't take long, and he worked further in the Amio area, he got a couple of people from Arawe. They also joined this work of his, because of this story that he told them, it went as follows: 'This, this work I'm doing now, we will have a lot of money, which they will, they will give to us.' Mhmh, that's what he said. Well, we did it now, did it, did it, did it, did it, did it with him.

Things went on and on and on, and at one time we went to his house, I went directly to his house, I was there and I said to him, to his face, I said: '*Kandere*, I don't believe too much in this work that you've done, I haven't really seen it with my own eyes.' And at one time, he went and carried a piece of a sack, filled up to here with the money that had been earned, and he came out, he carried it and came and I emptied it out now [inaudible], I looked at it, I didn't count this money either, I just looked at it, and we put it back into the sack. Well, he carried the sack back inside again. Well, we had come because of this, and we saw it with our own eyes. We went back again, and now we talked in the village now, we said: 'I suppose, this work of his, I suppose it is really true.' Because we had gone and we had seen part, part of the money, that's from the sack, he carried outside and we really saw it with our own eyes ... In his house, in a room. Well, that's how it was, whoever had heard this ...

Each man contributed money, as he wanted, for example, ten Toea or twenty Toea. It was not much money that went to him [Peter Paga] as a tax, our taxes were only just like that. Mhmh, well, things went on and on and on, all villages up to the oil palm plantations, the oil palm planters also paid taxes, paid them to Peter Paga. They did this and did this, all the Arawe people too paid taxes to him. And me, we too, we didn't think too much about this, ah, this work he was doing. I suppose it was just this money that we paid as taxes that he showed us – or not? So we didn't believe too much in this work, because even the two of us, I think, that, because it was our own money, that he, he had collected and shown to us when I first went there and looked, that's what I think about this.

Regarding this work, his mother had given him power, this power was just for him, but he spoiled it and gave it to us, all the people, and so on, he did it, he did it and did it and did it, it went totally wrong, it didn't go well any more, because he invited too many people, from the oil palm settlers up to the Ulamona area we all joined him, with this work of his, this story of his, that he did.

Well, we were there and at one time he said he would get the money and bring it to our area now, bring it to our area on the coast. Well, he gathered all the people, like, the people from Umua, Berema ... up to the Amio area ... all the villages from the bush area, they came down, they stayed in Ubae, they met in Ubae. Later they, they brought this money down with, to the coast, together with him, together with Peter Paga. Well, they came, they came quite slowly, they came along the road, they came, they came, they came, they invited us from Koimumu, we went with them again. We danced with them up to Vavua now, we walked on the road, we danced further, we were happy and happy, we shouted around and continued to do so, it went on and on, we went straight to Rapuri now. We wanted to look further, the government cars came, that was no joke, the police cars. Man, there we were now, and we stood there now, these police, the police cars came now, they stopped all of us now, in the street. Man, all the people, the, the Kaulong, they were all running around, they were afraid of the police now. They ran away. We were there, he called them and said: 'Hey, you can't run away, come, let's come together, because we begin, because of this thing you have already left your villages, come here, OK, stand up, the police should see all of us.' Mhmh, the police took us away, we met in the village now, in the village of Rapuri now. We were about to go, the police talked and talked, they finished talking, and Peter Paga also talked and talked, the police heard him out and the police said: 'OK, Big Man, get in the car.' They sat him in the car now in order to persecute him further ... The police took him now, took him, took him to a cell now, in Hoskins, he stayed there, he stayed, people went before the court ... went to prison.

He was in prison and came back, we did it again and we-we wanted to try to do it again and it, the court hauled us in again. I went before the court as well ... Me and his father, a married relative, a married relative of mine, we went before the court, a brother who has died since, Laia, and a mission carpenter, both of them, Reki and Kaumu, we went together to ... Vavua, we went before the court, we were there ... he said: 'Everything, you just put it on to me. It was I myself who gave you this story, and you brought it to all the villages.' And we went before the court now, we talked only at his expense, we blamed it on him alone, but this time we won the court, we came to the village. At this time he went to prison now, and I suppose he was a little bit afraid of the government and so gave up this work of his.

John Mataligi

John Mataligi talks about the origin of the *tumbuan* or *valuku* (Chapter 5).

Em ya, yu lukim maunten ya [inaudible], *i gat ples bilong ol i stap antap, sapos yumi go, i go insait long dispela bikbus ya ... wanpela man olsem mi, mama bilong en na papa bilong en i dai pinis, tumbuna tasol i lukautim, na em i sindaun na sindaun hait tasol na i lukluk long ol tumbuan ya i, sampela i hangamap, sampela i wokabaut tambolo ... Long maunten ya, long ples ya, ples ya, mi tok pastaim pinis long en ya. Orait, na ol i go, em i tok: 'Wanem kain tumbuan ya olsem? Ating bai mi sindaun na mi lukluk, bai lukim ol holim i kam.' Orait, ol i kam wok long wokabaut, em i sindaun tasol long as bilong diwai i stap, ol i lukim em, ol man dewel ya, i wok long lukim em ...*

Orait, na em i go, i go bek long ples, em i go na tokim pupu bilong en, tok: 'Pupu ... ol kain tumbuan ya i, mi no save lukim, na nau mi go sindaun na mi lukim ol, ol i wokabaut na sampela i hangamap yet long ol diwai na ol bun bilong ol tasol, ol i no karamapim ol, sampela ol i karamapim ol pinis tu na i hangamap, ol i no bilasim ol yet.' Na tumbuna bilong en tok: 'Orait, tumora bai yumitupela i go.' Orait, tupela i go nau na i go sindaun hait gen long ples bilong manki ya, long pupu bilong en ya, na lukim, lukluk long ol, ol i wokabaut gen i kam na tupela i go catchim ol nau, catchim ol i go i go, lukim olgeta kain tumbuan i kamap, olgeta kain tumbuan i kamap nau, orait, tupela i lukim ol pinis na tupela i go bek long ples, i go bek long ples na toktok insait long ples Mai, i no Mai tambolo ya, antap.

Em i wok long wokim tumbuan na ol tumbuan tru ya, ol man long bipo ya, ol i wokim na 'Mi tupela pupu bilong mi lukim ol pinis, bai yumi wokim ol' na, na ol i tok, askim bek: 'Orait, yupela i catchim gut ol?' Tok: 'Ah, mitupela i lukim ol ya, bun bilong ol tasol, ol i wokim na frame bilong ol, ol i wokim na i stap, ol i hangamapim ol na ol i no kisim skin diwai long karamapim ol yet.' Orait, tupela i go drawim tasol long graun, drawim long graun tasol, olgeta, olgeta man i go luklukim dispela kain tumbuan, olsem valuku ya, biriri ya na olgeta kain ya, Talemulitamala, olsem man i kraikrai bihain long papa bilong en long tupela i go long dog, em, orait na ... tupela i drawim, tupela pupu bilong en i drawim pinis na sharim long olgeta man na ol i lukim, tok: 'Oh, mipela dispela clan bai i wokim dispela.' Orait, 'mipela dispela clan bai wokim dispela', em nau, wanpela, ol i wokim traipela kaikai bai ol i karim ol, olgeta tumbuan, ol i redim pinis, bai ol i karim i go long ples, bai olsem olgeta ples i go, ol i salim tok long olgeta clan bilong ol i go, i go long Mai, bai ol i kisim, ol i go, sindaun, olgeta i go kamap, olsem olgeta yangpela man ya, olgeta inap, ol i go kamap long ples, kamap long ples long olgeta tumbuan, em nau, ol i go kamap long ples, wokabaut long ol olsem ol man long dewel ol i wokim pinis. Tok: 'Ol i wok olsem, orait, dispela tumbuan i i wok olsem na name bilong ol olsem.'

Em, em, orait, na taim nau long nait, bai ol i slip gen, bai, long nait bai ol i lukim, olgeta man i go sindaun long ai bilong wara ya, ol i troimwe uben, na, tasol ol tumbuan ya, ol i bihainim wara i kam daun, em Dage ya, ol i bihainim wara i kam daun long Dage na bai ol i bihainim welsan, ol i bihainim welsan nau bilong olgeta man, olgeta clan bai ol i catchim olgeta tumbuan ya, bai wanwan bilong ol, long wanem ples Mai bipo i bikpela ples, orait, olgeta clan nau i kisim ol, i holim pas ol. 'Dispela tumbuan bilong mipela' o 'dispela tumbuan bilong mipela dispela clan' o 'dispela tumbuan bilong mipela dispela clan', em, ol i wokim olsem ... Dage tasol i kamapim ol, na ol man long Talasea i, long, i no go daun long Talasea, long ol Kove, Bakovi tasol, em, em ol i catchim ol, na ... ol boi long mipela, ol lapunpun bipo ol i save go daun long Mai, ol i save kisim ol, kisim ol dispela tumbuan nau bai inapim olgeta ples long mipela ya, em. Em mi harim, inap ya, ol i, dispela kain stori.

There, you see that mountain there [inaudible], there is a village that belongs to them that is up there, if we go, if we go into this thick bush ... a man like me, his mother and father had died already, he had been brought up just by his grandfather, and he sat there and he just sat there hiding and looked at the *tumbuan*, some were hanging down, some were walking around down there ... On the mountain, in the village, I have talked about at first. Well, and they went, he said: 'What sort of *tumbuan* is that? I suppose I will sit down and I will look, I will see how they will hold them and come.' Well, they came and they were walking, he just sat down on a tree root and he sat down, they saw him, the spirits, they were seeing him ...

Well, and he went, went back to the village, he went and said to his *pupu*, he said: '*Pupu* ... the different kinds of *tumbuan*, I have never seen them, and now I went and sat down and saw them, they walked and some were still hanging down from the trees and it was just their frames, they had not yet been covered, some had been covered and they hang down, they had not yet been decorated.' And his grandfather said: 'Well, tomorrow we will both go.' Well, they both went now and went and sat down hiding again at the place of the boy, to his *pupu*, and they looked, they saw them, they walked again and they came and they both went and caught them now, caught them, caught them, caught them, saw all kinds of *tumbuan* emerging, all kinds of *tumbuan* emerged now, well, when they both had seen them they both went back to the village, they went back to the village and talked in the village of Mai, it wasn't Mai but below, above.

He was making the *tumbuan* and the real *tumbuan*, the people from before, they were making them and [he said]: 'Me and my *pupu* we have seen them, we will make them,' and, and they said, asked back: 'Well, have you caught them properly?' He said: 'Ah, we have both seen them, just their frames, they were making their frames, they continued to make them, they were hanging them down and they had not yet fetched the tree bark in order to cover them.' Well, they both drew it just on the ground, drew it just on the ground, all, all the men went there and saw these types of *tumbuan*, such as *valuku*, *biriri* and, and all types, Talemulitamala, like the man who cries after his father when they both walk with the dog, he, well, and ... they both drew, with his *pupu* he finished drawing and shared it with all the men and they looked, and said: 'Oh, we the people of this clan will make this,' that's it, a, they hosted a great feast in order to carry them, all the *tumbuan*, they completed their preparation, in order to carry them to the village, so that all the villages would, they sent messages to all their clans, sent them, sent them up to Mai, they would get them, they went, sat down, they all arrived, like all the young men, everyone without exception, they all arrived in the village, they arrived in the village with all the *tumbuan*, that's it, they arrived in the village, walked around with them like people among the spirits had done already. People said: 'They did it like that, well, this *tumbuan* works like this and his name goes like this.'

So, so, well, when it was night now, they were to sleep again, then, in the night they were to see, all the men who went and sat down at the mouth of the river, they threw out the net, and, but the *tumbuan*, they followed the river and came down, it was at Dage, they followed the river and came down to Dage and they would follow the beach, they followed the beach now so that all the men, all the clans would catch all the *tumbuan*, every one of them, because previously the village Mai has been a big village, well, all the clans caught them now, they kept them in their grip. 'This *tumbuan* belongs to us,' or 'this *tumbuan* belong to us as the members of this clan', or 'this *tumbuan* belong to us as the members of this clan', that's, that's how they did it ... Just Dage created them, and the men from Talasea, from, they didn't go down to Talasea, to the Kove, only to the Bakovi, so, so they caught them, and ... our boys, formerly the old people went down to Mai, they caught them, caught these *tumbuan* now in order to supply all our villages with them, so. That's what I heard, they, this kind of story.

Titus Mou

Titus Mou links the *tumbuan* or *valuku* with the cure of colds (Chapter 5).

Valuku ya, stori bilong en i kam long Dage … stat long Dage i kam olsem, na i stat tambolo, em bihainim frut … gallip … Taim mipela i no kaikai yet, ol i kaikai pinis long Dage, so i wok long wokabaut i kam, bihainim frut, long hap, long hap bilong Garua ol i wokim bilong ol, long hap bilong Bileki ol i wokim bilong ol, orait, taim Mapakuo i wok long kam olsem, ol i statim ol narapela tumbuan, bihainim ol nau i kam i kam i kam … Ol i save bihainim longpela rot ya. Bipo ol i no gat wok bisnis olsem tede, ol i no gat gaden, bai ol i busy nambaut long ol samting, ol i ken go sibi long Hoskins, ol i ken kam bek.

Orait, as bilong ol, long wokabautim, bihainim dispela gallip ya, bikos yu save, frut, taim gallip i ka-karim kaikai, em i save bringim sik, bringim ol kain flu na epidemic samting, ah? As bilong ol dispela tumbuan nau, bilong ranim ol dispela, olgeta masalai bilong galip ya, bai ranim ol i kam, i kam, i kam, troimwe ol i go daun long Kapeuru, i go pinis, em mining bilong en. Olsem bilong pinisim dispela sik, ah? Pinisim, olsem ranim ol dispela sik ya, ranim, ol i mas ranim, rausim ol i go. Olsem na valuku i stap long lalomaloma, i free long ol man i kam long biknait, yu slip pinis, ol i ran yet, bikos bai ol dispela sik nogut ya i no ken kam long ples o dewel nogut ya i no ken kam long ples, bai ol pretim tumbuan, ol i speed tasol i go long Kapeuru, dive i go daun i go long ples long solwara, em mining blong en.

The *valuku*, their story comes from Dage … it begins in Dage and goes like this, and it begins down there, it follows the fruits … almonds … When we haven't eaten them yet, people in Dage have eaten them already, so it is walking in this direction, following the fruits, there, in the area of the Garua they make them for themselves, in the area of the Bileki they make them for themselves, well, when the Mapakuo is about to come here, they begin with another *tumbuan*, later now they come, come, come … They usually follow a long way. Earlier people had not been busy earning money like today, they had no gardens, so that they would be busy with all kinds of things, they could make *sibi* in Hoskins, they could come back.

Well, their reason, for walking around, for following these almonds, because you know, when the almonds are-are ripe, this usually brings sickness, brings various kinds of flu and something like epidemics, ah? The reason for these *tumbuan* now, in order to chase these, all the bush spirits of the almonds, they would be chasing them here, chasing them here, chasing them here, throwing them down into the Kapeuru, to end it, that's its meaning. Like to end this sickness, ah? To end it, like to chase these sicknesses, chase them, they have to chase them, remove them. Thus, when the *valuku* are in the *lomaloma*, all men are free to come in the middle of the night, you are already asleep, they are still running around, because these evil sicknesses should not come into the village or the evil spirits should not come into the village, they would be afraid of the *tumbuan*, they would just hurry to go to the Kapeuru, dive down to go into the sea, that's its meaning.

Peter Tautigi

Peter Tautigi reproduces part of 'Lima's teaching' (Chapter 3).

Bilong en mi harharim tasol ol big man i toktok long en, i kam stori long mipela, i tok olsem: 'Olgeta poisen na kambang bilong poisen na kaware bilong poisen, aut! Yupela i no ken wokim moa na kilim nating man'. Orait, salim ol soldia bilong en, salim ol boi bilong i go, na ol i go mumut insait long haus ... bilong olsem i wanwan family, ol i go lukluk long insait long haus na painim wanem samting insait, kisim i go, troimwe long solwara, orait, long wanem dispela miting bilong en em i tok olsem, dispela miting: 'Yu no ken, yumi no ken traihat long wok, dispela kokonas yumi no ken planim, kokonas ya em i bilong kaikai bilong koki na ol kangal na em ol pisin nambaut, bai ol i kaikaim dispela kokonas, i no gat wanpela samting i kamap long kokonas.'

Tok bilong en, tok long Lima, em miting bilong en ... 'Bai putim oda tasol i go, samting i mas kamap. Orait, yu klinim olgeta samting insait long ... ples, olgeta samting i mas, i no gat kilim man na i no gat poisen, yu mas sindaun gut na tingting long lotu, OK, na yu ken kamap olsem, na samting insait long maus bilong yu, yu mas autim olgeta, ol poisen, yu mas autim olgeta, yu no ken holim' ... em i tok bai, ol i putim tasol oda i go long Rabaul na ol bringim kago i kam ... mipela yet i mas takis, putim moni i go na i givim em, em i mas odaim kago i kam ... 'Liklik wanshilling i stap long yupela, yupela i mas autim olgeta ... yu mas amamas wantaim kago, wantaim moni.'

As far as he is concerned, I have just heard what the Big Men had said about him, what they told us, they said the following: 'All witchcraft and lime used for witchcraft and the ginger used for witchcraft, get rid of it! You may not do that any more and kill people without reason.' Well, he sent his soldiers, sent his boys, and they dug in the houses ... of almost every family, they went looking inside the house and found whatever was there, they took it, threw it into the sea, well, because at this meeting of his he said the following, at this meeting: 'You may not, we may not try hard to work, we may not plant these coconut palms, coconut palms are food for cockatoos and the feathers and all kinds of birds, they will eat these coconut palms, there is not a single thing that comes from coconut palms.'

That's what he said, Lima said that, that was his meeting ... 'You will just give an order, something has to emerge. Well, you clean up everything within ... the village, everything has to, there will be no killing of people and there will be no witchcraft, you have to behave properly and think of Christianity, OK, and you can become like, and whatever is in your mouth, you must remove it completely, all the witchcraft, you must remove it completely, you may not keep it' ... he said that later orders would be sent to Rabaul and goods would be brought here ... we ourselves have to pay taxes, collect the money and give it to him, he has to order the goods to come here ... 'The bit of money you have, you have to give it away completely ... you have to be happy with the goods, with the money.'

Glossary

Nakanai

My transcription of Nakanai mostly follows the word lists of Chowning (n.d.) and Johnston (1980a: 281–92, 1980b: 144–51).

Atetu   Mean, egoistical

Kuruloto   Collection of materials for making masks

Lalomaloma   Place for making masks
Lamahela   Shame
Latilogo   Respect

Pupu   Grandparent in the female line, grandchild in the female line

Saveilevaluku   Spirits of the *valuku*
Sibi   Performance of masked dances, performing masked dances

Tahalolorivo   Men from the bush, spirits

Valuku   Masks, masked dances
Valuku barabara   Evil *valuku*
Valuku bisisi   Small *valuku*
Valuku ururu   Big *valuku*
Valukulorivo   *Valuku* from the bush

Tok Pisin

My transcription of Tok Pisin mostly follows the dictionary of Mihailic (1971). Any deviations from this correspond to the way the inhabitants of Koimumu and neighbouring talk at present.

As	Core, origin
Bagarap	Exhausted, damaged
Belhat	Furious, fury
Bet	Litter
Bikhet	Disobedience, insubordination, stubbornness
Bisnis	Economic undertaking, clan
Bun nating	Small, insignificant
Council	Local government council
Daunim	To disparage someone
Dirty olgeta	Completely ruined
Galip	Canarium nut
Garamut	Slit gong
Giaman tingting	False thought, mendacious thought
Greedy	Mean, egotistical
Han	Hand
Hap tok	Part of teaching
Haus boi	Men's house
Haus kiap	Building erected for the colonial administration
Isi	Obliging, approachable, simple
Kago kalt	Cargo cult
Kaikai bilong koki	Food for cockatoos
Kaikai bilong kotkot	Food for crows
Kaikai bilong ples	Food from the village
Kaikai bilong stua	Food from the store
Kandere	Matrilateral relative
Kapa	Corrugated iron
Kapupu	To pass intestinal wind, fart
Kiap	Government officer
Kliarim	To explain something
Kok	Member, penis
Komiti	Committee member
Kotim	To bring someone before the court

Kros	Angry, dispute
Lain	Group, clan
Laplap	Waistcloth
Las ples	Last village (term with which the inhabitants of Koimumu refer to their own village)
Liklik wanshilling	A little bit of money
Longlong	Confused, mad
Lotu	The Christian religion, church building, participation in services
Lukatutim family	To take care of family life
Lus	Lost
Mak bilong rispekt	Sign of respect
Man	Man, human being
Man tru	Proper man
Manki bilong Koimumu	Boy from Koimumu
Marasin	Medicine
Marimari	Sympathy, compassion
Masalai	Bush spirit
Maus	Mouth
Mipela inap	We have got enough.
Moa yet	A lot
Muni	Money
Namba	Marking, rank, number
Nambatri	Number Three
Nambatu	Number Two
Nambawan	Number One
Narakain liklik	A little bit different
Narakain olgeta	Completely different
Nau tasol	Just now
Ovaim	Exaggeration
Papa	Father
Pasin	Usage, custom
Pasin pamuk	Sexual offence
Paua	Power
Paulim	To distort something, to confuse something
Paulim meri	To seduce women
Pinis nating	Ending just like that
Pispis	To urinate
Poisen	Witchcraft, sorcery
Pulim	To monopolise someone

Raskal	Young criminal
Raunim	To circle around something
Rausim	To remove something, to remove someone
Rispekt	Respect
Samsam	To dance, dance
Samting	Thing, something
Samting tru	Something correct, something real, something effective
Save	Knowledge, aptitude, habit
Sem	Shame, to be ashamed
Sindaun bilong mipela	Our way of life
Sindaun bilong waitman	Way of life of the whites
Singautim	To call for someone
Singsing	Celebration, feast
Sori	I am sorry
Stadi	To learn, to reflect on
Stap gut	To behave properly
Strongim	To encourage someone
Susu	Breast, breasts
Swit tru	Very tempting
Taim	Time
Taim nogut	Bad time
Takis	Taxes
Tambu	Materials for making shell money, prohibition, affinal relative
Tanim	To twist something, to distort something
Tavur	Triton's trumpet
Tingting nating	To believe something just like that (without a reason)
Tingting nogut	Bad thought
Tok baksait	To speak badly of someone
Tok ples	Vernacular language
Tokaut	To disclose, to put something into the open
Toktok	Expression, talk, teaching
Trikim	To deceive someone
Tuhat	Sweat
Tumbuan	Masks, masked dances
Waitman	White (white man), whites (white men)
Welmasta	Wild white man, wild white men
Wok	Work

References

Interviews and conversations

I have arranged this list of interviews and conversations first according to the names of the respective main informants, and then chronologically. For each interview, the following information is listed: place (the numbers refer to the 'List of houses in Koimumu'), the names of those who were also present apart from the main informants (as far as is known or can be reconstructed) and the form in which the contents of the interview or conversation were recorded.

Anonymous. 28 July 1996; Rapuri beach; Titus Mou; notes (taken afterwards).
Ave, Francis. 6 July 1997; house 90; notes (taken simultaneously).
———. 15 July 1997; Koimumu *lomaloma*; Emil Avra (temporarily), other men; notes (taken afterwards).
———. 29 July 1997; house 90; notes (taken simultaneously).
———. 30 July 1997; Koimumu *lomaloma*; Julius Bauba (temporarily), Chris Gar (temporarily), John Gepoa, Raymond Mare (temporarily), Kenneth Kautu (temporarily), Joe Sakim (temporarily), Leo Tokayu, other men; notes (taken simultaneously).
Bai, Ambrose. 26 June 1996; house 90; Joe Vilei (temporarily), two children (temporarily); notes (taken simultaneously), recording (partial) and transcription.
———. 30 July 1996; house 90; notes (taken simultaneously).
———. 28 May 1997; house 85; Joe Kaveu, John Kaveu, Barth Sesega, other men, several women and children (temporarily); notes (taken simultaneously), recording (complete) and transcription.
Batari, Ursula. 23 June 1996; house 22; John Bubu, Ignes Vavala; notes (taken afterwards).
Bobore, Tomuga. 28 July 1996; Rapuri beach; Titus Mou; notes (taken simultaneously).
Boko, Robert. 28 June 1996; house 90; notes (taken afterwards).
———. 8 June 1997; Guria beach; other men; notes (taken afterwards).
Bole, Carolyn. 30 May 1996; house 90; other women, several children; notes (taken afterwards).
Bubu, Christoph. 24 June 1996; house 90; notes (taken afterwards).
Bubu, John Marerego. 5 June 1996; house 90; Ursula Batari; notes (taken afterwards).
———. 1 July 1996; house 22; Ursula Batari; notes (taken simultaneously).
———. 6 July 1997; house 5; Alphonse Mape, Hedwig Mape; notes (taken afterwards).
Dao, Andrew. 4 June 1996; house 90; Dominika Bauba; several children; notes (taken afterwards).
———. 16 June 1997; house 21; Dominika Bauba; several children; notes (taken afterwards).

Dimas, Angie. 29 April 1996; Papalaba guesthouse (Hoskins); Francis; notes (taken afterwards).

Dodo, Sophia. 19 July 1996; house 90; notes (taken afterwards).

Dumu, Antonia. 15 May 1997; house 16; other women; notes (taken afterwards).

Empen, P. Norbert. 22 July 2003; Missionaries of the Sacred Heart assembly room (Hiltrup); notes (taken afterwards).

Eppmann, P. Klaus. 19 April 1996; Klaus Eppmann's house (Valoka); notes (taken simultaneously).

———. 9 August 1997; Klaus Eppmann's house (Valoka); notes (taken simultaneously).

Gar, Ludwig Tautele. 18 April 1997; Guria beach; notes (taken afterwards).

———. 29 April 1997; house 90; notes (taken simultaneously).

Gar, Martin. 31 May 1997; Rapuri beach; Francis Ave, Joe Gar, Paul Gar, Michael Labu, Otto Puli, Joe Sogi, Lucas Viloa, other men; notes (taken simultaneously).

Gar, Paul. 24 May 1996; new school building; Leo Mape (temporarily), Peter Mape (temporarily), Joe Sogi; notes (taken simultaneously).

———. 18 June 1996; house 90; notes (taken simultaneously).

———. 7 August 1996; house 70; a relative of Paul Gar's from Tarobi, several women and children; notes (taken simultaneously), recording (complete) and transcription.

———. 11 August 1996; house 70; Emil Avra Gar (temporarily), Hedwig Bai Bauba; notes (taken afterwards).

———. 27 August 1996; house 70; notes (taken simultaneously).

———. 18 September 1997; Cosmas Gar's house (Port Moresby); Cosmas Gar, Maternus Gelu Mape, Janet Pue, several women and children; notes (taken simultaneously), recording (complete) and transcription.

Geloa, Pius. 31 August 1997; house 26; Roy Mou, Muimui Nenamur, Simon Taukibe, several women and children; notes (taken afterwards).

Gelu, Vincent. 22 April 1997; Vincent Gelu's store (opposite house 79.); two women; notes (taken afterwards).

Golumu, Fred. 26 May 1996; Fred Golumu's house (Tagaragara); Joe Sogi; notes (taken simultaneously).

———. 21 July 1996; Tagaragara beach; Titus Mou, other men, several women (temporarily); notes (taken simultaneously), recording (partial) and transcription.

Goodenough, Ward H. 30 November 2001; University of Pennsylvania Museum Archives (Philadelphia); Alex Pezzati; notes (taken simultaneously), recording (complete) and transcription.

Guvi, Leo. 9 July 1997; Makasili *lomaloma*; Caspar Biku, John Kaore, Ben Kautu, Benedikt Kavoa, John Mataligi, David Puso, Phidelius Puso, Lucas Viola, other men; notes (taken afterwards).

Hartmann, P. Alois. 7 July 1996; Alois Hartmann's house (Vavua); notes (taken afterwards).

———. 19 April 1997; Alois Hartmann's house (Vavua); notes (taken simultaneously), recording (partial) and transcription.

Ilo, Joe. 19 June 1996; house 48; Paul Gar; notes (taken simultaneously), recording (partial) and transcription.

———. 8 May 1997; house 48; Albert Garoka, Mathilda Ragi; notes (taken afterwards).

———. 26 May 1997; house 48; Albert Garoka, several women; notes (taken simultaneously), recording (partial) and transcription.

———. 4 September 1997; house 48; Michael Vavala; notes (taken simultaneously), recording (partial) and transcription.

Kaue, Regina. 18 August 1996; path through Koimumu; Michael Maito; notes (taken afterwards).

———. 26 May 1997; house 47; Michael Maito, Peter Mape (temporarily); notes (taken afterwards).

Kautu, Camillus. 21 July 1996; house 90; one woman and one child; notes (taken afterwards).

————. 24 August 1996; Koimumu *lomaloma*; John Bubu, Paul Gar, Fred Golumu, Joe Kaveu, Alphonse Mape, Peter Mape, Otto Puli, Joe Sogi; notes (taken simultaneously).
Kautu, Michael. 14 June 1997; Guria beach; other men; notes (taken afterwards).
Kaveu, Joe. 16 June 1996; house 85; Gertrud Waba; notes (taken afterwards).
Kikei, John. 16 August 1996; house 90; notes (taken afterwards).
Laili, Henry. 1 June 1996; Henry Laili's house (Rapuri); Marcus Valentine; notes (taken simultaneously).
Loko. 26 July 1996; Loko's house (Galilo); Titus Mou, other men; notes (taken simultaneously), recording (complete) and transcription.
Lowa, Albert. 5 June 1996; house 4; notes (taken afterwards).
————. 26 June 1996; house 4; Augustin Bauba (temporarily), Theodora Kalapoe; notes (taken simultaneously).
————. 16 June 1997; house 4; Leonie Boige, Anselma Mape, several women and children; notes (taken afterwards).
————. 19 August 1997; house 4; Philibert Mape; notes (taken afterwards).
Maito, Michael. 6 May 1997; house 47; Regina Kaue, Joe Tali; notes (taken afterwards).
Mape, Alphonse Ipa. 22 May 1996; new school building; Joe Sogi, other men; notes (taken afterwards).
————. 28 June 1996; house 5; other men, several women; notes (taken afterwards).
————. 13 July 1996; Lakuba assembly place; notes (taken afterwards).
————. 14 July 1996; house 5; Herrmann Mape, Otto Mape, Sabina Mape; notes (taken simultaneously).
————. 20 July 1996; trip to Rapuri; notes (taken afterwards).
————. 27 July 1996; house 90; notes (taken simultaneously).
————. 9 August 1996; house 90; notes (taken simultaneously), recording (partial) and transcription.
————. 1 April 1997; Kimbe; notes (taken afterwards).
————. 5 April 1997; Guria beach; other men; notes (taken afterwards).
————. 12 April 1997; trip from Kimbe to Gavui; Hedwig Mape, several women; notes (taken afterwards).
————. 22 May 1997; Guria *haus boi*; other men; notes (taken afterwards).
————. 19 July 1997; Port Moresby; one man; notes (taken afterwards).
Mape, Dominique. 13 April 1997; house 12; Leo Mape (temporarily), Michael Taumosi; notes (taken afterwards).
————. 22 June 1997; Guria beach; notes (taken afterwards).
————. 26 June 1997; house 5; Alphonse Mape; notes (taken afterwards).
Mape, Hedwig Tavilalili. 15 June 1997; house 5; notes (taken afterwards).
Mape, Hermann. 15 August 1996; Koimumu area; Christoph Bubu, Boas Mera, other men; notes (taken afterwards).
————. 1 April 1997; house 5; Hedwig Mape, Leo Mape, Peter Mape, Simon Mape, other men; notes (taken afterwards).
————. 1 May 1997; house 2; Otto Mape; notes (taken afterwards).
————. 9 June 1997; house 2; Peter Mape (temporarily), Justin Tiale Misile, one woman; notes (taken afterwards).
Mape, Leo Kalakulu. 20 July 1996; house 90; Paul Bubu, Bertha Vitolo; notes (taken afterwards).
Mape, Maternus Gelu. 17 September 1997; Australian National University guest house (Port Moresby); notes (taken afterwards).
Mape, Otto Valuku. 30 May 1996. house 1; notes (taken simultaneously).
————. 14 June 1996; house 90; Barth Sesega (temporarily); notes (taken afterwards).
————. 19 August 1996; house 1; one young man (temporarily), several women (temporarily); notes (taken simultaneously).
————. 22 August 1996; house 21; Andrew Dao, Domenika Bauba, several children; notes (taken afterwards).

———. 17 April 1997; house 40; other men, several women and children; notes (taken simultaneously).

Mape, Peter. 24 May 1996; new school building; Paul Gar, Leo Mape, Joe Sogi; notes (taken simultaneously).

———. 4 June 1996; new school building; Hermann Mape, Simon Mape; notes (taken simultaneously).

———. 20 June 1996; house 90; notes (taken afterwards).

———. 30 June 1996; Guria *haus boi*; Andrew Dao (temporarily), Paul Gar, Joe Sogi, George Tautigi, other men; notes (taken simultaneously).

———. 7 July 1996; Guria beach; John Bubu (temporarily), Andrew Dao (temporarily), Alphonse Mape, Joe Sogi (temporarily), other men; notes (taken simultaneously).

———. 23 July 1996; house 90; Philibert Mape (temporarily); notes (taken afterwards).

———. 19 May 1997; house 5; Francis Pakela; notes (taken afterwards).

———. 14 June 1997; Guria beach; John Bubu, Paul Gar, Pius Geloa, Michael Labu (temporarily), Bernhard Lome, Zacharias Malaga, Alphonse Mape (temporarily), Otto Mape, Thomas Paliavu, Jack Pigia, Thomas Sauli, Joe Sogi, Peter Tautigi, Joe Vilei (temporarily); notes (taken simultaneously).

———. 16 September 1997; house 5; Francis Ave, Alphonse Mape, Simon Mape, Peter Tautigi; notes (taken afterwards).

Mape, Philibert Batili. 5 July 1996; house 90; several children; notes (taken afterwards).

Mape, Sabina. 28 May 1996; Kimbe; notes (taken afterwards).

Mataligi, John. 10 July 1997; Makasili *lomaloma*; Ludwig Gar, John Kaore, Stephen Lima, Augustin Sande, Joe Togato, Otto Puli, David Puso, Thomas Puso, Lucas Viola, other men; notes (taken simultaneously), recording (partial) and transcription.

Mongi, Greg. 18 April 1996; Greg Mongi's office (Kimbe); John Glengme (temporarily), Angie Dimas (temporarily); notes (taken afterwards).

Mou, Francis. 12 June 1996; house 90; notes (taken afterwards).

———. 20 June 1996; house 74; notes (taken afterwards).

———. 5 July 1996; house 74; Jack Koro, several children; notes (taken simultaneously), recording (partial) and transcription.

Mou, Roy. 3 June 1996; house 90; Josepha Gar, several children; notes (taken afterwards).

———. 22 June 1996; house 23; notes (taken afterwards).

Mou, Titus. 28 June 1996; trip from Koimumu to Kimbe and back; Joe Kaveu, Alphonse Mape; notes (taken afterwards).

———. 4 July 1996; house 90; Alphonse Mape; notes (taken simultaneously), recording (partial) and transcription.

———. 22 July 1996; Titus Mou's house (Rapuri); other men; notes (taken afterwards).

———. 1 June 1997; Guria beach; John Bubu, Paul Gar, Joe Ilo, Bernhard Lome, Alphonse Mape, Peter Mape, Joe Vilei; notes (taken simultaneously).

Olpitarea, Lawrence. 27 May 1996; school office; notes (taken afterwards).

———. 6 June 1996; school office; notes (taken afterwards).

———. 8 June 1996; school office; notes (taken afterwards).

Olpitarea, Leoba. 30 May 1996; school office; notes (taken afterwards).

———. 18 July 1996; house 90; notes (taken afterwards).

———. 10 August 1996; school office; Lawrence Olpitarea; notes (taken afterwards).

———. 6 September 1997; trip from Koimumu to Kimbe; Alphonse Mape, Hedwig Mape, other women; notes (taken afterwards).

Paga, Pius. 26 April 1997; house 82; several women and children; notes (taken afterwards).

Paliavu, Francisca. 17 June 1996; house 28; notes (taken afterwards).

Puli, Otto. 21 July 1996; Rapuri beach; Martin Gar, Titus Mou, Tomuga Bobore (temporarily), other men; notes (taken simultaneously), recording (complete) and transcription.

———. 8 June 1997; Vavua church grounds; Martin Gar, other men, several women and children; notes (taken afterwards).

———. 21 June 1997; Vavua *lomaloma*; Lucas Boko, Martin Gar, Joachim Magelau, Phidelius Makokovu, Titus Mou (temporarily), Thomas, Ragi, Augustin Sande, Henry

Sesega, Gabriel Tagai (temporarily), Lucas Viola (temporarily); notes (taken simultaneously).

Sakim, Joe. 1 August 1996; house 90; notes (taken afterwards).

Sande, Augustin. 19 June 1997; Vavua *lomaloma*; other men; notes (taken simultaneously).

————. 22 June 1997; Vavua *haus boi*; Titus Mou, other men; notes (taken simultaneously), recording (partial) and transcription.

Sarere, Peter. 6 June 1997; Peter Sarere's house (Vavua); one man (temporarily), one woman (temporarily), several children (temporarily); notes (taken simultaneously), recording (partial) and transcription.

Sesega, Barth Umari. 19 July 1996; Gabriel Kaiwa's house (Rapuri); other men, several women; notes (taken afterwards).

————. 27 May 1997a; house 87; Petra Magea; notes (taken afterwards).

————. 27 May 1997b; house 36; John Kaveu, Kaose; several women; notes (taken afterwards).

Sogi, Joe Babo. 26 May 1996; house 90; two children; notes (taken afterwards).

————. 6 June 1996; house 90; notes (taken simultaneously).

————. 27 June 1996; path from Kapeuru to Koimumu; notes (taken afterwards).

————. 9 July 1996; house 31; notes (taken afterwards).

Tautigi, George Labu. 3 May 1996; Tailabolo assembly place; other men; notes (taken afterwards).

————. 2 June 1996; Guria beach; Alphonse Mape, Leo Mape, Peter Mape, Simon Mape, two men; notes (taken afterwards).

————. 29 June 1996; house 41; Cecilia Sugupolo, Joe Sogi (temporarily), several children; notes (taken afterwards).

————. 6 April 1997; house 41; Cecilia Sugupolo, Joe Kaveu, several women and children; notes (taken afterwards).

————. 13 June 1997; Guria beach; Pius Kua, Philibert Mape, Thomas Paliavu, Carol Taukomo; notes (taken simultaneously).

Tautigi, Peter. 2 September 1997; house 36; Michael Kautu (temporarily), one woman (temporarily), several children (temporarily); notes (taken simultaneously), recording (complete) and transcription.

Tauvato, Casimir. 11 June 1996; house 90; notes (taken afterwards).

Thomas, Gerry. 18 April 1996; Gerry Thomas's house (at Walindi's house); notes (taken afterwards).

Tomarum. 16 May 1997; house 90; John Kikei, one man; notes (taken afterwards).

Tubu, Thaddäus. 23 August 1997; Makasili *lomaloma*; other men; notes (taken simultaneously).

————. 27 August 1997; Karapi beach; Martin Laliso (temporarily), several children (temporarily); notes (taken simultaneously).

Varago. 26 July 1996; Varago's house (Galilo); Titus Mou, a man (temporarily), a woman (temporarily), several children (temporarily); notes (taken simultaneously), recording (complete) and transcription.

Vavala, Michael. 21 August 1996; house 30; one child; notes (taken afterwards).

Vilei, Joe. 3 April 1997; house 90; Sophia Dodo; notes (taken afterwards).

————. 9 May 1997; house 48; Joe Ilo; several women and children; notes (taken afterwards).

Archive material

Letters and email

Brinkmann, Fr. N. 29 August 1986, *Letter to Fr. Alfred Völler*, Münster, Archives of the Missionaries of the Sacred Heart, File '1985–1988'.

Goodenough, W.H. 1 February 2003, *Email to Holger Jebens*, Frankfurt am Main, Archives of Holger Jebens (HJ).

Limburg, Fr. H. 18 May 2004, *Letter to Holger Jebens*, HJ.

Schwartz, T. 20 February 1997, *Letter to Holger Jebens*, HJ.

Schweiger, Fr. S. 2 November 1947, *Letter to his Bishop*, Rabaul, Archives of the Archdiocese Rabaul, File '221 Valoka (1)', roll 59/60 (AR 1).

———. 5 December 1948, *Letter to his Bishop*, AR 1.

Stamm, Fr. J. 29 May 1922, *Letter to Father Lakaff*, Rabaul, Archives of the Archdiocese Rabaul, File '222 Valoka (2)', roll 61/62 (AR 2).

Valentine, B. 11 March 2003, *Letter to Holger Jebens*, HJ.

———. 2 October 2004, *Letter to Holger Jebens*, HJ.

Valentine, C.A. 31 March 1954, *Letter to Ward H. Goodenough*, Philadelphia, University of Pennsylvania Museum Archives, Lakalai (West Nakanai) 1954, File 'Nakanai–Miscellaneous' (UP N).

———. 23 February 1956, *Letter to Ward H. Goodenough*, UP N.

———. 24 August 1959, *Letter to Ward H. Goodenough*, HJ.

———. 8 November 1959, *Letter to Ward H. Goodenough*, HJ.

———. n.d., *Letter to his parents, Jess and Charles Valentine*, HJ.

Zwinge, P. 15 October 1923, *Letter to his Bishop*, AR 2.

Field notes

Chowning, A. (AC) 31 May 1954, [No title], Philadelphia, University of Pennsylvania Museum Archives, Lakalai (West Nakanai) 1954, File '64 State' (UP 64).

———. 5 August 1954, [No title], Philadelphia, University of Pennsylvania Museum Archives, Lakalai (West Nakanai) 1954, File '79 Ecclesiastical organization' (UP 79).

Goodenough, W.H. (WHG) 13 May 1954, [No title], Philadelphia, University of Pennsylvania Museum Archives, Lakalai (West Nakanai) 1954, File '78 Religious practices' (UP 78).

———. 19 May 1954, [No title], UP 79.

Valentine, C.A. (CV) 16 May 1954, [No title], UP 79.

———. 7 June 1954, [No title], UP 79.

———. 8 June 1954, [No title], UP 79.

———. 11 June 1954, [No title], UP 79.

———. 14 June 1954, [No title], UP 79.

———. 22 June 1954, [No title], Philadelphia, University of Pennsylvania Museum Archives, Lakalai (West Nakanai) 1954, File '72 War' (UP 72).

———. 17 July 1954, *Kivung at our house*, UP 79

———. 20 July 1954, *Kivung and Kabani at Banule: 'last day' movement among Bakovi*, UP 79.

———. 23 July 1954, *Discussion of Kabani policy*, UP 79.

———. 27 July 1954, *Confession and the personalities of the two Fathers*, UP 79.

———. 29 July 1954, *Masta Hitla (continued)*, UP 79.

———. 5 August 1954, *Masta Hitla (continued)*, UP 79.

———. 8 August 1954a, *The mysterious masta at Vunapope & elsewhere*, UP 79.

———. 8 August 1954b, *Contact with Americans at Malalia*, UP 79.

———. 9 August 1954, *Masta Hitla (continued) and subsequent developments (Batari)*, UP 79.

———. 12 August 1954, *The Kivung and Kabani*, UP 79.

———. 13 August 1954a, *Lima's life history continued, beginning the movement*, UP 79.

———. 13 August 1954b, *First arrival of white men and other stories*, Philadelphia, University of Pennsylvania Museum Archives, Lakalai (West Nakanai) 1954, File '66 Political behaviour' (UP 66).

———. 13 August 1954c, *The ship of the ancestors: a story told by Batili of the time when he was young*, UP 66.

———. 14 August 1954a, *More about Batari's movement*, UP 79.

———. 14 August 1954b, *First Europeans, origins of things, etc.*, UP 79.

———. 16 August 1954, [No title], UP 79.

———. 17 August 1954a, *Toktok bilong wanpela masta*, UP 79.

———. 17 August 1954b, *Present Kivung-Kabani*, UP 79.

———. 17 August 1954c, *Pago eruption, rival missions, myths of origin of cargo*, UP 79.

———. 17 August 1954d, *Romo and the Maleo*, UP 79.

———. 18 August 1954, *Pasin blong Astrelia na pasin blong Amerika*, UP 79.

———. 19 August 1954, *A totemistic (?) cargo movement and sequelae involving Batari's and Lima's movements*, UP 79.

———. 20 August 1954a, *The Kivung and Kabani*, UP 79.

———. 20 August 1954b, *The Batili myth as told by Boko's Father and how it was confirmed by the coming of the Europeans and Americans; identification of Europeans and Americans with the ancestors*, UP 79.

———. 21 August 1954a, *Mamare and I talk about getting information about the Kivung*, UP 79.

———. 21 August 1954b, *Cooperative Kivung in Central Nakanai*, UP 79.

———. 22 August 1954, *Lima tells all (?) about the Kivung and Kabani*, UP 79.

———. 23 August 1954a, *Lima tells all (?) (continued)*, UP 79.

———. 23 August 1954b, *A school on the talk of the big kivungs*, UP 79.

———. 27 August 1954a, *Kampani leaders gather to discuss coming of Americans with Lima and review some of the talks Fr. B has given them*, UP 79.

———. 27 August 1954b, *The dead & the origin of cargo*, UP 79.

———. 31 August 1954a, *Americans and natives in wartime*, UP 79.

———. 31 August 1954b, *Morning kivung in the haus kanu*, UP 79.

———. 1 September 1954a, *Deo-Sivava, the true lotu of the tubuna, the loss, the withholding [sic], and the return in the disguised tok-piksa form of Christianity*, UP 79.

———. 1 September 1954b, *Germans, Americans, Australians, and cargo*, UP 79.

———. 3 September 1954, *Americans and Australians talk at Talasea*, UP 79.

———. 5 September 1954, *Complains [sic] against Australians*, UP 79.

———. 7 September 1954, *The talk against Ragi, Fr. B. talks to Golumu, a Kivung, and distribution of the food which came on the Matoko*, UP 79.

———. 9 September 1954, *Select Kivung at Gavuvu*, UP 79.

———. 11 September 1954a, *A catalogue of Berger's giaman, introduced by grievances against Maynard; the coming, return of the dead, cargo made by the dead, e Suara, etc.*, UP 79.

———. 11 September 1954b, *More of the Father's doctrine: care of the matmats to please the dead, Patima, the big masta who stops all cargo, Fr. B. boasts of this wisdom, etc*, UP 79.

———. 12 September 1954a, *Cargo brought by the dead to pre-war Manus*, UP 79.

———. 12 September 1954b, *Sunday sermon by Munzlinger*, UP 79.

———. 14 September 1954, *I recommend the expulsion of Fr. Berger*, UP 79.

———. 15 September 1954, *Circumstances surrounding my talk about the Father*, UP 79.

———. 19 September 1954a, *Another fracas with Berger*, UP 79.

———. 19 September 1954b, *Paliau schooled in Rabaul by Masta Hitla and inspired by another German agitator, though he began with his own tingting*, UP 79.

———. 24 September 1954, *Who went with Berger to make court at Talasea and some of the methods of intimidation Berger is using to keep people away from me*, UP 79.

———. 27 September 1954, *Further methods of intimidation; I send out copies of Ward's talk*, UP 79.

————. 1 October 1954, *Lima bans the mankis from coming to our house*, UP 79.

————. 4 October 1954, *Berger's latest reactions of my campaign: more liew [sic] about me, threats, talks of reorganizing the Kivung*, UP 79.

————. 5 October 1954, *Rumblings within the Kivung*, UP 79.

————. 6 October 1954, [No title], UP 79.

————. 8 October 1954, *Reign of terror*, UP 79.

————. 16 October 1954, *Foley comes to Rapuri*, UP 79.

————. 21 October 1954, *Aftermath of the affair with Berger*, UP 79.

————. 24 October 1954, [No title], UP 79.

Valentine, E. (EV) 6 September 1954, [No title], UP 79.

Patrol reports

Patrol Report Hoskins (PRH). 1965/66-2, R. Allmark, West Nakanai, National Archives of Papua New Guinea (NA).

————. 1967/68-15, R. Tobia, West Nakanai Census Division, NA.

Patrol Report N (PRN). 1929-N/60/29, P.M. Penhalluriack, 'Report of a patrol to certain villages in East Nakanai' (31 October 1929), Pacific Manuscripts Bureau (PMB) 631.

Patrol Report Talasea (PRT). 1944/45-K2, J.K. White, West Nakanai Sub-Division (4 November 1944), NA.

————. 1952/53-7, E.S. Sharp, West Nakanai Sub-Division (25 February 1953), NA.

————. 1954/55-11, S.M. Foley, West Nakanai Sub-Division, NA.

————. 1956/57-6, P.F. Sebise, West Nakanai, NA.

————. 1961/62-11, C.S. Booth, West Nakanai Census Division (17 February 1962), NA.

Patrol Report Y (PRY) 1927-8, I.M Mack, West Nakanai, 27 August – 6 September 1927 (6 September 1927), PMB 1036.

Other sources

Allan, C.H. 1951, 'Marching rule: a nativistic cult of the British Solomon Islands', *Corona* 3: 93–100.

Allen, B.J. 1976, 'Information flow and innovation diffusion in the East Sepik District, Papua New Guinea' (Ph.D. diss., Australian National University).

Anonymous. 1904a, 'Bluttat auf Neupommern', *Deutsche Kolonialzeitung* 21(37): 371 (15 September 1904).

————. 1904b, 'Die Ermordung der Missionare in den Bainingbergen', *Deutsche Kolonialzeitung* 21(39): 388–89 (29 September 1904).

————. 1904c, 'Deutsch-Neu-Guinea', *Deutsches Kolonialblatt* 22: 667–69 (1 November 1904).

————. 1904d, 'Deutsch-Neu-Guinea', *Deutsches Kolonialblatt* 23: 705 (15 November 1904).

————. 1904e, 'Aus dem Bismarck-Archipel', *Deutsche Kolonialzeitung* 21(46): 458 (17 November 1904).

Arndt, S. 2002, *Weiß-Sein als Konstruktion des Rassimus und Kategorie*, http: //www2.hu-berlin.de/ffz/pdf-files/arndt.pdf [accessed 14 June 2005].

Assmann, A. 1991, 'Zur Metaphorik der Erinnerung', in *Mnemosyne: Formen und Funktionen der kulturellen Erinnerung*, eds A. Assmann and D. Harth, Frankfurt am Main, 13–35.

————. 1998, *Erinnerungsräume: Formen und Wandlungen des kulturellen Gedächtnisses*. Munich.

————. 2004, 'Zur Mediengeschichte des kulturellen Gedächtnisses', in *Medien des kollektiven Gedächtnisses: Konstruktivität – Historizität – Kulturspezifizität* (Media and Cultural Memory 1), eds A. Erll and A. Nünning, Berlin, 45–60.

Assmann, J. 1988, 'Kollektives Gedächtnis und kulturelle Identität', in *Kultur und Gedächtnis*, eds J. Assmann and T. Hölscher, Frankfurt am Main, 9–19.

————. 1991, 'Die Katastrophe des Vergessens: das Deuteronomium als Paradigma kultureller Mnemotechnik', in *Mnemosyne: Formen und Funktionen der kulturellen Erinnerung*, eds A. Assmann and D. Harth, Frankfurt am Main, 337–55.

————. 2000, *Das kulturelle Gedächtnis: Schrift, Erinnerung und politische Identität in frühen Hochkulturen*. Munich (orig. 1992).

————. 2004, 'Von Haus aus unzuverlässig. Johannes Fried erklärt das Erinnerungsvermögen aus einem Wechselspiel von Kultur und Gehirn', *Frankfurter Rundschau* 6 October 2004.

Bashkow, I. 1999, '"Whitemen" in the moral world of Orokaiva of Papua New Guinea' (Ph.D. diss., University of Chicago).

————. 2000, '"Whitemen" are good to think with: how Orokaiva morality is reflected on whitemen's skin', in 'Whiteness in the field', ed. J. Hartigan, *Identities* 7(3): 281–332.

————. 2006, *The meaning of whitemen: race and modernity in the Orokaiva cultural world*. Chicago.

Belshaw, C.S. 1950, 'The significance of modern cults in Melanesian development', *Australian Outlook* 4(2): 116–25.

Benjamin, C. 1977, 'Implications of further cash cropping on the settlement blocks of the Hoskins Oil Palm Scheme', in *Agriculture in the tropics: papers delivered at the tenth Waigani seminar*, eds B.A.C. Enyi and T. Yarghese, Waigani, 46–53.

————. 1985, 'Some food market influences of a large-scale small-holder development in the West New Britain area of Papua New Guinea', *Papua New Guinea Journal of Agriculture, Forestry and Fisheries* 33(3/4): 133–41.

Biermann, P.F. and P.H. Pittruff, eds. 1997, *Hundert Jahre Missionshaus Hiltrup und Deutsche Provinz der Herz-Jesu-Missionare: Dokumentation 1897–1997.* Münster.

Bley, P.B. 1925, *Die Herz Jesu-Mission in der Südsee: Geschichtliche Skizze über das Apostolische Vikariat Rabaul*. Hiltrup.

Bodrogi, T. 1951, 'Colonization and religious movements in Melanesia', *Acta Ethnographica Academiae Hungaricae* 3: 259–92.

Borsboom, A. and T. Otto. 1997, 'Introduction: transformation and tradition in Oceanic religions', in *Cultural dynamics of religious change in Oceania* (Verhandelingen van het Koninklijk Instituut voor Taal-, Land- en Volkenkunde 176), eds T. Otto and A. Borsboom, Leiden, 1–9.

Brown, M. 1996, 'On resisting resistance', *American Anthropologist* 98(4): 729–35.

Bubandt, N. 2004, 'Violence and millenarian modernity in Eastern Indonesia', in *Cargo, cult, and culture critique*, ed. H. Jebens, Honolulu, 92–116.

Burgmann, A. 1961, 'L. Bischofs Vokabulare der Ubili-Sprache (Neubritannien)', *Anthropos* 56(5/6): 930–33.

Burridge, K.O.L. 1960, *Mambu: a Melanesian millennium*. London.

Butzer, G. and M. Günter, eds. 2004, *Kulturelles Vergessen: Medien – Rituale – Orte* (Formen der Erinnerung 21). Göttingen.

Cancik, H. and H. Mohr. 1990, 'Erinnerung/Gedächtnis', in *Handbuch religionswissenschaftlicher Grundbegriffe*, vol. 2, eds H. Cancik, B. Gladigow and M. Laubscher, Stuttgart, 299–323.

Carlson, A.R. 1970, *German foreign policy, 1890–1914, and colonial policy to 1914: a handbook and annotated bibliography*. Metuchen, NJ.

Chinnery, E.W.P. and A.C. Haddon. 1917, 'Five new religious cults in British New Guinea', *The Hibbert Journal* 15(3): 448–63.

Chowning, A. 1958, 'Lakalai society' (Ph.D. diss., University of Pennsylvania).

————. 1965/66, 'Lakalai kinship', *Anthropological Forum* 1(3/4): 476–501.

————. 1983, 'Inspiration and convention in Lakalai paintings', in *Art and artists of Oceania*, eds S. Mead and B. Kernot, Palmerston, 91–104.

———. n.d., 'West Nakanai vocabulary', MS.

Chowning, A. and W.H. Goodenough. 1965/66, 'Lakalai political organization', *Anthropological Forum* 1(3/4): 412–73.

Clifford, J. 1997, 'A ghost among Melanesians', in J. Clifford, *Routes: travel and translation in the late twentieth century*, Cambridge, 47–51.

Corris, P. 1973, *Passage, port and plantation: a history of Solomon Islands labour migration 1870–1914*. Carlton.

Counts, D. 1989, 'Shadows of war: changing remembrance through twenty years in New Britain', in *The Pacific theater: island representations of World War II* (Pacific Islands Monograph Series 8), eds G.M. White and L. Lindstrom, Honolulu, 187–203.

Counts, D. and D.A. Counts. 1976, 'Apprehension in the backwaters', *Oceania* 46(4): 283–305.

Counts, D.A. 1972, 'The Kaliai and The Story: development and frustration in New Britain', *Human Organization* 31: 373–83.

———. 1978, 'Christianity in Kaliai: response to missionization in Northwest New Britain', in *Mission, church and sect in Oceania* (ASAO Monographs 6), eds J.A. Boutilier, D.T. Hughes and S.W. Tiffany, Lanham, 355–94.

Counts, D.A. and D. Counts. 2000, Book review 'A. Lattas: *Cultures of secrecy*, Madison 1998', *Paideuma* 56: 323–29.

Crowley, T. 2001, 'Language, culture, history and the fieldworker: what I did on my Christmas holidays on Malakula (Vanuatu)', *Anthropological Forum* 11(2): 195–215.

Dahmen, P.J. 1955, 'P. Dahmen berichtet von seiner Fahrt zur Nordküste von New Britain (13.–30. Juni)', *Chronik der Norddeutschen Provinz* 46: 6.

Dalton, D. 2000a, 'Cargo cults and discursive madness', in A critical retrospective on 'Cargo Cult': Western/Melanesian intersections, ed. D. Dalton, *Oceania* 70(4): 345–61.

———. 2004, 'Cargo and cult: the mimetic critique of capitalist culture', in *Cargo, cult, and culture critique*, ed. H. Jebens, Honolulu, 187–208.

———. ed. 2000b, 'A critical retrospective on "cargo cult": Western/Melanesian intersections', *Oceania* 70(4).

Dark, P. 2001, 'Kilenge aesthetics in art and ceremony', MS.

Devereux, G. 1967, *From anxiety to method in the behavioral sciences*. The Hague.

Dexter, D. 1968, *The New Guinea offensives* (Australia in the war of 1939–1945. Series 1.VI). Canberra (orig. 1961).

Dicks, P.J. 1905, 'Zu der Mordtat von St. Paul', *Monatshefte zu Ehren Unserer Lieben Frau vom hlst. Herzen Jesu* 22(March): 111–14.

Dunn, Sr. M., ed. 2004, 'Centenary of "martyrdom" at St. Paul's: remembering the historical event and reflecting afresh', MS.

Ealel, E.H.M. 1984, *West Nakanai (Kimbe) oil palm scheme* (Environmental Reports 20). Melbourne

Eckert, G. 1937, 'Prophetentum in Melanesien', *Zeitschrift für Ethnologie* 69: 632–33.

———. 1940, 'Prophetentum und Kulturwandel in Melanesien', *Baessler Archiv* 23: 26–41.

Editions du Signe ed. 1999, *Gottes Herz in der Welt: Missionsschwestern vom heiligsten Herzen Jesu von Hiltrup 1900–2000*. Strasburg.

Epstein, A.L. 1998, 'Tubuan: the survival of the male cult among the Tolai', *Journal of Ritual Studies* 12(2): 15–28.

Erll, A. 2004, *Kollektives Gedächtnis und Erinnerungskulturen: eine Einführung*. Stuttgart.

Esposito, E. 2002, *Soziales Vergessen: Formen und Medien des Gedächtnisses der Gesellschaft*. Frankfurt.

F.D. 1904, 'Eine Trauerbotschaft aus der Südsee-Mission', *Monatshefte zu Ehren Unserer Lieben Frau vom hlst. Herzen Jesu* 21(October): 447–54.

Fajans, J. 1985, 'They make themselves: life cycle, domestic cycle and ritual among the Baining' (Ph.D. diss., Stanford University).

Feldt, E. 1946, *The coast watchers*. Melbourne.

Firth, S. 1973, 'German firms in the Western Pacific Islands, 1857–1914', *The Journal of Pacific History* 8: 10–28.

————. 1978, 'Captain Hernsheim: Pacific venturer, merchant prince', in *More Pacific Islands portraits*, ed. D. Scarr, Canberra, 115–30.

————. 1982, *New Guinea under the Germans*. Carlton.

————. 1985, 'German New Guinea: the archival perspective', *The Journal of Pacific History* 20(2): 94–103.

Fischer, H. 1981, *Die Hamburger Südsee-Expedition: Über Ethnographie und Kolonialismus*. Frankfurt.

Fortune, R.F. 1932, *Sorcerers of Dobu: the social anthropology of the Dobu islanders of the Western Pacific*. London.

Franke, P.B. 1982, 'Mein Leben: geschrieben von P. Joseph Reischl', MS.

Fried, J. 2004, *Der Schleier der Erinnerung: Grundzüge einer historischen Memorik*. Munich.

Friederici, G. 1912, *Wissenschaftliche Ergebnisse einer amtlichen Forschungsreise nach dem Bismarck-Archipel im Jahre 1908* (Ergänzungsheft Nr. 5 der Mitteilungen aus den Deutschen Schutzgebieten), vol. 2. Berlin.

Gardiner, M. 1984, *Footprints on Malekula: a memoir of Bernard Deacon*. Edinburgh.

Gilliam, A. 1990, 'Obituary Charles A. Valentine', *Anthropology Newsletter* 31(7): 5.

Goodenough, W.H. 1952, 'Ethnological reconnaissance in New Guinea', *The University Museum Bulletin* 17(1): 5–37.

————. 1954, 'Some observations on the Nakanai people', in *Annual Report and Proceedings 1954*, ed. Papua and New Guinea Scientific Society, Port Moresby, 39–45.

————. 1955, 'The pageant of death in Nakanai: a report of the 1954 expedition to New Britain', *The University Museum Bulletin* 19(1): 19–43.

————. 1962, 'Foreword', in D.R. Swindler, *A racial study of the West Nakanai* (Museum Monographs, New Britain Studies), Philadelphia, vii–viii.

————. 1965, 'Personal names and modes of address in two Oceanic societies', in *Context and meaning in cultural anthropology*, ed. M.E. Spiro, New York, 265–76.

Gosden, C. and C. Knowles. 2001, *Collecting colonialism: material culture and colonial change*. Oxford.

Gray, A.C. 1999, 'Trading contacts in the Bismarck Archipelago during the whaling era, 1799–1884', *The Journal of Pacific History* 34(1): 23–43.

Griffin, J., H. Nelson and S. Firth. 1979, *Papua New Guinea: a political history*. Richmond.

Gründer, H. 1995, *Geschichte der deutschen Kolonien*. Paderborn.

Guiart, J. 1951a, '"Cargo cults" and political evolution in Melanesia', *Mankind* 4(6): 227–29.

————. 1951b, 'Forerunners of Melanesian nationalism', *Oceania* 22(2): 81–90.

————. 1951c, 'John Frum movement in Tanna', *Oceania* 22: 165–75.

Haddon, A.C. 1934, 'Preface', in B. Deacon, *Malekula: a vanishing people in the New Hebrides*, ed. C.H. Wedgwood, London, xiii–xxix.

Hanson, A. 1989, 'The making of the Maori: culture invention and its logic', *American Anthropologist* 91(4): 890–902.

Harding, T. 1967, 'A history of cargoism in Sio, North-East New Guinea', *Oceania* 38(1): 1–23.

Harple, T. 2000, Book review 'A. Lattas: *Cultures of secrecy*, Madison 1998', *The Asia Pacific Journal of Anthropology* 1(1): 142–43.

Hartigan, J. 1997, 'Establishing the fact of whiteness', *American Anthropologist* 99(3): 495–505.

————. 2000a, 'Whiteness in the field: introduction to a special issue of Identities', in 'Whiteness in the field', ed. J. Hartigan, *Identities* 7(3): 269–79.

————. ed. 2000b, 'Whiteness in the field', *Identities* 7(3).

Hees, P.F. 1913a, 'Brief des hochw. P. Hees an einen Freund', *Monatshefte. Vereinsorgan der Erzbruderschaft U. L. Frau vom hlst. Herzen und der Genossenschaft der Missionare vom hlst. Herzen Jesu* 30(March): 103–8.

————. 1913b, 'Geister- und Zauberwesen auf Neupommern. Erzählungen aus Kindermund', *Monatshefte. Vereinsorgan der Erzbruderschaft U. L. Frau vom hlst. Herzen und der Genossenschaft der Missionare vom hlst. Herzen Jesu* 30(July): 301–6; 30(August): 343–51.

————. 1914a, 'Altes und Neues vom Toriu', *Monatshefte. Vereinsorgan der Erzbruderschaft U. L. Frau vom hlst. Herzen und der Genossenschaft der Missionare vom hlst. Herzen Jesu* 31(April): 156–62.

————. 1914b, 'Unsere Nakanaijugend am Toriu', *Monatshefte. Vereinsorgan der Erzbruderschaft U. L. Frau vom hlst. Herzen und der Genossenschaft der Missionare vom hlst. Herzen Jesu* 31(May): 210–18.

————. 1915/16, 'Ein Beitrag aus den Sagen und Erzählungen der Nakanai (Neupommern, Südsee)', *Anthropos* 10/11: 34–64, 562–85, 861–87.

Hefele, F. 1927, 'Nautik und Meteorologie. Während der Reise in Melanesien', in *Ergebnisse der Südsee-Expedition 1908–1910*, vol. 2, ed. G. Thilenius, Hamburg, 361–402.

Hellwig, F.E. 1927, 'Tagebuch der Expedition', in *Ergebnisse der Südsee-Expedition 1908–1910*, vol. 1, ed. G. Thilenius, Hamburg, 43–359.

Hempenstall, P.J. 1978, *Pacific Islanders under German Rule: a study in the meaning of colonial resistance*. Canberra.

————. 1987, 'The neglected empire: the superstructure of the colonial state in German Melanesia', in *Germans in the tropics: essays in German colonial history* (Contributions in Comparative Colonial Studies 24), eds A.J. Knoll and L.H. Gann, New York, 93–129.

Hempenstall, P.J. and N. Rutherford. 1984, *Protest and dissent in the colonial Pacific*. Suva.

Hermann, E. 1992a, 'The Yali movement in retrospect: rewriting history, redefining "cargo cult"', in 'Alienating mirrors: Christianity, cargo cults and colonialism in Melanesia', ed. A. Lattas, *Oceania* 63(1): 55–71.

————. 1992b, 'Die Last der Vergangenheit. Erinnerungsbemühungen an die Yali-Bewegung', in *Abschied von der Vergangenheit: ethnologische Berichte aus dem Finisterre-Gebirge in Papua New Guinea*, ed. J. Wassmann, Berlin, 49–73.

————. 1995, *Emotionen und Historizität: Der emotionale Diskurs über die Yali-Bewegung in einer Dorfgemeinschaft der Ngaing, Papua New Guinea*. Berlin.

————. 1997, 'Kastom versus cargo cult: emotional discourse on the Yali movement in Madang Province, Papua New Guinea', in *Cultural dynamics of religious developments in Oceania* (Verhandelingen van het Koninklijk Instituut voor de Taal-, Land- en Volkenkunde 176), eds T. Otto and A. Borsboom, Leiden, 88–102.

————. 2004, 'Dissolving the self-other dichotomy in western "cargo cult" constructions', in *Cargo, cult, and culture critique*, ed. H. Jebens, Honolulu, 36–58.

Hiatt, L.R. 1988, 'Introduction', in 'In memoriam Peter Lawrence, 1921–1987', eds J.R. Beckett, L.R. Hiatt and F.C. Merlan, *Oceania* 59(1): 1–2.

Hiery, H.J. 1995a, *The neglected war: the German South Pacific and the influence of World War I*. Honolulu.

————. 1995b, *Das Deutsche Reich in der Südsee (1900–1921): Eine Annäherung an die Erfahrung verschiedener Kulturen* (Veröffentlichungen des Deutschen Historischen Institutes London 37). Göttingen.

————. 2001a, 'Die deutsche Verwaltung Neuguineas 1884–1914', in *Die deutsche Südsee 1884–1914: Ein Handbuch*, ed. H.J. Hiery, Paderborn, 277–311.

————. 2001b, 'Der Erste Weltkrieg und das Ende des deutschen Einflusses in der Südsee', in *Die deutsche Südsee 1884–1914: Ein Handbuch*, ed. H.J. Hiery, Paderborn, 805–54.

————. ed. 2001c, *Die deutsche Südsee 1884–1914: Ein Handbuch*. Paderborn.

Hobsbawm, E. 1983, 'Introduction: inventing traditions', in *The invention of tradition*, eds E. Hobsbawm and T. Ranger, Cambridge, 1–14.

Höltker, G. 1941, 'Die Mambu-Bewegung in Neuguinea: ein Beitrag zum Prophetentum in Melanesien', *Annali Lateranensi* 5: 181–219.

————. 1946, 'Schwarmgeister in Neuguinea während des letzten Krieges', *Neue Zeitschrift für Missionswissenschaft* 2(3): 201–16.

Howard, A. 1990, 'Cultural paradigms, history, and the search for identity in Oceania', in *Cultural identity and ethnicity in the Pacific*, eds J. Linnekin and L. Poyer, Honolulu, 259–79.

Hudson, W.J., ed. 1971, *Australia and Papua New Guinea*. Sydney.

Hüskes, P.J., ed. 1932, *Pioniere der Südsee: Werden und Wachsen der Herz-Jesu-Mission von Rabaul zum Goldenen Jubiläum 1882–1932*. Hiltrup-Salzburg.

Huizer, G. 1992, 'Cargo and charisma: millenarian movements in today's global context', in 'Imagining cargo cults', ed. T. Otto, *Canberra Anthropology* 15(2): 106–30.

Hulme, D. 1982, 'An economic appraisal of the Hoskins Oil Palm Scheme', MS.

Janssen, H. 1974, 'The Story cult of Kaliai', in 'The church and adjustment movements', ed. Melanesian Institute, *Point* 1: 4–28.

Janssen, P.C., ed. 1929, 'Zur 25. Wiederkehr des Todestages unserer Baininger Märtyrer', *Monatshefte. Vereinsorgan der Erzbruderschaft U. L. Frau vom hlst. Herzen und der Genossenschaft der Missionare vom hlst. Herzen Jesu* 46(August).

Jaspers, P.R. 1979, 'Historische Untersuchungen zu einem Mord an Missionaren auf New Britain (Papua New Guinea) 1904', *Zeitschrift für Missionswissenschaft und Religionswissenschaft* 63: 1–24.

———. 1984, 'The beginnings of the Catholic Church in Papua New Guinea', in 'Papers prepared for the visit of Pope John Paul II to Papua New Guinea, 7–10 May 1984', ed. The joint committee of the Catholic Church and the government for the visit of Pope John Paul II to Papua New Guinea, MS, 31–46.

Jebens, H. 1995, *Wege zum Himmel: Katholiken, Siebenten-Tags-Adventisten und der Einfluß der traditionellen Religion in Pairudu, Southern Highlands Province, Papua New Guinea* (Mundus Reihe Ethnologie 86). Bonn (English translation: *Pathways to heaven: contesting mainline and fundamentalist Christianity in Papua New Guinea*. Oxford, 2004).

———. 1997a, 'Catholics, Seventh-Day Adventists and the impact of tradition in Pairundu (Southern Highlands Province, PNG)', in *Cultural dynamics of religious developments in Oceania* (Verhandelingen van het Koninklijk Instituut voor der Taal-, Land- en Volkenkunde 176), eds T. Otto and A. Borsboom, Leiden, 33–44.

———. 1997b, 'Störenfriede und falsche Christen. Zur Konstruktion und Instrumentalisierung von *kastom* in der Southern Highlands Province von Papua-Neuguinea', in 'Gestern und Heute: Traditionen in der Südsee', ed. M. Schindlbeck, *Baessler Archiv* 45: 481–96.

———. 2000, 'Signs of the Second Coming: on eschatological expectation and disappointment in Highland and Seaboard Papua New Guinea', *Ethnohistory* (1): 171–204.

———. 2001a, 'Reo Franklin Fortune: Sorcerers of Dobu. London 1932', in *Hauptwerke der Ethnologie*, eds C.F. Feest and K.-H. Kohl, Stuttgart, 108–13.

———. 2001b, '"How the white man thinks": Peter Lawrence: *Road belong cargo*. Manchester 1964', *Paideuma* 47: 203–21.

———. 2001c, 'Valuku: Maskentänze in West New Britain (Papua-Neuguinea) als Aneignung des Eigenen', in *New Heimat*, eds K.-H. Kohl and N. Schafhausen, New York, 78–89.

———. 2002, 'Trickery or secrecy? On Andrew Lattas' interpretation of "Bush Kaliai cargo cults"', *Anthropos* 97: 181–99.

———. 2003a, 'Zur Dialektik von Selbst- und Fremdwahrnehmung in West New Britain (Papua-Neuguinea)', *Mitteilungen der Berliner Gesellschaft für Anthropologie, Ethnologie und Urgeschichte* 24: 41–54.

———. 2003b, 'Starting with the law of the *tumbuan*: masked dances in West New Britain (Papua New Guinea) as an appropriation of one's own cultural self', *Anthropos* 98: 115–26.

———. 2004a, 'Introduction: cargo, cult, and culture critique', in *Cargo, cult, and culture critique*, ed. H. Jebens, Honolulu, 1–13.

———. 2004b, '"Vali did that too": on western and indigenous cargo discourses in West New Britain (Papua New Guinea)', *Anthropological Forum* 14(2): 117–39.

———. 2004c, 'Talking about cargo cults in Koimumu (West New Britain Province, Papua New Guinea', in *Cargo, cult, and culture critique*, ed. H. Jebens, Honolulu, 157–69.

———. ed. 2004d, *Cargo, cult, and culture critique*. Honolulu.

Jebens, H. and K.-H. Kohl. 1999, 'Konstruktionen von "Cargo": Zur Dialektik von Fremd- und Selbstwahrnehmung in der Interpretation melanesischer Kultbewegungen', *Anthropos* 94: 3–20.

Johnston, R.L. 1973, *Lakalai anthropology essentials: an outline of the religion, social organization, and value system of the Lakalai people of West New Britain, contrasting traditional and modern patterns.* Ukarumpa.

———. 1976, 'Lakalai (Nakanai): Translated by Raymond Johnston', in *Legends from Papua New Guinea*, ed. K.A. McElhannon, Ukarumpa, 139–45 (orig. 1974).

———. 1980a, *Nakanai of New Britain: the grammar of an Oceanic language* (Pacific Linguistics B 70). Canberra.

———. 1980b, 'The languages and communities of the Kimbe bay region', in *Language, communication and development in New Britain*, ed. R.L. Johnston, Ukarumpa, 107–58.

———. ed. 1980c, *Language, communication and development in New Britain.* Ukarumpa.

Jolly, M. 1992, 'Specters of inauthenticity', *Contemporary Pacific* 4: 49–72.

Jolly, M. and N. Thomas. 1992a, 'Introduction', in 'The politics of tradition in the Pacific', eds M. Jolly and N. Thomas, *Oceania* 62(4): 241–48.

Jolly, M. and N. Thomas, eds. 1992b, 'The politics of tradition in the Pacific', *Oceania* 62(4).

Jonas, W.J.A. 1972, 'The Hoskins Oil Palm Scheme', *The Australian Geographer* XII(1): 57–58.

Jose, A.W. 1987, *The Royal Australian Navy 1914–1918* (The official history of Australia in the war of 1914–1918 10). St Lucia (orig. 1928).

Journal de la Société des Océanistes 1999, 'Les Politiques de la Tradition: identités culturelles et identités nationales dans le Pacifique'. Sous la direction d'Alain Babdzan, *Journal de la Société des Océanistes* 109(2).

Kämpf, H. 2003, 'Die Inversion des Blicks: Überlegungen zum Theorieeffekt ethnologischer Begriffe', *Paideuma* 49: 87–104.

———. 2005, 'Der Sinn fürs Scheitern. Ethnologische Bekenntnisliteratur zwischen Selbsterforschung und Selbstverlust', *Paideuma* 51: 133–51.

Kaplan, M. 1990, 'Meaning, agency and colonial history: Navosavakadua and the *Tuka* Movement in Fiji', *American Ethnologist* 17: 3–22.

———. 1995, *Neither cargo nor cult: ritual politics and the colonial imagination in Fiji.* Durham, NC.

Keck, V. 1993, 'Talk about a changing world: young Yupno men in Papua New Guinea debate their future', *Canberra Anthropology* 16(2): 67–96.

Keesing, R.M. 1982a, 'Kastom and anticolonialism on Malaita: "culture" as political symbol', in 'Reinventing traditional culture: the politics of kastom in Island Melanesia', eds R.M. Keesing and R. Tonkinson, *Mankind* 13(4): 357–73.

1982b, 'Kastom in Melanesia: an overview', in 'Reinventing traditional culture: the politics of kastom in Island Melanesia', eds R.M. Keesing and R. Tonkinson, *Mankind* 13(4): 297–301.

———. 1989, 'Creating the past: custom and identity in the contemporary pacific', *The Contemporary Pacific* 1(1/2): 19–42.

Keesing, R.M. and R. Tonkinson, eds. 1982, 'Reinventing traditional culture: the politics of kastom in Island Melanesia', *Mankind* 13(4).

Kempf, W. 1996, *Das Innere des Äußeren: Ritual, Macht und historische Praxis bei den Ngaing in Papua Neuguinea.* Berlin.

Kleintitschen, P.A. 1929, 'Die Bluttat in den Baininger Bergen am 13. August 1904', in 'Zur 25. Wiederkehr des Todestages unserer Baininger Märtyrer', ed. P.C. Janssen, *Monatshefte. Vereinsorgan der Erzbruderschaft U. L. Frau vom hlst. Herzen und der Genossenschaft der Missionare vom hlst. Herzen Jesu* 46(August): 236–59.

———. n.d., 'Der Tubuan', MS.

Knoll, A.J. and L.H. Gunn, eds. 1987, *Germans in the tropics: essays in German colonial history* (Contributions in Comparative Colonial Studies 24). New York.

Koch, G. 1979, 'Forschungen im Bergland von Neuguinea: das interdisziplinäre West-Irian Projekt' (Information paper for the exhibition 'Steinzeit-heute'). Berlin.

Kohl, K.-H. 1987, 'Fetisch, Tabu, Totem: zur Archäologik religionswissenschaftlicher Begriffsbildung', in K.-H. Kohl, *Abwehr und Verlangen: zur Geschichte der Ethnologie*, Frankfurt am Main, 89–102.

———. 2000, 'Prozesse kultureller Selbstbehauptung und die Rolle der Ethnologie', in *Die offenen Grenzen der Ethnologie: Schlaglichter auf ein sich wandelndes Fach*, eds S.M. Schomburg-Scherff and B. Heintze, Frankfurt am Main, 68–82.

———. 2004, 'German money and the tree of wealth in East Flores', in *Cargo, cult, and culture critique*, ed. H. Jebens, Honolulu, 79–91.

Kordt, P.J. 1960, [No title], MS.

Kühling, S. 1998, 'The name of the gift: ethics of exchange on Dobu island' (Ph.D. diss., Australian National University).

———. 2005, *Dobu: ethics of exchange on a Massim Island, Papua New Guinea*. Honolulu.

Laade, W. 1999, *Music and culture in south-east New Britain: UNESCO territorial survey of Oceanic music: report on field research conducted in August–October 1988*. Bern.

Langham, I. 1981, *The building of British social anthropology: W.H.R. Rivers and his Cambridge disciples in the development of kinship studies, 1898–1931* (Studies in the History of Modern Science 8). Dordrecht.

Lanternari, V. 1963, *The religions of the oppressed: a study of modern messianic cults*. London.

Larcom, J. 1982, 'The invention of convention', in 'Reinventing traditional culture: the politics of kastom in Island Melanesia', eds R.M. Keesing and R. Tonkinson, *Mankind* 13(4): 330–37.

———. 1983, 'Following Deacon: the problem of ethnographic reanalysis, 1926–1981', in *Observers observed: essays on ethnographic fieldwork* (History of Anthropology 1), ed. G.W. Stocking, London, 175–95.

Lattas, A. 1987, 'Savagery and civilisation: towards a genealogy of racism', *Social Analysis* 21: 39–58.

———. 1989, 'Trickery and sacrifice: tambarans and the appropriation of female reproductive powers in male initiation ceremonies in West New Britain', *Man* (N.S.) 24: 451–69.

———. 1990, 'Aborigines and contemporary Australian nationalism: primordiality and the cultural politics of otherness', *Social Analysis* 27: 50–69.

———. 1991a, 'Sexuality and cargo cults: the politics of gender and procreation in West New Britain', *Cultural Anthropology* 6(2): 230–56.

———. 1991b, 'Nationalism, aesthetic redemption and aboriginality', *The Australian Journal of Anthropology* 2(3): 307–24.

———. 1992a, 'The punishment of masks: cargo cults and ideologies of representation in West New Britain', *Canberra Anthropology* 15(2): 69–88.

———. 1992b, 'Skin, personhood and redemption: the double self in West New Britain cargo cults', in 'Alienating mirrors: Christianity, cargo cults and colonialism in Melanesia', ed. A. Lattas, *Oceania* 63(1): 27–54.

———. 1993, 'Sorcery and colonialism: illness, dreams and death as political languages in West New Britain', *Man* (N.S.) 28: 51–77.

———. 1996a, 'Introduction: mnemonic regimes and strategies of subversion', *Oceania* 66: 257–65.

———. 1996b, 'Memory, forgetting and the New Tribes Mission in West New Britain', *Oceania* 66: 286–304.

———. 1998, *Cultures of secrecy: reinventing race in Bush Kaliai cargo cults*. Madison.

———. ed. 1992c, 'Alienating mirrors: Christianity, cargo cults, and colonialism in Melanesia', *Oceania* 63(1).

Lātūkefu, S., ed. 1989, *Papua New Guinea: a century of colonial impact 1884–1984*. Boroko

Laufer, P.C. 1955, 'Schwarmgeister in der Südsee', *Hiltruper Monatshefte* 63(8): 175–79.

Lawrence, P. 1964, *Road belong cargo: a study of the cargo movement in the Southern Madang District New Guinea*. Manchester.

Leavitt, S.C. 1995, 'Political domination and the absent oppressor: images of Europeans in Bumbita Arapesh narratives', *Ethnology* 34(3): 177–89.

———. 2004, 'From "cult" to religious conversion: the case for making cargo personal', in *Cargo, cult, and culture critique*, ed. H. Jebens, Honolulu, 170–86.

Linckens, P.H. 1904, 'Die Mordtat auf Neupommern', *Monatshefte zu Ehren Unserer Lieben Frau vom hlst. Herzen Jesu* 21(November): 495–502.

———. 1905, 'Am Grabe der ermordeten Missionare und Missionsschwestern von St. Paul', *Monatshefte zu Ehren Unserer Lieben Frau vom hlst. Herzen Jesu* 22(July): 357–61.

———. 1921, *Streiflichter aus der Herz-Jesu-Mission (Neupommern)*. Hiltrup.

———. 1922, *Die deutsche Provinz der Missionare vom hlst. Herzen Jesu: kurze geschichtliche Denkschrift zu ihrem Silbernen Jubiläum 1897–1922*. Hiltrup.

Lindstrom, L. 1993, *Cargo cult: strange stories of desire from Melanesia and beyond*. Honolulu.

———. 1999, 'Mambu phone home', *Anthropological Forum* 9(1): 99–105.

———. 2004, 'Cargo cult at the third millennium', in *Cargo, cult, and culture critique*, ed. H. Jebens, Honolulu, 15–35.

Linnekin, J. 1990, 'The politics of culture in the Pacific', in *Cultural identity and ethnicity in the Pacific*, eds J. Linnekin and L. Poyer, Honolulu, 149–73.

———. 1992, 'On the theory and politics of cultural construction in the Pacific', in 'The politics of tradition in the Pacific', eds M. Jolly and N. Thomas, *Oceania* 62(4): 249–63.

Linnekin, J. and L. Poyer. 1990a, 'Introduction', in *Cultural identity and ethnicity in the Pacific*, eds J. Linnekin and L. Poyer, Honolulu, 1–16.

Linnekin, J. and L. Poyer, eds. 1990b, *Cultural identity and ethnicity in the Pacific*. Honolulu.

Lommel, A. 1953, 'Der "Cargo-Kult" in Melanesien: ein Beitrag zum Problem der "Europäisierung" der Primitiven', *Zeitschrift für Ethnologie* 78(1): 17–63.

Long, G. 1963, *The final campaign* (Australia in the war of 1939–1945. Series 1.VII). Canberra.

Longayroux, J.P., T. Fleming, A. Ploeg, R.T. Shand, W.F. Straamans and W. Jonas. 1972, *Hoskins development: the role of oil palm and timber* (New Guinea Research Bulletin 49). Canberra.

Lotman, J.M. and B.A. Uspenskij. 1984, 'The role of dual models in the dynamics of Russian culture (up to the end of the eighteenth century)', in J.M. Lotman and B.A. Uspenskij, *The semiotics of Russian culture* (Michigan Slavic Contributions 11), ed. A. Shukman, Ann Arbor, 3–35.

Macdonald, J. 2000, 'The Tikopia and "what Raymond said"', in *Ethnographic artifacts: challenges to a reflexive anthropology*, eds S.R. Jaarsma and M.A. Rohatynskyj, Honolulu, 107–23.

Mackenzie, S.S. 1987, *The Australians at Rabaul: the capture and administration of the German possessions in the South Pacific: with introduction by Hank Nelson and Michael Piggott* (The Official History of Australia in the War of 1914–1918 10). St Lucia (orig. 1927).

Mageo, J.M. 2001a, 'Introduction', in *Cultural memory: reconfiguring history and identity in the postcolonial Pacific*, ed. J.M. Mageo, Honolulu, 1–9.

———. 2001b, 'On memory genres: tendencies in cultural remembering', in *Cultural memory: reconfiguring history and identity in the postcolonial Pacific*, ed. J.M. Mageo, Honolulu, 11–33.

———. ed. 2001c, *Cultural memory: reconfiguring history and identity in the postcolonial Pacific*. Honolulu.

Mair, L.M. 1948, *Australia in New Guinea*. London (second edition: 1970, Melbourne).

Malinowski, B.K. 1922, *Argonauts of the Western Pacific: an account of native enterprise and adventure in the archipelagoes of Melanesian New Guinea*. London.

McCarthy, J.K. 1963, *Patrol into yesterday: my New Guinea years*. Melbourne.

———. 1964, 'Foreword', in P. Lawrence, *Road belong cargo: a study of the cargo movement in the Southern Madang District New Guinea*, Manchester, v–ix.

McDowell, N. 1988, 'A note on cargo and cultural constructions of change', *Pacific Studies* 11: 121–34.

————. 2000, 'A brief comment on difference and rationality', in 'A critical retrospective on "Cargo Cult": Western/Melanesian intersections', ed. D. Dalton, *Oceania* 70(4): 373–80.

McPherson, N.M. 2001, '"Wanted: young men, must like adventure": Ian McCallum Mack, Patrol Officer', in *In colonial New Guinea: anthropological perspectives* (ASAO Monograph Series 19), ed. N.M. McPherson, Pittsburgh, 82–110.

Mead, M. 1956, *New lives for old: cultural transformation – Manus, 1928–1953*. New York.

Mertens, P.B. 1932, 'Baining und das Blutbad von St. Paul', in *Pioniere der Südsee: Werden und Wachsen der Herz-Jesu-Mission von Rabaul zum Goldenen Jubiläum 1882–1932*, ed. P.J. Hüskes, Hiltrup-Salzburg, 33–46.

Mihailic, F. 1971, *The Jacaranda dictionary and grammar of Melanesian pidgin*. Port Moresby.

Miller, J. Jr. 1959, *Cartwheel: the reduction of Rabaul* (United States Army in World War II. The War in the Pacific 8). Washington, DC.

Missionare vom hlst. Herzen Jesu, ed. 1909, *Aus der deutschen Südsee: Mitteilungen der Missionare vom heiligsten Herzen Jesu*, vol. 1: P. *Matthäus Rascher, M.S.C. und Baining (Neu-Pommern) Land und Leute*. Münster.

————. 1917, *Festschrift zum Goldenen Jubiläum des Kleinen Liebeswerkes vom heiligsten Herzen Jesu, 2. Oktober 1867–2. Oktober 1917*. Münster.

————. 1954, *Gott ist größer als unser Herz: Hundert Jahre Missionare vom heiligsten Herzen Jesu*. Münster.

————. 1975, *75 Jahre Missionsschwestern vom heiligsten Herzen Jesu von Hiltrup 1900–1975*. Ariccia-Rome.

————. n.d., *1882–1982: Hundert Jahre Herz-Jesu-Missionare in der Südsee*. Münster.

Moses, J.A. and P.M. Kennedy, eds. 1977, *Germany in the Pacific and Far East, 1870–1914*. St. Lucia.

Mühlhäusler, P. 1985a, 'External history of Tok Pisin', in *Handbook of Tok Pisin (New Guinea Pidgin)* (Pacific Linguistics C 70), eds S.A. Wurm and P. Mühlhäusler, Canberra, 35–64.

————. 1985b, 'Internal development of Tok Pisin', in *Handbook of Tok Pisin (New Guinea Pidgin)* (Pacific Linguistics C 70), eds S.A. Wurm and P. Mühlhäusler, Canberra, 75–166.

Mühlmann, W.E. 1961, *Chiliasmus und Nativismus: Studien zur Psychologie, Soziologie und historischen Kasuistik der Umsturzbewegungen*. Berlin

Müller, P.H. 1932, 'Forschungsreisen und Erkundungsfahrten', in *Pioniere der Südsee: Werden und Wachsen der Herz-Jesu-Mission von Rabaul zum Goldenen Jubiläum 1882–1932*, ed. P.J. Hüskes, Hiltrup-Salzburg, 104–11.

Neumann, K. 1992, *Not the way it really was: constructing the Tolai past* (Pacific Islands Monograph Series 10). Honolulu.

————. 1998, 'The stench of the past: revisionism in Pacific Islands and Australian history', *The Contemporary Pacific* 10(1): 31–64.

Oddo, S., A. Schwab and H. Welzer. 2003, 'Erinnerung und Gedächtnis: ein Werkstattbericht aus einem interdisziplinären Forschungsprojekt', in *Jahrbuch des Kulturwissenschaftlichen Instituts 2002/2003*, ed. J. Rüsen, Essen, 342–55.

Otto, T. 1991, *The politics of tradition in Baluan: social change and the construction of the past in a Manus societ*. Nijmegen (reproduction of Ph.D. diss., Australian National University).

————. 1992a, 'The Paliau movement in Manus and the objectification of tradition', *History and Anthropology* 5: 427–54.

————. 1992b, 'Introduction: imagining cargo cults', in 'Imagining cargo cults', ed. T. Otto, *Canberra Anthropology* 15(2): 1–10.

————. 1999, 'Cargo cults everywhere?', *Anthropological Forum* 9: 83–98.

————. 2004, 'Work, wealth, and knowledge: enigmas of cargoist identifications', in *Cargo, cult, and culture critique*, ed. H. Jebens, Honolulu, 209–26.

————. ed. 1992c, 'Imagining cargo cults', *Canberra Anthropology* 15(2).

Panoff, M. 1987, 'Y eut-il des esclaves en Nouvelle-Bretagne? Une critique des témoignages', *Journal de la Société des Océanistes* 33(85): 133–55.

Parkinson, R. 1907, *Dreißig Jahre in der Südsee: Land und Leute, Sitten und Gebräuche im Bismarckarchipel und auf den deutschen Salomoinseln*, ed. B. Ankermann. Stuttgart.

Pos, H. 1950, 'The revolt of "Manseren"', *American Anthropologist* 52: 561–64.

Powell, W. 1884, *Unter den Kannibalen von Neu-Britannien: Drei Wanderjahre durch ein wildes Land: Frei übertragen durch Dr. F.M. Schröter*. Leipzig.

Read, K.E. 1958, 'A "cargo" situation in the Markham valley, New Guinea', *Southwestern Journal of Anthropology* 14: 273–94.

Reche, O. 1954, *Nova Britannia: 1. Teilband* (Ergebnisse der Südsee-Expedition 1908–1910. II. Ethnographie: A. Melanesien, vol. 4). Hamburg.

Reed, S.W. 1943, *The making of modern New Guinea: with special reference to culture contact in the mandated territory* (Memoirs of the American Philosophical Society 18). Philadelphia.

Robbins, J. 1998, 'Becoming sinners: Christian transformations of morality and culture in a Papua New Guinea Society', (Ph.D. diss., University of Virginia).

———. 2000, Book review 'A. Lattas: *Cultures of secrecy*, Madison 1998', *The Contemporary Pacific* 12(2): 540–42.

———. 2004a, *Becoming sinners: Christianity and moral torment in a Papua New Guinea society* (Ethnographic Studies in Subjectivity 4). Berkeley.

———. 2004b, 'On the critique in cargo and the cargo in critique: toward a comparative anthropology of critical practice', in *Cargo, cult, and culture critique*, ed. H. Jebens, Honolulu, 243–59.

Rohatynskyj, M.A. 2000, 'The enigmatic Baining: the breaking of an ethnographer's heart', in *Ethnographic artifacts: challenges to a reflexive anthropology*, eds S.R. Jaarsma and M.A. Rohatynskyj, Honolulu, 174–94.

Rowley, C.D. 1958, *The Australians in German New Guinea, 1914–1921*. Melbourne.

Rutschky, M. 1992, 'Nachrichten aus dem Beitrittsgebiet', *Merkur* 519: 465–80.

Sack, P.G. 1985, 'A history of German New Guinea: a debate about evidence and judgement', *The Journal of Pacific History* 20(2): 84–94.

———. ed. 1980, *German New Guinea: a bibliography*. Canberra.

Sack, P.G. and D. Clark, eds. 1979, *German New Guinea: the Annual Reports*. Edited and translated by Peter Sack and Dymphna Clark. Canberra.

Sax, W.S. 1998, 'The hall of mirrors: orientalism, anthropology, and the other', *American Anthropologist* 1000(2): 292–302.

Scarr, D. 1970, 'Recruits and recruiters: a portrait of the labour trade', in *Pacific Islands Portraits*, eds J.W. Davidson and D.A. Scarr, Canberra, 225–51.

Scharmach, P.L. 1953, *Manuale missionariorum*. Vunapope.

———. 1960, *This crowd beats us all*. Surry Hills.

Scheps, B. and W. Liedtke. 1992, *Bibliographie deutschsprachiger kolonialer Literatur zu Quellen der Ethnographie und Geschichte der Bevölkerung von Kaiser Wilhelms-Land, dem Bismarck-Archipel und den Deutschen Salomon Inseln 1880–1914, annotiert* (Ozeanien-Bibliographie 1). Dresden.

Schiefflin, E. and D. Gewertz. 1985, 'Introduction', in *History and ethnohistory in Papua New Guinea* (Oceania Monographs 28), eds E. Schiefflin and D. Gewertz, Sydney, 1–6.

Schindlbeck, M. 1984, 'Cargo-Bewegung, Tradition und Migration. Sozio-ökonomische Veränderungen bei den Sawos von Gaikorobi, Sepik-Gebiet, Papua-Neuguinea', *Paideuma* 30: 275–98.

———. 1990, 'Tradition and change in Kwanga villages', in *Sepik heritage: tradition and change in Papua New Guinea*, eds N. Lutkehaus, C. Kaufmann, W.E. Mitchell, D. Newton, L. Osmundsen and M. Schuster, Durham, 232–40.

Schmidlin, J. 1913, *Die katholischen Missionen in den deutschen Schutzgebieten*. Münster in Westfalen.

Schmidt, P.J., ed. 1947, *Die Hiltruper Märtyrer von Sankt Paul*. Münster.

Schütte, H. 1986, 'Methodistische Mission in Deutsch-Neuguinea: Aspekte des Beitrags der Missionen zum Übergang in neue gesellschaftliche Formen', in *Wok Misin 100 Jahre deutsche Mission in Papua-Neuguinea: Dokumentation der Tagung vom 30.4.–4.5.1986 in Neuendettelsau*, ed. Missionskolleg, Neuendettelsau, 95–116.

Schumm, P.R. 1932, 'Nakanai und die weitere Nordküste Neubritanniens', in *Pioniere der Südsee: Werden und Wachsen der Herz-Jesu-Mission von Rabaul zum Goldenen Jubiläum 1882–1932*, ed. P.J. Hüskes, Hiltrup-Salzburg, 73–80.

Schuster, M. 1990, 'Aspects of the Aibom concept of history', in *Sepik heritage: tradition and change in Papua New Guinea*, eds N. Lutkehaus, C. Kaufmann, W.E. Mitchell, D. Newton, L. Osmundsen and M. Schuster, Durham, 7–19.

Schwartz, T. 1962, 'The Paliau movement in the Admiralty Islands 1946–1954', *Anthropological Papers of the American Musuem of Natural History* 49: 207–421.

———. 1973, 'Cult and context: the paranoid ethos in Melanesia', *Ethos* 1(2): 153–74.

Schwarz, B. 1980, 'Seeking to understand cargo as a symbol', *Catalyst* 10(1): 14–27.

Schwester (Sr.) Brigitta. 1905, 'Die Mordtat von St. Paul', *Monatshefte zu Ehren Unserer Lieben Frau vom hlst. Herzen Jesu* 22(February): 61–67.

Senft, G. 2002, Book review 'H.J. Hiery ed.: *Die Deutsche Südsee 1884–1914*, Paderborn 2001', *Paideuma* 48: 299–303.

Simmons, R.T., J.J. Graydon, N.M. Semple and D.R. Swindler. 1956, 'A blood group genetical survey in West Nakanai, New Britain', *American Journal of Physical Anthropology* 14: 275–86.

Stanner, W.E.H. 1953, *The South Seas in transition: a study of post-war rehabilitation and reconstruction in three British Pacific dependencies*. Sydney.

Steffen, P. 2001, 'Die katholischen Missionen in Deutsch-Neuguinea', in *Die deutsche Südsee 1884–1914: Ein Handbuch*, ed. H.J. Hiery, Paderborn, 243–383.

Steinbauer, F. 1971, *Die Cargo-Kulte: als religionsgeschichtliches und missionstheologisches Problem*. Erlangen.

Stewart, K. and S. Harding. 1999, 'Bad endings: American apocalypsis', *Annual Review of Anthropology* 28: 285–310.

Stowe, D.W. 1996, 'Uncolored people: the rise of whiteness studies', *Lingua franca* 6: 68–77.

Strelan, J. 1977, *Search for salvation: studies in the history and theology of cargo cults*. Adelaide.

Swindler, D.R. 1962, *A racial study of the West Nakanai* (Museum Monographs. New Britain Studies. Philadelphia.

Taschner, F. 1985, *Pater Franz und seine Mamussi*. Hallbergmoos.

Thiele, S. 1993, 'Response to Lattas', *Oceania* 64(1): 77–78.

Thomas, N. 1992, 'The inversion of tradition', *American Ethnologist* 19(2): 213–32.

Threlfall, N. 1975, *One hundred years in the islands: the Methodist/United Church in the New Guinea Islands region*. Rabaul.

———. n.d., 'Methodist missionaries in the Nakanai area', MS.

Tonkinson, R. 1982, 'Kastom in Melanesia: introduction', in 'Reinventing traditional culture: the politics of kastom in Island Melanesia', eds R.M. Keesing and R. Tonkinson, *Mankind* 13(4), 302–5.

Trask, H.-K. 1991, 'Natives and anthropologists: the colonial struggle', *The Contemporary Pacific* 3(1): 159–67.

Trompf, G.W., ed. 1990, *Cargo cults and millenarian movements: transoceanic comparisons of new religious movements*. Berlin.

Uplegger, H. and W.E. Mühlmann. 1961, 'Die Cargo-Kulte in Neuguinea und Insel-Melanesien', in W.E. Mühlmann, *Chiliasmus und Nativismus: Studien zur Psychologie, Soziologie und historischen Kasuistik der Umsturzbewegungen*, Berlin, 165–89.

Valentine, B. 1978, *Hustling and other hard work: life styles in the ghetto*. New York.

Valentine, C.A. 1955a, 'Cargo beliefs and cargo cults among the West Nakanai of New Britain: a report to the Department of Territories (15th January 1955)', MS.

———. 1955b, 'Cargo beliefs and cargo cults among the West Nakanai of New Britain (March 1955)', MS.

———. 1956a, 'Cargo beliefs and movements in the Talasea Sub-District New Britain (December 1956)', MS.

———. 1956b, 'Health in a changing society: the West Nakanai of New Britain', MS.

———. 1958, 'An introduction to the history of changing ways of life on the island of New Britain' (Ph.D. diss., University of Pennsylvania).

———. 1959, 'Religion and culture change: reflections on an example from Melanesia', MS.

———. 1960a, 'Uses of ethnohistory in an acculturation study', *Ethnohistory* 7(1): 1–27.

———. 1960b, 'We were adopted by the Lakalai ... K.U. anthropologist initiated into primitive tribe', *Topeka Capitol Journal* 19(July): 142–43.

———. 1961a, *Masks and men in a Melanesian society: the valuku or tubuan of the Lakalai of New Britain*. Lawrence.

———. 1961b, 'Symposium on the concept of ethnohistory: comment', *Ethnohistory* 8: 271–80.

———. 1963a, 'Men of anger and men of shame: Lakalai ethnopsychology and its implications for sociopsychological theory', *Ethnology* 2: 441–77.

———. 1963b, 'Social status, political power, and native responses to European influence in Oceania', *Anthropological Forum* 1(1): 3–55.

———. 1965, 'The Lakalai of New Britain', in *Gods, ghosts and men in Melanesia: some religions of Australian New Guinea and the New Hebrides*, eds P. Lawrence and M.J. Meggitt, Melbourne, 162–97.

———. 1968, *Culture and poverty: critique and counterproposals*. Chicago.

———. 1978, 'Introduction', in Bettylou Valentine, *Hustling and other hard work: life styles in the ghetto*, New York, 1–10.

———. n.d., 'Spirits and men in the traditional world of the Lakalai', MS.

Valentine, C.A. and B. Valentine. 1975, 'Brain damage and the intellectual defence of inequality', *Current Anthropology* 16(1): 117–50.

Valentine, C.A. and B. Valentine. 1979a, 'Nakanai: villagers, settlers, workers and the Hoskins Oil Palm Project (West New Britain Province)', in *Going through changes: villagers, settlers and development in Papua New Guinea*, eds C.A. Valentine and B. Valentine, Port Moresby, 49–71.

Valentine, C.A. and B. Valentine. 1979b, 'Conclusions', in *Going through changes: villagers, settlers and development in Papua New Guinea*, eds C.A. Valentine and B. Valentine, Port Moresby, 90–102.

Valentine, C.A. and B. Valentine, eds. 1979c, *Going through changes: villagers, settlers and development in Papua New Guinea*. Port Moresby.

Valentine, C.A. and E. Valentine. 1956, 'Chronology of recorded events in and around New Britain with special reference to the Nakanai area', MS.

Van Rijswijck, O. 1966, *The Silanga resettlement project* (New Guinea Research Unit Bulletin 10). Canberra.

Verhaar, J.W.M. 1995, *Toward a reference grammar of Tok Pisin an experiment in corpus linguistics* (Oceanic Linguistics Special Publication 26). Honolulu.

Wagner, F.X. 1960, 'Ein Beispiel missionarischer Sozialarbeit in der Südsee', *Neue Zeitschrift für Missionswissenschaft* 16: 35–64.

———. 1996, *Mein Leben und Wirken als Herz-Jesu-Missionar in der Südsee 1950–1993*. Freilassing.

Wagner, R. 1981, *The invention of culture*. Chicago (orig. 1975).

———. 2000 'Our very own cargo cult', in 'A critical retrospective on "Cargo Cult": Western/Melanesian intersections', ed. D. Dalton, *Oceania* 70(4): 362–72.

Waldersee, J. 1995, *'Neither eagles nor saints': MSC missions in Oceania 1881–1975: with the collaboration of John F. McMahon MSC who wrote the last three chapters*. Sydney.

Walker, A.S. 1957, *The island campaigns* (Australia in the War of 1939–1945. Series 5.III). Canberra.

Weigl, P.J. 1955, 'Missionsschicksal', *Hiltruper Monatshefte* 63(9): 196–200; 63(10): 220–24.

Weinrich, H. 1997, *Lethe: Kunst und Kritik des Vergessens*. Munich.

Welzer, H. and H.J. Markowitsch. 2001, 'Umrisse einer interdisziplinären Gedächtnisforschung', *Psychologische Rundschau* 52(4): 205–14.

Wichmann, A. 1909, *Nova Guinea: Résultats de l'Expedition Scientifique Néerlandaise à la Nouvelle-Guinée en 1903*, vol. 1: *Entdeckungsgeschichte von Neu-Guinea (bis 1828)*. Leiden.

———. 1910, *Nova Guinea: Uitkomsten der Nederlandsche Nieuw-Guinea-Expeditie in 1903*, vol. 2.1. Leiden.

———. 1912, *Nova Guinea: Résultats de l'Expedition Scientifique Néerlandaise à la Nouvelle-Guinée en 1903*, vol. 2.2: *Entdeckungsgeschichte von Neu-Guinea (1885 bis 1902)*. Leiden.

Wigmore, L. 1968, *The Japanese thrust* (Australia in the war of 1939–1945. Series 1.IV). Canberra (orig. 1957).

Williams, F.E. 1934, 'The Vailala Madness in retrospect', in *Essays presented to C.G. Seligman*, eds E.E. Evans-Pritchard, R. Firth, B. Malinowski and I. Schapera, London, 269–379.

Williams, R.G. 1972, *The United Church in Papua, New Guinea, and the Solomon Islands: the story of the development of an indigenous church on the occasion of the centenary of the L.M.S. in Papua, 1872–1972*. Rabaul.

Wollrad, E. n.d, *Bibliography 'Whiteness'*, http: //uni-oldenburg.de/zfg/eff/docs/whiteness_literature.pdf [accessed 14 June 2005].

Worsley, P. 1957, *The trumpet shall sound: a study of "cargo" cults in Melanesia*. London.

Wright, M. 1965, *If I die: coastwatching and guerilla warfare behind Japanese lines*. Melbourne.

Zinser, H. 1985, 'Probleme und Grenzen der Anwendung psychoanalytischer Begriffe in der Religionswissenschaft', *Paideuma* 46: 189–206.

Index